Learning and Leading with
Habits *of* Mind

Learning and Leading with
Habits *of* Mind

16 Essential Characteristics for Success

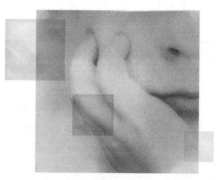

Edited by

Arthur L. Costa and Bena Kallick

ASCD

Alexandria, Virginia USA

1703 N. Beauregard St. • Alexandria, VA 22311-1714 USA
Phone: 800-933-2723 or 703-578-9600 • Fax: 703-575-5400
Web site: www.ascd.org • E-mail: member@ascd.org
Author guidelines: www.ascd.org/write

Gene R. Carter, *Executive Director*; Nancy Modrak, *Publisher*; Julie Houtz, *Director of Book Editing & Production*; Darcie Russell, *Project Manager*; Georgia Park, *Senior Graphic Designer*; Mike Kalyan, *Production Manager*; Barton Matheson Willse & Worthington, *Typesetter*

Printed in the United States of America. Cover art copyright © 2008 by ASCD. ASCD publications present a variety of viewpoints. The views expressed or implied in this book should not be interpreted as official positions of the Association.

All Web links in this book are correct as of the publication date but may have become inactive or otherwise modified since that time. If you notice a deactivated or changed link, please e-mail books@ascd.org with the words "Link Update" in the subject line. In your message, please specify the Web link, the book title, and the page number on which the link appears.

PAPERBACK ISBN: 978-1-4166-0741-0   ASCD product #108008   n12/08
Also available as an e-book through ebrary, netLibrary, and many online booksellers (see Books in Print for the ISBNs).

Quantity discounts for the paperback edition only: 10–49 copies, 10%; 50+ copies, 15%; for 1,000 or more copies, call 800-933-2723, ext. 5634, or 703-575-5634. For desk copies: member@ascd.org.

Library of Congress Cataloging-in-Publication Data

Learning and leading with habits of mind : 16 essential characteristics for success / edited by Arthur L. Costa and Bena Kallick

    p. cm.
  Includes bibliographical references and index.
   ISBN 978-1-4166-0741-0 (pbk. : alk. paper)   1. Thought and thinking—Study and teaching.   2. Cognition in children.   3. Success   I. Costa, Arthur L.   II. Kallick, Bena.

  LB1590.3.L423 2008
  370.15'24—dc22

                                      2008032561

18 17 16 15   6 7 8 9 10 11 12

Native peoples teach that the ultimate norm for morality is the impact our choices have on persons living seven generations from now. If the results appear good for them, then our choices are moral ones; if not, they are immoral.

We therefore dedicate *Learning and Leading with Habits of Mind* to our children, our grandchildren, and their children's children.

Deep down you know you can be remarkable. You shouldn't settle for anything less than your best self, reaching ever closer to your potential—whether as a leader or in any other part of your life.

—*Kevin Eikenberry, author*

Learning and Leading with
Habits *of* Mind

16 Essential Characteristics for Success

Foreword: Thinking on the Road of Life xi
David Perkins

Preface xvi
Arthur L. Costa and Bena Kallick

Acknowledgments xxv

Suggestions for Using This Book xxvi
Arthur L. Costa and Bena Kallick

PART I: DISCOVERING AND EXPLORING HABITS OF MIND

Introduction 1
Arthur L. Costa and Bena Kallick

1. Changing Perspectives About Intelligence 5
   Arthur L. Costa and Bena Kallick

2. Describing the Habits of Mind 15
   Arthur L. Costa

3. Habits of Mind in the Curriculum 42
   Arthur L. Costa and Bena Kallick

4. Habits of Mind: A Journey of Continuous Growth 59
   James Anderson, Arthur L. Costa, and Bena Kallick

5. Is Your Instruction Habit Forming? 69
   James Anderson and Arthur L. Costa

PART II: BUILDING A THOUGHT-FULL ENVIRONMENT

Introduction 95
Arthur L. Costa and Bena Kallick

6. Creating "Thought-Full" Environments 97
Arthur L. Costa and Bena Kallick

7. Toward a Mindful Language of Learning 117
Arthur L. Costa and Bena Kallick

8. Using Questions to Challenge Students' Intellect. 135
Arthur L. Costa and Bena Kallick

9. Thinking Maps: Visual Tools for Activating Habits of Mind . . . 149
David Hyerle

PART III: ASSESSING AND REPORTING ON HABITS OF MIND

Introduction 175
Arthur L. Costa and Bena Kallick

10. Defining Indicators of Achievement 177
Arthur L. Costa and Bena Kallick

11. Assessing Habits of Mind 190
Arthur L. Costa and Bena Kallick

12. Learning Through Reflection 221
Arthur L. Costa and Bena Kallick

13. Wondering to Be Done 236
Steve Seidel

14. Reporting Growth in Habits of Mind 258
Arthur L. Costa and Bena Kallick

PART IV: LEADING SCHOOLS WITH HABITS OF MIND

Introduction 269
Arthur L. Costa and Bena Kallick

15. Creating a Culture of Mindfulness 271
Arthur L. Costa and Bena Kallick

16. Habits of Mind for the Systems-Savvy Leader 291
    Jennifer Abrams

17. Leading Is a Habit of Mind 307
    William A. Sommers and Diane P. Zimmerman

PART V: LEARNING FROM MINDFUL SCHOOLS

Introduction 317
    Arthur L. Costa and Bena Kallick

18. Habits of Mind in North Carolina:
    Increasing Intellectual Capacity of Disadvantaged Students . . . 319
    Mary P. Hargett and Margaret Evans Gayle

19. Bringing a Vision to Life 333
    Curtis Schnorr and Thommie DePinto Piercy

20. A "Throwaway" School No More 342
    Bertie Simmons

21. The Mindful Culture of Waikiki Elementary School 348
    Bonnie Tabor, Sandra Brace, Matt Lawrence, and Arnold Latti

22. Integrating the Habits of Mind: A District Perspective 362
    Nancy Skerritt, Emilie Hard, and Kristin Edlund

APPENDIXES

A. Bringing Habits of Mind to Life 379
B. Leading Schools with Habits of Mind 387
C. When Have Habits of Mind Become Infused? 390
D. Inventories and Checklists 395
E. Resources Related to Habits of Mind 402

Index 404
About the Editors and Other Contributors 415

Foreword:
Thinking on the Road of Life

David Perkins

While driving into town a few years ago, I found myself behind a young man in a red convertible. Like many people, I have certain expectations about young men in red convertibles, but this young man surprised me. When we reached a railroad crossing, he was painfully careful. He slowed down as he approached the tracks. The closer he got to the tracks, the more he slowed. As his car passed over the tracks, it hardly was moving at all. At this point, with great care, the young man looked to the left, and then he looked to the right. No train was coming. Satisfied with his safety, he gunned the engine and sped off. The young man was careful—and yet he wasn't. Surely, the middle of the tracks isn't the best position from which to scan for oncoming trains!

This man's behavior provides a kind of metaphor for the mission of *Learning and Leading with Habits of Mind*. When on the road of life, we ought to be thoughtful about what we are doing. For example, we ought to manage impulsivity and strive for accuracy, two of the worthwhile Habits of Mind this book describes. Yet if good thinking is to help us out in life, it has to go on the road with us. The trouble is, good thinking often gets left behind altogether, or it's exercised in flawed ways and so doesn't do quite the right job, as this young man demonstrated.

How can we encourage ourselves and others—particularly students—to take good thinking on the road? *Learning and Leading with Habits of*

Mind explores one answer to that challenge: the cultivation of habits of mind, or habits of thought, as John Dewey (1933) called them. The idea is that we should have habits of mind such as persistence and flexible thinking, just as we have habits like brushing our teeth or putting the dog out or being kind to people. Habits are not behaviors we pick up and lay down whimsically or arbitrarily. They are behaviors we exhibit reliably on appropriate occasions, and they are smoothly triggered without painstaking attention.

The very notion of habits of mind, however, poses a conceptual puzzle. By definition, habits are routine, but good use of the mind is not. The phrase "habits of mind" makes for a kind of oxymoron, like "loud silence" or "safe risk." Indeed, the story of the young man in the convertible illustrates what can go wrong with cultivating habits of mind. Here you have a habit of mind (being careful) played out in a way that misses the point (the man looks for the train from the middle of the tracks). The very automaticity of a habit can undermine its function. Habits like that don't serve us well on a literal highway—or on the metaphorical road of life.

Can one have a habit of mind that truly does its work? The resolution to this puzzle is not very difficult. There's a difference between the thinking required to manage a mental process and the thinking done by the process. A habitual mental process does not require a lot of management to launch and sustain it, but that process itself may involve mindful thinking. It may involve careful examination of alternatives, assessment of risks and consequences, alertness to error, and so on. For example, I have a simple, well-entrenched habit for the road of life: looking carefully when I depart a setting to be sure that I'm not leaving anything behind. This habit triggers and runs off reliably, with very little need for mindful management. But the behaviors deployed by the habit are highly mindful: scrutinizing the setting, glancing under chairs for concealed objects, and peering into drawers and closets for overlooked items.

In all fairness, the man in the convertible displayed a habit with something of this quality, too. It was good that he looked both ways with care. No doubt his scan of the tracks was precise and sensitive. He certainly would have detected any oncoming train. The difficulty was that his habit included a bug, rather like a bug in a computer program. Although his

habit had a thoughtful phase (scanning the tracks), he was not thoughtful about his habit (choosing the point where he should scan the tracks).

Thus, the idea of habits of mind is not self-contradictory. A behavior
can be habitual in its management but mindful in what it does. Still, one
might ask, "Why not have it all? Ideally, shouldn't thinking processes
always be mindfully managed for that extra edge?" Probably not. At least
three things are wrong with this intuitively appealing ideal.

First, having to manage a thinking process mindfully would likely
reduce the thoughtfulness of the process itself. As Herbert Simon (1957)
and many other psychologists have emphasized, we humans have a limited capacity for processing information. Committing the management
of a thinking process to routine is one way to open up mental space for the
work the process has to do.

Second, life has many distractions and preoccupations. A well-
developed habit is more likely to make its presence felt than a practice that
always must be deployed with meticulous deliberateness.

The third objection to this ideal of thoroughly mindful thinking goes
beyond these pragmatic considerations to a logical point. Suppose the
general rule is that thinking processes need mindful management. Surely
managing a thinking process is itself a thinking process, so that process,
too, needs mindful management. And the process of managing that needs
mindful management, and so on. It is mindful management all the way
up, an infinite tower of metacognition, each process managed by its own
mindfully managed manager. Clearly this approach won't work. Enter
habits of mind, an apt challenge to a misguided conception of thinking
as thoroughly thoughtful.

The notion of habits of mind also challenges another conception:
intelligence. Most of the research on human intelligence is emphatically
"abilities centric" (Perkins, 1995; Perkins, Jay, & Tishman, 1993). As mentioned in Chapter 1, the IQ tradition sees intelligence as a pervasive,
monolithic mental ability, summed up by IQ and Charles Spearman's
(1904) "g" factor, a statistical construct representing general intelligence.
A number of theorists have proposed that there are many kinds of mental
ability (2 to 150, according to one model developed by Guilford [1967]).
Although this book is not a setting where these models bear review (see

Perkins, 1995), most of these models have something in common: they treat intelligence as an "ability on demand." Intelligence becomes a matter of what we can do when we know what it is that we're supposed to try to do (such as complete this analogy, decide whether this inference is warranted, or find the best definition for this word).

Thinking in everyday life is a different matter. We not only have to solve problems, we also have to find them amid an ongoing, complex stream of demands and distractions. On the road of life, our thinking is not just a matter of the thinking we can do when we know a peak performance is demanded. It also is a matter of our sensitivity to occasions and our inclination to invest ourselves in them thoughtfully. High mental ability alone may serve us well when we're sitting at a desk, our pencils poised; but good habits of mind keep us going in the rest of the world. This point is underscored by scholars such as philosopher Robert Ennis (1986) with his analysis of critical thinking dispositions, psychologist Jonathan Baron (1985) with his dispositional model of intelligence, and psychologist Ellen Langer (1989) with her conception of mindfulness.

A program of empirical research on thinking dispositions, which I've conducted with Ron Ritchhart, Shari Tishman, and other colleagues over several years, underscores what's at stake here (see, for example, Perkins & Ritchhart, 2004; Perkins & Tishman, 2001). Working with students from middle to late elementary school, we investigated their performance on a variety of critical and creative thinking tasks involving narratives. Over and over again we found that they *could* do far better than they *did* do when they explored options, considered pros and cons, and performed similar tasks. Their performance was limited because they often did not detect when such moves were called for. When they did detect what they should do or when the places were pointed out, they easily could show the kind of thinking called for. They didn't lack intelligence in the sense of ability on demand, but they lacked the habits of mind that provide for ongoing alertness to shortfalls in thinking.

In that spirit, this book speaks not just to intelligence in the laboratory but also to intelligent behavior in the real world. It addresses how we can help youngsters get ready for the road of life, a sort of "drivers education" for the mind. Imagine what life would be like without good habits of various sorts. Our teeth would rot, our bodies collapse, our gardens wither, our tempers sour, and our friends drift away. We do better to the extent that we get direction from good habits, including habits of mind. When today's students hit the road, the ideas in *Learning and Leading with Habits of Mind* can help them ride on smooth mental wheels, checking for trains *before* they start over the tracks!

References

Baron, J. (1985). *Rationality and intelligence*. New York: Cambridge University Press.

Dewey, J. (1933). *How we think: A restatement of the relation of reflective thinking to the education process*. New York: D. C. Heath.

Ennis, R. H. (1986). A taxonomy of critical thinking dispositions and abilities. In J. B. Baron & R. S. Sternberg (Eds.), *Teaching thinking skills: Theory and practice* (pp. 9–26). New York: W. H. Freeman.

Guilford, J. P. (1967). *The nature of human intelligence*. New York: McGraw-Hill.

Langer, E. J. (1989). *Mindfulness*. Reading, MA: Addison-Wesley.

Perkins, D. N. (1995). *Outsmarting IQ: The emerging science of learnable intelligence*. New York: Free Press.

Perkins, D. N., Jay, E., & Tishman, S. (1993). Beyond abilities: A dispositional theory of thinking. *The Merrill-Palmer Quarterly, 39*(1), 1–21.

Perkins, D. N., & Ritchhart, R. (2004). When is good thinking? In D. Y. Dai & R. J. Sternberg (Eds.), *Motivation, emotion, and cognition: Integrative perspectives on intellectual functioning and development* (pp. 351–384). Mahwah, NJ: Erlbaum.

Perkins, D. N., & Tishman, S. (2001). Dispositional aspects of intelligence. In S. Messick & J. M. Collis (Eds.), *Intelligence and personality: Bridging the gap in theory and measurement* (pp. 233–257). Mahwah, NJ: Erlbaum.

Simon, H. A. (1957). *Models of man: Social and rational*. New York: Wiley.

Spearman, C. (1904). General intelligence, objectively defined and measured. *American Journal of Psychology, 15*, 201–209.

❖ ❖ ❖

Preface

Arthur L. Costa and Bena Kallick

Donna Norton Swindal, a resource teacher in Burnsville, Minnesota, shared an interesting story about a 4th grader who brought a newspaper clipping to class. The article described genocide in a troubled African country. After a lively discussion about what was happening there, one concerned classmate stated, "If those people would just learn to persist, they could solve their problems."

His philosophical colleague added, "If they would learn to listen with understanding and empathy, they wouldn't have this problem."

Yet another young activist suggested, "We need to go over there and teach them the Habits of Mind!"

What are the "Habits of Mind" these concerned young citizens were so eager to share? They are the overarching theme of *Leading and Learning with Habits of Mind*, and they are the heart of the book you hold in your hands.

The Beginning

The idea for the Habits of Mind started in 1982. In our beginning conversations, we referred to them as "intelligent behaviors." In our daily work with students and staff, these ideas flourished into rich experiences. We soon realized that these concepts and experiences needed to be documented and disseminated to others. We discovered that we needed a common terminology for the behaviors that would be expected from one another if, indeed, we were living in a productive learning organization. In 1999 we became entranced with Lauren Resnick's statement (1999) that "one's intelligence is the sum of one's habits of mind." That's it, we thought! We don't want *behaviors*; we want *habits*. Learning the behaviors of problem solving, for example, is not the goal. We want to *habituate* effective problem solving. Performing a behavior once is not enough. We want students to appreciate the value of and to develop the propensity for skillful problem solving using a repertoire of mindful strategies applied in a variety of settings. So we came to call these dispositions Habits of Mind, indicating that the behaviors require a discipline of the mind that is practiced so it becomes a habitual way of working toward more thoughtful, intelligent action.

In 2000 we created a developmental series of four books, published by the Association for Supervision and Curriculum Development, to inspire the work of others. They were

- *Book 1: Discovering and Exploring Habits of Mind*
- *Book 2: Activating and Engaging Habits of Mind*
- *Book 3: Assessing and Reporting on Habits of Mind*
- *Book 4: Integrating and Sustaining Habits of Mind*

The intent of Habits of Mind: A Developmental Series was to help educators teach toward these Habits of Mind, which we see as broad, enduring, and essential lifespan learnings that are as appropriate for adults as they are for students. Our hope was that by teaching students (and adults) the Habits of Mind, students would be more disposed to draw upon the habits when they face uncertain or challenging situations. And, ultimately, we hoped the habits would help educators develop thoughtful, compassionate, and cooperative human beings who can live productively in an increasingly chaotic, complex, and information-rich world (as the 4th graders in the anecdote at the start of this preface so aptly demonstrate).

That was 10 years ago. Since that time the Habits of Mind have been embraced by school faculties around the world. The word is spreading to universities, businesses, parents, and other community members. Research has been conducted to demonstrate the positive impact of the

Habits of Mind on students, individuals, and entire school staffs. We have been amazed and delighted with the innovations, elaborations, and applications that have sparked teachers, parents, and school leaders to create children's stories, poetry, limericks, songs, school plays, videos, and performances extolling the virtues of the Habits of Mind.

We continue to expand our work through a process we call "a spiral of reciprocal learning." The work that we write about is translated into classroom reality. The realities of the classroom, in turn, inform our writing. Although we occasionally work alongside teachers in their classrooms, we more often work alongside the work that they send to us. As we study their work, we develop an enhanced theory of learning about the habits. The Habits of Mind have influenced not only school practices but also the entire culture of schools. (The stories from Friendship Valley Elementary School, Waikiki School, Furr High School, and Tahoma School District presented in Chapters 19 through 22 are examples.) We need to continue to tell the classroom stories, as they help to crystallize a theory of practice with the Habits of Mind. This book, *Learning and Leading with Habits of Mind*, is intended to serve that purpose.

A Dual Purpose

The most powerful learning communities use these Habits of Mind to guide all their work. Yet sometimes the practicality of school life requires that people make individual commitments with the hope that their beliefs and behaviors will affect the whole. Teaching with the Habits of Mind requires a shift toward a broader conception of educational outcomes and how they are cultivated, assessed, and communicated. *Learning and Leading with Habits of Mind* aims to help you work toward and achieve a move from "individual" to "systems" in your thinking.

In this book, we provide the following:

• Descriptions and examples of the Habits of Mind.

• Instructional strategies intended to foster acquisition of these habits at school and at home.

• Assessment tools that provide a way to gather evidence of student growth in the Habits of Mind.

• Suggestions for ways to involve students, teachers, and parents in communicating progress toward acquiring the Habits of Mind.

• Descriptions from schools, teachers, and administrators about how they have incorporated the Habits of Mind into their practice.

• Examples of the effects that the Habits of Mind have had on students, staffs, individual teachers, and their work, as well as on the culture of the school.

• Descriptions of qualities of leadership necessary for the Habits of Mind to become successfully infused into school cultures and classrooms.

Our true intent for this book, however, is far more panoramic, pervasive, and long-range. It works at two levels. The first level encompasses immediate and practical considerations that promote using the Habits of Mind in classrooms and schools every day. The second level addresses a larger, more elevated concern for creating a learning culture that considers the Habits of Mind as central to building a thoughtful community and world. We have divided the book into separate sections, each addressing the levels as follows:

Part I: Discovering and Exploring Habits of Mind

Level 1: Defining the Habits of Mind and understanding the significance of developing these habits as a part of lifelong learning.

Level 2: Encouraging schools and communities to elevate their level and broaden their scope of curricular outcomes by focusing on more essential, enduring life span learnings.

Part II: Building a Thought-Full Environment

Level 1: Learning how to teach the habits directly and to reinforce them throughout the curriculum.

Level 2: Enhancing instructional decision making to employ content not as an end of instruction but as a vehicle for activating and engaging the mind.

Part III: Assessing and Reporting on Habits of Mind

Level 1: Learning about a range of techniques and strategies for gathering evidence of students' growth in and performance of the Habits of Mind.

Level 2: Using feedback to guide students to become self-assessing and to help school teams and parents use assessment data to cultivate a more thoughtful culture.

Part IV: Leading Schools with Habits of Mind in Mind

Level 1: Learning strategies for extending the impact of the Habits of Mind throughout the school culture and community.

Level 2: Forging a common vision among all members of the educational community from kindergarten through postgraduate work: teachers, administrative teams, administrators, librarians, staff developers, teacher educators, school board members, and parents. This vision describes the characteristics of efficacious and creative thinkers and problem solvers.

Part V: Learning from Mindful Schools

Level 1: Learning from other schools and agencies about the powerful effects of the Habits of Mind on student learning, staff members, and the culture of the school.

Level 2: Becoming intrigued and inspired to pursue and experience the impact of the Habits of Mind as a transformational tool to create professional learning communities.

The Habits of Mind

The following list contains the 16 Habits of Mind. The habits begin with the individual and move out to the entire community. Keep in mind, however, that the list is not complete. As our conversations continue—and as you work with the habits—we are likely to identify other habits that should be added to this list.

Although they are elaborated in Chapter 2, the 16 Habits of Mind we have identified can be described briefly as follows:

1. *Persisting*. Stick to it. See a task through to completion, and remain focused.

2. *Managing impulsivity*. Take your time. Think before you act. Remain calm, thoughtful, and deliberate.

3. *Listening with understanding and empathy*. Seek to understand others. Devote mental energy to another person's thoughts and ideas.

Hold your own thoughts in abeyance so you can better perceive another person's point of view and emotions.

4. *Thinking flexibly.* Look at a situation another way. Find a way to change perspectives, generate alternatives, and consider options.

5. *Thinking about thinking (metacognition).* Know your knowing. Be aware of your own thoughts, strategies, feelings, and actions—and how they affect others.

6. *Striving for accuracy.* Check it again. Nurture a desire for exactness, fidelity, craftsmanship, and truth.

7. *Questioning and posing problems.* How do you know? Develop a questioning attitude, consider what data are needed, and choose strategies to produce those data. Find problems to solve.

8. *Applying past knowledge to new situations.* Use what you learn. Access prior knowledge, transferring that knowledge beyond the situation in which it was learned.

9. *Thinking and communicating with clarity and precision.* Be clear. Strive for accurate communication in both written and oral form. Avoid overgeneralizations, distortions, and deletions.

10. *Gathering data through all senses.* Use your natural pathways. Gather data through all the sensory paths: gustatory, olfactory, tactile, kinesthetic, auditory, and visual.

11. *Creating, imagining, innovating.* Try a different way. Generate novel ideas, and seek fluency and originality.

12. *Responding with wonderment and awe.* Let yourself be intrigued by the world's phenomena and beauty. Find what is awesome and mysterious in the world.

13. *Taking responsible risks.* Venture out. Live on the edge of your competence.

14. *Finding humor.* Laugh a little. Look for the whimsical, incongruous, and unexpected in life. Laugh at yourself when you can.

15. *Thinking interdependently.* Work together. Truly work with and learn from others in reciprocal situations.

16. *Remaining open to continuous learning.* Learn from experiences. Be proud—and humble enough—to admit you don't know. Resist complacency.

Finding an Internal Compass

In teaching toward the Habits of Mind, we are interested in not only how many answers students know but also how students behave when they don't know an answer. We are interested in observing how students produce knowledge rather than how they merely reproduce it. A critical attribute of intelligent human beings is not only having information but also knowing how to act on it.

By definition, a problem is any stimulus, question, task, phenomenon, or discrepancy, the explanation for which is not immediately known. Intelligent behavior is performed in response to such questions and problems. Thus, we are interested in focusing on student performance under those challenging conditions—dichotomies, dilemmas, paradoxes, polarities, ambiguities, and enigmas—that demand strategic reasoning, insightfulness, perseverance, creativity, and craftsmanship to resolve.

Teaching toward the Habits of Mind is a team effort. Because the acquisition of these habits requires repeated opportunities over a long period, the entire staff must dedicate itself to teaching toward, recognizing, reinforcing, discussing, reflecting on, and assessing them. When students encounter these habits at each grade level in the elementary years and in each classroom throughout the secondary day—and when the habits also are reinforced and modeled at home—they become internalized, generalized, and habituated. They become an "internal compass" to guide and direct us toward more efficacious, empathic, and cooperative actions.

We need to find new ways of assessing and reporting growth in the Habits of Mind. We cannot measure process-oriented outcomes using old-fashioned, product-oriented assessment techniques. Gathering evidence of performance and growth in the Habits of Mind requires "kid watching." As students interact with real-life, day-to-day problems in school, at home, on the playground, alone, and with friends, teaching teams and other adults can collect anecdotes and examples of written and visual expressions that reveal students' increasingly skillful, voluntary, and spontaneous use of these Habits of Mind in diverse situations and circumstances. This work takes time. The habits are never fully mastered, though they do become increasingly apparent over time and with repeated experiences and opportunities to practice and reflect on their performance.

Student Outcomes for the 21st Century

Learning and innovation skills are what separate students who are prepared for increasingly complex life and work environments in the 21st
century from those who are not. Students in our schools today live in a
technology- and media-driven environment marked by access to an abun-
dance of information, rapid changes in technology tools, and the need to
collaborate and make individual contributions as they prepare for both
the workplace and participation in democracy. Today's life and work environments require far more than thinking skills and content knowledge.

To be effective in the 21st century, citizens and workers must be able
to communicate, to team, to continuously learn, and to function in a
visual, data-rich society. The school and community must emphasize the
increasing importance of learning to learn in light of the shift to a digital
age that values intellectual capital. This vision redefines the purpose of
public education. The school's vision must seek to create learners who
have the self-confidence, independence, and high-tech proficiencies to
continuously learn—meeting challenges innovatively and creatively (Partnership for 21st Century Skills, 2007).

According to the vision, students need to be prepared with the following skills:

- Creativity and innovation.
- Critical thinking and problem solving.
- Communication and collaboration.
- Flexibility and adaptability.
- Initiative and self-direction.
- Social and cross-cultural skills.
- Productivity and accountability.
- Leadership and responsibility.

Leading and Learning with Habits of Mind can help you start down
a path to that vision. It provides a road map for individuals, for classrooms,
and ultimately for a full-system approach to enhanced curriculum,
instruction, and assessment. For our purposes, we think a "system" is
approached when the Habits of Mind are integrated throughout the
culture of the organization—that is, when all individual members of a

learning community share a common vision of the attributes of effective and creative problem solvers not only for their students but for themselves as well; when resources are allocated to the development of those dispositions; when strategies to enhance those characteristics in themselves and others are planned; and when members of the organization join in efforts to continuously assess, refine, and integrate those behaviors in their own and the organization's practices. The result of a full-system approach is exemplified by this excerpt from a 5th grader's valedictorian address during graduation from Friendship Valley Elementary School in Westminster, Maryland:

> I can tell you right now that we will never be able to forget the Habits of Mind. They helped us so much! They taught us better ways of doing things and how to resolve problems! We learned respect and manners. My mother was so very impressed with this teaching. Also we learned that you need to get along with others and not to disrespect them either.

References

Partnership for 21st Century Skills. (2007). *Framework for 21st century learning*. Tucson, AZ: Author. Available: www.21stcenturyskills.org.

Resnick, L. (1999, June 16). Making America smarter. *Education Week*, pp. 38–40.

❖   ❖   ❖

Acknowledgments

We wish to express our appreciation to the many contributors to this book. The descriptions of their experiences, lessons, implementation strategies, vignettes, and artwork are what give meaning, expression, and practicality to the Habits of Mind. To them we are eternally grateful.

We wish to thank Scott Willis, Nancy Modrak, Darcie Russell, and other members of the ASCD publishing staff who encouraged and guided us throughout this project, and Kathleen Florio for her attention to detail.

We pay particular tribute to Bena's husband, Charles, and Art's wife, Nancy, who tolerated our time away from them. Their love, encouragement, and understanding provided the support base for our success.

Finally, we wish to acknowledge the many teachers, administrators, and parents in the numerous schools and communities throughout the United States and abroad who have adopted and implemented the Habits of Mind and have found them a meaningful way to organize learning. The future world will be a more thoughtful, compassionate, and cooperative place because of their dedication to cultivating the Habits of Mind in students and modeling them in their own behavior.

❖   ❖   ❖

Suggestions for Using This Book

Arthur L. Costa and Bena Kallick

As we all know, the social construction of knowledge about a book often invites finding deeper meaning in the text. Perhaps that is why book reading groups are so popular. We recommend that you use *Learning and Leading with Habits of Mind* as a book around which you may construct meaning. We suggest that you read designated parts of the book and meet with some regularity with others to (1) dig more deeply into its meaning and (2) reflect on your practice as you try some of what is suggested in the text. It is our hope that this is not just another book to be read. Rather, we hope that it is a book that you read, question, and revisit; and whose ideas you will use, with the ultimate goal of developing a vision of, and practices for, a thoughtful school.

Protocols for Chapter Study Groups

Given our hope for how you will use this book, we offer the following protocols for studying each chapter.

Protocol 1

Have each member of the group read the chapter individually. For the group discussion, ask the following questions:

• What is the author's purpose? What have you learned about the culture of this school or district?

• How did the habits serve as a catalyst for a change in the school culture? What did you observe about the leadership?

• What did you find intriguing? Challenging? Unique? Controversial?

• What did you learn from this chapter that might be applicable to your situation?

Protocol 2

Have each member of the group read the chapter individually. In preparation for the discussion, ask each member to use a two-column note-taking format. In the first column, record your response to the text. In the second column, note what was specifically stated in the text.

During the group discussion, use the following process:

• First, ask each member of the group to share one entry from the notes. There is no discussion at this time. Each person just shares individual thoughts.

• Second, ask each person to share one entry that he would like the group to discuss. A timekeeper limits the discussion of each question to five minutes (the time may vary depending on the size of the group and the amount of time available).

• Third, ask this overall question: What have we learned based on this analysis of the text?

Protocol 3

Have each member of the group read the chapter individually. When the group comes together, ask each member to work with a partner to identify where the chapter says something that

• Confirms what you thought.
• Contradicts what you thought.
• Raises a question.

- Confuses you.
- Seems important.
- Is new or interesting.

Have each pair share one question that the group tries to answer. Finally, discuss your thoughts as a group and imagine how this reading might influence your work.

Protocol 4

Have each member of the group read the chapter individually. As a group, use the following format to analyze the text before discussion:

- What if . . . ?
- Why did . . . ?
- How did . . . ?
- What would happen if . . . ?
- What might . . . ?
- Why do you think . . . ?
- What implications . . . ?
- Why is . . . ?
- How can . . . ?
- How can we know whether . . . ?

In addition to providing a way to find deeper meaning in the text, all four protocols will give the group an opportunity to practice the following Habits of Mind:

- Listening with understanding and empathy.
- Thinking flexibly.
- Remaining open to continuous learning.
- Thinking and communicating with clarity and precision.

Literature Circles

Penn Valley School in Lower Merion, Pennsylvania, created literature circles to study a book that included information about the Habits of Mind. You might consider forming your own literature circles to study this book. Literature circles are small, temporary discussion groups whose members have chosen to read the same story, poem, article, or book. The group members determine which portion of the text they will read either during or outside the meeting. As they read, members prepare to fulfill specific responsibilities in the upcoming discussion. Each comes to the group with the notes needed to help perform that specific job.

The circles have regular meetings, with discussion roles rotating for each session. When they finish a book, circle members plan a way to share highlights of their reading with the wider community. Then they trade members among groups, select more reading, and move into a new cycle. Once readers are comfortable with successfully conducting their own wide-ranging, self-sustaining discussions, formal discussion roles may be dropped.

Based on Daniels (1994) and Routman (1991), we have identified these key features of literature circles:

- Participants choose their own materials.
- Small, temporary groups are formed on the basis of book or chapter choice.
- Different groups read different books (or chapters).
- Groups meet on a regular schedule to discuss their reading.
- Participants use written or drawn notes to guide both their reading and their discussion.
- Participants generate discussion topics.
- Group meetings aim to foster open, natural conversations. Though group members may play specific roles in a discussion, personal connections, digressions, and open-ended questions are welcome.
- In newly forming groups, participants play a rotating assortment of task roles.
- The leader serves as a facilitator, not as a group member or an instructor.
- Self-evaluation occurs.
- A spirit of playfulness and fun pervades the room.
- When members complete a book, they share with one another (and with the community). Then new groups form around new reading choices.

Also based on Daniels (1994) and Routman (1991), we have identified the following group roles:

- Discussion Director: Creates a list of questions for the group.
- Passage Picker: Chooses parts of the book to be read aloud.
- Connector: Finds connections between the book and the classroom as well as the book and the school community.

You may want to create other roles to satisfy your group's needs. Whatever form your group takes, literature circles are a powerful way to explore information in a relaxed but dynamic setting. They provide opportunities to practice thinking and communicating with clarity and precision, listening with understanding and empathy, and thinking flexibly by examining alternative points of view. They also offer an experience in continuous learning.

References

Daniels, H. (1994). *Literature circles: Voice and choice in the student-centered classroom.* York, ME: Stenhouse.

Routman, R. (1991). *Invitations: Changing as teachers and learners K–12.* Portsmouth, NH: Heinemann.

❖   ❖   ❖

Part I

Discovering and Exploring
Habits of Mind

Many people have played themselves to death. Many people have eaten and drunk themselves to death. Nobody ever thought himself to death.

—*Gilbert Highet, educator and author*

Welcome to the Habits of Mind. As we embark on this journey together, our deepest wish is that this will be a generative experience—one that deepens your thinking about what is important to teach students for their future. We hope that it will nurture new possibilities for your work in education.

The intent of Part I of this book, Discovering and Exploring Habits of Mind, is to let you know where we're coming from. In Chapter 1 we start with a brief history of how society's perspectives of what constitutes "intelligence" have changed over the years and where the Habits of Mind fit into the more modern conception of intelligence.

Chapter 2 describes the 16 Habits of Mind. This list was derived from studies of what successful, "intelligent" people do when they are confronted with problems to solve, decisions to make, creative ideas to generate, and ambiguities to clarify. These successful people are from all walks of life and include physicians, teachers, auto mechanics, entrepreneurs, artists, and scientists. We propose that if these are the attributes of successful people, then we should help our students acquire these attributes as well. They are the characteristics that will predict students' success if they go on to college, if they take a job, if they become active in their community, and if they marry and raise a family.

Chapter 3 describes the place of the Habits of Mind in the curriculum. We believe that the Habits of Mind do not displace the agreed-upon standards of learning that have been developed and adopted by the school. Rather, the content that is taught serves as a vehicle and provides an opportunity for learning the Habits of Mind. What is unique about the Habits of Mind is that they provide a common terminology for communication by all members of the school community: parents, teachers, administrators, and students. Thus, the Habits of Mind provide a shared vision of the attributes and characteristics of the graduates of the school. In that way, staff members from diverse departments and grade levels can work together even though the students and the content they teach may be different.

Chapter 4 describes a journey of continued growth in the Habits of Mind. Five dimensions contribute to that growth. These dimensions become the focus of instruction and assessment to help learners progress toward the internalization of the Habits of Mind. The intent of this chapter is to provide a map that a staff or school district can use in planning for the continual modification of learning experiences so they become more complex, sophisticated, and appropriate for students' development over time.

Chapter 4 is coauthored with our colleague James Anderson, who worked to infuse the Habits of Mind with hundreds of teachers throughout Australia under the auspices of the Australian National Schools Network. They observed that all students use the Habits of Mind; some use them intuitively, whereas others have learned them because of instruction or modeling by parents and previous teachers. However, they also noted that those same students might not use the habits skillfully or strategically. They may not fully realize the value of them, or they may use the habits in a limited range of situations. However, these educators found that over time and with increasingly sophisticated instruction, students seem to progress as they mature, become more skillful, and develop greater inclination toward and value for the Habits of Mind. This journey also provides a basis for the instructional design described in Chapter 5 and for the assessment strategies described in Part III of this book.

Building on the dimensions of growth described in Chapter 4, Chapter 5 describes a range of instructional approaches and strategies. The intent is for teachers to develop a repertoire of instructional designs to teach the Habits of Mind with increasing complexity and sophistication. We wouldn't want to keep teaching students at the "Exploring Meanings" level.

The purpose of Part I, therefore, is to orient you to the Habits of Mind—their power and their value—and to provide insights into curriculum and instruction intended to enhance their development.

—*Arthur L. Costa and Bena Kallick*

1

Changing Perspectives About Intelligence

Arthur L. Costa and Bena Kallick

What is intelligence if not the ability to face problems in an unprogrammed (creative) manner? The notion that such a nebulous socially defined concept as intelligence might be identified as a "thing" with a locus in the brain and a definite degree of heritability—and that it might be measured as a single number thus permitting a unilinear ranking of people according to the amount they possess[—]is a principal error ... [,] one that has reverberated throughout the country and has affected millions of lives.

—Stephen Jay Gould

The changing conception of intelligence is one of the most powerful, liberating forces ever to influence the restructuring of education, schools, and society. It also is a vital influence behind the development of the Habits of Mind, which are detailed more fully in the next chapter. To better understand those habits, though, it is important to grasp how the concept of intelligence has changed over the last century. This chapter traces the evolution of conceptions of intelligence. It also considers how some significant researchers, educators, and psychologists influenced and transformed mental models of the intellect.

Intelligence for a Bygone Era

At the turn of the 19th century in the United States, society was undergoing great shifts. Masses of immigrants poured into the nation, moving inland from their ports of entry or staying in the large eastern cities to fill the needs of the job-hungry Industrial Revolution. In retrospect, it is easy to see that the society of that day was elitist, racist, and sexist, its actions fueled by a fear of diluting "Anglo-Saxon purity." Employers of the time believed they needed a way to separate those who were educable and worthy of work from those who should be relegated to menial labor (or put back on the boat and shipped to their country of origin).

World War I contributed to homogenizing classes, races, and nationalities. Through military travels, enhanced communication, and industrialization, our population was becoming more cosmopolitan. A popular song of the time, "How 'Ya Gonna Keep 'Em Down on the Farm After They've Seen Paree?" alerted the aristocracy to the impending trend toward globalization. Metaphorically the song proclaimed that to protect the existing separation of the masses into their "rightful" places, there was a need to analyze, categorize, separate, distinguish, and label human beings who were "not like us." Some means was necessary to measure individuals' and groups' "mental energies," to determine who was "fit" and who was not (Gould, 1981; Perkins, 1995).

Thanks to a mentality ruled by ideas of mechanism, efficiency, and authority, many came to believe that everything in life needed to be measured. Lord Kelvin, a 19th century physicist and astronomer, stated, "If you cannot measure it, if you cannot express it in numbers, your knowledge is of a very meager and unsatisfactory kind." Born in this era was Charles Spearman's theory of general intelligence. His theory was based on the idea that intelligence is inherited through genes and chromosomes and that it can be measured by one's ability to score sufficiently on Alfred Binet's Stanford-Binet Intelligence Test, yielding a static and relatively stable IQ score (Perkins, 1995, p. 42).

Immersed in the "efficiency" theories of the day, educators strived for the *one* best system for curriculum, learning, and teaching. Into this scene of educational management entered Edward L. Thorndike from Columbia University. He went beyond theory to produce usable educational tools including textbooks, tests, curriculums, and teacher training.

Thorndike continues to wield a tremendous influence on educational practice. His "associationist" theory suggests that knowledge is a collection of links between pairs of external stimuli and internal mental responses. In this context, learning is thought to be a matter of increasing the strength of the "good," or correct, bonds and decreasing the strength of the incorrect ones. Spearman's and Thorndike's theories still serve educators as a rationale for procedures such as tracking students according to high and low aptitude, the bell curve, drill and practice, competition, frequent testing, ability grouping, IQ scores as a basis for special education, task-analyzing learning into separate skills, and reinforcement of learning by rewards and external motivations.

When people view their intelligence as a fixed and unchangeable entity, they strive to obtain positive evaluations of their ability and to avoid displaying evidence of inadequate ability. They believe their intelligence is demonstrated in task performance: they either have or lack ability. This negative self-concept influences effort. Effort and ability are negatively related in determining achievement, and having to expend great effort with a task is taken as a sign of low ability (Resnick & Hall, 1998).

Toward a New Vision

Clearly, something new is needed if schools are to break out of this traditional, aptitude-centered mentality and make it possible for young people to acquire the kinds of mental habits needed to lead productive, fulfilling lives. We need a definition of intelligence that is as attentive to robust habits of mind as it is to the specifics of thinking processes or knowledge structures. We need to develop learning goals that reflect the belief that ability is a continuously expandable repertoire of skills, and that through a person's efforts, intelligence grows incrementally.

Incremental thinkers are likely to apply self-regulatory, metacognitive skills when they encounter task difficulties. They are likely to focus on analyzing the task and trying to generate and execute alternative strategies. They will try to garner internal and external resources for problem solving. When people think of their intelligence as something that grows incrementally, they are more likely to invest the energy to learn something new or to increase their understanding and mastery of tasks. They display continued high levels of task-related effort in response to difficulty. Learning goals are associated with the inference that effort and ability are positively related, so that greater efforts create and make evident more ability.

Children develop cognitive strategies and effort-based beliefs about their intelligence—the habits of mind associated with higher-order learning—when they continually are pressed to raise questions, accept challenges, find solutions that are not immediately apparent, explain concepts, justify their reasoning, and seek information. When we hold children accountable for this kind of intelligent behavior, they take it as a signal that we think they are smart, and they come to accept this judgment. The paradox is that children become smart by being treated as if they already are intelligent (Resnick & Hall, 1998).

A body of research deals with factors that seem to shape these habits, factors that have to do with people's beliefs about the relation between effort and ability. Self-help author Liane Cordes states: "Continuous effort—not strength or intelligence—is the key to unlocking our potential" (Cordes, n.d.). The following discussion traces the historical pathways of influential theories that have led to this new vision of intelligent behavior (Fogarty, 1997).

Intelligence Can Be Taught

Ahead of his time, Arthur Whimbey (Whimbey, Whimbey, & Shaw, 1975) urged us to reconsider our basic concepts of intelligence and to question the assumption that genetically inherited capacities are immutable. Whimbey argued that intelligence could be taught, and he provided evidence that certain interventions enhance the cognitive functioning of students from preschool to college level. Through instruction in problem solving, metacognition, and strategic thinking, Whimbey's students not only increased their IQ scores but also displayed more effective approaches to their academic work. Participants in such studies, however, ceased using the cognitive techniques as soon as the specific conditions of training were removed. They became capable of performing the skill that was taught, but they acquired no general *habit* of using it and no capacity to judge for themselves when it was useful (Resnick & Hall, 1998).

To accommodate new learning, the brain builds more synaptic connections between and among its cells. It has been found that IQ scores have increased over the years (Kotulak, 1997). These increases demonstrate that instead of being fixed and immutable, intelligence is flexible and subject to great changes, both up and down, depending on the kinds of stimulation the brain gets from its environment.

Structure of the Intellect

J. P. Guilford and R. Hoeptner (1971) believed that all students have intelligence, but they defined it in terms of "what kind" instead of "how much." Guilford and his associates believed that intelligence consists of more than 120 thinking abilities that are combinations of operations, contents, and products. Operations include such mental capabilities as comprehending, remembering, and analyzing; contents refer to words, forms, and symbols; and products refer to complexity: single units, groups, and relationships.

Twenty-six of these factors were found to be relevant to school success. Tests were developed to profile students' abilities, and curriculum units and instructional strategies were developed to target, exercise, and enhance each of the 26 intellectual capacities. Guilford believed that through these interventions, a person's intelligence could be amplified.

Theory of Cognitive Modifiability

Iconoclast Reuven Feuerstein, working with disadvantaged children in Israel, challenged the prevailing notion of a fixed intelligence with his theory of cognitive modifiability. Feuerstein believes that intelligence is not a fixed entity but a function of experience and mediation by significant individuals (parents, teachers, caregivers) in a child's environment.

This modern theory underlies a fresh view of intelligence as modifiable; it contends that intelligence can be taught, that human beings can continue to enhance their intellectual functioning throughout their lifetimes, and that all of us are "gifted" and all of us are "retarded" simultaneously (Feuerstein, Rand, Hoffman, & Miller, 1980).

Multiple Forms of Intelligence

Howard Gardner (1983, 1999, 2006) believes that there are many ways of knowing, learning, and expressing knowledge. Gardner has identified several distinct intelligences that function in problem solving and in the creation of new products: verbal, logical/mathematical, kinesthetic, musical, spatial, naturalistic, interpersonal, intrapersonal, and existential.

Gardner also believes that these intelligences can be nurtured in all human beings. Although each individual may have preferred forms, all of us can, with proper mediation and experience, continue to develop these capacities throughout our lifetime.

Intelligence as Success in Life

Robert Sternberg (1984) found that "mythological" IQ scores had little predictive quality in regard to success in later life. He argues for three types of intelligence:

• *Analytical intelligence* in which comparisons, evaluations, and assessments are made.

• *Creative intelligence* involving imagination, design, and invention.

• *Practical intelligence* in which use, practicality, and demonstration are paramount.

Sternberg believes that all human beings have the capacity to continue growing in these three domains, and he encourages educators to enhance them all (Sternberg, Torff, & Grigorenko, 1998).

Learnable Intelligence

David Perkins (1995) further supports the theory that intelligence can be taught and learned. He believes that three important mechanisms underlie intelligence:

• *Neural intelligence* is the "genetically determined, hard-wired original equipment" that one has inherited and that determines the speed and efficiency of one's brain. Neural intelligence cannot be altered much.

• *Experiential intelligence* is context-specific knowledge that is accumulated through experience. It means knowing one's way around the various settings and contexts in which one functions. A person's reservoir of experiential intelligence can be expanded.

• *Reflective intelligence* is the "good use of the mind; the artful deployment of our faculties of thinking." It includes self-managing, self-monitoring, and self-modifying. Perkins refers to this capacity as "mindware" (p. 264), and it can and should be cultivated.

Emotional Intelligence

Drawing on vast amounts of brain research, Daniel Goleman (1995) asserts that the intellect and emotions are inextricably intertwined. One cannot be developed without the other. Educating the emotions may be as important as educating the intellect. Developing self-awareness, managing impulsivity and emotions, empathizing, and developing social skills are the most basic forms of intelligence. If these capacities are neglected, inadequacies may cause people to fall short of developing fuller intellectual capacities.

Moral Intelligence

Robert Coles (1997) believes that children can become "more intelligent" by developing their inner character. He believes students develop a social/moral intelligence by learning empathy, respect, reciprocity, cooperation, and how to live by the Golden Rule through the example of others and through explicit dialogue about moral issues. Coles believes that every child grows up by building a "moral archeology," a moral code of ethics through interactions with parents, peers, and significant others. He believes that this capacity can continue to be developed throughout a person's lifetime.

A Fully Developed Intellect

Luis Alberto Machado (1980), former Venezuelan minister of intellectual development, reminds us that all human beings have a basic right to the full development of their intellect. More and more government leaders in the United States and other nations are realizing that the level of a country's overall development depends on the level of its people's intellectual development. Industrial leaders realize that to survive and progress, any corporation must invest in its intellectual capital by continuing to enhance the mental resources of its employees. Educators, too, are realizing that our minds, bodies, and emotions must be engaged and transformed for learning to occur.

Social Intelligence

Daniel Goleman (2006) cites neurological research that suggests that the human brain is a "social brain" with an innate capacity to bond with others, to empathize with others, to engage in social reasoning, and to have concern for others. He suggests that social prowess, not cognitive or physical superiority, is what allowed *Homo sapiens* to achieve its highest evolutionary accomplishments. Goleman makes the case that intelligence is not all "cognitive" but rather is composed of emotional and social intelligence as well.

Habits of Mind

Carol Dweck (1999) found that the highest achievers in school

- Have the highest vulnerability to helplessness.
- Are most likely to believe their intelligence is a fixed trait.
- Are more likely to want tasks they are sure they can do well.
- Are more likely to blame their abilities and show impairment in the face of difficulties.
- Aren't well served in long-term learning such as in college or careers.

She states:

> You might think that students who were highly skilled would be the ones who relish a challenge and persevere in the face of setbacks. Instead, many of these students are the most worried about failure, and the most likely to question their ability and to wilt when they hit obstacles. (p. 1)

Increasingly we are adopting the mental model that intelligence is a set of teachable, learnable behaviors that all human beings can continue to develop and improve throughout their lifetimes. We must help students think powerfully about ideas, learn to critique as well as support others' thinking, and become thoughtful problem solvers and decision makers. The Habits of Mind provide a set of behaviors that discipline intellectual processes. Taken as a whole, the many definitions and interpretations of what is meant by intelligence lead us to conclude that the habits can be cultivated, articulated, operationalized, taught, fostered, modeled, and assessed. They can be an integral component of instruction in every school subject, and they may determine achievement of any worthy goal as one moves out into life.

We need to do such work if we truly are to be guided by the rhetoric "all kids can learn." We need to modify that slogan to "all kids do learn *but not on the same day and not in the same way.*" Then, we have to understand what it means not only to say that phrase but also to put it into operation in classrooms. We can no longer be satisfied with a system that is willing to classify, categorize, and sort students on the basis of misaligned test scores.

As Lauren Resnick (1999) stated, "One's intelligence is the sum of one's habits of mind."

References

Coles, R. (1997). *The moral intelligence of children: How to raise a moral child.* New York: Random House.

Cordes, L. (n.d.). Retrieved from www.bestmotivation.com/quotes-1/of/Liane_Cordes.htm

Dweck, C. (1999). *Self theories: The role of motivation, personality and development.* New York: Random House.

Feuerstein, R., Rand, Y., Hoffman, M. B., & Miller, R. (1980). *Instrumental enrichment: An intervention program for cognitive modifiability.* Baltimore, MD: University Park Press.

Fogarty, R. (1997). *Brain compatible classrooms.* Arlington Heights, IL: SkyLight Training and Publishing.

Gardner, H. (1983). *Frames of mind: The theory of multiple intelligences.* New York: Basic Books.

Gardner, H. (1999, July). Multiple intelligences. Speech delivered at the Thinking for a Change Conference; 7th International Thinking Conference, Edmonton, Alberta, Canada.

Gardner, H. (2006). *Multiple intelligences: New horizons.* New York: Basic Books.

Goleman, D. (1995). *Emotional intelligence: Why it can matter more than IQ.* New York: Bantam Books.

Goleman, D. (2006). *Social intelligence: The new science of human relationships.* New York: Bantam Books.

Gould, S. J. (1981). *The mismeasure of man.* New York: W. W. Norton.

Guilford, J. P., & Hoeptner, R. (1971). *The analysis of intelligence.* New York: McGraw-Hill.

Kotulak, R. (1997). *Inside the brain: Revolutionary discoveries of how the mind works.* Kansas City, MO: Andrews McMeel.

Machado, L. A. (1980). *The right to be intelligent*. New York: Pergamon Press.

Perkins, D. N. (1995). *Outsmarting IQ: The emerging science of learnable intelligence*. New York: Free Press.

Resnick, L. B. (1999, June 16). Making America smarter. *Education Week*, pp. 38–40.

Resnick, L., & Hall, M. (1998, Fall). Learning organizations for sustainable education reform. *DAEDALUS: Journal of the American Academy of Arts and Sciences*, 89–118.

Sternberg, R. (1983). *How can we teach intelligence?* Philadelphia, PA: Research for Better Schools.

Sternberg, R. J. (1984). *Beyond I.Q.: A triarchic theory of human intelligence*. New York: Cambridge University Press.

Sternberg, R. J., Torff, B., & Grigorenko, E. (1998, May). Teaching for successful intelligence raises school achievement. *Phi Delta Kappan*, 79(9), 667–669.

Whimbey, A., Whimbey, L. S., & Shaw, L. (1975). *Intelligence can be taught*. New York: Erlbaum.

2

Describing the Habits of Mind

Arthur L. Costa

> When we no longer know what to do we have come to our real work, and when we no longer know which way to go we have begun our real journey. The mind that is not baffled is not employed. The impeded stream is the one that sings.
>
> —Wendell Berry

This chapter contains descriptions for 16 of the attributes that human beings display when they behave intelligently. In this book, we refer to them as Habits of Mind. They are the characteristics of what intelligent people do when they are confronted with problems, the resolutions to which are not immediately apparent.

These Habits of Mind seldom are performed in isolation; rather, clusters of behaviors are drawn forth and used in various situations. For example, when listening intently, we use the habits of thinking flexibly, thinking about our thinking (metacognition), thinking and communicating with clarity and precision, and perhaps even questioning and posing problems.

Do not conclude, based on this list, that humans display intelligent behavior in only 16 ways. The list of the Habits of Mind is not complete. We want this list to initiate a collection of additional attributes. In fact, 12 attributes of "Intelligent Behavior" were first described in 1991 (Costa,

1991). Since then, through collaboration and interaction with many others, the list has been expanded. You, your colleagues, and your students will want to continue the search for additional Habits of Mind to add to this list of 16.

Habits of Mind as Learning Outcomes

Educational outcomes in traditional settings focus on how many answers a student knows. When we teach for the Habits of Mind, we are interested also in how students behave when they *don't know* an answer. The Habits of Mind are performed in response to questions and problems, the answers to which are not immediately known. We are interested in enhancing the ways students *produce* knowledge rather than how they merely *reproduce* it. We want students to learn how to develop a critical stance with their work: inquiring, editing, thinking flexibly, and learning from another person's perspective. The critical attribute of intelligent human beings is not only having information but also knowing how to act on it.

What behaviors indicate an efficient, effective thinker? What do human beings do when they behave intelligently? Vast research on effective thinking, successful people, and intelligent behavior by Ames (1997), Carnegie and Stynes (2006), Ennis (1991), Feuerstein, Rand, Hoffman, and Miller (1980), Freeley (as reported in Strugatch, 2004), Glatthorn and Baron (1991), Goleman (1995), Perkins (1991), Sternberg (1984), and Waugh (2005) suggests that effective thinkers and peak performers have identifiable characteristics. These characteristics have been identified in successful people in all walks of life: lawyers, mechanics, teachers, entrepreneurs, salespeople, physicians, athletes, entertainers, leaders, parents, scientists, artists, teachers, and mathematicians.

Horace Mann, a U.S. educator (1796–1859), once observed that "habit is a cable; we weave a thread of it each day, and at last we cannot break it." In *Learning and Leading with Habits of Mind*, we focus on 16 Habits of Mind that teachers and parents can teach, cultivate, observe, and assess. The intent is to help students get into the habit of behaving intelligently. A Habit of Mind is a pattern of intellectual behaviors that leads to productive actions. When we experience dichotomies, are confused by

FIGURE 2.1
Dimensions of the Habits of Mind

The Habits of Mind incorporate the following dimensions:

Value: Choosing to employ a pattern of intellectual behaviors rather than other, less productive patterns.

Inclination: Feeling the tendency to employ a pattern of intellectual behaviors.

Sensitivity: Perceiving opportunities for, and appropriateness of, employing the pattern of behaviors.

Capability: Possessing the basic skills and capacities to carry through with the behaviors.

Commitment: Constantly striving to reflect on and improve performance of the pattern of intellectual behaviors.

Policy: Making it a policy to promote and incorporate the patterns of intellectual behaviors into actions, decisions, and resolutions of problematic situations.

dilemmas, or come face-to-face with uncertainties, our most effective response requires drawing forth certain patterns of intellectual behavior. When we draw upon these intellectual resources, the results are more powerful, of higher quality, and of greater significance than if we fail to employ such patterns of intellectual behavior.

A Habit of Mind is a composite of many skills, attitudes, cues, past experiences, and proclivities. It means that we value one pattern of intellectual behaviors over another; therefore, it implies making choices about which patterns we should use at a certain time. It includes sensitivity to the contextual cues that signal that a particular circumstance is a time when applying a certain pattern would be useful and appropriate. It requires a level of skillfulness to use, carry out, and sustain the behaviors effectively. It suggests that after each experience in which these behaviors are used, the effects of their use are reflected upon, evaluated, modified, and carried forth to future applications. Figure 2.1 summarizes some of these dimensions of the Habits of Mind, which are elaborated in Chapter 3. The following sections describe each of the 16 Habits of Mind.

Persisting

Success seems to be connected with action. Successful people keep moving. They make mistakes, but they never quit.

—*Conrad Hilton*

Efficacious people stick to a task until it is completed. They don't give up easily. They are able to analyze a problem, and they develop a system, structure, or strategy to attack it. They have a repertoire of alternative strategies for problem solving, and they employ a whole range of these strategies. They collect evidence to indicate their problem-solving strategy is working, and if one strategy doesn't work, they know how to back up and try another. They recognize when a theory or an idea must be rejected and another employed. They have systematic methods for analyzing a problem, which include knowing how to begin, what steps must be performed, what data must be generated or collected, and what resources are available to assist. Because they are able to sustain a problem-solving process over time, they are comfortable with ambiguous situations.

Students often give up when they don't immediately know the answer to a problem. They sometimes crumple their papers and throw them away, exclaiming "I can't do this!" or "It's too hard!" Sometimes they write down *any* answer to get the task over with as quickly as possible. Some of these students have attention deficits. They have difficulty staying focused for any length of time; they are easily distracted, or they lack the ability to analyze a problem and develop a system, structure, or strategy of attack. They may give up because they have a limited repertoire of problem-solving strategies, and thus they have few alternatives if their first strategy doesn't work.

Managing Impulsivity

Goal-directed, self imposed delay of gratification is perhaps the essence of emotional self-regulation: the ability to deny impulse in the service of a goal, whether it be building a business, solving an algebraic equation, or pursuing the Stanley Cup.

—Daniel Goleman

Effective problem solvers are deliberate: they think before they act. They intentionally establish a vision of a product, an action plan, a goal, or a destination before they begin. They strive to clarify and understand directions, they develop a strategy for approaching a problem, and they withhold immediate value judgments about an idea before they fully understand it. Reflective individuals consider alternatives and consequences of several possible directions before they take action. They decrease their need for trial and error by gathering information, taking time to reflect on an answer before giving it, making sure they understand directions, and listening to alternative points of view.

Often, students blurt out the first answer that comes to mind. Sometimes they shout an answer, start to work without fully understanding the directions, lack an organized plan or strategy for approaching a problem, or make immediate value judgments about an idea (criticizing or praising it) before they fully understand it. They may take the first suggestion given or operate on the first idea that comes to mind rather than consider alternatives and the consequences of several possible directions. Research demonstrates, however, that less impulsive, self-disciplined students are more successful. For example, Duckworth and Seligman (2005) found

> Highly self-disciplined adolescents outperformed their more impulsive peers on every academic performance variable, including

report-card grades, standardized achievement test scores, admission to a competitive high school and attendance. Self-discipline measured in the fall predicted more variance in each of these outcomes than did IQ, and unlike IQ, self-discipline predicted gains in academic performance over the school year. (p. 940)

Listening with Understanding and Empathy

Listening is the beginning of understanding. . . . Wisdom is the reward for a lifetime of listening. Let the wise listen and add to their learning and let the discerning get guidance.

—Proverbs 1:5

Highly effective people spend an inordinate amount of time and energy listening (Covey, 1989). Some psychologists believe that the ability to listen to another person—to empathize with and to understand that person's point of view—is one of the highest forms of intelligent behavior. The ability to paraphrase another person's ideas; detect indicators (cues) of feelings or emotional states in oral and body language (empathy); and accurately express another person's concepts, emotions, and problems—all are indicators of listening behavior. (Piaget called it "overcoming egocentrism.")

People who demonstrate this Habit of Mind are able to see through the diverse perspectives of others. They gently attend to another person, demonstrating their understanding of and empathy for an idea or a feeling by paraphrasing it accurately, building upon it, clarifying it, or giving an example of it.

Senge, Roberts, Ross, Smith, and Kleiner (1994) suggest that to listen fully means to pay close attention to what is being said beneath the words—listening not only to the "music" but also to the essence of the person speaking; not only for what someone knows but also for what that person is trying to represent. Ears operate at the speed of sound, which is far slower than the speed of light the eyes take in. Generative listening is the art of developing deeper silences in oneself, slowing the mind's hearing to the ears' natural speed and hearing beneath the words to their meaning.

We spend 55 percent of our lives listening, but it is one of the least taught skills in schools. We often say we are listening, but actually we are rehearsing in our head what we are going to say when our partner is finished. Some students ridicule, laugh at, or put down other students' ideas. They interrupt, are unable to build upon, can't consider the merits of, or don't operate on another person's ideas.

We want students to learn to devote their mental energies to another person and to invest themselves in their partner's ideas. We want students to learn to hold in abeyance their own values, judgments, opinions, and prejudices so they can listen to and entertain another person's thoughts. This is a complex skill requiring the ability to monitor one's own thoughts while at the same time attending to a partner's words. Listening in this way does not mean we can't disagree with someone. Good listeners try to understand what other people are saying. In the end, they may disagree sharply, but because they have truly listened, they know exactly the nature of the disagreement.

Thinking Flexibly

Of all forms of mental activity, the most difficult to induce even in the minds of the young, who may be presumed not to have lost their flexibility, is the art of handling the same bundle of data as before, but placing them in a new system of relations with one another by giving them a different framework, all of which virtually means putting on a different kind of thinking-cap for the moment. It is easy to teach anybody a new fact. . . . but it needs light from

heaven above to enable a teacher to break the old framework in
which the student is accustomed to seeing.

—*Arthur Koestler*

An amazing discovery about the human brain is its plasticity — its ability to
"rewire," change, and even repair itself to become smarter. Flexible people have the most control. They have the capacity to change their minds
as they receive additional data. They engage in multiple and simultaneous
outcomes and activities, and they draw upon a repertoire of problem-
solving strategies. They also practice style flexibility, knowing when thinking broadly and globally is appropriate and when a situation requires
detailed precision. They create and seek novel approaches, and they have
a well-developed sense of humor. They envision a range of consequences.

Flexible people can address a problem from a new angle using a
novel approach, which de Bono (1991) refers to as "lateral thinking." They
consider alternative points of view or deal with several sources of information simultaneously. Their minds are open to change based on additional
information, new data, or even reasoning that contradicts their beliefs.
Flexible people know that they have and can develop options and alternatives. They understand means-ends relationships. They can work within
rules, criteria, and regulations, and they can predict the consequences of
flouting them. They understand immediate reactions, but they also are
able to perceive the bigger purposes that such constraints serve. Thus,
flexibility of mind is essential for working with social diversity, enabling an
individual to recognize the wholeness and distinctness of other people's
ways of experiencing and making meaning.

Flexible thinkers are able to shift through multiple perceptual positions at will. One perceptual orientation is what Jean Piaget called *egocentrism*, or perceiving from our own point of view. By contrast, *allocentrism*
is the position in which we perceive through another person's orientation. We operate from this second position when we empathize with
another's feelings, predict how others are thinking, and anticipate potential misunderstandings.

Another perceptual position is *macrocentric*. It is similar to looking
down from a balcony to observe ourselves and our interactions with others. This bird's-eye view is useful for discerning themes and patterns from

assortments of information. It is intuitive, holistic, and conceptual. Because we often need to solve problems with incomplete information, we need the capacity to perceive general patterns and jump across gaps of incomplete knowledge.

Yet another perceptual orientation is *microcentric*, examining the individual and sometimes minute parts that make up the whole. This worm's-eye view involves logical, analytical computation, searching for causality in methodical steps. It requires attention to detail, precision, and orderly progressions.

Flexible thinkers display confidence in their intuition. They tolerate confusion and ambiguity up to a point, and they are willing to let go of a problem, trusting their subconscious to continue creative and productive work on it. Flexibility is the cradle of humor, creativity, and repertoire. Although many perceptual positions are possible—past, present, future, egocentric, allocentric, macrocentric, microcentric, visual, auditory, kinesthetic—the flexible mind knows when to shift between and among these positions.

Some students have difficulty considering alternative points of view or dealing with more than one classification system simultaneously. *Their* way to solve a problem seems to be the *only* way. They perceive situations from an egocentric point of view: "My way or the highway!" Their minds are made up: "Don't confuse me with facts. That's it!"

Thinking About Thinking (Metacognition)

When the mind is thinking it is talking to itself.

—*Plato*

The human species is known as *Homo sapiens sapiens*, which basically means "a being that knows their knowing" (or maybe it's "knows *they're* knowing"). What distinguishes humans from other forms of life is our capacity for metacognition—the ability to stand off and examine our own thoughts while we engage in them.

Occurring in the neocortex, metacognition, or thinking about thinking, is our ability to know what we know and what we don't know. It is our ability to plan a strategy for producing the information that is needed, to be conscious of our own steps and strategies during the act of problem solving, and to reflect on and evaluate the productiveness of our own thinking. Although inner language, thought to be a prerequisite for metacognition, begins in most children around age 5, metacognition is a key attribute of formal thought flowering at about age 11.

The major components of metacognition are, when confronted with a problem to solve, developing a plan of action, maintaining that plan in mind over a period of time, and then reflecting on and evaluating the plan upon its completion. Planning a strategy before embarking on a course of action helps us keep track of the steps in the sequence of planned behavior at the conscious awareness level for the duration of the activity. It facilitates making temporal and comparative judgments; assessing the readiness for more or different activities; and monitoring our interpretations, perceptions, decisions, and behaviors. An example would be what superior teachers do daily: developing a teaching strategy for a lesson, keeping that strategy in mind throughout the instruction, and then reflecting upon the strategy to evaluate its effectiveness in producing the desired student outcomes.

Intelligent people plan for, reflect on, and evaluate the quality of their own thinking skills and strategies. Metacognition means becoming increasingly aware of one's actions and the effect of those actions on others and on the environment; forming internal questions in the search for information and meaning; developing mental maps or plans of action; mentally rehearsing before a performance; monitoring plans as they are employed (being conscious of the need for midcourse correction if the plan is not meeting expectations); reflecting on the completed plan for self-evaluation; and editing mental pictures for improved performance.

Interestingly, not all humans achieve the level of formal operations. As Russian psychologist Alexander Luria found, not all adults metacogitate. Although the human brain is capable of generating this reflective consciousness, generally we are not all that aware of how we are thinking, and not everyone uses the capacity for consciousness equally (Chiabetta, 1976; Csikszentmihalyi, 1993; Whimbey, Whimbey, & Shaw, 1975; Whimbey, 1980). The most likely reason is that all of us do not take the time to reflect on our experiences. Students often do not take the time to wonder why they are doing what they are doing. They seldom question themselves about their own learning strategies or evaluate the efficiency of their own performance. Some children virtually have no idea of what they should do when they confront a problem, and often they are unable to explain their decision-making strategies (Sternberg & Wagner, 1982). When teachers ask, "How did you solve that problem? What strategies did you have in mind?" or "Tell us what went on in your head to come up with that conclusion," students often respond, "I don't know. I just did it."

We want students to perform well on complex cognitive tasks. A simple example might be drawn from a reading task. While reading a passage, we sometimes find that our minds wander from the pages. We see the words, but no meaning is being produced. Suddenly, we realize that we are not concentrating and that we've lost contact with the meaning of the text. We recover by returning to the passage to find our place, matching it with the last thought we can remember, and once having found it, reading on with connectedness. This inner awareness and the strategy of recovery are components of metacognition.

Striving for Accuracy

A man who has committed a mistake and doesn't correct it is committing another mistake.

—Confucius

Whether we are looking at the stamina, grace, and elegance of a ballerina or a carpenter, we see a desire for craftsmanship, mastery, flawlessness, and economy of energy to produce exceptional results. People who value truthfulness, accuracy, precision, and craftsmanship take time to check over their products. They review the rules by which they are to abide, they review the models and visions they are to follow, and they review the criteria they are to use to confirm that their finished product matches the criteria exactly. To be craftsmanlike means knowing that one can continually perfect one's craft by working to attain the highest possible standards and by pursuing ongoing learning to bring a laserlike focus of energies to accomplishing a task.

These people take pride in their work, and they desire accuracy as they take time to check over their work. Craftsmanship includes exactness, precision, accuracy, correctness, faithfulness, and fidelity. For some people, craftsmanship requires continuous reworking. Mario Cuomo, a great speechwriter and politician, once said that his speeches were never done; it was only a deadline that made him stop working on them.

Some students may turn in sloppy, incomplete, or uncorrected work. They are more eager to get rid of the assignment than to check it over for accuracy and precision. They are willing to settle for minimum effort rather than invest their maximum. They may be more interested in expedience rather than excellence.

Questioning and Posing Problems

> The formulation of a problem is often more essential than its solution, which may be merely a matter of mathematical or experimental skill. . . . To raise new questions, new possibilities, to regard old problems from a new angle, requires creative imagination and marks real advances.
>
> —*Albert Einstein*

One of the distinguishing characteristics of humans is our inclination and ability to *find* problems to solve. Effective problem solvers know how to ask questions to fill in the gaps between what they know and what they don't know. Effective questioners are inclined to ask a range of questions:

- What evidence do you have?
- How do you know that's true?
- How reliable is this data source?

They also pose questions about alternative points of view:

- From whose viewpoint are we seeing, reading, or hearing?
- From what angle, what perspective, are we viewing this situation?

Effective questioners pose questions that make causal connections and relationships:

- How are these (people, events, or situations) related to each other?
- What produced this connection?

Sometimes they pose hypothetical problems characterized by "if" questions:

- What do you think would happen *if* . . . ?
- *If* that is true, then what might happen *if* . . . ?

Inquirers recognize discrepancies and phenomena in their environment, and they probe into their causes.

- Why do cats purr?
- How high can birds fly?
- Why does the hair on my head grow so fast, while the hair on my arms and legs grows so slowly?
- What would happen if we put the saltwater fish in a freshwater aquarium?
- What are some alternative solutions to international conflicts, other than wars?

Some students may be unaware of the functions, classes, syntax, or intentions in questions. They may not realize that questions vary in complexity, structure, and purpose. They may pose simple questions intending to derive maximal results. When confronted with a discrepancy, they may lack an overall strategy to search for and find a solution.

Applying Past Knowledge to New Situations

I've never made a mistake. I've only learned from experience.
—*Thomas A. Edison*

Intelligent humans learn from experience. When confronted with a new and perplexing problem, they will draw forth experiences from their past. They often can be heard to say, "This reminds me of . . ." or "This is just like the time when I . . . ." They explain what they are doing now with analogies about or references to their experiences. They call upon their store of knowledge and experience as sources of data to support, theories to explain, or processes to solve each new challenge. They are able to abstract meaning from one experience, carry it forth, and apply it in a novel situation.

Too often, students begin each new task as if it were being approached for the first time. Teachers are dismayed when they invite students to recall how they solved a similar problem previously—and students don't remember. It's as if they had never heard of it before, even though they recently worked with the same type of problem! It seems each experience is encapsulated and has no relationship to what has come before or what comes after. Their thinking is what psychologists refer to as an "episodic grasp of reality" (Feuerstein et al., 1980); that is, each event in life is separate and discrete, with no connections to what may have come before or no relation to what follows. Their learning is so encapsulated that they seem unable to draw it forth from one event and apply it in another context.

Thinking and Communicating with Clarity and Precision

I do not so easily think in words. . . . After being hard at work having arrived at results that are perfectly clear . . . I have to translate my thoughts in a language that does not run evenly with them.

—*Francis Galton, geneticist*

Language refinement plays a critical role in enhancing a person's cognitive maps and ability to think critically, which is the knowledge base for efficacious action. Enriching the complexity and specificity of language simultaneously produces effective thinking.

Language and thinking are closely entwined; like either side of a coin, they are inseparable. Fuzzy, vague language is a reflection of fuzzy, vague thinking. Intelligent people strive to communicate accurately in both written and oral form, taking care to use precise language; defining terms; and using correct names, labels, and analogies. They strive to avoid overgeneralizations, deletions, and distortions. Instead, they support their statements with explanations, comparisons, quantification, and evidence.

We sometimes hear students and adults using vague and imprecise language. They describe objects or events with words like *weird, nice,* or *OK.* They name specific objects using such nondescriptive words as *stuff, junk, things,* and *whatever.* They punctuate sentences with meaningless interjections like *ya know, er,* and *uh.* They use vague or general nouns and pronouns: "*They* told me to do it," "*Everybody* has one," or "*Teachers* don't understand me." They use nonspecific verbs: "Let's *do* it." At other times, they use unqualified comparatives: "This soda is *better;* I like it *more*" (Shachtman, 1995).

Gathering Data Through All Senses

Observe perpetually.

—*Henry James*

The brain is the ultimate reductionist. It reduces the world to its elementary parts: photons of light, molecules of fragrance, sound waves, vibrations of touch—all of which send electrochemical signals to individual brain cells that store information about lines, movements, colors, smells, and other sensory inputs.

Intelligent people know that all information gets into the brain through sensory pathways: gustatory, olfactory, tactile, kinesthetic, auditory, and visual. Most linguistic, cultural, and physical learning is derived from the environment by observing or taking it in through the senses. To know a wine it must be drunk; to know a role it must be acted; to know a game it must be played; to know a dance it must be performed; to know a goal it must be envisioned. Those whose sensory pathways are open, alert, and acute absorb more information from the environment than those whose pathways are withered, immune, and oblivious to sensory stimuli.

The more regions of the brain that store data about a subject, the more interconnection there is. This redundancy means students will have more opportunities to pull up all those related bits of data from their multiple storage areas in response to a single cue. This cross-referencing of data strengthens the data into something that's learned rather than just memorized (Willis, 2007).

We are learning more and more about the impact of the arts and music on improved mental functioning. Forming mental images is important in mathematics and engineering; listening to classical music seems to improve spatial reasoning. Social scientists use scenarios and role playing;

scientists build models; engineers use CAD-CAM; mechanics learn through hands-on experimentation; artists explore colors and textures; and musicians combine instrumental and vocal music.

Some students, however, go through school and life oblivious to the textures, rhythms, patterns, sounds, and colors around them. Sometimes children are afraid to touch things or get their hands dirty. Some don't want to feel an object that might be slimy or icky. They operate within a narrow range of sensory problem-solving strategies, wanting only to describe it but not illustrate or act it, or to listen but not participate.

Creating, Imagining, Innovating

The future is not some place we are going to but one we are creating. The paths are not to be found, but made, and the activity of making them changes both the maker and the destination.

—John Schaar, political scientist

All human beings have the capacity to generate novel, clever, or ingenious products, solutions, and techniques—*if* that capacity is developed (Sternberg, 2006). Creative human beings try to conceive solutions to problems differently, examining alternative possibilities from many angles. They tend to project themselves into different roles using analogies, starting with a vision and working backward, and imagining they are the object being considered. Creative people take risks and frequently push the boundaries of their perceived limits (Perkins, 1991). They are intrinsically rather than extrinsically motivated, working on the task because of the aesthetic challenge rather than the material rewards.

Creative people are open to criticism. They hold up their products for others to judge, and they seek feedback in an ever-increasing effort to refine their technique. They are uneasy with the status quo. They constantly strive for greater fluency, elaboration, novelty, parsimony, simplicity, craftsman-ship, perfection, beauty, harmony, and balance.

Students, however, often are heard saying "I can't draw," "I was never very good at art," "I can't sing a note," or "I'm not creative." Some people believe creative humans are just born that way and that genes and chromosomes are the determinants of creativity.

Responding with Wonderment and Awe

The most beautiful experience in the world is the experience of the mysterious.

—*Albert Einstein*

Describing the 200 best and brightest of *USA Today*'s All USA College Academic Team, Tracey Wong Briggs (1999) states, "They are creative thinkers who have a passion for what they do." Efficacious people have not only an "I can" attitude but also an "I enjoy" feeling. They seek intriguing phenomena. They search for problems to solve for themselves and to submit to others. They delight in making up problems to solve on their own, and they so enjoy the challenge of problem solving that they seek perplexities and puzzles from others. They enjoy figuring things out by themselves, and they continue to learn throughout their lifetimes. One efficacious person is chemist Ahmed H. Zewail, a Nobel Prize winner, who said that he had a passion to understand fundamental processes: "I love molecules. I want to understand why do they do what they do" (Cole, 1999).

Some children and adults avoid problems and are turned off to learning. They make such comments as "I was never good at these brain teasers," "Go ask your father; he's the brain in this family," "It's boring," "When am I ever going to use this stuff," "Who cares," "Lighten up, teacher; thinking is hard work," or "I don't do thinking!" Many people never enrolled in another math class or other "hard" academic subject after they weren't required to in high school or college. Many people perceive thinking as hard work, and they recoil from situations that demand too much of it.

We want students to be curious, to commune with the world around them, to reflect on the changing formations of a cloud, to feel charmed by the opening of a bud, to sense the logical simplicity of mathematical order. Intelligent people find beauty in a sunset, intrigue in the geometric shapes of a spider web, and exhilaration in the iridescence of a hummingbird's wings. They marvel at the congruity and intricacies in the derivation of a mathematical formula, recognize the orderliness and adroitness of a chemical change, and commune with the serenity of a distant constellation. We want students to feel compelled, enthusiastic, and passionate about learning, inquiring, and mastering (Costa, 2007).

Taking Responsible Risks

There has been a calculated risk in every stage of American development—the pioneers who were not afraid of the wilderness, businessmen who were not afraid of failure, dreamers who were not afraid of action.

—*Brooks Atkinson*

Risk takers seem to have an almost uncontrollable urge to go beyond established limits. They are uneasy about comfort; they live on the edge of their competence. They seem compelled to place themselves in situations in which they do not know what the outcome will be. They accept confusion, uncertainty, and the higher risks of failure as part of the normal process, and they learn to view setbacks as interesting, challenging, and growth producing. However, responsible risk takers do not behave impulsively. Their risks are educated. They draw on past knowledge, are thoughtful about consequences, and have a well-trained sense of what is appropriate. They know that all risks are not worth taking.

Risk takers can be considered in two categories: those who see the risk as a *venture* and those who see it as *adventure*. The venture part of risk taking might be described in terms of what a venture capitalist does. When a person is approached to take the risk of investing in a new business, she will look at the markets, see how well organized the ideas are, and study the economic projections. If she finally decides to take the risk, it is a well-considered one.

The adventure part of risk taking might be described by the experiences from Project Adventure. In this situation, there is a spontaneity, a willingness to take a chance in the moment. Once again, a person will take the chance only if experiences suggest that the action will not be life threatening or if he believes that group support will protect him from harm (e.g., checking out the dimensions of weight, distance, and strength of a bungee cord before agreeing to the exhilaration of a drop). Ultimately, people learn from such high-risk experiences that they are far more able to take actions than they previously believed. Risk taking becomes educated only through repeated experiences. It often is a cross between intuition, drawing on past knowledge, striving for precision and accuracy, and a sense of meeting new challenges.

Bobby Jindal, then executive director of the National Bipartisan Commission on the Future of Medicare, stated, "The only way to succeed is to be brave enough to risk failure" (Briggs, 1999, p. 2A). When people hold back from taking risks, they miss opportunities. Some students seem reluctant to take risks. They hold back from games, new learning, and new friendships because their fear of failure is far greater than their desire for venture or adventure. They are reinforced by the mental voice that says, "If you don't try it, you won't be wrong," or "If you try it and you are wrong, you will look stupid." The other voice that might say, "If you don't try it, you will never know," is trapped by fear and mistrust. These students are more interested in knowing whether their answer is correct or not than in being challenged by the process of finding the answer. They are unable to sustain a process of problem solving and finding the answer over time, and therefore they avoid ambiguous situations. They have a need for certainty rather than an inclination for doubt.

We hope that students will learn how to take intellectual as well as physical risks. Students who are capable of being different, going against the grain of common thinking, and thinking of new ideas (testing them with peers and teachers) are more likely to be successful in an age of innovation and uncertainty.

Finding Humor

You can increase your brain power three to fivefold simply by laughing and having fun before working on a problem.

—Doug Hall

Why we laugh, no one really knows. Laughing is an instinct that can be traced to chimps, and it may reinforce our social status (Hubert, 2007). Humor is a human form of mutual playfulness. Beyond the fact that laughing is enjoyable, it may have medicinal value as well. Laughing, scientists have discovered, has positive effects on physiological functions: blood vessels relax, stress hormones disperse, and the immune system gets a boost, including a drop in the pulse rate. Laughter produces secretion of endorphins and increased oxygen in the blood. Humor has been found to have psychological benefits as well. It liberates creativity and provokes such higher-level thinking skills as anticipating, finding novel relationships, visual imaging, and making analogies. People who engage in the mystery of humor have the ability to perceive situations from an original and often interesting vantage point. They tend to initiate humor more often, to place greater value on having a sense of humor, to appreciate and understand others' humor, and to be verbally playful when interacting with others. Having a whimsical frame of mind, they thrive on finding incongruity; perceiving absurdities, ironies, and satire; finding discontinuities; and being able to laugh at situations and themselves.

Some students find humor in all the wrong places—human differences, ineptitude, injurious behavior, vulgarity, violence, and profanity. They employ laughter to humiliate others. They laugh at others yet are unable to laugh at themselves. We want students to acquire the habit of finding humor in a positive sense so they can distinguish between those situations of human frailty and fallibility that require compassion and those that truly are funny (Dyer, 1997).

Thinking Interdependently

Take care of each other. Share your energies with the group. No one must feel alone, cut off, for that is when you do not make it.
—*Willie Unsoeld, mountain climber*

Humans are social beings. We congregate in groups, find it therapeutic to be listened to, draw energy from one another, and seek reciprocity. In groups we contribute our time and energy to tasks that we would quickly tire of when working alone. In fact, solitary confinement is one of the cruelest forms of punishment that can be inflicted on an individual.

Collaborative humans realize that all of us together are more powerful, intellectually or physically, than any one individual. Probably the foremost disposition in our global society is the heightened ability to think in concert with others, to find ourselves increasingly more interdependent and sensitive to the needs of others. Problem solving has become so complex that no one person can go it alone. No one has access to all the data needed to make critical decisions; no one person can consider as many alternatives as several people.

Some students may not have learned to work in groups; they have underdeveloped social skills. They feel isolated, and they prefer solitude. They say things like "Leave me alone—I'll do it by myself," "They just don't like me," or "I want to be alone." Some students seem unable to contribute to group work and are job hogs; conversely, other students let all the others in a group do all the work.

Working in groups requires the ability to justify ideas and to test the feasibility of solution strategies on others. It also requires developing a willingness and an openness to accept feedback from a critical friend. Through this interaction, the group and the individual continue to grow. Listening, consensus seeking, giving up an idea to work with someone else's, empathy, compassion, group leadership, knowing how to support group efforts, altruism—all are behaviors indicative of cooperative human beings.

Remaining Open to Continuous Learning

The greater our knowledge increases the more our ignorance unfolds.

—John F. Kennedy

In a world that moves at warp speed, there is more to know today than ever before, and the challenge of knowing more and more in every succeeding day, week, month, and year ahead will only continue to expand exponentially. The quest for meaningful knowledge is critical and never ending.

Intelligent people are in a continuous learning mode. They are invigorated by the quest of lifelong learning. Their confidence, in combination with their inquisitiveness, allows them to constantly search for new and better ways. People with this Habit of Mind are always striving for improvement, growing, learning, and modifying and improving themselves. They seize problems, situations, tensions, conflicts, and circumstances as valuable opportunities to learn (Bateson, 2004).

A great mystery about humans is that many times we confront learning opportunities with fear rather than mystery and wonder. We seem to feel better when we know rather than when we learn. We defend our biases, beliefs, and storehouses of knowledge rather than invite the unknown, the creative, and the inspirational. Being certain and closed gives us comfort, whereas being doubtful and open gives us fear. As G. K. Chesterton so aptly expressed, "There is no such thing on earth as an uninteresting subject; there are only uninterested people."

Because of a curriculum employing fragmentation, competition, and reactiveness, students from an early age are trained to believe that deep learning means figuring out the truth rather than developing capabilities for effective and thoughtful action. They have been taught to value certainty rather than doubt, to give answers rather than to inquire, to know which choice is correct rather than to explore alternatives. Unfortunately, some adults are content with what they already believe and know. Their childlike curiosity has died. They exhibit little humility because they believe they are all knowing. They do not seek out or discover the wisdom of others. They do not know how or when to leverage a love of and lust for learning. As a result, they follow a path of little value and minimal opportunity.

Our wish is for creative students and people who are eager to learn. This Habit of Mind includes the humility of knowing that we don't know, which is the highest form of thinking we will ever learn. Paradoxically, unless we start off with humility, we will never get anywhere. As the first step, we must already have what eventually will be the crowning glory of all learning: to know—and to admit—that we don't know and to not be afraid to find out.

The Right Stuff

> The beautiful thing about learning is that nobody can take it away
> from you.
>
> —B. B. King

The 16 Habits of Mind just described were drawn from research on human effectiveness, descriptions of remarkable performers, and analyses of the characteristics of efficacious people. These Habits of Mind can serve as mental disciplines. Students, parents, and teachers, when confronted with problematic situations, might habitually use one or more of these Habits of Mind by asking themselves, "What is the most *intelligent* thing I can do right now?" They also might consider these questions:

- How can I learn from this? What are my resources? How can I draw on my past successes with problems like this? What do I already know about the problem? What resources do I have available or need to generate?

- How can I approach this problem flexibly? How might I look at the situation in another way? How can I draw upon my repertoire of problem-solving strategies? How can I look at this problem from a fresh perspective (lateral thinking)?

- How can I illuminate this problem to make it clearer, more precise? Do I need to check out my data sources? How might I break this problem down into its component parts and develop a strategy for understanding and accomplishing each step?

- What do I know or not know? What questions do I need to ask? What strategies are in my mind now? What am I aware of in terms of my own beliefs, values, and goals with this problem? What feelings or emotions am I aware of that might be blocking or enhancing my progress?

- How does this problem affect others? How can *we* solve it together? What can I learn from others that would help me become a better problem solver?

Community organizer Saul Alinsky coined a very useful slogan: "Don't just do something . . . stand there!" Taking a reflective stance in the midst of active problem solving is often difficult. For that reason, each of these Habits of Mind is situational and transitory. There is no such thing as perfect realization of any of them. They are utopian states toward which we constantly aspire. Csikszentmihalyi (1993) states, "Although every human brain is able to generate self-reflective consciousness, not everyone seems to use it equally" (p. 23). Few people, notes Kegan (1994), ever *fully* reach the stage of cognitive complexity, and rarely before middle age.

These Habits of Mind transcend all subject matters commonly taught in school. They are characteristic of peak performers in all places: homes, schools, athletic fields, organizations, the military, governments, churches, or corporations. They are what make marriages successful, learning continual, workplaces productive, and democracies enduring. The goal of education, therefore, should be to support others and ourselves in liberating, developing, and habituating these Habits of Mind more fully. Taken together, they are a force directing us toward increasingly authentic, congruent, and ethical behavior. They are the touchstones of integrity and the tools of disciplined choice making. They are the primary vehicles in the lifelong journey toward integration. They are the "right stuff" that make human beings efficacious.

References

Ames, J. E. (1997). *Mastery: Interviews with 30 remarkable people*. Portland, OR: Rudra Press.

Bateson, M. (2004). *Willing to learn: Passages of personal discovery*. Hanover, NH: Steerforth Press.

Briggs, T. W. (1999, February 25). Passion for what they do keeps alumni on first team. *USA Today*, pp. 1A–2A.

Carnegie, J., & Stynes, J. (2006). *Finding heroes: Be inspired by the stories of amazing journeys*. East Melbourne, Victoria, Australia: Allen & Unwin.

Chiabetta, E. L. A. (1976). Review of Piagetian studies relevant to science instruction at the secondary and college levels. *Science Education 60*, 253–261.

Cole, K. C. (1999, October 13). Nobel prizes go to Caltech chemist, Dutch physicists. *Los Angeles Times*, pp. 1, 15.

Costa, A. (1991). The search for intelligent life. In A. Costa (Ed.), *Developing minds: A resource book for teaching thinking* (Rev. ed., Vol. 1, pp. 100–106). Alexandria, VA: ASCD.

Costa, A. (2007). Aesthetics: Where thinking begins. In A. Costa (Ed.), *The school as a home for the mind* (Ch. 2). Thousand Oaks, CA: Corwin.

Covey, S. (1989). *The seven habits of highly effective people: Powerful lessons in personal change*. New York: Simon & Schuster.

Csikszentmihalyi, M. (1993). *The evolving self: A psychology for the third millennium*. New York: HarperCollins.

de Bono, E. (1991). The CoRT thinking program. In A. Costa (Ed.), *Developing minds: Programs for teaching thinking* (Rev. ed., Vol. 2, pp. 27–32). Alexandria, VA: ASCD.

Duckworth, A. L., & Seligman, M. E. P. (2005). Self-discipline outdoes IQ in predicting academic performance of adolescents. *Psychological Science, 16*, pp. 939–944.

Dyer, J. (1997). Humor as process. In A. Costa & R. Liebmann (Eds.), *Envisioning process as content: Toward a renaissance curriculum* (pp. 211–229). Thousand Oaks, CA: Corwin.

Ennis, R. (1991). Goals for a critical thinking curriculum. In A. Costa (Ed.), *Developing minds: A resource book for teaching thinking* (Rev. ed., Vol. 1, pp. 68–71). Alexandria, VA: ASCD.

Feuerstein, R., Rand, Y., Hoffman, M. B., & Miller, R. (1980). *Instrumental enrichment: An intervention program for cognitive modifiability*. Baltimore, MD: University Park Press.

Glatthorn, A., & Baron, J. (1991). The good thinker. In A. Costa (Ed.), *Developing minds: A resource book for teaching thinking* (Rev. ed., Vol. 1, pp. 63–67). Alexandria, VA: ASCD.

Goleman, D. (1995). *Emotional intelligence: Why it can matter more than IQ*. New York: Bantam Books.

Hubert, C. (2007, August 12). Why we laugh. *Sacramento Bee*, p. L3.

Kegan, R. (1994). *In over our heads: The mental complexity of modern life*. Cambridge, MA: Harvard University Press.

Perkins, D. (1991). What creative thinking is. In A. Costa (Ed.), *Developing minds: A resource book for teaching thinking* (Rev. ed., Vol 1, pp. 85–88). Alexandria, VA: ASCD.

Senge, P. M., Roberts, C., Ross, R. B., Smith, B. J., & Kleiner, A. (1994). *The fifth discipline fieldbook: Strategies and tools for building a learning organization*. New York: Doubleday/Currency.

Shachtman, T. (1995). *The inarticulate society: Eloquence and culture in America*. New York: Simon & Schuster.

Sternberg, R. J. (1984). *Beyond I.Q.: A triarchic theory of human intelligence*. New York: Cambridge University Press.

Sternberg, R. J. (2006, February 22). Creativity is a habit. *Education Week*, pp. 47, 64.

Sternberg, R., & Wagner, R. (1982). "Understanding intelligence: What's in it for education?" Paper submitted to the National Commission on Excellence in Education.

Strugatch, W. (2004, December 5). Entrepreneurs tell their success stories. *New York Times*.

Waugh, S. (2005). *Chase your dreams*. An interactive DVD/video program. Canberra: Australian Government Department of Education, Science and Training, and Team Duet.

Whimbey, A. (1980, April). Students can learn to be better problem solvers. *Educational Leadership*, 37(7).

Whimbey, A., Whimbey, L. S., & Shaw, L. (1975). *Intelligence can be taught*. New York: Lawrence Erlbaum.

Willis, J. (2007). *Research-based strategies to ignite student learning: Insights from a neurologist and classroom teacher*. Alexandria, VA: ASCD.

3

Habits of Mind
in the Curriculum

Arthur L. Costa and Bena Kallick

Good schools focus on habits, on what sorts of intellectual activities will and should inform their graduates' lives.
—*Theodore R. Sizer,* Horace's School, *1992*

Schools are about learning, and the Habits of Mind offer a set of valued
intellectual dispositions toward which teachers and students consciously
and consistently work. The habits provide guidelines for a process for
interaction. Loyalty to a process for interaction is as significant as loyalty
to the decisions that are a result of that process. We seek to operate in a
world that is civil, that respects individuality and differences, and that provides a path for consistency, not uniformity. Senge (1990) suggests that a
culture is people thinking together. As individuals share meaning, they
negotiate and build a culture. As groups become more skillful in employing the Habits of Mind, the habits create a renegotiation of the organization by pervading the value system. This change results in the changing
of practices and beliefs of the entire organization. By employing the
Habits of Mind, the group mind illuminates issues, solves problems, and

---

Note: Many of the ideas presented in this chapter are drawn from the article "Maturing Outcomes" by Arthur L. Costa and Robert J. Garmston, published in *Encounter: Education for
Meaning and Social Justice,* Vol. 11, No. 1, Spring 1998.

accommodates differences. Also through the Habits of Mind, the group builds an atmosphere of trust in human relationships, trust in the processes of interaction, and trust throughout the organization. The Habits of Mind facilitate the creation of a shared vision (Senge, 1990).

Sharing a Vision for Process

As a school adopts a vision about the Habits of Mind that is shared by the entire staff, grade levels and subject areas are transcended. The vision leads to a commitment to a consistent set of behaviors that build a learning community. These behaviors and dispositions are more likely to be achieved because they are reinforced, transferred, and revisited at school throughout the grades and subject areas, at home, and in the community.

With a focus on the Habits of Mind, educators overcome the historical isolation, disparity, and episodic nature of teaching and learning. Each class can reinforce the values put forth by the Habits of Mind. For example, persistence is as valued in social sciences as it is in music, math, and physical education. All teachers, regardless of subject area or grade level, can agree on these desirable qualities. The transcendent qualities of systems thinking about outcomes can be found in such Habits of Mind as enhancing one's capacities for persisting; managing impulsivity; creating, imagining, innovating; thinking about thinking (metacognition); striving for accuracy; listening with understanding and empathy; taking responsible risks; and responding with wonderment and awe (Costa, 1991; Tishman & Perkins, 1997).

In *The Power of Their Ideas*, Debbie Meier (1995) affirms the habits' broad applicability:

> Lawyers tell us these "habits" are very lawyerly, but journalists and scientists tell us they are basic to what they do as well. As a historian I recognize them as being at the heart of my field. As a principal I find them useful when "naughty" kids are sent to my office. I ask them to put their version of the story on one side and that of whoever sent them to me on the other; then we discuss whether what's happened is part of a pattern, how else it might have been dealt with, and, finally, why it matters. (pp. 50–51)

Sharing Common Beliefs

Many programs and curriculum designs can be enriched by integrating the Habits of Mind into them. For example, Dimension 5 in the Dimensions of Learning Program (Marzano, 1992, pp. 131–152) is entitled "Productive Habits of Mind." The habits of mind that are named in Marzano's book are similar to the ones in this book. When teachers are developing units using *Understanding by Design* (Wiggins & McTighe, 2005), a focus on the thinking dispositions will strengthen the student's capacity for deeper understanding. When teachers are developing a program that focuses on social and emotional learning, the Habits of Mind become a set of behaviors that foster more thoughtful interactions (Elias, 2006). Thus we see that the Habits of Mind fit within a pattern of educational trends and programs that share a common philosophy of teaching toward broader, more panoramic, encompassing, and lifelong learning.

We are witnessing an educational refocusing away from teaching unrelated, fragmented, short-term content toward teaching broader, more enduring, essential, life-span learnings. Lauren Resnick (2001) writes that positive results were achieved when "cognitive researchers began to shift their attention to educational strategies that immerse students in demanding, long-term intellectual environments. . . . In experimental programs and in practical school reforms, we are seeing that students, who, over an extended period of time, are treated as if they are intelligent, actually become more so" (p. 4).

Elevating the Curriculum

The current focus on standards and accountability has led many educators away from a constructivist approach to curriculum and instruction. Instead, curriculum designers have emphasized coverage of content and drill in test-related knowledge. As a school staff begins to embrace the Habits of Mind, thinking becomes the focus of curriculum, instruction, and assessment. For many educators, this is a mind shift. For example, if the intent of instruction is behavioral and assumes that there is a body of knowledge students need to learn and be tested on, then only certain habits would be necessary. Students would need to strive for accuracy, use clear and precise language, and remain open to continuous learning.

The learning, however, would be teacher-directed and would not require many of the other habits.

If, on the other hand, instruction is concerned with students' developing a sense of curiosity, wonderment, and awe; creating, imagining, and innovating; and becoming more metacognitive about what and how they are learning, then a constructivist curriculum is more likely to provide the sort of challenging, cognitive tasks that require higher levels of thinking.

The curriculum requirements and standards need to be studied to identify where they can broaden student knowledge by "covering" the curriculum and where they can deepen student knowledge by allowing students to "uncover" the curriculum. These curricular decisions always present a tension in terms of time. The question is usually "Will I have enough time for students to dig more deeply into the curriculum?" We suggest that often it is not time that is the issue as much as process. Twenty minutes of a generative discussion may lead to better understanding and longer-lasting knowledge than will 20 minutes of detailed coverage of information. Such generative discussion can lead to project-based learning, which provides opportunities for students to become more self-directed and responsible for their learning. If we expect students to work more thoughtfully in class, then coaching is required. And as soon as we raise the expectation for higher-level thinking, the Habits of Mind become a necessary part of the curriculum. Practicing the Habits of Mind in this context promotes students' recognition of the greater benefits and values of using the habits.

The Habits of Mind are the dispositions that we want students to develop so that they are more capable of successfully working at a higher level. The habits are not another layer that is added on to an already over-crowded curriculum. Rather they are a significant part of the generative curriculum—a curriculum that engages students so that they are thinking beyond the test or the final exam to find application in other subjects, in their future careers, and in their lives.

Designing Curriculum with the Habits of Mind in Mind

Whenever educators set about putting their vision for more mindful schools into operation, they begin with the question of curriculum. The work of Heidi Hayes Jacobs suggests that it is powerful to begin an examination of curriculum with "curriculum mapping" (Jacobs, 1997). In this process, teachers detail what they currently teach and consider how it builds on the foundations of previous learnings and anticipates those of future years. They define the content, skills, and assessments that presently guide their instructional decisions. As teachers share their maps across grades, subjects, and schools, they consider what might be excessive, repetitious, necessary, or missing.

Jacobs suggests that the entire faculty engage in this process, not just a small committee. Curriculum mapping provides a rich opportunity for building curriculum as a decision-making process. The power of these conversations comes from the five basic groups of decisions that teachers consider:

- Deciding on content, strategies, and skills.
- Deciding on a focus for habits of mind.
- Deciding on materials, resources, and organizational patterns.
- Deciding on measures of student learning.
- Deciding on outcomes, goals, intentions, and purposes.

These decisions about what should be taught, how it should be taught, and how it should be assessed shape the minds of all children. The character of their minds, in turn, helps shape the culture in which we all live. Eliot Eisner (1997) states that schools serve children best when they help students broaden their understanding of content in meaningful ways. We suggest that to achieve this goal, Habits of Mind must be considered among all the varying curriculum goals and outcomes.

Broad Educational Outcomes

Anthropologist Gregory Bateson (1972) formulated an early notion of relating systems of learning to human growth. Dilts (1994) then applied this form of systems thinking to education. The major concepts are as follows:

- Any system of activity is a subsystem embedded in another system. This system also is embedded in an even larger system, and so on.
- Learning in one subsystem produces a type of learning relative to the system in which one is operating.

• The effect of each level of learning is to organize and control the information on the level below it.

• Learning something on an upper level will change things on lower levels, but learning something on a lower level may or may not inform and influence levels above it.

These insights led to a realization that authentic outcomes are subsystems embedded inside other subsystems. In such arrangements, different types and magnitudes of learning occur relative to the system in which one operates. Each more overarching, complex, and abstract level has a greater impact upon the learning of the levels within it. Because each level affects the interpretation of the levels below, changing meaning on an upper level changes decisions and actions at lower levels; changing something at a lower level, however, does not necessarily affect the upper levels.

When educators make decisions about curriculum, instructional methodologies, and assessment strategies, they hold in their minds at least four nested levels of outcomes. Each one is broader and more encompassing than the levels within, and each represents greater authenticity. We might consider these levels to be working like a digital camera in which we can zoom in to any one level or zoom out to get a panoramic view of the whole. Skillful teachers learn to maintain the vision of the whole, or zoom out, as they work in each level simultaneously. In the following sections, we zoom in on each level.

Figure 3.1 summarizes the landscape.

Content

Teachers must focus on the coherence and cumulative effects of activities in the classroom. Curriculum design work starts by answering questions such as this: What concepts and principles should students be learning? State, provincial, and school district standards of learning often help with this decision. While teachers maintain interest in day-to-day activities, the learning activities are now employed as vehicles to learn content. Teachers ask: "What concepts or understandings do I want my students to know as a result of this activity? What will I do to help them understand? How will I know they understand the concepts?"

FIGURE 3.1
Four Levels of Educational Outcomes

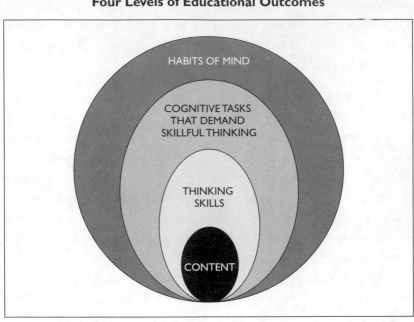

For example, when studying the American Revolution, students learn some fundamental facts about the revolution. In addition, they learn about the concepts associated with a revolution as a means for change. Lessons and activities bring the students to an enlarged understanding of what indicators and triggers exist that cause a revolution and consider whether other options might be possible as we learn from history.

Thinking Skills

Drawing upon state, district, and organizational standards of learning, teachers begin to select content for its generative qualities (Perrone & Kallick, 1997). Content, however, is not the end. Standards also apply to thinking skills and *abilities* that students are expected to display in such learnings. Types of thinking are often embedded in subject matter standards using specific thinking *verbs* that describe what students are to do in meeting the content standard (e.g., "*analyze* the differences" between two kinds of government or "*draw conclusions*" from a certain kind of experiment). Thus, the content becomes a vehicle for experiencing, practicing, and applying the processes needed to think creatively and critically: observing and collecting data, formulating and testing hypotheses, drawing conclusions, and posing questions.

Here's an example from Virginia's secondary school standards in history and social science:

> The student will develop skills for historical and geographical analysis, including the ability to
>   **analyze** documents, records and data . . .
>   **evaluate** the authenticity, authority and credibility . . .
>   **formulate historical questions** and **defend** findings based on **inquiry** and **interpretation** (Virginia Department of Public Instruction, 2001, p. 38)

Other thinking skills appear in statements that specify what students are to do to demonstrate that they have mastered a specific kind of content, as, for example, in a standard-related statement such as this:

> Students should be able to demonstrate how the "second industrial revolution" changed the nature and conditions of work by:
>   (7–12) **assessing** the effects of the rise of big business on labor . . .
>   (7–12) **analyzing** how working conditions changed . . .
>   (5–12) **analyzing the causes and consequences** of the employment of children (National Center for History in the Schools, 1996, p. 152)

These standards not only present us with a pressing need to provide instruction in thinking; they also *legitimatize* taking the time to provide the kind of instruction necessary to accomplish this goal. Furthermore, they suggest that successful instruction in skillful thinking should be done *while* teaching subject matter instead of *in addition to* teaching subject matter. Thinking and subject matter content are neither separate from nor in opposition to each other.

The following is an expanded list of thinking words that we have culled from educational standards articulated in various part of the United States, Canada, and elsewhere:

Analyze	Evaluate	Observe
Apply	Generalize	Organize
Classify	Hypothesize	Predict
Compare	Identify	Solve
Conclude	Inquire	Summarize
Connect	Interpret	Test
Contrast	Judge	

The standards from which these "thinking words" have been extracted represent a random sampling of standards included in present-day curricular objectives. The implication is that a student cannot demonstrate mastery of any of these required standards without performing one or more important thinking skills.

Process outcomes, therefore, are of greater valence than the outcomes of subject-specific content because to be literate in the content, students must know and practice the processes by which that content came into being (Paul & Elder, 1994; Tishman & Perkins, 1997). At this level, teachers decide: What processes do I want my students to practice and develop? What thinking skills will be required to activate the mind about the big ideas I am presenting? How can I directly teach those thinking skills and processes?

Considering the U.S. history example, students might develop a thinking map that examines the sequence of events that led to the American Revolution. They might be asked to understand the frustration of the people at that time by examining the causes and effects of the Boston Tea Party. They might be encouraged to hypothesize about what might have happened if people had waited instead of revolting.

Cognitive Tasks That Demand Skillful Thinking

Once teachers have clearly identified the content and thinking skills, they need to design the cognitive tasks that will require students to engage in deeper thinking. Many people refer to this as "backward planning"

(Wiggins & McTighe, 2005). Planning from this perspective means that each level will deepen students' thinking about the subject as they process material to meet the expectations of the cognitive task.

Earlier in this book we stated that the Habits of Mind are drawn forth in response to problems, the answers to which are not immediately known. Teachers, therefore, design rich tasks requiring strategic thinking, long-range planning, creating something new, making a decision, resolving discrepancies, clarifying ambiguities, constructing the meaning of a phenomenon, conducting research to test theories, or ameliorating polarities. If the task is not sufficiently authentic, engaging, and challenging, then students will revert to merely reproducing knowledge. When students are sufficiently challenged, they give meaning to the work, produce new knowledge, and draw upon the Habits of Mind. (See Chapter 5 for further elaboration of cognitively demanding tasks.)

In the U.S. history example, students might plan a research project to support their theories that evolutionary change need not lead to revolutionary change. Students could plan and present an exhibit demonstrating their understandings and develop rubrics for judging the exhibits and working together effectively. Additionally, they might reflect on and evaluate themselves both individually and collectively, considering how well they met criteria for the project's completion and for thinking and working interdependently.

Habits of Mind

From the broadest perspective of the curriculum landscape, students not only must use the Habits of Mind to succeed in the cognitive task that is assigned; they also learn that success is ensured by mindfully applying these habits. Through reflection and self-evaluation, they begin to see how the application of the habits transfers to all subject areas.

In the example of the U.S. history project, students attend to communicating with accuracy and precision, persisting, and listening with understanding and empathy. As they work in their groups, they experience interdependent thinking. Finally, upon completion of the task, students think about their thinking. They might be asked reflective questions such as these:

• What metacognitive strategies did you employ to manage and monitor your listening skills during your work in teams?

• What effect did striving for accuracy and precision have on your product?

• How did thinking interdependently contribute to your task accomplishment?

Questions might also be asked that invite transfer to situations beyond this learning:

• In what other classes would it be important to strive for accuracy and precision?

• In what other situations beyond school would thinking interdependently contribute to your success?

This attention leads to a process of internalization. Continuous explicit reference to the habits, practice in applying the habits in their work, identifying and analyzing the skills underlying each of the habits, and appreciating the value that the habits bring to their lives lead students to finally make the habits a part of all that they do. (For additional examples of these types of questions and lessons leading toward internalization, see Chapter 5.)

We are proposing, therefore, that teachers deliberately adopt and assess the Habits of Mind as outcomes of their curriculum and instruction. Focusing on, teaching, and encouraging growth in the Habits of Mind changes the design of activities, determines selection of content, and enlarges assessments. The bigger the circle in which the outcomes live, the more influence they exert on the values of each learning (Meadows, 1997). If we wish to influence an element deeper within the system, each tiny adjustment in the environment surrounding it produces profound effects on the entire system. This realization allows us to search beyond the Habits of Mind for systems to which we naturally aspire in our journey of human development, which, if affected, also would influence our capacity to learn (Garmston, 1997).

Designing Curriculum to Focus on the Habits of Mind

It is important to realize that the effects of teaching the Habits of Mind are not immediate. Forming the Habits of Mind requires many experiences, encounters, reflections, rehearsals, practice sessions, and instructions. To accomplish this goal, teachers must also get into the habit of teaching the vocabulary of the Habits of Mind, deliberately structuring questions and inviting students to plan for and reflect on their use of the habits. Students soon begin using that vocabulary—even in preschool and kindergarten. They learn to recognize the performance (or absence) of the Habits of Mind in themselves and others—in characters in books and films, in playground experiences, and even in politicians and other public figures. They discuss ways that performance could be improved. Teachers and students grow beyond the conscious stage as they internalize the Habits of Mind. The habits become intuitive, ultimately reaching automaticity. The individual strands (behaviors) eventually are woven into a strong cable (habit).

In addition to integrating the Habits of Mind into the already existing curriculum, teachers know that students go through an evolution of learning in relation to the habits. We describe this evolution in Chapter 4, "Habits of Mind: A Journey of Continuous Growth." Although this journey is neither linear nor prescriptive, the description nonetheless provides a framework or map for increasing integration, beginning with a foundation of merely being aware of what the habits are and recognizing them in various situations, employing and finding value in using them, adopting them, reflecting on and evaluating their use, and finally internalizing them.

This journey provides teachers with a map to serve as a guide toward increasing instructional complexity. The function of a map is to provide a view of the territory: a starting place, alternative routes, signposts and mile markers along the way, and a destination toward which we are heading. Keeping the map in mind or in view during the journey allows us to see where we've been and to anticipate where we are going. Consider the following example.

In a typical middle school consisting of grades 6, 7, and 8, the staff might start implementing the Habits of Mind by building the foundation with all students—by helping them become aware of and explore the meanings of the Habits of Mind, and identifying what they look like and sound like. Posters illustrating the Habits of Mind with logos and quotations might be placed around the school and classrooms as reminders. Teachers might have students define the habits in their own terms and provide examples from their own lives and experiences. (Students are generally very adept at this.) Once students know what the Habits of Mind are, teachers might ask students to find examples of them in novels, films, videos, newspapers, and cartoons, and on the athletic field.

Teachers often provide a way for students to begin to assess where they are with the habits. Are they using the habits as they work with others in a group? Are they using the habits when they study? Once students understand the Habits of Mind, they can map their own journey of development. Teachers may choose to provide only whole-class lessons intent on building awareness. This might be all that is accomplished in the classrooms throughout the school.

In the next school year, the students have all advanced one grade. The 8th graders have gone on to high school. While the new 7th and 8th graders may need a brief review of the Habits of Mind, teachers would *not* want to spend the year at the stage of becoming aware of and exploring the meanings of the Habits of Mind. Rather, they would want to focus more on the strategic applications of the Habits of Mind. They might invite students to be alert to and aware of their use of the Habits of Mind as they work on complex problems and rich, cognitively demanding tasks. They might discuss the value of the habits and how the habits served them in working toward greater skills in problem solving and decision making. They would invite students to transfer the habits to life situations beyond the school.

Meanwhile, a new crop of 6th graders has entered the school. They may know nothing about the Habits of Mind and would therefore have to be introduced to them, as the 6th graders were the previous year.

Again as the third school year begins, the original 6th graders have now become 8th graders and are becoming well skilled in the Habits of Mind as a result of the staff's coordination, articulation, and reinforcement across the various subjects and classes that students have taken. Now those 8th graders need to expand their capacities, to extend the value, and to build commitment to continuous growth in the Habits of Mind. The teachers stress metacognition by discussing with students what they are thinking about to guide their decisions, actions, and thoughts. Values and benefits of using the Habits of Mind are continually explored. By now, students autonomously and without prompting employ the Habits of Mind, assess themselves, and develop goals and strategies for their improvement.

Meanwhile, the 6th graders have become 7th graders and are ready for their strategic application of the Habits of Mind—to build alertness, skillfulness, and valuing of the habits. And yet another crop of 6th grade students are new to the school and are introduced to the experiences designed to explore meanings.

Obviously this same map could be employed by an elementary or a secondary school staff. Ideally, we envision a sequence of learning about the Habits of Mind, with students becoming more skillful and more spontaneous in their use, and using them more widely, in a setting beginning in kindergarten (or even the preschool level) and continuing through graduation from high school. (See the Tahoma story by Skerritt, Hard, and Edlund in Chapter 22.)

The map we've described provides an idealized view of the journey. Realistically it doesn't always work quite that way and is not that linear. What the map does suggest, however, is that when teaching the Habits of Mind directly, there needs to be a sequential development of the kind of curricular lessons that will be offered to the whole class. At the same time, teachers need to differentiate based on the individual needs of students. Students are at varying levels: advanced in some of the Habits of Mind yet novices in others. Some students come to school with well-developed habits, whereas others may have fewer opportunities to see role models and to develop the habits. As students become better at self-assessing, teachers can provide richer coaching examples so that all students are mapping their own roads to internalizing the habits.

When students who have never heard of the Habits of Mind transfer in from other schools, they need to become aware of what the habits are and how they define the school culture. The map provides an overview that also allows teachers to individualize depending on students' emerging knowledge of and display of the Habits of Mind.

In Summary

School staffs view the habits as the most panoramic view of the curriculum when they understand the long-range, cumulative, enduring nature of learning. They understand that success is desired not only in school but also in life. When all staff members share this kind of vision, their work transcends grade levels and subject areas. Panoramic outcomes are more likely to be achieved because they are reinforced, transferred, and revisited throughout the school, at home, and in the community.

It should be emphasized that learning activities are still taught. Content is selected for its generative nature, and processes are practiced, but they now accumulate into grander, more long-range, and lifelong outcomes. Activities, content, and thinking processes become vehicles for achieving these larger, more enduring, and essential Habits of Mind. Instead of a single teacher asking, "What do I want?" instructional teams now decide, "Which Habits of Mind do we want students to develop and employ? What will we do to assist their development? How might we work collaboratively to determine if students are developing increased skillfulness in such dispositions over time? What will we see or hear in student behaviors as evidence of their growth? How might we practice and assess our own growth toward these Habits of Mind through our work together?"

Staff and students learn to draw upon the Habits of Mind to organize and direct their intellectual resources as they confront and resolve problems, observe human frailty in themselves and others, plan for the most productive interventions in groups, and search out the motivations of their own and others' actions. The habits become the desirable meta-outcomes for the entire community—staff and students.

The following letter from Peter King, a graduate of Smoky Hills High School in Aurora, Colorado, illustrates his transcendence to a more "panoramic view" of educational outcomes:

> In the packet I read about "intellects," it says that people who behave intelligently are great problem solvers who are not necessarily mathematicians or scientists. Some are people like mechanics. The skills it takes to be a good mechanic are all listed in this packet. And when I say that, I disgust myself in thinking that all mechanics are morons. I'm talking about how hypocritical it is to say that mechanics are stupid when I'm one myself. Everybody is a mechanic in a way, but me in particular because

I had industrial arts and automotive classes since 9th grade. My passion is fixing my car, making it go faster and better. So how could I think badly about mechanics? Well, it's that little thing known as peer pressure. My parents, friends, and a majority of people look down on people who fix cars. So, I look down on myself; I hide my hobby like it was a crime. People don't realize the massive amount of problem-solving power it takes to fix someone else's mess.

All of these characteristics of intelligent behavior are used by "industrial artists." But don't get me wrong, there are definitely bad mechanics. That's why I fix my car myself. I believe the same skills I use in my Critical Thinking/Discussion Class are the ones I use to diagnose an engineering problem:

- Persevering when the solution is not readily apparent. (It took me months to fix a vibration the car made that no other mechanic could fix.)
- Checking for Accuracy
- Problem Posing
- Working with Past Knowledge
- Ingenuity and Creativity (Ask Mr. Ferrari about this one!)

These I believe are the most-used skills. We are all "mechanics" in a way. It's just that some of us get our hands greasy.

In this age of accountability and "other-directed learning," school curriculum is derived from the selection of content from the disciplines, including history, geography, mathematics, biology, physics, literacy, and the fine arts. At the same time, we develop statements of goals of education in terms of desired characteristics of students as effective learners: skillful problem solvers, responsible citizens, team players. It is assumed that if students learn all the subject matter, meet the standards, do well on tests and stay in school, somehow students will become the kind of people we want them to become.

Embracing the Habits of Mind proposes that learning of content is not only an outcome, but that learning such content also provides opportunities to experience, practice, and value those larger, more enduring and essential learnings that students need to enable them to participate effectively in their future.

References

Bateson, G. (1972). *Steps to an ecology of mind*. San Francisco: Chandler.

Costa, A. (2008). Habits of mind: Learnings that last. In A. Costa (Ed.), *The school as a home for the mind* (pp. 29–48). Palatine, IL: Thousand Oaks, CA: Corwin.

Dilts, R. (1994). *Effective presentation skills*. Capitola, CA: META Publications.

Eisner, E. (1997, January). Cognition and representation: A way to pursue the American dream? *Phi Delta Kappan, 78*(5), 348–353.

Elias, M. (2006). The connection between academic and social-emotional learning. In M. J. Elias & H. Arnold (Eds.), *The educator's guide to emotional intelligence and academic achievement* (pp. 4–14). Thousand Oaks, CA: Corwin.

Garmston, R. (1997, Spring). Nested levels of learning. *Journal of Staff Development, 18*(2), 66–68.

Jacobs, H. H. (1997). *Mapping the big picture: Integrating curriculum and assessment K–12*. Alexandria, VA: ASCD.

Marzano, R. J. (1992). *A different kind of classroom: Teaching with Dimensions of Learning*. Alexandria, VA: ASCD.

Meadows, D. (1997, Winter). Places to intervene in a system (in increasing order of effectiveness). *Whole Earth*, pp. 79–83.

Meier, D. (1995). *The power of their ideas*. Oakland, CA: Coalition of Essential Schools.

National Center for History in the Schools. (1996). *National standards for United States history, grades 5–12* (Expanded ed.). Los Angeles: University of California Press.

Paul, R., & Elder, L. (1994). All content has a logic: That logic is given by a disciplined mode of thinking, Part 1. *Teaching Thinking and Problem Solving, 16*(5), 1–4.

Perrone, V., & Kallick, B. (1997). Generative topics for process curriculum. In A. Costa & R. Liebmann (Eds.), *Supporting the spirit of learning: When process is content* (pp. 23–24). Thousand Oaks, CA: Corwin.

Resnick, L. B. (2001). Making America smarter: The real goal of school reform. In A. L. Costa, (Ed.), *Developing minds: A resource book for teaching thinking* (pp. 3–6). Alexandria, VA: ASCD.

Senge, P. (1990). *The fifth discipline: The art and practice of the learning organization*. New York: Doubleday/Currency.

Sizer, T. (1992). *Horace's school*. Oakland, CA: Coalition of Essential Schools.

Tishman, S., & Perkins, D. (1997, January). The language of thinking. *Phi Delta Kappan, 78*(5), 368–374.

Virginia Department of Education. (2001). *History and social science standards of learning for Virginia schools*. Richmond, VA: Author.

Wiggins, G., & McTighe, J. (2005). *Understanding by design* (2nd ed.). Alexandria, VA: ASCD.

4

Habits of Mind:
A Journey of Continuous Growth

James Anderson, Arthur L. Costa, and Bena Kallick

Developing our Habits of Mind is a lifelong journey; a journey in which we continually explore and deepen our understanding of the habits; a journey of continuously becoming more attuned to situations in which the habits would benefit our own behavior as well as the behavior of others; a journey of a growing capacity to be more skillful and strategic as we use the habits, a journey of developing our ability to critically self-reflect as we focus on our own behavior and the behavior of others.

It is easy to think of a Habit of Mind as something that we either use or don't use. It would be more accurate, however, to refer to how well or poorly we use the habit. Most people will engage in the habits to a degree, but they sometimes lack the skills to execute them well. They may not understand or appreciate the benefits that accrue when the habits are mindfully applied. They may be unaware of opportunities or not have the sensitivity to recognize opportunities to engage one or more of the Habits of Mind as well as to encourage others to use them.

As we observe students in our schools and classrooms, we quickly recognize that some are more adept, more skillful, and more effective at applying one or more of the habits than are others. As we observe students over time, it is our desire that they move through schooling and into adulthood getting better at using the habits. A description of exactly how this journey takes place may be quite elusive.

In most areas of schooling we have a clear understanding of what improvement looks like. We need only refer to our state and provincial curriculum documents to see how development is described in standards, rubrics, and benchmarks for such subject areas as mathematics, history, music, and physical education. However, until now we may have lacked a clear guide to and description of development and improvement in the Habits of Mind. Following are descriptions of five dimensions within which learners can grow in relation to their Habits of Mind.

Five Dimensions of Growth

An understanding of these five dimensions of growth allows us to plan curriculum designed to develop the habits. The dimensions can also guide our efforts in assessment and suggest effective pedagogies in which teachers might engage learners to facilitate their growth.

Exploring Meanings

This dimension concerns a student's ability to articulate the meanings of the Habits of Mind. As students explore meaning they develop a greater capacity to articulate more sophisticated definitions and acquire more concepts associated with the Habits of Mind. They develop a basic literacy around the language of the habits. They are able to draw upon a greater range of examples and to build more complex analogies, and they begin to connect the habits to their own experiences and recognize them in others. They become able to reflect on times when they have (or should have) used a particular habit.

For example, in the early primary years students may define persistence as "sticking to it and not giving up." They may cite the examples from books such as *The Little Engine That Could*. They might reflect on times when they played games or did their homework and persisted. However, as they are exposed to more experiences and develop a deeper understanding of persistence, we would want to see and hear them deepening their meaning. They might define persistence in terms of keeping goals in mind, identifying obstacles toward achieving the goals, and finding effective ways around them. They might cite more contemporary examples from the media, raising questions about their observations of persistence in others and becoming even more fluent in using synonyms and analogies for persistence. Students may advocate the need for persistence as a necessary ingredient to solve world problems.

Expanding Capacities

As students learn and practice the Habits of Mind, they become more skillful. They develop a large repertoire of strategies that they can call upon. As the skills and tools are repeated, students also grow more adept at selecting and sequencing the most appropriate strategies at the appropriate time. They refine their ability to apply each of these skills and strategies in complex and sophisticated ways. Learners begin to develop internal, metacognitive strategies and "self-talk" about using the Habits of Mind when confronted with problems, decisions, and ambiguous situations. Furthermore, as students expand their capacities in regard to the Habits of Mind, they are able to call upon different habits in sequence and employ them more effectively and strategically. Persistence, for example, is not just a word. Rather, it is found to be a composite of numerous skills and strategies. Learners employ techniques that help them stay with a task in the face of uncertainty. When it is difficult to complete a task, learners develop new ways of encouraging themselves to stick with it.

Increasing Alertness

To engage in any of the Habits of Mind, we must first be sensitive to cues from the environment. We must recognize that a problematic situation exists and that the opportunity for engaging one or more of the Habits of Mind has presented itself. Students must build some guiding principles or criteria upon which they become increasingly alert to opportunities to engage in the Habits of Mind.

Students will initially find it easy to engage in the Habits of Mind in familiar, often simple contexts. However, over time we want them to be able to be alert to opportunities in new, novel, and complex situations. Furthermore, students will often rely on external prompts from teachers or others to indicate when to engage in the Habits of Mind. As they develop their alertness, they will become more self-directed and apply the appropriate habits spontaneously. As students' competence in persisting increases, for example, they realize that persistence is not appropriate in every situation. Although it is important to persist to accomplish a task, it is not appropriate to persist with an argument in the face of contradictory and important evidence that does not support an argument.

Extending Values

As learners connect success to the effective application of the Habits of Mind, they begin to make predictions about when and why it might be appropriate to use a particular habit. In doing so they also deepen their valuing of the habits because they can understand why using a habit would be important in these situations. They can reflect back upon the use of the habit and see that when the habit has been appropriately used, it has led to greater success. Continuous experiences in which the habits show real benefits for successful interactions with work and with others create a better sense of self-confidence. As a result, the individual not only values the habits but also makes a commitment to using them. As learners extend the value they place on the Habits of Mind, they express a belief that the habit is important not just in particular situations, but also more universally as a pattern of behavior in their life, and they express a desire for the Habits of Mind to be adopted in the lives of others and in the community at large.

Building Commitment

Building a commitment to continuous improvement in the use of the Habits of Mind occurs when learners increasingly become self-directed. Self-improvement in this dimension is recognized as learners become self-managing by setting goals for themselves, self-monitoring as they "observe themselves" in action, and more self-reflective as they evaluate themselves, modify their behaviors, and set new and increasingly higher standards for their own performance. Self-evaluation moves from being the quantitative recognition of the use of the Habits of Mind in themselves to being increasingly more descriptive and qualitative. Movement through this dimension indicates significant improvement, but for many students the improvement stops after a period of time.

Internalization

Although the Habits of Mind are never fully mastered, for continuous learners they are continually practiced, modified, and refined. If they are truly "habituated," they are performed automatically, spontaneously, and

FIGURE 4.1

Dimensions of Growth

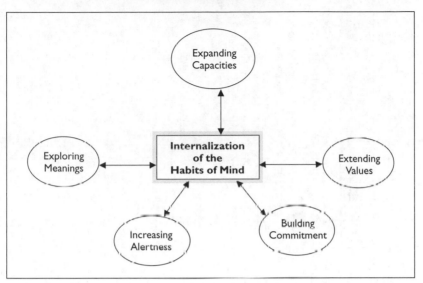

without prompting. They become an "internal compass" to guide actions, decisions, and thoughts. When confronted with complex decisions, ambiguous tasks, challenging problems, or perplexing dilemmas, learners ask themselves questions such as these:

- What is the most flexible thing I can do right now?
- What strategies do I have at my disposal that could benefit me now?
- What questions do I need to ask myself and others?
- Who else do I need to think about?
- How can I refine the problem to make it clearer?
- What intrigues me about this problem?

This type of internalization happens as learners develop along each of the five dimensions and commit themselves to continuous growth in these dimensions, as illustrated in Figure 4.1. The point we strive toward when developing, improving, extending, and becoming more effective in the use of the Habits of Mind is to become truly internalized and committed to continual growth in each of these dimensions. Figure 4.2 provides a framework for teaching and assessing growth in each of the dimensions.

FIGURE 4.2

Framework for Teaching and Assessing Growth in Dimensions of the Habits of Mind (HOM)

Dimension	Developmental Learning Tasks	Teacher Facilitation	Assessment of Desired Results
Exploring Meanings	• To extend the meanings and uses of the HOM. • To increase understanding of what are HOM. • To clarify and build upon meanings and definitions, and to find increasing examples of HOM in self and others.	• Provide activities that build meaning. • Introduce and build terminology, definitions, concept acquisition, including the use of nonexamples. • Connect to other experiences through word splash, finding examples in books, films, newspapers; on playground; in community. • Recognize and label student use of the HOM. • Model the HOM. • Design charts and posters/using icons. • Teach HOM directly. *Sample questions:* • What does (HOM) mean to you? • What might be an example of (HOM)? • What are some other words or phrases that might mean the same as (HOM) for you? • In what ways has your understanding of the HOM grown since we last thought about its meaning?	The student develops a broader, deeper understanding of the Habits of Mind. Growth in this dimension will be recognized by learners being able to … • Use the HOM terminology correctly. • Translate/interpret the HOM in their own vernacular. • Make more complex analogies and cite more examples. • Articulate a more complex, detailed understanding of the HOM. • Self-report the use of the HOM.

FIGURE 4.2   *(continued)*

Framework for Teaching and Assessing Growth in Dimensions of the Habits of Mind (HOM)

Dimension	Developmental Learning Tasks	Teacher Facilitation	Assessment of Desired Results
Expanding Capacities	• To become more skillful in the application of the HOM. • To self-monitor which skills and strategies are being used and which ones need to be perfected and employed. • To build an ever-increasing repertoire of tools and strategies. • To apply the HOM in sequence and in concert.	• Teach new strategies, refine old ones, and help learners to select appropriate ones. • Provide guidance in integrating the use of the HOM in groups and sequences. • Invite students to describe what skills and strategies helped them when they needed to, for example, persist, manage their impulsivity, think flexibly. • Unpack each HOM to identify the metacognitive skills and strategies appropriate to each; for example, use mind maps to answer the question "What can I do when I get stuck?" *Sample questions:* • What goes on in your head when you use the habit of ___? • What are you talking to yourself about when you ___? • What will you be aware of in your own thinking as you ___? • What habit did you find yourself using when you were ___? • What skills and strategies might you employ when you know you need to (persist, strive for accuracy, empathize, manage impulsivity, etc.)?	The student increases use of a widening range of strategies, skills, and tools and does so with greater sophistication in sequence, accuracy, stamina, and elegance. Growth in this dimension will be recognized by learners being able to … • Select the appropriate tool at the appropriate time. • Orchestrate appropriate sequences and groupings of HOM. • Use greater numbers of supporting strategies with increasing sophistication and skill. • Increasingly use HOM in concert and in sequence. • Apply the HOM to new contexts and areas in their life.

FIGURE 4.2   *(continued)*

Framework for Teaching and Assessing Growth in Dimensions of the Habits of Mind (HOM)

Dimension	Developmental Learning Tasks	Teacher Facilitation	Assessment of Desired Results
Increasing Alertness	• To become increasingly vigilant to an expanding range of situations in which to apply the HOM. • To become more sensitive to cues from a widening range, variety, and number of situations and environments as signals to engage one or more of the HOM.	• Build criteria for learners to carry internally that help them recognize new situations in which to apply the HOM; provide new situations and guide the application of the HOM in these settings. • Use transfer strategies to help learners move the HOM to new areas, contexts, and domains. *Sample questions:* • In what other situations might it be important to employ this HOM? • What cues were you aware of in this situation that indicated to you that it would be appropriate to use _____? • If you were to _____, which of the habits would serve you? • What are some reasons a person might want to use the HOM of _____ in this situation? • How might a _____ use the HOM when _____? • What predictions would you make if _____ failed to use the HOM of _____?	The student becomes more astute in the ability to increasingly recognize, without prompting, when to apply the Habits of Mind. Growth in this dimension will be recognized by learners being able to … • Apply the HOM to new settings. • Recognize increasingly diverse, complex, and novel situations in which to apply the HOM. • Spontaneously draw forth appropriate HOM when confronted with ambiguous, perplexing situations. • Recognize a wider range of situations in which to apply the HOM. • Recognize novel and complex situations in which to apply the HOM, without assistance. • Articulate the criteria upon which these decisions are made. • Describe the metacognitive strategies employed while using the HOM.

FIGURE 4.2 (continued)

Framework for Teaching and Assessing Growth in Dimensions of the Habits of Mind (HOM)

Dimension	Developmental Learning Tasks	Teacher Facilitation	Assessment of Desired Results
Extending Values	• To increasingly find the values and benefits of using the HOM and therefore to spontaneously choose to employ them. • To advocate their use to others.	• Make HOM a learning outcome; ensure that success in the classroom is connected to application of the HOM. • Facilitate discussions and reflections on the values and benefits. • Encourage students to capture their reflections, insights, and values through such means as portfolios, journal entries, and essays. *Sample questions:* • Why would it be important to employ this HOM in this situation? • If you were to _____, why would (HOM) serve you? • What are some of the reasons a _____ might want to use the HOM of _____? • How might a _____ use the HOM when _____? • What values are you expressing when you choose to employ HOM? • What would be some of the benefits f _____ chose to employ HOM? • Which HOM would serve _____ in a situation like this? Why?	The student develops deeper appreciation of the positive results achieved when applying the HOM. Growth in this dimension will be recognized by learners increasingly being able to . . . • Express valuing of the HOM not only for self in the moment, but also generalized to the lives of other persons and universal situations. • Display an increased propensity and inclination for applying the HOM. • Choose to use the HOM instead of other less productive patterns of behaviors and explain why. • Articulate their choice to use the HOM, reflecting the value they place on it.

FIGURE 4.2   (continued)

Framework for Teaching and Assessing Growth in Dimensions of the Habits of Mind (HOM)

Dimension	Developmental Learning Tasks	Teacher Facilitation	Assessment of Desired Results
Building Commitment	• To "internalize" the HOM as a way of life. • To become increasingly more autonomous in the improved use of the HOM. • To become more effective at reflecting, self-evaluating, self-modifying, self-prescribing. • To set goals for self-improvement and more skillful use of the HOM. • To experiment with ways to improve use, to continuously learn more about the power and effects of the HOM. • To model the HOM to others. • To employ the HOM as a lens to analyze, understand, and resolve world problems.	• Provide appropriate scaffolding and assessment structures that move learners toward self-directedness and qualitative assessment. • Apply the HOM in many rich, challenging tasks that engage the learner's intellect, imagination, and metacognition. • Apply the HOM in interdisciplinary learnings at school, at home, and in the community. *Sample questions:* • As you reflect on this situation, which of the HOM served you the most? • What were some of the effects your use of (HOM) had on _____? • As you anticipate future situations, what commitments or action plans do you have in mind to improve your use of (HOM)? • What are some of the ways your use of HOM has changed in the past year? • How have the HOM influenced your decisions about _____? • As you envision your future, which of the HOM might you work on in your personal growth plans? • What strategies of self-improvement might you design?	Individuals are characterized by the HOM when they are empathic, continual, creative, persistent learners who are willing to take risks and to admit they don't know but want to find out. To be characterized as such, evidence is gathered through observation of patterns of behavior in numerous settings over an extended period of time. Growth in this dimension will be recognized by learners increasingly being able to … • Self-report the effective or ineffective use of the HOM. • Admit that the HOM are never perfected or developed fully. • Employ the HOM without reminding or prompting. • Become more self-directed in choosing to evaluate and extend their use of the HOM. • Choose and apply increasingly qualitative strategies to evaluate their use of the HOM. • Express criteria for choosing a course of action based on the HOM.

5

Is Your Instruction Habit Forming?

James Anderson and Arthur L. Costa

Creative, powerful teachers have a repertoire of teaching strategies and techniques. They draw forth strategies from this repertoire depending on the lesson's content and purposes, the students' levels of development, the current interests of the students, the adopted standards, and the agreements of the staff and school about what should be taught when. Also, effective teachers remain alert to that "teachable moment" when students are ready, excited, and open to the learning at hand.

How, then, might we design instruction, lessons, and units of work that help students progress along the journey of continual growth toward internalizing the Habits of Mind described in Chapter 1? What follows are several suggestions that might be included in the design of lessons.

Designing Instruction with Habits of Mind in Mind

Armed with an understanding of how students acquire the Habits of Mind through a continuous journey of growth over time, we can develop a repertoire of instructional strategies and use a range of approaches to lesson design that will skillfully craft learning experiences that develop the Habits of Mind.

As we plan our lessons, we usually have in mind the learning goals for our students. We have a clear idea of the evidence that would indicate the students have achieved these learning goals. We take into account the students' prior knowledge and level of achievement. We may have an idea of common errors or misconceptions and plan for these to be addressed. With all of this forethought, we plan a series of learning activities designed to build students' understandings, skills, and knowledge so the students can achieve these learning goals.

When it comes to teaching Habits of Mind, we use the same planning process as we do for other aspects of our teaching. We make the Habits of Mind an explicit outcome of our teaching. We consider the students' current level of achievement and prior knowledge of the Habits of Mind we are addressing. We plan for common misconceptions or difficulties to be addressed, and, most important, we sequence a series of learning experiences designed to develop students' Habits of Mind so they can become the skillful and effective problem solvers we would like them to be.

Although effective teachers have a clear vision of what development and improvement of their students' learning looks like, describing the development of a Habit of Mind may be more difficult. In Chapter 4 we described five dimensions of growth. Not only do we want students to explore the meanings of the Habits of Mind, we also want them to become more skillful in their application of a Habit of Mind. We want them to apply the Habits of Mind in increasingly diverse situations, we want them to place an ever-higher value on these habits above other patterns of behavior, and we want them to continuously strive for self-improvement. Once recognized, these dimensions can help us design activities to develop our students' Habits of Mind.

In designing appropriate activities, the first two approaches to consider are the following:

- Cognitively Demanding Tasks.
- Building Intuitive Awareness.

These approaches to lesson design might be labeled "teaching *for* the Habits of Mind" because they simply create classroom conditions in which the Habits of Mind will be encountered, labeled, recognized, and reinforced. When a school's curriculum is rich in these cognitively demanding tasks and when teachers use the language, the development of the Habits of Mind is expected or hoped for. We refer to this situation as "repeated exposure." Although such instruction may result in some degree of improvement in learning, we know that carefully designed programs that identify specific outcomes, employ targeted strategies, recognize current ability, and assess the degree that learning has taken place will be more effective.

If our goal is to truly develop skillfulness, alertness, valuing, and commitment rather than simply recognizing and labeling Habits of Mind, the "repeated exposure" approach alone is not satisfactory. Other complementary approaches are also required if we are to effectively and efficiently develop students' Habits of Mind. Therefore, we include three approaches to lesson design.

- Exploring Meanings of the Habits of Mind.
- Strategic Application of the Habits of Mind.
- Building Depth, Complexity, and Elegance.

These three approaches might be classified as "teaching *of* the Habits of Mind" because the habits become explicit goals and outcomes of the instruction.

A third category of instructional design we might label "teaching *with* the Habits of Mind." We include two approaches in this category:

- Diagnosing and Assessing Students' Level of Mastery of the Habits of Mind.
- Modeling the Habits of Mind.

The following sections describe the purposes, strategies, and assessments associated with each of these approaches to lesson design.

Cognitively Demanding Tasks

As described in Chapter 2, the Habits of Mind come forth in response to problems whose resolutions are not immediately known. Therefore, this approach to lesson design calls upon teachers to present students with problems, dilemmas, and dichotomies whose resolutions are not readily apparent.

Purpose. The purpose of this lesson design is to plan for, experience, and reflect upon the use of the Habits of Mind when presented with cognitive tasks—or when problems may emerge from the environment—that are challenging, controversial, ambiguous, or enigmatic, and whose answers are not immediately known.

Strategies. A cognitively demanding task, such as those described in the following examples, engages students skillfully in a variety of authentic, rich activities that require strategic planning, creative approaches, and the application of organized, multiple, and complex thinking skills and Habits of Mind. These activities might include solving a problem, making a difficult decision, resolving polarities, creating something new, or investigating an unknown. Here are three examples:

• A secondary science teacher asks her students to consider a scenario in which a 15-year-old boy obtains a hair sample from a person he believes is his father, without that person's permission. The students are then asked to answer the question "Should paternity exclusion testing be allowed without the authorization of the people involved?" (Moulds, 2006).

• A 5th grade teacher asks his students to compare and contrast two versions of the famous story of Pocahontas and John Smith by reading the fictionalized account *The Double Life of Pocahontas* by Jean Fritz (1987) and watching the Disney movie. Students work in groups to take accurate notes about the characters, setting, plot, and events that are depicted in the movie and to extract precise details from the text. Students draw conclusions about the accuracy of historical events after finding significant patterns in the similarities and differences between the two sources (Reagan, 2009).

• A 1st grade teacher organizes the class into small groups and presents each group with a strong horseshoe magnet and a wide variety of objects made of different elements: wood, metals, glass, cloth, ceramics, and paper. She asks her students to group the materials according to those that a magnet will or will not pick up. From their classification and experiments, students will describe the properties of each group of objects and draw conclusions as to which materials are attracted to magnets.

According to Moulds (2006), cognitively demanding tasks

• Are culminating performances that are purposeful and have value in the real world.

• Involve students in solving problems.

• Require students to develop and use complex reasoning processes (higher-order thinking processes such as analysis and problem solving).

• Engage students in the learning process.

• Draw on widely accepted topics in subject areas.

• Connect to the world beyond the classroom.

• Are rich in their application as they represent an outcome of substantial intellectual and educational value.

Effective teachers frequently include these kinds of cognitively demanding tasks throughout their lessons and units of work. In fact, when schools first come across the Habits of Mind, their initial response may be that they already "do" habits of mind. The difference is that the task provides a vehicle not only to engage in provocative, intriguing content and to use skillful problem solving, but also to explicitly experience the benefits of using one or more of the Habits of Mind.

After introducing the task, teachers may alert the students to the use of one or more of the Habits of Mind:

• You'll be working in groups on this task. Let's review some of the skills we learned about *thinking interdependently*.

• Since we are trying to determine historical truth, it will be very important to strive for *accuracy and precision and to communicate our ideas with clarity*.

During the activity, teachers may wish to remind students about the use of the particular habit the class is focusing on:

• Alicia, how did your sharing the information about Pocahontas that you found on the Internet further your group's thinking?

• Assad, tell us how you thought about the magnet experiment. What was the metacognitive process you used?

Then, upon completion of the task, the teacher invites the group to reflect upon its application of and skillfulness in using the Habits of Mind, and the value of the habits. Teachers will want to invite students to reflect on which additional habits were drawn upon, and to establish some goals for further refinement of their use of the Habits of Mind:

- So, during this task, we were focusing on *thinking interdependently* and *striving for accuracy*. What were some indicators in your group that you thought interdependently?
- What might we work on next to get even better at it?
- The intent of this unit was to determine historical truth. How did *striving for accuracy and precision* assist in drawing your conclusions?
- Besides *thinking interdependently* and *striving for accuracy and precision*, what other Habits of Mind served you as you worked on this task?
- When else in your life would it be important to be mindful of these *interdependent thinking* skills?

Assessment. Cognitively demanding tasks provide rich opportunities for students to self-assess by documenting their reflections and insights in journals, portfolios, PowerPoint presentations, interviews, and exhibits. (See Chapter 11 for more about assessing the Habits of Mind.) Students should not only monitor and record their understanding of and interest in the content that is studied; they should also record and reflect on their use of the Habits of Mind. When students share their portfolios and journals, teachers gain greater insight into their level of understanding of, degree of commitment to, and skillfulness in the use of the Habits of Mind. Next steps along the journey of continuous growth can thereby be planned.

Building Intuitive Awareness

To build this experiential awareness of the Habits of Mind at a more intuitive level, the teacher uses the terminology and models appropriate use of the habits both in and out of the classroom. This modeling will often include using Habits of Mind that are not the current focus of the class, or using them in ways not required by the students at this time. Students see and hear effective application of the Habits of Mind in a range of contexts. They also come to recognize that the Habits of Mind are a valued part of the way teachers approach their role.

Purpose. The purpose of this lesson design is to lay the groundwork for introducing the Habits of Mind at a later time in a more formal way. The intent is to show that the Habits of Mind are a valued and purposeful part of the teacher's life and to alert students to new and diverse situations where the Habits of Mind might be applied.

Strategies. Using the language of the Habits of Mind is a powerful strategy and helps students learn to recognize opportunities to engage in the habits. Using the language of the Habits of Mind also reinforces that they represent an expected and valued way of behaving at the school. Students will also learn to associate the application of the habits with success in the curriculum and thereby further deepen their valuing of them.

Drawing upon standards and typical content appropriate for the developmental level of the students, the teacher presents students with cognitively demanding tasks. As the students are working on these tasks, the teacher recognizes and labels the students' use of one or more of the Habits of Mind:

• You really *persisted* with this problem. You hung in there until you were satisfied with your solution.

• You need to go back and *check for accuracy.*

• Let me tell you what's *going on in my mind* as I think about this problem.

• What *questions* are you asking yourself as you solve this problem?

• In what ways might you *think flexibly* about this problem—approach it in other ways?

• What *intrigues* you about this problem? What are you continuing to *wonder* about?

• *Thinking interdependently* allowed you to divide up the task, making it easier for each person to succeed.

• What was *going on inside your head* when you came to that conclusion?

Teachers might wish to read to students (at the primary grades) or have students read books that have one or more of the Habits of Mind as a theme (for a list of such books, go to www.habits-of-mind.net). For example, the story of *The Little Engine That Could* (Piper, 1976) is a prime example of *persistence* and would provide an appropriate introduction for kindergarten and early-grade students. In elementary grades, teachers might read with the class *The True Story of the Three Little Pigs by A. Wolf* (Scieszka, 1989) and then discuss the meaning of *empathy*. For more mature students, *The Diary of Anne Frank* (Goodrich, 1993) could become an object lesson on *managing impulsivity* and *persistence*. Maya Angelou's *I Know Why the Caged Bird Sings* (2002) could be a focus for discussion with secondary school students on *drawing on past knowledge*.

Hearing these identifying terms as students are performing one or more of the habits creates an awareness of their own behavior. This strategy creates a foundation on which an understanding of the Habits of Mind can later be built.

Assessment. Teachers will want to keep anecdotal records and checklists to respond to questions such as these:

- Are students attending and participating?
- Are students beginning to use the terminology of the Habits of Mind?
- Are students reflecting on their experiences?
- Are students talking about and discussing their feelings and perceptions as they reflect on the task?
- Are students aware of and analyzing their own and others' behaviors?

Exploring Meanings of the Habits of Mind

Early in students' acquaintance with the Habits of Mind, teachers will want to establish definitions and to explore the meanings of the Habits of Mind.

Purpose. The purpose of this lesson design is to help students become familiar with, understand the meanings and purposes of, and be able to use the language of the Habits of Mind. As a result of these types of lessons, students should be able to cognitively label the Habits of Mind they use and to recognize use of the habits by others. Although teachers will sometimes use this type of lesson to introduce all 16 Habits of Mind, we can also assume that a lesson may focus on just one or two.

In this type of lesson, teachers can also begin to diagnose where the students' development of the Habits of Mind lies in relation to the journey of continuous growth described in Chapter 4 and to prescribe some next goals for students.

Employing this lesson design means that class time, independent of content lessons, is devoted to the explicit teaching of the Habits of Mind. Students undertake a range of activities designed to help them gain a deeper understanding of the habit and to acquire an array of examples and analogies. Some strategies, such as the use of Y-charts to help students identify what a habit looks like, sounds like, and feels like, are equally applicable to all the habits. Other activities may lend themselves to just one habit. (See Part II for additional suggestions.)

Students first build meaning around the habit. They build a working definition of *what* the habit is and connect this to prior understandings. This definition acts as a kind of cognitive anchor for the student, who can then use the language to build on this understanding in a meaningful way.

Once students have a working definition of the habit, they are able to recognize it being applied by others and then by themselves. They begin to recognize *how* others go about applying the habit in different situations; and they begin to recognize some of the strategies, skills, and tools used when applying the habit. Many teachers have found that using the Habits of Mind as a character analysis tool can be powerful at this point. Book and film characters, media personalities, heroes and heroines, and people familiar to the student (including peers, teachers, and family members) all can be used to discuss how people use the Habits of Mind. Judi Roach, a 4th grade teacher at Central Elementary School in Sidney, Nebraska, provides this example:

> I immediately saw a direct connection between the Habits of Mind and Iditarod mushers, specifically Jeff King, the four-time Iditarod champion. Jeff King has visited the Sidney schools many times because Cabela's, Jeff's main sponsor, is located in Sidney. In 2006, my 4th graders wrote a book for Jeff and how he uses the Habits of Mind. I had 17 kids, so it worked out great. Each student wrote on one habit and how Jeff used it during the Iditarod race.

The 17th student wrote the dedication page and did the artwork for the cover. Last year, I began teaching Habits of Mind all year long. The students became very familiar with them and authored their own personal book on how they used the HOM throughout their life. Of course, I once again engaged the Iditarod mushers as people who incorporate these thinking strategies into their lives.

This recognition of the use of the Habits of Mind in others allows students to begin discussing and recognizing *when* it is appropriate to use particular Habits of Mind and to develop sensitivity to these situations. Recognition of the habits in others and in themselves leads students to make judgments about the value of these habits—*why* they are important to use instead of other less productive patterns of behaviors.

Within this lesson design, focusing activities on the what, how, when, and why of the Habits of Mind is a useful strategy. Teachers will, of course, inject their own examples and personal vignettes, definitions, and applications to assist students' awareness and understanding.

Strategies. The terminology, meanings, values, and uses of the Habits of Mind are explicitly introduced to the student through a wide range of activities. They are described and explored in a general way to both reveal and expand upon students' current understanding.

Some teachers have found it useful to introduce the class to all 16 Habits of Mind by posting a list with a brief description of what they are and why the class is focusing on them. The teacher might then explore one or two habits more deeply. Most teachers have found that introducing all 16 at once, however, may be a bit overwhelming.

Some staffs have prioritized the list based upon the needs of their students. In departments at the secondary level, some teams have chosen to focus on the habit most needed and displayed by scholars in their discipline. In math, for example, questioning and problem posing, metacognition, striving for accuracy, persisting, thinking and communicating with clarity and precision, and drawing on past knowledge might be of particularly high value. In the arts, thinking flexibly, creating, imagining and innovating, questioning and problem posing, and striving for precision and accuracy might be stressed.

Teachers might prompt the students' awareness and understanding of the Habits of Mind with questions such as these:

- What does [Habit of Mind] mean to you?
- What might be an example of [Habit of Mind]?
- What are some other words or phrases that might mean the same as [Habit of Mind] for you?

To prompt students' recognition of the Habits of Mind, teachers might ask questions such as these:

- What might you see (hear) someone doing (saying) if they were using [Habit of Mind]?
- In the story, what were some of the Habits of Mind the character displayed? How did you recognize them?
- What Habit of Mind is _____ using when you see her doing _____?
- Which of the Habits of Mind is this story about?
- List the three Habits of Mind you feel you are best at. What are some of the things you do that show you're good at this habit?

Students can be involved in developing meaning for the Habits of Mind by doing a number of things, including the following:

- Looking up the meanings of their defining terms in the dictionary and then preparing a PowerPoint presentation to share with the class.
- Making posters and charts.
- Making analogies ("Thinking interdependently is like a chain because . . .").
- Drawing cartoons illustrating each of the Habits of Mind and posting them in the classroom and throughout the school.
- Completing a "word splash" by generating synonyms, phrases, or other terms that are similar in meaning to a particular Habit of Mind.
- Completing "Looks Like, Sounds Like, Feels Like" charts for each of the Habits of Mind.

To increase their understanding of the various Habits of Mind, teachers can invite students to describe times in their lives when they found that one or more of the habits was of value to them. The following are some excerpts from journals kept by students at Sir Francis Drake High School in the Tamalpais Union High School District in San Anselmo, California:

Listening with Understanding and Empathy
Listening before prejudging someone's contribution makes sense. Being patient helps. I was surprised at the great ideas and how much everyone added.

Metacognition
I sometimes have to talk to myself and tell myself to work harder, or to stop slacking.

They give us time to think about everything—all of our actions and work and that is something that really helps. Not many kids get that; it's so neat.

And a 4th grader at Crow Island School in the Winnetka Public Schools in Illinois wrote this:

Persisting
I have used my perseverance. When I was doing long division. It was very long and hard but I did it. I still want to improve for the future when I'm in high school.

Once students know what the Habits of Mind are and why they are valued, teachers can be alert and seize opportunities to practice and apply the Habits of Mind. Questions can be designed to call attention to one or more of the habits, to develop awareness of them, and to reflect on their use.

Before beginning a learning activity, questions such as these may be posed to cue and focus on the importance of and use of one or more of the Habits of Mind:

• As you anticipate your projects, which of the Habits of Mind might we need to use?

• In working on these math problems, which of the Habits of Mind will help us?

• As we are reading, which of the Habits of Mind will we be using to help understand the story?

After a learning activity, questions such as these can stimulate reflection on and synthesis of the Habits of Mind:

• As you reflect on your work on this project, which of the Habits of Mind did you find yourself using?

• As you were solving these problems, which of the Habits of Mind did you employ? How did they help you? How did they affect your work?

• As you were working in groups to design a plan, what metacognitive strategies did you use to monitor your performance of the Habits of Mind?

Transferring and applying the Habits of Mind to other settings and situations may also be cued through well-constructed questions such as these:

• In what other classes might you use these Habits of Mind?

• In what other situations in your life would your use of these Habits of Mind be beneficial?

• In what careers or professions would people have to use these Habits of Mind?

Other intriguing questions to stimulate discussion of the Habits of Mind might ask how an intelligent person would use the Habits of Mind to, for example, choose a doctor, purchase a car, read a newspaper, watch television, or vote.

Assessment. Teachers can use journals, writing samples, and checklists to determine if students can

• Define what is meant by each of the Habits of Mind.
• Give examples of them in settings other than school.
• Describe what a particular Habit of Mind looks like, feels like, and sounds like.

- Give examples from their own experience.
- Identify, when asked to reflect on a task, which of the Habits of Mind they drew upon.
- Identify which Habit of Mind they "forgot to use" during problematic situations.
- Identify which of the Habits of Mind characterizes the main characters in a story.
- Recognize examples of the Habits of Mind in movies, television programs, newspaper articles, advertising, and books.

Although this instructional approach may serve as an introduction to exploring meanings on the journey of continuous growth (see Chapter 4), it can also be revisited from time to time. It has a place in the context of a unit of work where the habits are being infused and developed alongside traditional content knowledge. The intent is to help establish the Habits of Mind as a valued learning outcome of the unit. The approach should extend and add to students' previous definitions and understandings. For example, a teacher in an early primary class that focuses on the habit of *persistence* might be satisfied if the students build a definition that consists of "don't give up" and cite the example of *The Little Engine That Could*. However, a teacher at the upper-secondary level would want students to develop a deeper definition and more complex examples of persistence, including such elements as the search for alternatives, keeping the goal in mind, and using a range of strategies. For these reasons, lessons of this type are appropriate in any unit of work in which developing the Habits of Mind is a part. These units may seek to help students develop

- Increasingly sophisticated and insightful meanings for the habits.
- Better internal criteria for self-assessment.
- Sensitivity to situations where it is appropriate to use the habits and transference to a range of new, novel, and complex situations.
- A range of strategies for use when employing the Habits of Mind.
- Recognition of the valuing of the habits by others.

Teaching *of* the Habits of Mind is an essential component of a curriculum design that aims to develop one of the habits. Such teaching helps establish the habit as part of the learning outcomes of the unit, and it also extends and develops students along several of the developmental continuums. However, a unit of study that included only this sort of lesson approach would fail to give students the opportunity to employ the habit in meaningful, authentic ways and would not necessarily teach or refine new skills and strategies. In a "thought-full" curriculum, this lesson design is just one of several that will come together to fully develop a student's Habits of Mind.

Strategic Application of the Habits of Mind

The intent of the approaches described so far is to create and deepen an awareness, understanding, and appreciation of the Habits of Mind. However, we want students to advance beyond the level of merely understanding. We want them to use the habits skillfully, to value the habits, and to use them appropriately in an increasingly wide range of situations. Obviously instruction that is intended to develop this strategic use of the Habits of Mind will need to be more advanced, complex, and sophisticated, with lessons that "lift" students beyond the awareness and recognition stages.

Strategic application of the Habits of Mind differs from the "Cognitively Demanding Tasks" approach in that it is far more focused on individual habits and the aspects of these habits that have been targeted for development. Rather than simply labeling the Habits of Mind that the task may call upon, teachers are actively guiding students' skillful use of the habit.

Purpose. The purpose of this lesson design is to help students to develop skillfulness in the repertoire of strategies they possess; to get better at selecting appropriate skills, tools, and strategies; to build greater alertness to situations when it is appropriate to engage in one or more of the Habits of Mind; and to extend their valuing of the Habits of Mind.

These skills, tools, and strategies will first be applied outside the content of the unit of work so that students can practice before applying the habits to the subject matter. Students will benefit from having time to see how they can transfer strategies from old contexts to new ones.

Strategies. Appropriate assessment and reflection strategies should also be incorporated in this approach. The instruction explicitly includes not only the use of the Habits of Mind, but also the specific skills, tools, and strategies that are involved. These are identified and labeled, along with the specific times at which they are called for. Figure 5.1 shows the work of one group of 4th graders who created a mind map of some skills and strategies for "Persisting: What to do when I get stuck."

Here are some sample questions to prompt students to predict the use and value of the Habits of Mind in a range of situations:

- In what other situations might it be important to employ this Habit of Mind?
- If you were to _____, which of the Habits of Mind would serve you?
- What are some of the reasons a _____ might want to use the Habit of Mind of _____?
- How might a _____ use the Habit of Mind when _____?
- What predictions would you make if _____ failed to use the Habit of Mind of _____?

Because we want these habits to become internalized, questions of a more metacognitive nature are appropriate. Here are some examples of questions intended to prompt students' metacognitive application of the Habits of Mind:

- What goes on in your head when you use the Habit of Mind of _____?
- What are you talking to yourself about when you [Habit of Mind]?
- What will you be aware of in your own thinking as you [Habit of Mind]?
- What Habit of Mind did you find yourself using when you were _____?
- What cues will you be aware of that might prompt your use of this Habit of Mind in the future?

Lessons in this category should explore the effects of the use of various strategies that are basic to each of the Habits of Mind. They should include opportunities not only to explore alternative strategies, but also to predict

FIGURE 5.1

Skills and Strategies for Persisting

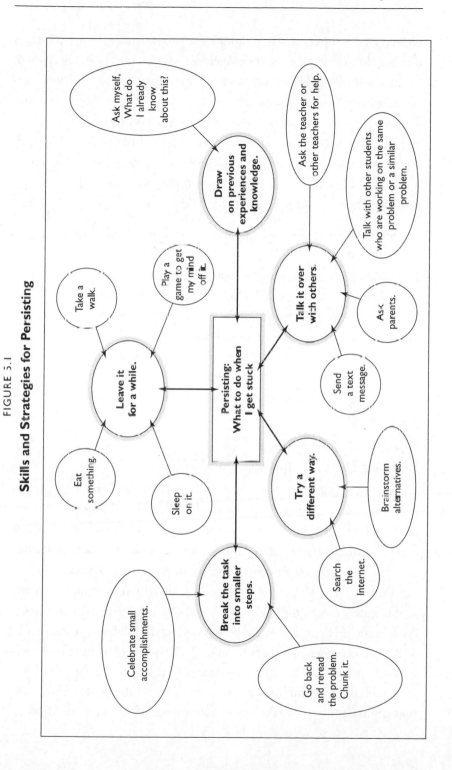

consequences for each. They should teach new strategies and focus on transfer, linkage, sequences, and situations in which the habits are applied.

Assessment. Assessment at this stage can occur through teacher observation of performance, journals, writing samples, and interviews, *and* through self-observation, as students assess their own use of the habits. Rubrics, portfolios, and journaling can be part of the process. Sophisticated assessments intended to reveal students' degree of internalization of the Habits of Mind are necessary. For example, assessments should determine whether students can do the following:

- Demonstrate the application of the Habits of Mind in problematic situations.
- Develop rubrics and operational definitions of the Habits of Mind.
- Predict situations in which the Habits of Mind will be useful.
- Analyze current events, books, stories, and situations in world affairs in which the Habits of Mind were or were not brought into play.
- Demonstrate how the Habits of Mind are clustered and related to one another.
- Describe the steps and strategies they use when drawing upon the Habits of Mind.

Building Depth, Complexity, and Elegance

The intent of the instructional strategies described so far is to create and deepen an awareness of, understanding of, and skillfulness in employing the Habits of Mind in an increasingly wide and diverse range of situations. Ultimately we want students to use the habits, without prompting, as a guide to govern their own decisions, thoughts, and actions.

Purpose. The purpose of this lesson design is to move students to more sophisticated use of the Habits of Mind—to help them become more "panoramic" in their views of situations in which the Habits of Mind may be applied; to help them build greater value in the habits; to increase their inclination to use the habits more spontaneously, without prompting; to cause them to make a commitment to self-monitor, self-evaluate, self-modify, and thus continually improve their own performance of the Habits of Mind.

These lessons should provide new, novel, or more complex opportunities in which students may apply the Habits of Mind. The degree of guidance from the teacher will typically decrease over time as students improve in their ability to recognize situations, choose strategies, and self-assess. Teachers' strategies will shift from telling students when and how to apply the habit, to prompting students to be alert for upcoming opportunities to engage in the habit, and finally to asking students to reflect on when they applied the habit and if they were able to do so successfully.

Lessons in this category will often have a strong focus on self-assessment and building commitment to using the habits. Students will, initially with assistance, develop skills in recognizing and evaluating their application of the habits. This evaluation will be based on the dimensions described in Chapter 4; that is, are students becoming more skillful, better able to recognize and apply the habits in new situations? Are they building greater appreciation of the value of the habits and improving their ability to self-assess? In these lessons students will develop criteria to evaluate their performance. Over time they will be expected to set learning goals and to reflect critically on their application of the habits.

The content of these lessons is firmly embedded in the subject area being taught. To the students' eye, the new learning that takes place in these lessons will be overtly from the subject area. The process of guiding the application of the habits will strengthen the habits while enhancing acquisition of content knowledge.

Strategies. In this instructional design, students identify which Habits of Mind will be essential to completing the task. Teachers ask students what those habits might look like and sound like as they work on the task. Students are alerted to be aware of their use of the particular habits and to monitor and record their observations of themselves and others. Upon completion of the lesson, students are invited to reflect on what they were aware of, which other Habits of Mind they used, what effects the use of the Habits of Mind had on their work, which habits they need to improve upon, and where else in school, life, and work those particular Habits of Mind might be useful. Students are encouraged to keep a journal of their thoughts, to create and use such self-assessment tools as portfolios, rubrics, checklists, anecdotal records, and inventories.

The teacher can present students with cognitively demanding problems, the answers to which are not immediately apparent. A more effective strategy, however, would be to ask students to become aware of, identify, and describe problems to pose for themselves. The teacher basically allows the students to manage their own problem solving, monitor and report their own progress, and modify their own strategies based on feedback from the teacher, the environment, experts in the field, and the experimental data itself. The teacher will, of course, serve as a catalyst, a resource, and a facilitator. The teacher will also be a keen observer to determine the level of the students' application of the Habits of Mind.

The following scenario describes how a teacher might approach this kind of lesson when the emphasis is on the habit of *thinking interdependently*:

> *Teacher*: We have been working in groups and learning how to share resources and take turns. These are important skills when we work in groups. Now we are going to learn some more strategies that help us work in even more sophisticated ways. In particular, we are going to learn how to take different roles in the group so we can make the most of individual strengths.

The teacher then goes on to discuss different thinking/learning styles and the values of each, the types of roles in groups and how they might be assigned, and other relevant points. In the process, students develop a deeper understanding of the nature of working in groups. An important part of this type of lesson design is that the strategy is taught explicitly:

> *Teacher*: Today, we were focusing on thinking interdependently. You met in groups to generate and evaluate alternative courses of action as we explored skillful decision making. Let's reflect now and analyze how you monitored yourselves and your group as you worked interdependently. Here are some questions to ponder: [Writes on board.]
>
> • While you were working in your groups, what metacognitive processes did you find yourselves using to manage your own and your group's interdependent thinking?

• What effects did this thinking have on your group's pro-ductiveness and efficiency?

• What are some indicators and evidence of that productiveness?

• From this reflection and analysis, what will you carry forth to future group work?

Let's now return to your small groups and respond to these questions.

After allowing students to interact with each other about these questions, the teacher invites discussion.

Teacher: Share with us what metacognitive strategies you employed.
Student 1: I found that I had to manage my impulsivity. I wanted to talk a lot and was tempted to tell the group all of my ideas. But I restrained myself. I listened to their ideas. I think by doing this I learned a lot more and heard ideas that I would never have thought of.
Student 2: Frankly, I was bored with the whole project. I thought the right decision was obvious. I wanted to get on with it rather than explore all those alternatives. However, I told myself that not everybody thought the same way as I did or saw it in the same way I did. I knew they'd come around if I just gave them time and continued to "hang in" with them. The result was that every-body agreed that the decision we chose was the best one. I think if I had dominated, we wouldn't have achieved a consensus.
Student 3: I thought our group was very creative in the alterna-tives they generated. That's because we listened to and built upon each other's ideas. I thought it was cool how one idea sparked another and another; we started generating ideas and almost couldn't stop. Our problem was having to choose one alternative from so many neat ideas.
Student 4: I found that I was easily distracted, and being the recorder in the group was difficult. I was always tempted to jump in to give my opinion, but that was not my role. It's hard to stay

with a role when you're really interested and concerned with the topic. I can see why it is important to match a role with a person's strengths.

The discussion continues, ending with an assignment asking students to write in their journals. The teacher provides the following prompts:

• Describe a problem that exists in (this school), (your home), (this community), (our country), (the world) that could be solved more satis-factorily if people employed the skills necessary to think interdependently.
• Describe ways you could take action to teach those skills to others.
• In future situations, what clues will alert you to know that this is a good time to think interdependently?

Questions to encourage students to reflect on and evaluate their use of the Habits of Mind might include the following:

• What were some of the effects your use of [Habit of Mind] had on _____?
• The next time you _____, how might you employ [Habit of Mind] differently or more effectively?
• What commitments or action plans do you have to improve your use of [Habit of Mind]?

Questions to extend the value of the Habits of Mind might include the following:

• What are some of the ways your use of the Habits of Mind has changed in the past year?
• How have the Habits of Mind influenced your decisions about _____?
• As you envision your future, which of the Habits of Mind might you work on in your personal growth plans?
• What strategies of self-improvement will you design in order to _____?

Assessment. Assessment may take place through observation, inter-views, self-analysis, and self-reporting in journals. The goal should be to determine whether students can do the following:

• Describe how they are using the Habits of Mind spontaneously in their lives.

• Observe, give feedback on, advocate, and teach others the Habits of Mind.

• Employ the Habits of Mind spontaneously without prompting.

The Habits of Mind may serve as mental disciplines. Ideally, when confronted with problematic situations, students would habitually use one or more of these Habits of Mind by asking themselves, "What is the most *intelligent thing* I can do right now?" They also may ask more specific questions related to specific Habits of Mind, such as these:

• How can I learn from this? What are my resources? How can I draw on my past successes with problems like this? What do I already know about the problem? What resources do I have available or need to generate? (*Applying past knowledge to new situations*)

• How can I approach this problem flexibly? How might I look at the situation in another way? How can I draw upon my repertoire of problem-solving strategies? How can I look at this problem from a fresh perspective? (*Thinking flexibly*)

• How can I illuminate this problem to make it clearer, more precise? Do I need to check out my data sources? How might I break this problem down into its component parts and develop a strategy for understanding and accomplishing each step? (*Thinking and communicating with clarity and precision*)

• What do I know or not know? What questions do I need to ask? What strategies are in my mind now? What am I aware of in terms of my own beliefs, values, and goals that relate to this problem? What feelings or emotions am I aware of that might be blocking or enhancing my progress? (*Thinking about thinking [metacognition]*)

• How does this problem affect others? How can we solve it together? What can I learn from others that would help me become a better problem solver? (*Thinking interdependently*)

Assessment at this level of development is self-assessment and is mostly metacognitive. Students can keep journals, complete "process logs," and create exhibitions of their work. When sharing and reflecting, they would describe their metacognitive strategies and their findings of power and efficacy as learners using the Habits of Mind. These assessment tools are elaborated on in Part III, Chapter 11.

Diagnosing and Assessing Students' Journey Toward Internalization of the Habits of Mind

The ultimate goal of instruction in the Habits of Mind is students' using them spontaneously—applying them without direction or prompting from the teacher. Taking a reflective stance in the midst of active problem solving, however, is often difficult. For that reason, each of the Habits of Mind is situational and transitory. There is no such thing as perfect realization and mastery of any of them. Few people ever *fully* reach the stage of cognitive complexity. Mastery is a utopian state toward which we constantly aspire. Furthermore, although all human beings have the capacity and potential to be self-reflective and conscious of their own habits and behaviors, not everyone seems to use that capacity and potential equally.

Purpose. The purpose of this lesson design is to determine where students are in their journey of growth toward internalization of the Habits of Mind.

Strategy. The teacher provides a cognitively demanding task as an opportunity for students to display their understanding of, application of, valuing of, and skillfulness with the Habits of Mind. The intent is to have students demonstrate that they are alert to new and diverse situations where the Habits of Mind might be applied, and that the Habits of Mind are valued and have become a purposeful part of their life.

Assessment. The design of the lessons in this category is similar to those in the category "Building Intuitive Awareness." Now, however, instead of modeling, labeling, and describing the Habits of Mind, the teacher observes to see if the students are modeling, labeling, and applying the habits. Are the students persisting, thinking interdependently, self-correcting, using clear and precise language, clarifying each other's language, and exemplifying other habits as well?

Modeling the Habits of Mind

Setting an example is not the main means of influencing another, it
is the only means.

—Albert Einstein

Children learn best through imitation. Because most dispositional
learnings are "caught, not taught," teachers must "walk the talk." The
Habits of Mind are not just "kid stuff." Teachers and students together
can get better at their Habits of Mind.

Purpose. The purpose of this lesson design is to provide consistent
instruction in which the Habits of Mind are modeled by the teacher and
integrated into the norms of the classroom and into the instructional
strategies. This category is teaching *with* the Habits of Mind.

Strategies. In this category, the strategies are simply the various behaviors the teacher demonstrates in day-to-day instruction. Here are some
examples:

• Teachers design and pose powerful questions so that students
experience, analyze, and compose powerful questions themselves (see
Chapter 8).

• Teachers listen to students with understanding and empathy so that
students will experience the feelings and benefits of being listened to with
understanding and empathy.

• Teachers share their thinking and planning so that students will
gain insight into the power of metacognition.

• Teachers manage their impulsivity so that students will develop a
vision of what it is like for a mindful adult to feel frustration, to control
anger, and to resist temptation.

• Teachers design activities that cause students to work in groups to
promote interdependent thinking.

• Teachers laugh at themselves and guarantee that no lesson is successful without finding humor.

• Teachers monitor their own questions, directions, and communications to ensure clarity and precision.

• Teachers find their subjects awesome, wondrous, and intriguing and express their sense of mystery and their exuberance and delight in the presence of their students.

• Teachers exhibit the humility of admitting they do not know all there is to know about teaching, learning, and the Habits of Mind, and they develop strategies for continuous learning and improving their own craft of teaching.

Assessment. Although these intangibles are difficult to measure, one would expect that, as a result of modeling over time, students would exhibit greater excitement about school, greater intrigue with problems to solve, stronger bonds with classmates, more self-directedness, and more enthusiasm for continued learning.

In Summary

We have described seven instructional approaches intended to focus on the gradual development of the Habits of Mind. Combined and sequenced appropriately, and coupled with your own ingenuity and successful past teaching and learning experiences, these instructional approaches can be used to infuse the development of Habits of Mind into units of work. Certainly these are not all of the ways that the habits are taught. As continual learners, it would be important for school staffs to share their strategies, to create electronic archives of successful lessons for all to share, and to continue to refine and craft the lessons with more powerful strategies and assessments. (For further suggestions for sharing among school staff members, see Chapter 15.)

References

Angelou, M. (2002). *I know why the caged bird sings.* New York: Random House.

Fritz, J. (1987). *The double life of Pocahontas.* New York: Puffin Books.

Goodrich, F. (1993). *The diary of Anne Frank.* New York: Harcourt School.

Moulds, P. (2006, December). Rich tasks: Developing student learning around important tasks. *Educational Leadership, 61*(4), 75–78.

Piper, W. (1976). *The little engine that could.* New York: Platt & Monk.

Reagan, R. (2009). Cognitive composition: Thinking-based writing. In A. Costa & B. Kallick (Eds.), *Habits of mind across the curriculum: Practical and creative strategies for teachers.* Alexandria, VA: ASCD.

Scieszka, J. (1989). *The true story of the three little pigs by A. Wolf.* New York: Putnam/Penguin.

Part II

Building a
Thought-Full Environment

Keep in mind always the present you are constructing. It should be
the future you want.

—Alice Walker

We begin Part II of *Learning and Leading with Habits of Mind* by considering classrooms and schools where the Habits of Mind flourish. How
have the educators in these classrooms and schools created thoughtful
environments where students encounter, think about, and develop the
Habits of Mind? Specifically, how have teachers created environments
where children discover the Habits of Mind and realize the benefits of
using the habits in school, in life, and as continuous learners? How have
teachers helped children gain insight about their own Habits of Mind
based on what they've learned from others? Exactly what characterizes
these kinds of rich learning environments? Part II provides suggestions
for teaching the Habits of Mind as well as creating classroom conditions
in which students can learn and practice the habits.

Because we know that language and thinking are closely entwined,
we start, in Chapter 6, by stressing that the language of thinking and the
Habits of Mind terminology should become part of the everyday dialogue
in classroom interaction. Thus, as children mature, they hear, then use,
and then think with those cognitive terms in mind. The Habits of Mind
become a normal part of students' dialogue. (By the way, we have found
that children at a very early age love using the terminology!)

If we want children to take responsible risks, to think creatively, and to think interdependently with others, then what learning conditions must be established to cultivate these qualities? Chapter 7 describes how teachers might use their verbal language to build trust, to establish warmth, and to promote students' self-esteem. In addition, it is more likely that students will learn to listen with understanding and empathy if their teachers model good listening skills as well.

Chapter 8 continues to explore teachers' language by focusing on classroom questions. Criteria for constructing intentionally complex questions are provided. Teachers learn how to construct questions that are designed to elicit certain Habits of Mind, and many examples are provided. Of utmost importance, however, is the need to teach students the art of skillful questioning as well.

One of the most powerful means of helping students know how to think, question, and become more aware of their thinking is to display their metacognition visually. In Chapter 9, David Hyerle, the foremost developer, researcher, and teacher of Thinking Maps®, provides rich examples of these visual tools and shares many connections with and implications of the maps for the Habits of Mind.

—*Arthur L. Costa and Bena Kallick*

6

Creating "Thought-Full" Environments

Arthur L. Costa and Bena Kallick

I am looking at a behavior called persistence. It means like people that never give up. For an example, Christopher Columbus sailed to the Indies to look for gold. He kept on going back to the Indies to search for gold. He never found it. But the thing he did, he never gave up looking for it. That's what persistence means.

And another book I read is *Katy and the Big Snow.* One day it was snowing bad and the snow was about 18 inches tall. The whole town couldn't get out of their houses because the snow was covering it. When Katy saw all the snow she decided to take all the snow out. It took her one day to clean up the snow. She didn't sleep. She didn't even get tired. She never stopped taking out all the snow. I learned that people who never give up are very brave.

—Student at Hidden Valley Elementary School, Burnsville, Minnesota

A unique attribute of the human brain is its neocortex—that convoluted top layer that surrounds the brain's hemispheres. It is the location of such higher mental functions as problem solving, experimentation, symbol manipulation, anticipation of the future, and creativity.

The neocortex of the brain shuts down by degrees under stress. The greater the stress, the greater the shutdown. Under great stress, we lash out, run away in terror, or freeze up; the brain experiences an altered blood flow and changes in activity patterns. The body-mind functioning is minimized. We become less flexible and more predictable, and survival patterns override pattern detection and problem solving. We "lose our train of thought" and our resourcefulness.

Mindful teachers, therefore, strive to maintain a classroom environment of trust, safety, and comfort for students. Such Habits of Mind as risk taking, questioning, listening with understanding and empathy, remaining open to continuous learning, creating and imagining, and finding humor cannot flourish under stressful conditions.

Mindful teachers know that all forms of communication—verbal and nonverbal—are important. They pay attention to physical signals from their students, noticing their nervousness, withdrawal, or fear. Alert to these cues, teachers use this information to modify their own classroom behavior to become more empathic and congruent with students' feelings. Such subtleties as a teacher's body language, voice tone, pauses in speech, breathing, implied value judgments, and presuppositions embedded in language all have an effect on students' comfort and cognition. These nonverbal signals and feelings are as important to thinking processes as they are to establishing a trusting relationship necessary for self-reflective learning.

Teachers know they can use specific nonverbal and verbal behaviors to nurture relationships. For example, direct eye contact and a concerned voice and facial expression are better at conveying empathy than are words (Burgoon, Buller, & Woodall, 1996). The teacher's gestures, posture, and voice qualities contribute to maintaining a trustful classroom environment. Taken together, these have an enormous impact on feelings of connectedness and rapport. Some scientists refer to this phenomenon as "mental state resonance," a state of alignment that permits a nonverbal form of communication that the students are being "understood" in the deepest sense; they are "feeling felt" by the teacher (Caine & Caine, 2001). And the safer one feels, the greater the access to neocortical functioning (see Damasio, 1994; see also Csikszentmihalyi, 1993; Damasio, 2000; and Pert, 1997).

What Is a "Thought-Full" Environment?

When we say the classroom must be a "thought-full environment," we are playing on the meaning of the word *thoughtful*: (1) to be "full of thought" and (2) to be caring and sensitive, to be "thoughtful" of others. The manner in which teachers and administrators respond to students can create and sustain a thoughtful environment that creates trust; allows risk taking; and is experimental, creative, and positive. This environment requires listening to each other's ideas, remaining nonjudgmental, and having rich data sources.

When Lisa Davis-Miraglia was a teacher at West Orchard Elementary School in Chappaqua, New York, she described her experiences with a thoughtful environment this way:

> Habits of Mind are a natural part of my classroom community because they are the attributes that my students and I strive to embrace as learners on a daily basis. Early in my career, I knew that I didn't want to respond to my students by saying, "Good answer" or "Great work." I didn't want to use those comments because they have little meaning, except to imply that the child's answer *prior* to the "great one" wasn't as good. Or it tells the child who might have answered next to give up because the "great answer" already has been given.
>
> Taking my cues from an art education course, I knew that if I could be specific in my praise it would have a more meaningful effect. For example, if you say to a child, "That's a great painting," the child might temporarily feel good about the praise. If you say, however, "I like the way you mixed the colors blue, white, and green in the ocean. It gives me a feeling of movement," the child is required to engage and reflect on the comment. Even if she disagrees, she is still engaged in a thought process that, more than likely, will trigger the idea of "movement" the next time she attempts a similar task.
>
> Evaluative comments tend to shut down thinking, and "thin comments," as my 4th graders refer to them, don't give the learner any information. My question, then, became, "How can I respond with 'thick,' or meaningful, praise in the classroom without being evaluative?" The Habits of Mind helped me be specific in my praise by making me focus on what's important. While the right

answer is a "good" thing to strive for, it's really the process one goes through to get the right answer that interests me.

In my own teaching, I've tried to get away from saying, "Good answer" or "Right." Instead, I try to note when a child is using an intelligent behavior. It's like saying, "Nice job!" to a child who is painting, instead of being specific and saying, "I like the choice of color here; it gives me a warm feeling." My comments are much more meaningful, but better than that is seeing kids recognize their peers. I have often found that the child that might be slower in completing work or has a difficult time grasping new concepts is thought to be not as smart by his or her peers. Now students hear me say, "[Kenny], you are a persistent problem solver." [Kenny] is being rewarded for his persistence, not just his answer.

Key Conditions and Behaviors

As we consider building a thought-full environment, it is important to recognize some key conditions and behaviors that signal to students that there is trust for critical and creative thinking. We describe these in the sections that follow.

A Deeply Held Belief

In classrooms where the Habits of Mind succeed, we find a deeply held belief that all students can continue to learn and improve. For many years, educators and parents alike believed that thinking skills programs were intended to challenge the intellectually gifted. Indeed, some thought that any child whose IQ fell below a certain score was doomed to reme-dial work or compensatory drill and practice. Much research, however, with hydrocephalic, Down syndrome, senile, and brain-damaged persons demonstrates that almost anyone can achieve amazing growth in intelli-gent behavior with proper intervention (see Chapter 1 and Feuerstein, Feuerstein, & Schur, 1997).

In classrooms that embrace the Habits of Mind, we also find a belief that the habits aren't just "kid stuff." Teachers, parents, and administrators can also monitor and modify their own Habits of Mind, such as manag-ing impulsivity, thinking about thinking (metacognition), listening with understanding and empathy, and thinking flexibly. We never fully master the Habits of Mind. Though we begin work with the habits as children, we continue to develop and improve them throughout our lives.

The Importance of Time

In many schools, educational innovations are seldom sustained. The focus continually shifts, making it difficult to determine what is most important: "Last year we were focused on differentiation, the year before we were concerned with authentic assessments, and before that we were focused on writing across the curriculum." Many educators make a statement such as "We already did thinking . . ." without realizing that thinking is central to the authentic practices and performances they now pursue so fervently. Each innovation is brought to the district as if it were unique, and considerable energy goes toward getting teachers on board with the new practices. Although each practice has merit, only a cluster of practices, well conceived and purposefully pursued, can lead to improved learning for students.

The power of the Habits of Mind is that the habits transcend any particular practice, and when used by both adults and students in the school, they serve to ensure the necessary dispositions for thoughtful change. Therefore, a school needs to keep a consistent focus on the Habits of Mind. Experience and research tell us it takes about three to four years of well-defined instruction with qualified teachers and carefully constructed curriculum materials for the Habits of Mind to become infused in the school culture. After three or four years, we start to observe significant and enduring changes in students' behavior.

If students are to internalize the Habits of Mind, they must encounter them again and again throughout the elementary and secondary years, in every subject and in every classroom as well as outside school. Educators must teach the Habits of Mind and thinking skills deliberately.

A Rich, Responsive Environment

Students must work in a rich, responsive environment if they are to make the Habits of Mind their own. They need access to a variety of resources that they can manipulate, experience, and observe. For example, the classroom should be filled with a variety of data sources: books, ency-clopedias, almanacs, thesauruses, CD-ROMs, and databases. Students should have contact with knowledgeable people in the community. Tech-nology provides rich opportunities for students to contact others through the Internet to explore theories and test their ideas. Field trips are impor-tant, too, not just for their content but because they provide students oppor-tunities to plan for and reflect on learning.

Students must manage more information and resources than ever before. As they move into adulthood, they will need the discipline of the Habits of Mind to guide their higher education and their careers. A rich, responsive classroom environment helps prepare them for all these experiences.

Attention to Readiness and Sequence

Theorists have clearly established both the nature of thinking capa-bilities and the sequence in which they appear in human beings. Too often, however, educators disregard these theories and present learning activities before students are ready for them developmentally. To find suc-cess, educators must introduce curriculum for the Habits of Mind in a sequence that matches children's development.

One of the chief causes for failure in formal education is that educa-tors begin with abstractions through print and language rather than with real, material action. Learning progresses through stages of increasing complexity (the number of ideas and factors we can think about) and increasing abstraction (progressing from a concrete object to a pictorial representation of the object, to a symbol that stands for the object, to a spoken word that stands for the symbol). Curriculum and instruction—including work with the Habits of Mind—are more meaningful if they are sequenced in a manner consistent with the stages of cognitive devel-opment (Lowery, 2001; see also Chapter 4).

Erik Erikson (1963) reminds us that as children proceed through differ-ent stages of development, they are focused on specific psychological, social, and emotional tasks. He reminds us that learners are simultaneously expe-riencing new learning that is accessible for us metacognitively, behaving as learners in a way that is observable to others, and internalizing the learning for future reference. As teachers, we must attend to all aspects of a student's development as we develop our curriculum, instruction, and assessments.

Keeping Track of Learning

In schools where the Habits of Mind are successfully in place, students keep track of their learning. Children write about, illustrate, and reflect on the use of the Habits of Mind in a personal log or diary. This work allows them to synthesize their thoughts and actions and to translate them into symbolic form. Reflection helps students truly make the Habits of Mind their own.

A log or diary also provides students the opportunity to revisit their initial perceptions about the Habits of Mind. Then they can compare any changes in those perceptions. Students also can chart the processes of strategic thinking and decision making, identifying "blind alleys" and recalling successes and "tragedies" of experimentation. For a variation on written journals, students can create electronic portfolios, Keynote or PowerPoint presentations, or video or audio recordings of projects and performances. (See Part III, Assessing and Reporting on Habits of Mind.)

Classroom Discussions

Guided discussions are always a useful way for teachers to offer insight about the Habits of Mind. Discussions also provide an opportunity for students to process their learning. Talking about situations in which Habits of Mind were, are, or could be applied is enormously helpful as students learn more and more about the habits. Teachers can guide specific discussions of students' problem-solving processes, inviting them to share their metacognition, reveal their intentions, and examine plans for solving a problem.

Frequent Infusion of the Habits

Teachers who are successful with the Habits of Mind use every possible opportunity to teach the habits. They are always on the lookout for occasions when the Habits of Mind would be useful to solve a problem, resolve a conflict, make a decision, or manage a polarity (Johnson, 1996). Have students noticed the Habits of Mind (or lack thereof) in their favorite television shows? Can they find them in the literature they're reading for

English class? Are the Habits of Mind evident in news events? Occasionally it's useful to set up simulations that require using the Habits of Mind. Such activities reinforce the concept that students always must be ready to call on these dispositions.

The Habits of Mind are most evident when we ask students to manage their own learning. Consider all the different Habits of Mind involved when we ask students to choose the group they will join, the topic they will study, and the ways that they will manage themselves to meet a deadline. Every occasion of self-directed learning is a rich opportunity for students to practice the Habits of Mind.

Using Praise and Rewards

It is important to consider the use of praise and rewards in the classroom. In all conversations with students, keep in mind that praise and rewards can be counterproductive if motivation already is evident when a student is engaged in desired behaviors. Praise uses positive value judgments conveyed through terms such as *good, excellent,* and *great*. Additional praise actually can reduce enthusiasm rather than reinforce it and increase motivation. Unfortunately, many students lack motivation, and some teachers use rewards to try to instill motivation. Rewards, however, are not the entire answer.

Joyce and Showers (1988) state "Praise and rewards, which are often associated with moderate class mean gains, were negatively correlated with both high and low achievers" (p. 56). Using rewards and praise to motivate student learning increases the students' dependency on others for learning. They don't come to find the learning inherently satisfying, and they don't come to value the acquisition or exercise of skills (Deci, 1995; Kohn, 1994; Lepper & Green, 1978). Praise builds conformity, and it makes students dependent on others for their worth. Praise also has been found to be a detriment to creativity (Amabile, 1979; Bronson, 2007).

Carol Dweck (2007) states:

Praising students for their intelligence . . . hands them not motivation and resilience but a fixed mind-set with all its vulnerability. In contrast, effort or "process" praise (praise for engagement, perseverance, strategies, improvement, and the like) fosters hardy motivation. It tells students what they've done to be successful and what they need to do to be successful again in the future. Process praise sounds like this:

•"You really *strived for accuracy* with your report, and your improvement shows it. You read the material over several times, outlined it, and tested yourself on it. That really worked!"

•"I like the way you *thought flexibly* by trying all kinds of strategies on that math problem until you finally got it."

•"It was a long, hard assignment, but you *persisted* and got it done. You stayed at your desk, kept up your concentration, and kept working. That's great!"

Although we acknowledge some of the problems related to praise, we do not suggest eliminating praise altogether. Praise is entirely appropriate at some times and can be used judiciously. For example, praise might be appropriate when students have obeyed rules or changed behaviors to the benefit of themselves and the class. Or praise can be useful in developmentally appropriate instances with young children. Praising seems best used with certain students and for certain tasks.

If praise is offered, it is important to describe the criteria for the praise. What makes an act "good" or "excellent" must be communicated along with the praise. This way, students understand the reason or criteria that makes the act acceptable, and they can repeat the performance. Consider these examples:

• "Your answer was good because you gave your reasons and rationale for your statements."

• "Your paragraph was well formed because you started with a topic sentence, then provided the evidence to support your conclusions."

Most teachers enjoy rewarding and praising their students. Brophy (1981), however, found that the one person in the classroom for whom praise has the most beneficial effect is the teacher. It is understandable, therefore, that research studies showing the detrimental effects of rewards are met with resistance.

Accepting Without Judgment

Nonjudgmental teachers accept what students say and do. When they accept, they give no clues through posture, gesture, or word whether a student's idea, behavior, or feeling is good, bad, better, worse, right, or wrong.

Nonjudgmentgal acceptance of students' ideas or actions provides a psychologically safe place where children can take risks, make decisions for themselves, and explore the consequences of their actions. Acceptance provides conditions in which students are encouraged to examine and compare their own data, values, ideas, criteria, and feelings with others' as well as the teacher's.

Mindful teachers use the following four kinds of nonjudgmental response behaviors to create an atmosphere in which students experience and practice the Habits of Mind: (1) pausing, (2) paraphrasing, (3) clarifying, and (4) providing data. When teachers model these skills, students also learn how to practice the skills when listening to and responding to one another.

Pausing. Some teachers dominate classroom talk by asking lower-level questions at a rapid-fire pace. A teacher may wait less than one second after posing a question before doing one of several things: repeating the question, commenting on a student's answer, redirecting the question to a new student, answering the question, or starting a new questioning sequence. In these kinds of exchanges, student answers are often terse or fragmentary, or the student's tone of voice may show a lack of confidence. Students have little opportunity for second thoughts or to extend their ideas. Many teachers appear programmed to accept only one, predetermined, "right" answer. They leave little room for alternate answers or differing opinions. Students receive the message that "the teacher's way of knowing is the *only* way of knowing."

Silence, or wait time, is one answer to this situation. Mary Budd Rowe (1969, 1974) first explored the concept of wait time in the late 1960s. During classroom observations, she noticed that some teachers used "purposeful pauses" as they conducted lessons and class discussions. In these classrooms, she noted students making speculations, holding sustained conversational sequences, posing alternative explanations, and arguing over the interpretation of data. She also noted positive changes in the affective climate and the quality of classroom interactions. She observed an increase in the level of cognitive functioning and academic achievement and a decrease in the number of behavior problems.

Using silence or wait time before responding to or asking a question enhances message delivery and acceptance by allowing the speaker and the listeners to breathe while the message is delivered. Breathing is essential for supporting cognition—not to mention life in general! The importance of breathing can best be understood by recognizing that the human brain accounts for approximately 3 percent of body mass and can consume up to 37 percent of the oxygen taken in. When we hold our breath, the carbon dioxide levels in the blood increase. The body reacts to the carbon dioxide increase in much the same way that it responds to threat by releasing hormones that support the fight-or-flight response. In addition, the human brain is hardwired to detect threat, which results in decreasing blood flow to the frontal lobes and increasing flow to the brain stem. When we hold our breath or perceive a threat, thinking is negatively affected (Garmston & Wellman, 2008). Action, not thought, becomes the priority. Pausing in appropriate places during the delivery of content supports group breathing and establishes a low-threat environment, thus allowing both presenter and audience to think more clearly and effectively (Zoller, 2005).

Additional research, including that of Goleman (2006) and Kendon (1990), has shown many positive changes in classrooms where the teacher uses increased wait time:

• The length of student responses increases 300 to 700 percent.

• The number of unsolicited but appropriate student responses increases.

• The number of failures to respond decreases.

• Student confidence increases, and there are fewer inflected responses.

• Speculative responses increase.

• Student-to-student interaction increases. Teacher-centered show-and-tell decreases.

• Teacher questions change in number and kind: the number of divergent questions increases, and teachers ask higher-level questions (as described by Bloom's *Taxonomy* [1956]).

- Teachers probe less for clarification because students make inferences and spontaneously support them with data.
- Students ask more questions.

As this list suggests, using wait time stimulates more complex thinking, enhances dialogue, and improves decision making.

Rowe (1974) has described three kinds of wait time. "Wait Time I" is the length of time a teacher pauses after asking a question. "Wait Time II" is the length of time a teacher waits after a student replies or asks another question. A minimum three-second pause is recommended. With higher-level cognitive tasks, five seconds or more of wait time may be required to achieve positive results. "Wait Time III" is the pausing and modeling of thoughtfulness that occurs after the student asks the teacher a question.

Rowe also examined the use of longer pauses in whole-group lecture settings. Students need time for mental processing in information-dense subjects like chemistry, physics, and geology. Her research indicates that retention and understanding increase when students are provided with 2 to 3 minutes for discussion, clarifying notes, and raising questions after every 8 to 10 minutes of instruction. (All unresolved student questions should be reserved for the last five minutes of the class period.) Many people call this strategy "think-pair-share" (McTighe & Lyman, 2001).

Wait time is an important factor in several of the Habits of Mind. When teachers specifically attend to the Habit of Mind of questioning and posing problems, they must also attend to wait time. Students need time to be able to think flexibly or creatively. Using longer pauses in group discussions provides students with the necessary think time to help them manage their impulsivity and take responsible risks as they answer questions posed either by the teacher or by the work they are studying.

Sometimes periods of silence in the classroom seem interminably long. But if trust is the goal, then students must have the opportunity to do their own thinking and problem solving. A teacher's silence after asking a question communicates the message "I regard you as sufficient. I trust your processes and knowledge; also, I trust that you know best the time you need to formulate a response."

Paraphrasing. Simply stated, paraphrasing can be defined as responding to what the student says or does by rephrasing, recasting, translating, empathizing, or summarizing. Teachers use this response when they want to extend, build upon, synthesize, or give an example based on the student's answer. Though the teacher may use words that are different from those of the student, the teacher strives to maintain the intent and accurate meaning of the student's idea. This is an active kind of acceptance and acknowledging because the teacher demonstrates that the student's message was received *and* understood. Here are examples of paraphrasing:

- "Your explanation is that if the heat were increased, the molecules would move faster and therefore disperse the food coloring faster."
- "Your idea is that we should all write our legislators rather than send them one letter from the group."
- "Shaun's idea is that the leaves could be classified according to their shapes, while Sarah's way is to group them by size."
- "An example of what you mean was when we arranged our rock collection according to several different classification systems."

Paraphrasing lets others know that the teacher is listening, that she understands or is trying to understand them, and that she cares. A well-crafted paraphrase communicates the message "I am trying to understand you— and therefore, I value what you have to say," and it establishes a relationship between people and ideas. Thus, questions preceded by paraphrases will be perceived similarly. Questions by themselves, no matter how artfully constructed, put a degree of psychological distance between the asker and the asked. Paraphrasing aligns the parties and creates a safe environment for thinking (Perkins, 2003).

Paraphrases reflect the speaker's content and the speaker's emotions about the content, and they frame a logical level for holding the content. The paraphrase reflects content back to the speaker for further consideration and connects that response to the flow of discourse emerging within the group. Such paraphrasing creates permission to probe for details and elaboration. Without the paraphrase, probing may be perceived as interrogation.

To paraphrase effectively, teachers must (1) *listen and observe* carefully to calibrate the content and emotions of the speaker and (2) *signal their intention* to paraphrase, by opening with a reflective sentence stem. Such stems put the focus and emphasis on the speaker's ideas, not on the paraphraser's interpretation of those ideas. For example, reflective paraphrases should not use the pronoun *I*. The phrase "What I think I hear you saying . . ." signals to many speakers that their thoughts no longer matter and that the paraphraser is now going to insert his own ideas into the conversation. Instead, the following paraphrase stems signal that a paraphrase is coming:

- "You're suggesting that . . . ."
- "You're proposing that . . . ."
- "So, what you're wondering . . . ."
- "So, you are thinking . . . ."
- "Um, you're pondering on the effects of . . . ."
- "And your hunch is . . . ."

If the paraphrase is not completely accurate, the student will offer corrections:

Teacher: So, you're concerned about the field trip and you want to get early input from the entire class.
Student: No. Before we go I think we should get input from the museum about what we'll see so that we can be prepared.

Summarizing and organizing a class's or group's thoughts by offering themes is an especially important form of paraphrase. Here are two examples:

- "We all seem to be concerned about two issues here. One is resource allocation and the other is the impact of those decisions on student learning."
- "So our major goal here is to define fairness in settling disputes in our classroom."

Empathizing. Teachers show empathy by responding in a way that acknowledges cognition *and* accepts feelings. Teachers respond this way when they especially want to recognize a student's feelings, emotions, or behaviors. Often teachers show empathy when they label a student's feelings. This response communicates that the teacher hears not only the student's idea but also the emotions underlying it. Here are some examples of empathic responses:

- "You're confused because those directions were unclear."
- "You're frustrated because you didn't get a chance to share your idea and you'd like us all to take turns. That requires patience. It's hard to wait when you're eager to share."
- [A student enters the room and slams a workbook on a desk.] "You're really upset today. Did you have difficulty with that assignment?"

Responding empathically can be important because many students come to school from dysfunctional, impoverished environments. The emotions and feelings they bring to school affect their learning and motivation. Empathizing does not mean a teacher condones acts of aggression or destructive behavior. Empathy simply means the teacher acknowledges both emotion and cognition.

Clarifying. Paraphrasing and clarifying are similiar in that both kinds of responses reflect the teacher's concern for fully understanding the student's idea. Clarifying signals that the teacher cares enough to want to understand what a student is saying. While paraphrasing, the teacher can demonstrate understanding. Clarifying, however, means the teacher does not understand what the student is saying and needs more information.

Clarifying is not meant to be a devious way to change or redirect what a student is thinking or feeling. It is not a subtle way of expressing criticism of something the student has done. It is not a way to direct the student's attention to the "correct answer." The intent of clarifying is to help the teacher better understand the student's ideas, feelings, and thought processes. Clarifying assists the teacher's understanding and also sharpens the perceptions and understandings of the student. (See also "Thinking and Communicating with Clarity and Precision" in Chapter 2.) Clarifying that is preceeded by a paraphrase helps make clear that the probe for more detail is for understanding, not judgment or interrogation. Clarifying contributes to trust because it communicates to students that their ideas are worth exploring and considering; the full meaning of those ideas, however, may not yet be understood.

If a student uses unusual terminology, expresses a confused concept or idea, or asks a question that the teacher does not understand, the teacher will want to clarify both the content of that idea and possibly the process by which that idea was derived. The teacher may express a lack of understanding of the student's idea and seek further explanation; invite the student to be more specific by requesting that the student elaborate on or rephrase the idea; or seek to discover the thinking processes underlying the production of that idea.

Clarifying is often stated as an interrogative, but it also could be a statement inviting further illumination. Here are examples:

- "Could you explain to us what you mean by *charisma?*"
- "So you're saying that you'd rather work by yourself than in a group. Is that correct?"
- "Go over that one more time, Shelley. I'm not sure I understand you."
- "You say you are studying the situation. Tell us just exactly what you do when you 'study' something."
- "Explain to us the steps you took to arrive at that answer."

By clarifying, teachers show students that their ideas are worthy of exploration and consideration. Clarifying demonstrates that the teacher is interested in, values, and wants to pursue students' thinking. When a teacher responds to students' comments by encouraging them to elaborate further, students become more purposeful in their thinking and behaving.

Providing information and feedback. Feedback in an environment of trust can contribute to students' development of the Habits of Mind over time. Students need feedback on their use of the habits, and a sense of trust in how that feedback is delivered stimulates motivation and self-directed learning—both of which support further development of the habits. Carol Sanford (1995) writes, "The ability to be self-correcting or self-governing is dependent on the capability to be self-reflecting [and] to see one's own processes as they play out." To support this aim, students must be involved in creating the criteria and processes for gathering and reporting the feedback (see Chapter 11). Sanford adds that feedback should be done based only on a previous agreement that specifies the principles and areas to be covered.

Providing information is also an important factor in the development of a specific and powerful Habit of Mind—remaining open to continuous learning. We must nurture the student's capacities for processing information by comparing, inferring, or drawing causal relationships. It is the acquisition of information that drives the spiral of continuous learning (see Chapter 11). Rich information must be readily available for the student to process. To contribute to the maintenance of trust, information should meet several conditions. Data must

- Be requested or needed.
- Be stated in observable terms.
- Be relevant.
- Allow for interpretation by the student, not the teacher.

Providing information means that the teacher actually supplies the information or helps students acquire it on their own. The teacher creates a climate that is responsive to the student's quest for information. Teachers can create this climate in several different ways:

1. Sometimes they provide feedback about a student's performance:
   - "No, 3 times 6 is not 24; 3 times 8 is 24."
   - "Yes, you have spelled *rhythm* correctly."

2. Sometimes they provide personal information, often in the form of "I" messages:
   - "I want you to know that chewing gum in this classroom really disturbs me."
   - "John, your pencil tapping is distracting me."
   - "The way you painted the tree makes me feel like I'm on the inside looking out."

3. Sometimes teachers make it possible for students to experiment with equipment and materials to find information for themselves:
   - "Here's a larger test tube if you'd like to see how your experiment would turn out differently."
   - "We can see the videoclip again if you want to check your observations."

4. At other times, teachers make primary and secondary sources of information accessible:

- "Mary, this almanac gives information you will need for your report on the world's highest mountain ranges."
- "Here's the dictionary. The best way to verify the spelling is to look it up."

5. Teachers also respond to student requests for information. For example, when a student asks, "What's this thing called?" the teacher replies, "This piece of equipment is called a bell jar."

6. During some exchanges, the teacher surveys the group for students' feelings or to gather information:

- "On this chart we have made a list of what you observed in the video. We can keep this chart in front of us so that we can refer to it as we classify our observations."
- "Let's go around the circle and share some of the feelings we had when we found out the school board is considering closing our school."

7. On some occasions, the teacher labels a thinking process, a Habit of Mind, or a behavior:

- "That is a *hypothesis* you are posing, Gina."
- "Sharing your ideas like that is an example of *thinking interdependently*, Mark."
- "Xavier, even though it was difficult, your *persisting* with this problem really paid off."
- "Nuyen, you *strived for accuracy* by providing evidence to support your theory."

Information must be presented in a nonjudgmental, behaviorally descriptive fashion and given only after the students have had an opportunity to recall as much as they can. Receiving information can be rewarding in itself (Bandura, 1997) and can be the source of energy for self-improvement (Garmston & Wellman, 2009). For example, here's a statement that could motivate students to improve their listening skills:

- "During the first five minutes presenting our reports, five students interrupted the speaker."

Having offered information, the teacher does not interpret but rather asks the students to construct meaning:

• "Of the six students in your group, Natasha spoke four times, Tyrone spoke two times, Nuyen spoke once, and the remaining three not at all. What do you make of that?"

The Importance of Modeling

Imitation and emulation are the most basic forms of learning. Teachers, parents, and administrators must realize the importance of their own display of desirable Habits of Mind in the presence of learners. In day-to-day events and when problems arise in schools, classrooms, and homes, children must see adults using the Habits of Mind. Without this consistency, a credibility gap is likely to develop. As Ralph Waldo Emerson is often quoted as saying, "What you do speaks so loudly, they can't hear what you say."

In Summary

A "thought-full" environment is a confluence of certain conditions and behaviors. It is more likely that students will better understand, develop the capacities for, and learn to value and to apply the Habits of Mind if they are in a trustful, risk-taking, creative classroom environment. Teachers and administrators are encouraged to monitor the climate of their school and classrooms to ensure these conditions are sustained.

References

Amabile, T. (1979). Effects of external evaluation on artistic creativity. *Journal of Personality and Social Psychology, 37*(2), 221–233.

Bandura, A. (1997). *Cognitive functioning in self-efficacy: The exercise of control.* New York: Freeman.

Bloom, B. (Ed.). (1956). *Taxonomy of educational objectives: Classification of educational goals.* New York: Longman, Green.

Bronson, P. (2007, February 12). How not to talk to your kids: The inverse power of praise. *New York Magazine.*

Brophy, J. E. (1981, October). *Teacher praise: A functional analysis* [Occasional Paper No. 28]. East Lansing, MI: Michigan State University Institute for Research on Teaching.

Burgoon, J., Buller, D., & Woodall, W. (1996). *Nonverbal communication: The unspoken dialogue* (2nd ed.). New York: McGraw-Hill.

Caine, G., & Caine, R. (2001). *The brain, education and the competitive edge.* Lanham, MD: Scarecrow Education.

Csikszentmihalyi, M. (1993). *The evolving self: A psychology for the third millennium*. New York: HarperCollins.

Damasio, A. (1994). *Descartes' error: Emotion, reason and the human brain*. New York: Putnam.

Damasio, A. (2000). *The feeling of what happens: Body and emotion in the making of consciousness*. Orlando, FL: Harcourt.

Deci, E. (1995). *Why we do what we do*. New York: Grosset Putnam.

Dweck, C. (2007, October). The perils and promises of praise. *Educational Leadership, 65*(2), 34–39.

Erikson, E. (1963). *Childhood and society*. New York: Norton.

Feuerstein, R., Feuerstein, R., & Schur, Y. (1997). Process as content in education of exceptional children. In A. Costa & R. Liebmann (Eds.), *Supporting the spirit of learning when process is content* (pp. 1–22). Thousand Oaks, CA: Corwin.

Garmston, R., & Wellman, B. (2008). *The adaptive school*. Norwood, MA: Christopher Gordon.

Goleman, D. (2006). *Social intelligence*. New York: Bantam.

Johnson, B. (1996). *Polarity management: Identifying and managing unsolvable problems*. Amherst, MA: HRD.

Joyce, B., & Showers, B. (1988). *Student achievement through staff development*. New York: Longman.

Kendon, A. (1990). *Conducting interaction: Patterns of behavior in focused encounters*. New York: Cambridge University Press.

Kohn, A. (1994). *Punished by rewards: The trouble with gold stars, incentive plans, A's, praise and other bribes*. New York: Houghton Mifflin.

Lepper, M., & Green, D. (Eds.). (1978). *The hidden cost of rewards: New perspectives on the psychology of human motivation*. New York: Erlbaum.

Lowery, L. (2001). The biological basis for thinking. In A. Costa (Ed.), *Developing minds: A resource book for teaching thinking* (3rd ed., pp. 234–244). Alexandria, VA: ASCD.

McTighe, J., & Lyman, F. (2001). Cueing thinking in the classroom: The promise of theory-embedded tools. In A. Costa (Ed.) *Developing minds: A resource book for teaching thinking* (3rd ed., pp. 384–392). Alexandria, VA: ASCD.

Perkins, D. (2003). *King Arthur's round table: How collaborative conversations create smart organizations*. New York: Wiley.

Pert, C. (1997). *Molecules of emotion: The science behind mind-body medicine*. New York: Simon & Schuster.

Rowe, M. B. (1969). Science, silence and sanctions. *Science and Children 6*, 11–13.

Rowe, M. B. (1974). Wait time and rewards as instructional variables: Their influence on language, logic and fate control. *Journal of Research in Science Teaching 11*, 81–94.

Sanford, C. (1995). *Feedback and self-accountability: A collision course*. Battle Ground, WA: Springhill Publications.

Zoller, K. (2005). The new science of non-verbal skills. In R. Garmston (Ed.), *The presenter's fieldbook: A practical guide* (2nd ed., pp. 119–138). Norwood, MA: Christopher Gordon.

7

Toward a Mindful
Language of Learning

Arthur L. Costa and Bena Kallick

Years of research have demonstrated the close, intertwined relationship of language and thought. In fact, the cognitive processes that children derive are embedded in the vocabulary, inflections, and syntax of adults' language. From birth, children imitate the sounds, words, phrases, and thought patterns of the significant adults in their lives (Feuerstein, 1980; Flavell, 1977; Vygotsky, 1962). Through these interactions in their formative years, children develop foundations of thought that endure throughout their lives.

Environments and interactions that demand and provide models of complex language and thought contribute to children's abilities to handle complex thinking processes as they mature (Sternberg & Caruso, 1985). This research interests us because the past several decades have seen significant transformations in U.S. families. With more working parents, broken homes, latchkey kids, and text messaging, it is surprising how little time parents and children actually spend talking together. Family life in the United States today often lacks the meaningful verbal interaction necessary to build a foundation for thinking, learning, and communicating in school. When children enter school lacking the complexity of language and thought needed to master academic demands, they often are disadvantaged.

Language is a foundation for the Habits of Mind. A person must have both *inner language* and *expressive language* to be able to develop the habits. For example, if students do not have inner language (the ability to talk to themselves), they will have difficulty thinking through a problem or being aware of their own thinking so they can use what they have learned in other situations. If they do not have expressive language (the ability to talk to others), they will be unable to participate in social thinking or to articulate questions.

Success in school and daily life depends upon the spontaneous application of the Habits of Mind during problem solving, innovating, and decision making. As adults, we can stimulate, engage, and help children practice the Habits of Mind by subtly and carefully using language with selected syntax, presuppositions, vocabulary, and intonations.

For example, teachers can consciously select key cognitive terminology so students encounter the words in common, everyday dialogue. They can formulate questions that lead students to exercise certain Habits of Mind. They can provide data that students must interpret for themselves. They can remain nonjudgmental so children must make their own judgments. In other words, educators can become more mindful of their own use of language.

We all can develop the habit of thinking and communicating with clarity and precision. In so doing, we educate students' cognitive structures, which ultimately leads to increased academic performance. This chapter contains suggestions for

• Building fluency in and a repertoire for the labels of the Habits of Mind.
  • Monitoring our own language.
  • Intentionally using language that will enhance awareness and performance of the Habits of Mind during daily interactions in classrooms and schools.

A "Word Splash"

We begin this chapter with a "word splash," which is intended to build fluency with the terms and phrases related to each Habit of Mind. Reproducing the exact wording of the habits as explicated in this book is not necessary in the classroom. Each Habit of Mind has a cluster of terms with similar meanings, and the student who can't remember *persisting* may well remember the habit of *stick to it*. What is important is learning what the habit means so that students can associate the appropriate behavior with the habit. One way students—and adults—can make these connections is through a word splash.

A word splash is a collection of key terms, synonyms, and phrases that convey meanings similar to a particular term (Lipton & Wellman, 1999). It enhances fluency with the terms and elaborates their meaning. A word splash also enhances flexibility by providing a group of terms rather than restricting someone to use of a single term. A word splash expands the range of questioning and paraphrasing, and it allows students and teachers to communicate with others using common terminology.

Each of the following word splashes was generated by groups of teachers as they considered key terms, synonyms, and word phrases that stand for and convey meanings similar to the terms we use for the Habits of Mind. To get started, here is a word splash for the phrase *Habits of Mind*:

Characteristics	Character traits	Attitudes
Virtues	Mental disciplines	Proclivities
Dispositions	Inclinations	Propensities
Qualities		

The following sections contain word splashes for each of the 16 Habits of Mind. These vocabulary lists are by no means complete. Invite students and colleagues to add to them. For example, students might make a glossary for the Habits of Mind and then use a thesaurus to add synonyms to their lists. Incorporate these words in spelling lists, or invite students to go on a scavenger hunt to find additional words and enlarge their mindful vocabulary.

Word Splash for *Persisting*

Never give up	Relentless	Stand your ground
Perseverance	Undaunted	Sustained
Indefatigable	Drive	Systematic
Focused	Resiliant	Hang in there

Diligence	Reliant	Try and try again
Continuing	Enduring	Stick-to-it-iveness
Stamina	Tenacity	Hang tough

Word Splash for *Managing Impulsivity*

Think before you act	Meditate	Reflective
Deliberate	Patient	Controlled
Thoughtful	Calm	Count to 10
Strategic	Planned	Wait time
Take a deep breath	Mindful	Considered
Self-regulated		

Word Splash for *Listening with Understanding and Empathy*

Empathic	Caring	Concentration
Tuned in	Paraphrase	Summarizing
Mirroring	Respectful	Compassionate
Attentive	Focused	Concentrate
Attuned		

Word Splash for *Thinking Flexibly*

Adaptable	Expandable	Lateral thinking
Bendable	Plasticity	Variety
Options	Diversity	Alternatives
Changing	Pliable	Growing
Open-minded	Creative	Multiple solutions
Different points of view	Resilient	Repertoire
Different perspectives	Fluent	Many possibilities

Word Splash for *Thinking About Thinking (Metacognition)*

Knowing what you know and what you don't know	Mindful	Talking to yourself
	Mental maps	Self-monitoring
	Cognizance	Inside your head
Talk-aloud problem solving	Alertness	Self-evaluative
	Consciousness	Self-awareness

Have a plan in mind

Self-aware

Thinking about
   your thinking

Inner feelings

Inner thoughts

Inner dialogue

Awareness

Thinking aloud

Reflective

Strategic planning

Word Splash for *Striving for Accuracy*

Specific	Quality	Ensure
Stamina	Fit	Mastery
Uncompromising	Finished	Check it out
Flawless	Proof	Sharp
Effortless	Fidelity	Perfection
Quality control	Correct	On target
Craftsmanlike	Surety	Exactness
Zero tolerance	Refined	Correctness
Hit the bull's-eye	Adroit	Elegant

Word Splash for *Questioning and Posing Problems*

Interested	Delving	Quest
Probing	Qualify	Clarifying
Investigative	Inquiry	Curious
Interrogative	Seeking	Inquisitive
Skeptical	Curious	Cautious
Puzzled	Query	Speculative
Perplexing	Proof	Hypothetical

Word Splash for *Applying Past Knowledge to New Situations*

Prior knowledge	Reuse	Recycled
Know your resources	Draw forth	Remember
Reservoir of knowledge/ experiences	Recall	Transfer
Just like the time when . . .	Bridge	Transform
Utilize memory for the future	Use again	Translate
Implementation	Scaffolding	Similar situations
	Apply	Reminds me

Word Splash for *Thinking and Communicating with Clarity and Precision*

Define your terms	Enunciate	Choice of words
Grammatically correct	Eloquent	Communicative
Command of the language	Editing	Articulate

Word Splash for *Gathering Data Through All Senses*

Engaged	Sensations	Involvement
Hands-on	Move it	Sensing
Touch	Clarity	Interactive
Physical, visual, tactual, kinesthetic	Experiential	Concrete
	Dance	Feel it
Auditory, gustatory, olfactory	Sensitivity	Perceptual acuity
	Sensitivities	Perceptions

Word Splash for *Creating, Imagining, Innovating*

Unconventional	Unique	Productive
Spontaneous	Fertile	Generative
Brainstorm	Artistic	Prolific
Imaginative	Clever	New
Fresh	Fluent	Ingenious
Innovative	Novel	Fecund
Divergent	Inventive	Engender

Word Splash for *Responding with Wonderment and Awe*

Wondrous	Insatiable	Alive
Sensation	Mysterious	Aha!
Amazed	Obsessed	Amazement
Appreciation	Enthralled	Far out
Astounding	Transfixed	Fascination
Excitement	Wide-eyed	Phenomenon
Awesome	Visionary	Passionate
Marvel	Motivated	Exuberant
Way cool	Surprise	Miraculous
Mesmerized	Energized	Challenged

Word Splash for *Taking Responsible Risks*

Do your thing	Challenged	Adventuresome
Courageous	Roving	New pathways
Exploration	Venture	Daring
Pathfinders	Vagabond	Unconventional
Individualistic	Gamble	Free-spirited
Living on the edge	Bold	Just do it

Word Splash for *Finding Humor*

Merry disposition	Laughable	Funnybone
Laugh at yourself	Funny	Comic
Comedian	Jokester	Absurd
Bizarre	Satirical	Pun
Capricious	Playful	Irony
Fanciful	Comedy	Caricature
Wittiness	Clown	Whimsical

Word Splash for *Thinking Interdependently*

Ohana (Hawaiian word for family, team, or spirit of community)	Social	Harmonious
	Family	Interdependence
	Mutual	Support group
	Reciprocity	Collegial
Cooperative	Amicable	Collaborative
Congenial	Teamwork	Reciprocal
Sense of community	Interconnected	Synergistic
Companionship		

Word Splash for *Remaining Open to Continuous Learning*

Continuous learning	Mastery	Problem finding
Autopoesis	Kaizen	Insatiable
Inquisitive	Dissatisfied	Self-modifying
Learning from experience	Self-help	Self-evaluating
	Commitment	Lifelong learning
Perpetual student	Self-actualizing	Failing forward
Continual learner		

Building "Mindful" Language

Once the language for naming the Habits of Mind has been expanded, the next step is to use language tools and strategies intentionally to enhance students' awareness and performance of these intelligent behaviors. Following are several ways to encourage the habits through specific, mindful use of language (Costa & Marzano, 2001).

Thinking Words

We often hear teachers admonish students to think: "Think hard!" Students sometimes are criticized for not having the inclination to think: "These kids just go off without thinking!" Actually, the term *think* is a vague abstraction covering a wide range of mental activities. Thus, students may not appear to think because

- The vocabulary is a foreign language to them.
- They may not know how to perform the specific skills that the term implies.

When adults speak mindful language, using specific, cognitive terminology and instructing students in ways to perform certain skills, students are more inclined to use those skills (Astington & Olson, 1990; Langer, 1997). Consider the following examples:

Instead of saying . . .	Use *mindful language* by saying . . .
"Let's look at these two pictures."	"Let's COMPARE these two pictures."
"What do you think will happen when . . . ?"	"What do you PREDICT will happen when . . . ?"
"How can you put those into groups?"	"How can you CLASSIFY . . . ?"
"Let's work this problem."	"Let's ANALYZE this problem."
"What do you think would have happened if . . . ?"	"What do you SPECULATE would have happened if . . . ?"

"What did you think of this story?"

"What CONCLUSIONS can you draw about this story?"

"How can you explain . . . ?"

"What HYPOTHESES do you have that might explain . . . ?"

"How do you know that's true?"

"What EVIDENCE do you have to support . . . ?"

"How else could you use this . . . ?"

"How could you APPLY this . . . ?"

"Do you think that is the best alternative?"

"As you EVALUATE these alternatives . . . ."

As children hear these cognitive terms in everyday use and experience the cognitive processes that accompany these labels, they internalize the words and use them as part of their own vocabulary. Teachers will also want to give specific instruction in the cognitive functions so that students possess experiential meaning along with the terminology (Beyer, 1991).

Communicating and Reinforcing Terminology

A 5th grade teacher standing yard duty on the playground noticed the beginnings of a scuffle between two 6th grade boys. She immediately scurried over to break up the fight. Before she got there, however, she overheard one of her 5th graders intervene and say, "Hey, you guys! Manage your impulsivity!"

—Marilyn Tabor, Irvine Unified School District, Irvine, California

Children love to use the Habits of Mind terminology. Teach them what *metacognition, persistence,* and *impulsivity* mean. Ask them to create posters listing the Habits of Mind. Invite them to create logos and symbols for each habit, and display both the posters and the logos on the classroom walls.

When students use one or more of the Habits of Mind, be quick to offer a label. The word splashes provided earlier offer a range of labels that have similar meanings. Here are examples of what to say:

- "You really *persisted* on that problem."
- "You *listened* to Danielle and *empathized* with her feelings."
- "I'll give you some more time. I know you are *metacogitating*."
- "That is an intriguing *problem* you are posing."
- "I see that in your *checking* over your story for accuracy, you found some errors needing correction."
- "That problem really *intrigues* you."
- "You were thinking *interdependently* when you worked with Nicholas."

Discipline

When disciplining children, decide which behaviors to discourage and which to reinforce. Disciplining is another opportunity to speak mindful language and to pose questions that cause children to examine their own behavior, search for the consequences of that behavior, and choose more appropriate actions (Bailis & Hunter, 1985). Consider the following examples:

Instead of saying . . .	Use *mindful language* by saying . . .
"Be quiet!"	"The noise you're making is disturbing us."
"Sarah, get away from Catherine!"	"Sarah, can you find another place to do your best work?"
"Stop interrupting!"	"Since it's Maria's turn to talk, what do you need to do?"
"Stop running!"	"Why do you think we have the rule about always walking in the halls?"

Teachers and other adults must discuss courtesy, appropriate behavior, and classroom and school rules with children if the children are to learn appropriate alternatives. Then, when students forget, they can search their memory for what was learned. Soon they will monitor their own behavior, an important dimension of metacognition (Costa, 2001).

Providing Data, Not Solutions

Sometimes we rob children of the opportunity to take charge of their own behavior by providing solutions, consequences, and appropriate actions for them. If instead we would merely provide data as input for children's decision making, they could learn to act more autonomously, become aware of the effects of their behavior on others, and become more empathic in sensing others' verbal and nonverbal cues.

We can speak mindful language by giving data, divulging information about ourselves, or sending "I" messages. Consider the following examples:

When children . . .	Use *mindful language* by saying . . .
Make noise by tapping their pencil	"I want you to know that your pencil tapping is disturbing me."
Interrupt	"I like it when you take turns to speak."
Whine	"It hurts my ears."
Are courteous	"I liked it when you came in so quietly and went right to work."
Chew gum	"I want you to know that gum chewing in my class disturbs me."

Some children, of course, don't recognize these forms of data as cues for self-control. In such cases, it may be necessary to provide more specific directions for appropriate behavior. Start, however, by giving students the chance to control themselves.

Classroom Management

Too often, teachers give all the information necessary to do a task, so that students merely perform the task without having to infer meaning. It's preferable to use mindful language that will lead students to analyze the task, decide on what is needed, and then act autonomously. Consider the following examples:

Instead of saying . . .	**Use *mindful language* by saying . . .**
"For our field trip, remember to bring spending money, comfortable shoes, and a warm jacket."	"What must we remember to bring with us on our field trip?"
"The bell has rung; it's time to go home. Clear off your tables, slide your chairs under the table quietly, and line up at the door."	"The bell has rung. What must we do to get ready to go home?"
"Get 52 cups, 26 scissors, and 78 sheets of paper. Get some butcher paper to cover the desks."	"Everyone will need two paper cups, a pair of scissors, and three sheets of paper. The desktops will need to be protected. Can you figure out what you'll need to do?"
"Remember to write your name in the upper-right-hand corner of your paper."	"So that I easily can tell who the paper belongs to, what must you remember to do?"
"You need to start each sentence with a capital letter and end with a period."	"This sentence would be complete with two additions. Figure out what they are."

Metacognition

Thinking about thinking begets more thinking (Costa, 2001). When children describe the mental processes they are using, the data they are lacking, and the plans they are formulating, they think about their own thinking, or metacogitate. When teachers use mindful language, they cause the covert thought processes students experience to become overt. Whimbey and Lochhead refer to this as "Talk Aloud Problem Solving" (Lochhead, 2001; Whimbey, 1985). Consider the following examples:

When students say . . .	Use *mindful language* by saying . . .
"The answer is 43 pounds, 7 ounces."	"Describe the steps you took to arrive at that answer."
"I don't know how to solve this problem."	"What can you do to get started?"
"I'm comparing . . . ."	"What goes on in your head when you compare?"
"I'm ready to begin."	"Describe your plan of action."
"We're memorizing our poems."	"What do you do when you memorize?"
"I like the large one best."	"What criteria are you using to make your choice?"
"I'm finished. I've got the answer."	"How do you know you're correct?"

As teachers invite students to describe what's going on inside their heads when thinking takes place, children become more aware of their own thought processes. As they listen to other students describe their metacognitive processes, they develop flexibility of thought and come to appreciate that there are several ways to solve the same problem.

Presuppositions

Language can be interpreted in terms of its *surface* meaning and its *structural* meaning. Surface meaning refers to word definitions, syntax, semantics, grammar, verb forms, and modifiers. Structural meaning refers to the subtle nuances, connotations, feelings, and images the words convey. A presupposition is a hidden, covert, or implicit meaning buried within the structure of the statement or sequence of language. For example, a teacher says, "Even Richard could pass that course." Several meanings are hidden within the substructure of this sentence: that Richard is not too bright a student and, further, that the course must be a cinch! Neither of these pieces of information is overtly present in the surface structure of the sentence. The sentence does not say, "Even Richard, who is not too bright a student, could pass that course, which is a cinch!" The implicit meaning or presupposition, however, is blatant (Elgin, 1980).

Over time, these kinds of messages seep into children's awareness. Usually the children are unaware that such verbal violence is being used against them, but they feel hurt or insulted in response to language that may sound, on the surface, like a compliment. Interestingly, people behave in response to others' perceptions of them: they behave as if they are expected to behave that way. Over time, negative presuppositions accumulate, and they influence students' poor self-esteem and negative self-concepts as thinkers. Negative behavior follows.

Using positive presuppositions is possible. Teachers can purposely select language to convey a positive self-concept as a thinker: "As you plan your project, what criteria for your research report will you keep in mind?" Notice the positive presuppositions: that you are planning, that you know the criteria for the research report, that you can keep them in your mind, and that you can apply them as you work.

Teachers never purposely set out to deprecate a student's self-esteem. These negative presuppositions, however, may creep into the language of classroom interaction. Teachers who speak mindful language monitor their own words to offer positive presuppositions. Consider the following examples:

Instead of saying . . .	Use *mindful language* by saying . . .
"Why did you forget to do your assignment?"	"As you plan for your assignment, what materials will you need?"
"Why don't you like to paint?"	"We need you to paint a picture to add to our gallery."
"Did you forget again?"	"Tell us what you will do to help you remember."
"When will you grow up?"	"As we grow older, we learn how to solve these problems from such experiences."

"Here, I'll give you an easier puzzle; then you'll be successful."

"As the puzzles get more difficult, how will you use planning like this again?"

Studying Mindful Language

Like any language, mindful language is dynamic. Mindful language can be created, analyzed, refined, and transmitted to others; it can also become archaic. Students, too, can explore the linguistic structure of mindful language. They can focus on word clusters or syntax cues within the language; such things signal what cognitive operations those words evoke. Sometimes this approach is referred to as *discourse analysis*, which includes such cognitive processes as concept formation, relationship identification, and pattern recognition.

For example, students can search for relationships as a way of linking information. They can find the word or word cluster that cues the thinking process of that relationship. This process is called *relationship identification*. Relationship identification requires students to

- Identify separate ideas that are related within a sentence.
- Identify the type of relationship between the ideas: addition, comparison, causality, sequence, or contrast.
- Identify the linguistic cues for the performance of that cognitive relationship. Words such as *both, same,* and *similar* indicate comparing. Words such as *however, but,* or *on the other hand* indicate contrasting. Words such as *first, next, after,* and *a while later* indicate sequencing.

Here's another way to look at relationship identification:

Cognitive Process	Type of Relationship	Example of Linguistic Cue
ADDITION	Two ideas go together in the same way.	"He is intelligent AND he is kind."
COMPARISON	Common attributes are shared.	"Shaun AND Sarah BOTH play the violin."

CONTRAST	Two ideas don't go together.	"He is healthy BUT he doesn't exercise."
CAUSALITY	One event causes another.	"Peter went home BECAUSE his work was finished."
SEQUENCE	One event happens before, during, or after another event.	"He went home, THEN he went to the library."

Teaching students to be alert to the cognitive process embedded in written and spoken language can help them become aware of their own language and thought. This instruction also can help them decode the syntactic, semantic, and rhetorical signals found in all languages, and learn to integrate the complex interaction of language, thought, and action (Marzano & Hutchins, 1985).

In Summary

Language is a tool for enhancing others' development. Speaking mindful language simply means that we consciously use communication to help students develop the Habits of Mind. We speak mindful language for a variety of reasons:

• Using a variety of terms, phrases, and slogans that are synonymous with the Habits of Mind builds conceptual fluency.

• Using specific cognitive terminology provides a good model for thinking and communicating with clarity and precision.

• Posing questions that cause children to examine their own behavior, search for the consequences of that behavior, and choose more appropriate actions serves as a rich model for questioning and posing problems as well as problem solving.

• Giving data, divulging information about ourselves, or sending "I" messages so that students must process the information themselves helps them develop self-control, flexible thinking, and the habit of listening with understanding and empathy.

• Causing students to analyze a task, decide on what is needed, and then act autonomously helps them with their social thinking and builds their questioning skills.

• Causing others to define their terms, become specific about their actions, make precise comparisons, and use accurate descriptors represents the habit of thinking and communicating with clarity and precision.

• Causing students' covert thought processes to become overt develops the habit of thinking about thinking (metacognition).

• Using positive presuppositions to enhance self-concept reinforces the dispositions necessary for the Habits of Mind.

• Helping children study and become alert to language cues that evoke thought processes develops their ability to gather data through all senses.

We stimulate and enhance others' thinking by asking questions, selecting terms, clarifying ideas and processes, providing data, and withholding value judgments. These strategies all contribute to mindful language, which is the language we use to grow the Habits of Mind.

References

Astington, S., & Olson, D. (1990). Metacognition and metalinguistic language: Learning to talk about thought. *Applied Psychology: An International Review, 39*(1), 77–87.

Bailis, M., & Hunter, M. (1985, August 14). Do your words get them to think? *Learning.*

Beyer, B. (1991). Practical strategies for the direct teaching of thinking skills. In A. Costa (Ed.), *Developing minds: A resource book for teaching thinking* (pp. 274–279), Alexandria, VA: ASCD.

Costa, A. (2001). Mediating the metacognitive. In A. Costa (Ed.), *Developing minds: A resource book for teaching thinking* (pp. 408–412). Alexandria, VA: ASCD.

Costa, A., & Marzano, R. (2001). Teaching the language of thinking. In A. Costa (Ed.), *Developing minds: A resource book for teaching thinking* (pp. 379–383). Alexandria, VA: ASCD.

Elgin, S. (1980). *The gentle art of verbal self-defense.* New York: Dorset Press.

Feuerstein, R. (1980). *Instrumental enrichment.* Baltimore, MD: University Park Press.

Flavell, J. (1977). *Cognitive development.* Englewood Cliffs, NJ: Prentice Hall.

Langer, E. (1997). *The power of mindful learning.* Cambridge, MA: Da Capo Press.

Lipton, L., & Wellman, B. (1999). *Pathways to understanding.* Guilford, VT: Pathways Publishing.

Lochhead, J. (2001). *Thinkback: A user's guide to minding the mind*. Hillsdale, NJ: Lawrence Erlbaum.

Marzano, R., & Hutchins, C. L. (1985). *Thinking skills: A conceptual framework*. Aurora, CO: McREL.

Sternberg, R., & Caruso, D. (1985). Practical modes of knowing. In E. Eisner (Ed.), *Learning and teaching the ways of knowing* (pp. 133–158). 84th yearbook of the National Society for the Study of Education. Chicago: University of Chicago Press.

Vygotsky, L. S. (1962). *Thought and language*. Cambridge, MA: Massachusetts Institute of Technology Press.

Whimbey, A. (1985). Test results from teaching thinking. In A. Costa (Ed.), *Developing minds: A resource book for teaching thinking* (pp. 269–271). Alexandria, VA: ASCD.

8

Using Questions to Challenge Students' Intellect

Arthur L. Costa and Bena Kallick

Thinking is an engagement of the mind that changes the mind.
—*Martin Heidegger,* What Do We Mean

When we ask teachers what they want their students to be able to do, they invariably emphasize the importance of thinking and problem solving. Yet given the high degree of apathy among today's students, how can we engage students' minds or, as Sizer suggests, guide them to "use their minds well" (1992, p. 73)?

A student's mind generally is engaged through some form of cognitive dissonance: a provocation or an inquiry. Effective teachers create this dissonance in two ways: (1) by raising a point of uncertainty or discrepancy in the content or (2) by pressing students to raise such points as they try to understand what is being presented. Ultimately engagement occurs through student interest, and we can only foster the conditions in which students' interest might be piqued.

Questioning strategies provide a rich opportunity for developing student engagement. All questioning should focus on drawing students into the learning process. Learners must be presented with problems and questions, the answers to which are not readily known, if they are to become aware of, draw forth, practice, and apply the Habits of Mind.

Careful, intentional, productive questioning is one of the most powerful tools a skillful teacher possesses. Engaging students by posing questions is a clear signal that the teacher is "democratizing" knowledge in the room, conveying a sense that every student is capable of knowing. When a teacher begins a question with "Who can tell me . . . ?" it immediately signals that only certain students have the answer. If the teacher begins the question with "What do we know about . . . ?" the words signal that all students have something to offer. If a teacher poses questions to which the answers already are known, students try to guess what's in the teacher's head and search for conformity, agreement, and certainty. But if neither the teacher nor the students know the answers, they can share sincere, collaborative inquiry as they search for solutions.

This chapter describes powerful questioning strategies that are intended to equip teachers with the linguistic skills and metacognitive maps to do the following:

   • Monitor their own questions, to ensure the question's clarity of purpose, level of complexity, and positive intention.
   • Formulate and pose powerful questions that intentionally challenge and engage students' intellect and imagination.
   • Enhance students' self-esteem.
   • Observe the effects of the questions on students' thinking.
   • Engage students' use of one or more of the Habits of Mind.
   • Serve as a model for students to emulate in their questioning.

Remember that one of the ultimate purposes of asking questions is to help students increase their own habit of questioning and posing problems. The following criteria, diagrams, and examples can be shared with students so that students will not only understand a teacher's questioning strategy, but also become skillful in posing powerful questions themselves. To encourage such development, teachers must intentionally model complex questions presented in language students can understand.

Some Questioning "Don'ts"

We start by inviting teachers to heighten their awareness of their current questioning patterns. Are you miscuing, confusing, or limiting student thought? Some questions limit other people's thinking. These limits must be avoided for students (and adults) to use the Habits of Mind.

At least five types of questions miscue or stifle students' thinking because the questions send confusing and mixed messages. They do not belong in lessons designed to engage the Habits of Mind. Here are examples:

1. *Verification questions*, the answers to which already are known by the teacher or by the student:
  - "What is the name of . . . ?"
  - "How many times did you . . . ?"

2. *Closed questions*, which can be answered "yes," "no," or "I can":
  - "Can you recite the poem?"
  - "Can you tell us the name of . . . ?"
  - "Who can remember . . . ?"
  - "Who can state the formula for . . . ?"

3. *Rhetorical questions*, in which the answer is given within the question:
  - "In what year was the War of 1812 fought?"
  - "Since when has Mikhail Gorbachev had his birthmark?"
  - "Who led Sherman's march through Georgia?"
  - "How long did the Seven Years War last?"
  - "What time does the two o'clock bus depart?

4. *Defensive questions*, which lead to justification, resistance, and self-protection:
  - "Why didn't you complete your homework?"
  - "Why would you do a thing like that?"
  - "Are you misbehaving again?"

5. *Agreement questions*, the intent of which is to invite others to agree with an opinion or answer:
  - "This is really the best solution, isn't it?"
  - "Let's do it my way, OK?"
  - "We really should get started now, shouldn't we?"
  - "Who can name the three basic parts of a plant? Root, stems, and leaves, right?"

Questions That Stimulate Complex Thinking

Questions invite different levels and complexity of thinking. Early in children's lives, they learn to be alert to certain syntax cues to know how to behave or think. Teachers will want to use linguistic tools deliberately to engage and challenge complex, creative thinking. The following vignette by Oliver Wendell Holmes captures the levels of thinking at increasingly complex levels:

The Three-Story Intellect

There are one-story intellects, two-story intellects, and three-story intellects with skylights.

All fact collectors, who have no aim beyond their facts, are one-story men.

Two-story men compare, reason, generalize, using the labors of the fact collectors as well as their own.

Three-story men idealize, imagine, predict—their best illumination comes from above, through the skylight. (Costa, 2001, p. 361)

Holmes reminds us that all three levels of thinking are important. Teachers will want to design and pose questions that elicit all three. The graphic representation of Holmes's story in Figure 8.1 can be used as a mental map to help teachers pose questions. On the first story are the data-gathering cognitive operations. On the second story we find cognitive operations that help students make meaning of the data: the processing level. The third story of the house invites students to go beyond the skylights to speculate, elaborate, and apply concepts in new and hypothetical situations. In the following sections we offer examples of questions that invite specific cognitive operations at each level of the three-story intellect.

Data Gathering

Data-gathering questions are designed to draw from students the concepts, information, feelings, or experiences acquired in the past and stored in long- or short-term memory. These questions can also be designed to

FIGURE 8.1

The Three-Story Intellect Model

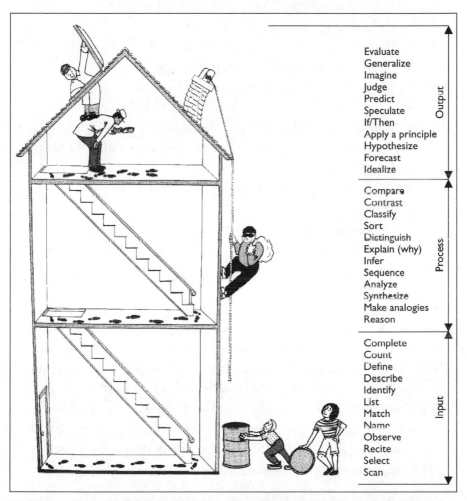

Adapted by permission of the publisher from the "Three-Story Intellect Model" from *Brain Compatible Classrooms* by Robin Fogarty, © SkyLight Training and Publishing, Inc.

activate the senses to gather data for processing at the next-higher level. Several cognitive processes are included at this level of thinking: recalling, completing, identifying, observing, counting, listing, reciting, defining, matching, scanning, describing, naming, and selecting. Here are examples of questions and statements designed to elicit these cognitive objectives:

- "Name the states that border California." (Naming)
- "How does the picture make you feel?" (Describing)
- "What word does this picture go with?" (Matching)
- "Define the word *haggard*." (Defining)
- "What did you see the man doing in the film?" (Observing)
- "Which ball is the blue one?" (Identifying)
- "How does the Gettysburg Address begin?" (Reciting)
- "How many coins are in the stack?" (Counting)
- "Which words in this list rhyme?" (Selecting)
- "The Mexican houses were made of mud bricks called . . . what?" (Completing)
- "Watch what color it turns when I put the litmus paper in the liquid." (Observing)
- "List the first four numbers in a set of positive integers." (Listing)
- "How did you feel about the grade you received in science?" (Recalling)

Processing

Teachers can guide students to process data in many ways. Sometimes teachers design questions and statements to seek cause-and-effect relationships. Other questions lead students to synthesize, analyze, summarize, compare, contrast, or classify. Several other cognitive processes are included at this level of thinking: distinguishing, making analogies, categorizing, experimenting, organizing, explaining, sequencing, grouping, and inferring. Here are examples of questions designed to elicit cognitive objectives at the processing level:

- "In what ways do you see the Civil War as being like the Revolutionary War?" (Comparing)
- "What suggests to you that Columbus believed he could get to the East by sailing west?" (Explaining)
- "From our experiments with food coloring in different water temperatures, what might you infer about the movement of molecules?" (Inferring)
- "How might you arrange the rocks in the order of their size?" (Sequencing)

- "What do you think caused the liquid to turn blue?" (Explaining)
- "Arrange in groups the things that a magnet will and will not pick up." (Grouping)
- "What other machines can you think of that work in the same way that this one does?" (Making analogies)
- "What are some characteristics of Van Gogh's work that make you think this painting is his?" (Distinguishing)
- "What might you do to test your idea?" (Experimenting)
- "In what ways are pine needles different from redwood needles?" (Contrasting)
- "In what ways might you arrange the blocks so that they have a crowded effect?" (Organizing)
- "What data are we going to need to solve this problem?" (Analyzing)
- "Arrange the following elements of a set in ascending order: ¾, ½, ⅙, ⅘." (Sequencing)
- "How does the formula for finding the volume of a cone compare with the formula for the volume of a pyramid?" (Comparing)

This level of cognition also is important when students do research projects. Often students simply copy or paraphrase the text in a resource book or from the Internet. When students understand that research is, by definition, inquiry, they learn to raise questions that can be answered only through true research. The cognitive processes listed at the start of this section can guide students to raise questions at a more complex level. Thus an assignment might read, "As you *analyze* the development of machines, what were some of their *effects* on the people living at that time?" Or, "How does the main character in this novel *compare* with the main character in that novel?"

If a whole unit is being planned, an essential question at this level might be this: "How did the invention of the wheel affect our lives today?"

Speculating, Elaborating, and Applying Concepts

Other questions and statements are designed to have students go beyond the concept or principle and use it in a novel or hypothetical situation. This application invites students to think creatively and hypothetically, to use their imagination, to expose a value system, or to make a judgment. These questions lend themselves most powerfully to the research process because their answers cannot be found in books or other data sources. Students must make sense of the resource material and answer an inquiry that requires them to invest in the material. Verbs that describe this cognitive level include applying, imagining, evaluating, judging, hypothesizing, generalizing, model building, predicting, extrapolating, speculating, forecasting, and transferring. For example, consider these questions:

• "What do you suppose will happen to our weather if a high-pressure area moves in?" (Forecasting)

• "If our population continues to grow as it has, what might life be like in the 22nd century?" (Speculating)

• "Because the amount of heat does affect the speed of movement of the molecules, what do you predict will happen when we put the liquid in the refrigerator?" (Predicting)

• "Imagine what life would be like if we had no laws to govern us." (Imagining)

• "What might you say about all countries' economies that are dependent upon only one crop?" (Generalizing)

• "Design a way to use this bimetal strip to make a fire alarm." (Applying)

• "How could you use this clay to make a model of a plant cell?" (Model building)

• "What would be a fair solution to this problem?" (Evaluating)

• "What makes this painting unique?" (Judging)

• "Given what we have learned, what other examples of romantic music can you cite?" (Applying)

• "What do you think might happen if we placed the saltwater fish in the tank of fresh water?" (Hypothesizing)

Here are examples of typical research questions at this level:

• "As you consider the periodic table and the invention of the microscope, which was more essential to organizing chemistry?"

- "How is rap music like another form of poetry?"
- "How were the inventions of the industrial age a necessary form of development for a culture?"

An essential question at this level might be this: "Is there such a thing as a 'good' war?"

Composing Powerful Questions

Desirable questions elicit in students an awareness and engagement of the Habits of Mind. If we want students to develop flexibility, remain open to continuous learning, and think creatively, the questions that we compose and present to them must signal conditional learnings rather than absolute truths. Our questions must enable students to become more open to novelty, alert to distinctions, sensitive to different contexts, and aware of multiple perspectives. Our questions, therefore, should guard against premature conclusions and routine ways of thinking and perceiving (Siegel, 2007). In fact, many educators have turned to the practice of asking essential questions (Wiggins & McTighe, 2005) that have the desirable characteristics described here in order to stimulate inquiry throughout a unit of study.

These kinds of questions have three characteristics (Costa & Garmston, 2007, pp. 44–47):

1. *The questions are invitational.* The teacher uses an approachable voice, with a lilt and melody rather than a flat, even tenor. Plurals are used to invite multiple, rather than singular, concepts:
   - "What are *some* of your *goals*?"
   - "What *ideas* do you have?"
   - "What *outcomes* do you seek?"
   - "What *alternatives* are you considering?"

The teacher selects words that express tentativeness or uses the conditional tense:
   - "What *hunches* do you have to explain this situation?"
   - "What conclusions *might* you draw?"
   - "What *may* indicate his acceptance?"

The teacher also uses invitational stems to enable the thinking skill to be performed:

- "As you *recall* . . . ."
- "As you *consider* . . . ."
- "As you *reflect* on . . . ."

Positive presuppositions assume capability and empowerment:

- "What are *some* of the *benefits you will derive* from *engaging* in this activity?"
- "*As you anticipate* your project, what will be *some indicators* that you are progressing and *succeeding?*"

2. *The questions engage specific cognitive operations, as previously described in the three levels: data gathering; processing; and speculating, elaborating, and applying concepts.*

3. *The questions address content that is either external or internal to the person being addressed.* External content might be what is going on in the environment around the student: lesson content, another student, a project, or a playground or home experience. Internal content might be what is going on inside the student's mind: satisfaction, puzzlement, frustration, thinking processes (metacognition), feelings, or emotions.

Teachers can compose powerful questions by putting these three elements together. Each question should have an invitational stem, a cognitive operation, and content (see Figure 8.2).

Here are examples of rich, complex questions:

- "As you reflect on what you've learned in this unit, what additional questions are you curious about?"
- "As you compare this project with others that you have done . . . ."
- "How might you sequence these events in such a way as to . . . ?"
- "What led you to these inferences about your performance's success?"
- "In what ways might your emotions have influenced your decisions about . . . ?"

FIGURE 8.2
Composing Powerful Questions: Three Linguistic Components

To compose powerful questions, choose one stem from each column.
For example, "As you/recall/what feelings . . ."

Invitational Stem	Cognitive Operation	Content
As you . . .	*Input:* At the data-gathering level, choose such words as	In seeking internal content, ask about students'
What are some of . . .	• Recall	
How might you . . .	• Define	• Reactions
	• Describe	• Feelings
What led to . . .	• Identify	• Thoughts
	• Name	• Emotions
What possible . . .	• List	
		In seeking external content, ask about the
What might . . .	*Process:* At the processing level, use words such as	
How might . . .	• Compare	• Project
	• Contrast	• Other students
How should . . .	• Infer	• Group
	• Analyze	• Event
	• Sequence	• Goals
	• Synthesize	• Lesson
	• Summarize	
	Output: At the output level, use words such as	
	• Predict	
	• Evaluate	
	• Speculate	
	• Imagine	
	• Envision	
	• Hypothesize	

Categorical Questions to Engage the Habits of Mind

If we want students to become more mindful of the Habits of Mind and
to practice them, teachers and parents must learn to pose questions that
help children draw forth or become aware of one or more of the habits.

We offer examples of "categorical questions" that are intended to draw forth one of the Habits of Mind. Please notice the invitational stems, the positive presuppositions, the plural and tentative language, the level of cognition, and the content. In these examples, the specific Habit of Mind is shown in parentheses:

• "While you were reading, what was going on inside your head to monitor your understanding of the story?" (Thinking about thinking [metacognition])

• "If you were John, how do you think you might react to what you said about him?" (Listening with understanding and empathy)

• "What might be some other ways you could solve this problem?" (Thinking flexibly)

• "What questions might you ask to gather the data you need to solve this problem?" (Questioning and posing problems)

• "How do you know your answer is correct?" (Striving for accuracy)

• "What intrigues you about this experiment?" (Responding with wonderment and awe)

• "As a result of your learning about the topics we've explored in this unit of study, what will you continue to ponder and want to learn more about?" (Remaining open to continuous learning)

The following cross-categorical questions are intended to invite someone to draw upon at least two or more of the Habits of Mind:

• "As you listen to others' points of view, what metacognitive strategies do you use to see the situation from their perspective?" (Thinking about thinking [metacognition]; listening with understanding and empathy; thinking flexibly)

• "As you read, what do you do when your mind wanders but you want to remain on task?" (Persisting; thinking about thinking [metacognition])

• "When you find yourself tempted to respond emotionally to a situation, what alternatives do you consider?" (Managing impulsivity; thinking flexibly)

• "When you are communicating with others, what indicators are you aware of in yourself and others that signal you are being understood?"

(Thinking and communicating with clarity and precision; thinking about thinking [metacognition])

• "As you talked to yourself about this problem, what new insights were generated?" (Thinking about thinking [metacognition]; creating, imagining, innovating)

Rachel Billmeyer (2009) suggests that questioning to engage the Habits of Mind while reading is a powerful strategy:

Applying past knowledge to new situations:
How does the passage relate to events or experiences that you have had? How does knowing the findings of the scientist help you to understand the physical world?
Questioning and posing problems:
What problems led the scientist to pursue experimentation?
Thinking about thinking:
How did the author cause you to think? To feel?

Developing Students' Skillfulness in Questioning and Posing Problems

Students can develop skillfulness in questioning by being asked to compose questions for various purposes, including for tests and quizzes, for study guides, to guide observations while watching an instructional video, or to prepare for a field trip. For example, teachers might invite students to read the "Three-Story Intellect Model" in Figure 8.1 and then to compose three first-story, second-story, and third-story questions to be included in a quiz or a test. Some teachers ask students to prepare questions in a group to be given to another group. The second group then answers the questions, and the first group evaluates those answers along with the original questions. This activity serves two important purposes. First, students ask more difficult questions because they want to make them "hard" for the other group. Second, they must be able to answer their own questions, which challenges their own thinking as well.

Whatever the subject area, it is helpful for students to pose study questions for themselves before and during their reading of textual material.

Self-generating questions facilitate comprehension. We know that reading with a purpose stimulates a more focused mind. Questioning while reading provides an opportunity for the reader to predict what is coming next in the story. Many students find it useful to keep their questions in a response log or a reading log. Then they can begin to answer the questions raised as they reflect on the reading and seek other sources.

Sometimes the most significant questions are generated through the research process. Students can learn that a thoughtful way to end their research paper is with a set of questions generated as a result of their inquiry. Students gain much when they realize that there is always more to know! (See also Koechlin & Zwaan, 2006.)

In Summary

Skillful teachers compose and monitor their questions with the specific intention of having students engage one or more of the Habits of Mind. These kinds of questions build heightened consciousness. Students hear the specific vocabulary, and they soon learn that the habits are valued and can be used throughout their lives. Furthermore, hearing and responding to complex questions provides the linguistic models that students will soon incorporate in their own questioning. Thus they become more skillful in composing questions and posing problems.

References

Billmeyer, R. (2009). Creating thoughtful readers through habits of mind. In A. Costa (Ed.), *Habits of mind across the curriculum: Practical and creative strategies for teachers.* Alexandria, VA: ASCD.

Costa, A. (2001). Teacher behaviors that enable student thinking. In A. Costa (Ed.), *Developing minds: A resource book for teaching thinking* (pp. 359–369). Alexandria, VA: ASCD.

Costa, A., & Garmston, R. (2007). *Cognitive coaching foundation seminar learning guide* (7th ed.). Revised by J. Elison & C. Hayes. Norwood, MA: Christopher Gordon.

Koechlin, C., & Zwaan S. (2006). *How to empower students to ask questions and care about answers.* Portland, ME: Stenhouse.

Siegel, D. (2007). *The mindful brain.* New York: W. W. Norton.

Sizer, T. R. (1992). *Horace's school.* New York: Houghton Mifflin.

Wiggins, G., & McTighe, J. (2005). *Understanding by design* (2nd ed.). Alexandria, VA: ASCD.

9

Thinking Maps:
Visual Tools for Activating
Habits of Mind

David Hyerle

Learners construct knowledge as they build cognitive maps for
organizing and interpreting new information. Effective teachers help
students make such maps by drawing connections among different
concepts and between new ideas and learners' prior experience.
            —*Linda Darling-Hammond,* The Right to Learn *(1997)*

In early 1995, 4th graders at Friendship Valley Elementary School in Carroll County, Maryland, responded to a narrative writing prompt on the
Maryland Performance-Based Assessment. The school had been built five
years before on the principles of "the school as a home for the mind" and
had strengthened its program through a range of high-quality teaching
and learning strategies (see Chapter 19).

If you had been standing in a certain hallway of Friendship Valley
on the morning of that test—normally a stressful few hours for all
involved—you would have been startled by an ecstatic teacher running out of a room exclaiming, "They're using them on the test!" Many
of her students, without coaching, had used Thinking Maps® to generate

FIGURE 9.1
Student Flow Map

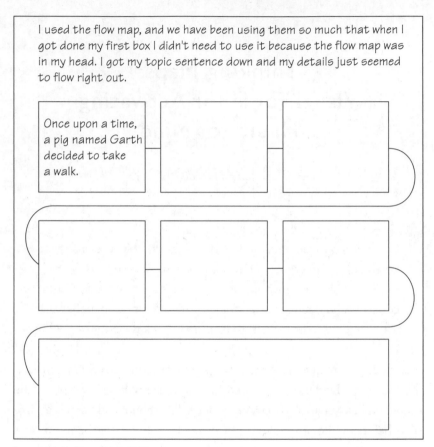

I used the flow map, and we have been using them so much that when I got done my first box I didn't need to use it because the flow map was in my head. I got my topic sentence down and my details just seemed to flow right out.

Once upon a time, a pig named Garth decided to take a walk.

Source: Adapted from Hyerle, 2000.

and organize information to complete the prompt. After the testing documents were collected, the teacher asked students to write about strategies they used during the test. One student responded with a note and a flow map, one of the eight Thinking Maps that students had been taught (see Figure 9.1).

By the time the student and her peers sat down for the writing test, they were relatively fluent with using flow maps to direct and construct networks of knowledge on the way to final products. In addition, they had developed the disposition for creativity and flexibility. They were able to persist, and they could call on a highly developed system for reflection and metacognition. In the end, these students' test scores were second across the whole state of Maryland on the combined scoring of six performance assessments—well beyond the mark where students in the school had performed previously. Exactly how was it that the student and her classmates, in the midst of a stressful test, were able to pull up a Thinking Map in their mind's eye?

Thinking Maps: A Common Visual Language for Learning

It is easy for us to recognize that carpenters, cooks, and computer programmers—and their mentors—have particular tools in hand for transforming raw materials into unique final products. The well designed, efficient home, the thoughtfully placed array of items on the plate, and the user-friendly interface of a software program are engendered with both practicality and, in the most effective cases, artistry. Over their careers these craftspeople develop methods and strategies as they move from novice to expert use in these tools. They also develop an interdependent array of habits of mind that enrich their capacities to use the tools of the trade strategically, purposefully, and with a sense of design that often integrates mind, heart, and soul.

As we look into the classroom, though, we may ask: What are the tools of cognition for teachers to use to directly facilitate the *specific* thinking skills of apprentice learners so they move from being novice thinkers to expert thinkers and develop lifelong Habits of Mind? This is the animating question for this chapter. An answer surfaces from Linda Darling-Hammond's insight about how "cognitive maps" are at the intersection of effective teaching and improved student performance. In this chapter, we investigate a common visual language found in eight fundamental cognitive tools called *Thinking Maps*. This theory-embedded language offers pre-K to college students—as well as teachers, leadership teams, and business people—a coherent, consistent, and flexible model of visual tools for

• *Representing* cognitive patterns as connected to prior experience and content knowledge.

• *Constructing* abstract concepts and practical products of thinking.

• *Facilitating* the full range of Habits of Mind within and across disciplines.

As shown in Figure 9.2, in isolation each of the eight Thinking Maps is grounded in a specific, fundamental cognitive process. When used together as a dynamic, interdependent visual language, these tools concretely support interactive teaching and learning, higher-order thinking and metacognition, and Habits of Mind across linear and nonlinear patterns of thinking. How is this different from most classroom practice? In a nutshell, most classroom practice *implies* cognitive skills instruction through "content" instruction, whereas use of Thinking Maps explicitly *defines and animates* such skills for students, so they become aware, cognitive actors in the classroom of learning.

FIGURE 9.2

Thinking Maps: A Common Visual Language

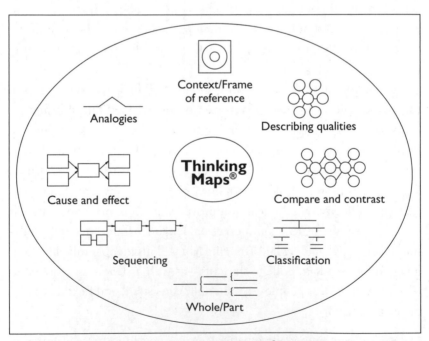

Source: Reprinted by permission of the publisher from *Thinking Maps® Training of Trainers Resource Manual* by David Hyerle, © 2000 Thinking Maps, Inc.

The Visual Brain

The brain is capable of absorbing 36,000 images every minute. How can this incredible figure be true? It is because the sophisticated, front-loaded wiring of our brain system is well beyond our imagination. Research approximates that between 80 and 90 percent of the information received by the brain comes through the eyes. Though our auditory and kinesthetic modes of sensing are complex and integrated with visual processing, the dominant mode is visual. Such dominance may seem a radical departure from the idea that we need to somehow balance instruction across multiple modalities. Yet the reality is that the human brain has evolved to become positively *imbalanced* toward visual imaging for information processing.

Even if we believe that some individuals are more kinesthetic, auditory, or visual learners—or more global or analytic—we need to consider research showing that each of us still processes far more information visually than through other modalities We must help students use their visual strengths.

Visual Tools for Constructing Knowledge

Metacognition means thinking about thinking. It means knowing what we know—and what we don't know—and how we know that. Metacognition also refers to an awareness and control of one's cognitive processes and the regulatory mechanisms used to solve problems. Metacognition anchors strategies for students so that they can apply them in life situations beyond school.

When students represent their cognitive strategies with visual tools, they practice metacognition, a principle of learning in which they describe the thinking processes they use to organize content knowledge into patterns and to solve problems (Hyerle, 1996). Three types of visual tools aid this metacognition: brainstorming webs, task-specific graphic organizers, and thinking-process maps (see Figure 9.3).

As noted earlier, carpenters and chefs have particular tools for different operations; in much the same way, thinkers turn to different visual tools to activate certain Habits of Mind. In the examples that follow, we see that students can develop their capacities to be creative and flexible,

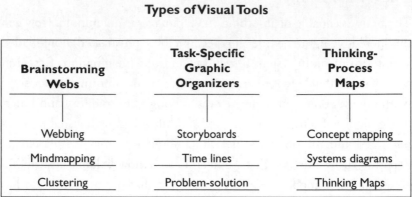

FIGURE 9.3

Types of Visual Tools

Brainstorming Webs	Task-Specific Graphic Organizers	Thinking-Process Maps
Webbing	Storyboards	Concept mapping
Mindmapping	Time lines	Systems diagrams
Clustering	Problem-solution	Thinking Maps

Source: Adapted from Hyerle, 2000.

to persevere, to be systematic, and to be aware of and reflective about metacognitive patterns to the degree that they can fluently apply these patterns to classroom challenges.

Visual tools enable students to look into their own thinking ("displayed metacognition" [Costa, 1991]), as they might look at their own reflection in a pool of water. With visual tools, students see their thinking displayed. From this public display, all students can readily share in one another's thinking and become self-reflective on the process, content, and, most important, evolving *form* of their thinking.

Brainstorming Webs

Although brainstorming webs appear in infinite forms, most learners start in the center of a blank page and branch out, creating idiosyncratic designs as an idea expands. The open form and purpose of brainstorming webs promote creative generation of ideas without blinders. Most brainstorming webs are used for thinking "outside the box," and they spark a high degree of open-ended networking and associative thinking.

After students become fluent with webbing, or with Tony Buzan's more specific techniques called Mindmapping™ (Buzan, 1994), it becomes clear that a cluster of intelligent behaviors, centered around creative thinking, is actively engaged and facilitated. Although educators have found it easy to identify verbal and written fluency as key objectives in school, it is more difficult for us to see that these two forms—speech and writing—are essentially linear representations. With brainstorming webs, students have self-generated, nonlinear tools for activating fluent thinking, which reflects the holistic networking capacity of the human brain.

Students call upon their disposition for ingenuity, originality, and insightfulness to express this form of thinking. Brainstorming webs provide the tools for venturing to the edge of our thinking—and thinking beyond the edge. Brainstorming also opens other Habits of Mind, such as thinking flexibly and wonderment.

Many teachers have a particular concern about brainstorming: What happens after the storm? Students need to move beyond the generation of ideas. They need to gain organizational control over ideas, and they need self-control to support more systematic and analytical thinking. To address this concern, another type of visual tool supports another cluster of Habits of Mind.

Task-Specific Graphic Organizers

Unlike webs, which facilitate thinking *outside* the box, most graphic organizers are structured so that students think *inside* the box. A teacher may create or take from a teacher's guide a specific visual structure that students follow and fill in as they proceed through a complex series of steps. Teachers often match these organizers with specific patterns of content or the development of content skills; thus, they are called "task-specific organizers." These highly structured graphics may seem constraining at times, yet each can be fruitful for students as they systematically approach a task, organize their ideas, and stay focused (especially when the task is complex).

For example, many organizers are sequential, showing the steps for solving a word problem, organizing content information for a research report, learning a specific process for a certain kind of writing prompt, or highlighting essential skills and patterns for comprehending a story. Because these types of visual tools are highly structured, they directly facilitate several Habits of Mind: persisting, managing impulsivity, striving for accuracy, and thinking and communicating with clarity and precision.

The visual/spatial structure guides students through the steps, box by box or oval by oval. Teachers report that one of the main outcomes of using graphic organizers is that they provide a concrete system and model for proceeding through a problem that students would otherwise abandon because they have not developed their own organizational structures for persisting. An obvious reason for this advantage is that the visual structure reveals a whole view of the process and—an important feature—an end point.

This kind of structuring also provides visual guidelines, much like a rope students can grasp. They don't impulsively jump outside the problem to what Benjamin Bloom (1956) calls "one-shot thinking." The visual modeling shows students that they can manage their impulsivity and stay in the box when they need to focus on following through to a solution. This kind of modeling also lends itself to greater accuracy and precision of language. Students usually don't have a record of their thinking, along with the steps and missteps they took along the way. They also have a hard time differentiating one idea from the next. By visually capturing their thinking, students can look back on their ideas, refine them, and share them with others to get feedback.

Both brainstorming webs and graphic organizers help students become familiar and fluent with networking and patterning information. Such work leads to a question about the relationships between thinking skills instruction and visual tools: Are there common patterns of thinking keyed to questions we ask every day in schools that could—if represented visually—deepen students' understanding and extension of their own thinking and Habits of Mind?

Thinking-Process Maps

A third kind of visual tool simultaneously supports thinking inside and outside the box. These tools—which I call thinking-process maps— are designed to reflect common patterns of thinking, from fundamental cognitive skills such as comparison, classification, and cause-effect reasoning to integrated visual languages such as Concept Mapping™ (Novak & Gowin, 1984), systems diagramming, and Thinking Maps.

Although these dynamic tools often *look* much like some static graphic organizers we see in classrooms, the differences in the purpose, introduction, application, and outcomes are significant. Thinking-process maps scaffold many Habits of Mind related to brainstorming webs and organizers, but these tools focus explicitly on different forms of concept development. They facilitate more explicitly four Habits of Mind: questioning and posing problems, gathering data through all senses, thinking about thinking (metacognition), and listening with understanding and empathy. When students are transforming information into knowledge using Thinking Maps, they are in dynamic congruence—or a dance—with what is already going on in their networking brain. Pat Wolfe summarizes the connection between brain research and Thinking Maps: "Neuroscientists tell us that the brain organizes information in networks and maps. What better way to teach students to think about ideas and organize and express their ideas than to use the very same method that the brain uses" (Hyerle, 2004, p. xi).

Thinking Maps and the Habits of Mind

Although it may appear obvious that using Thinking Maps, like many other approaches, will at some level support the development of the Habits of Mind, deep interdependencies link the activation of these 8 cognitive patterns as visual representations and the 16 intellectual behaviors. To create an organizing framework for making connections between thinking maps and the Habits of Mind, I have organized the habits into four informal groups: reflecting, attending, generating, and projecting (see Figure 9.4). In the following analysis, I use these categories to interpret how a classroom of 1st grade students improved their Habits of Mind as they independently and interdependently mapped out, comprehended, and wrote paragraphs about a book they had read.

At Mt. Airy Elementary School in Carroll County, Maryland, the principal, Dr. Thomasina DePinto Piercy, guided the simultaneous development and use of the Habits of Mind and Thinking Maps across her whole school. Through Dr. Piercy's interactions with Art Costa and me, all of the teachers in this K–5 school were trained in Thinking Maps,

FIGURE 9.4

A Tree Map of the Habits of Mind

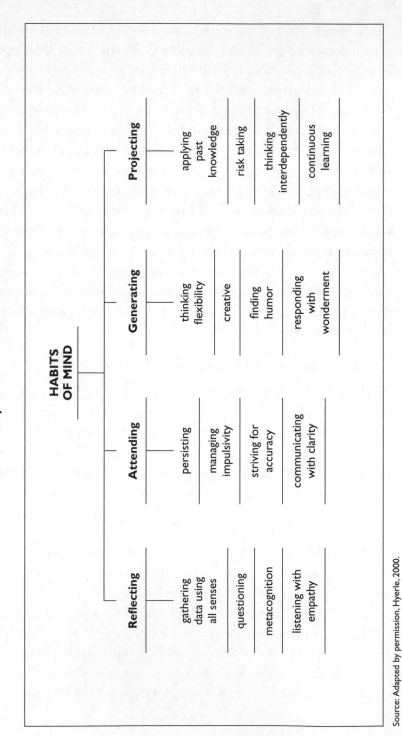

Source: Adapted by permission, Hyerle, 2000.

with the required follow-up coaching over a 12-month period. Teachers worked as a whole faculty and met in grade-level teams, attending workshops and receiving ongoing classroom support for focusing on both approaches. The eight Thinking Maps were posted in every classroom along with the vocabulary of the Habits of Mind to remind teachers and students to consciously apply and integrate the maps and habits in their daily work.

With this background of professional development in mind, imagine you are stepping into a classroom with Dr. Piercy and me some years ago, as we observed and videotaped a classroom of 1st graders who had recently finished reading the book *How Leo Learned to Be King*. (To view this video in edited form as you read, you may also go to www.thinking foundation.org.)

As the class began, the students were asked to respond to this question posed by their teacher, Ms. Smith: "How would you organize your thinking about this book?" Most high school students would have trouble with this question! But these young students had become fluent with Thinking Maps over the previous 18 months, so when Ms. Smith asked this question, they responded thoughtfully with ideas about which cognitive tool they would use to organize their thinking, how they would use the maps, and why. After a 30-minute small-group discussion, students were asked to return to their own desks, to choose the Thinking Map they thought would be most useful, and to begin mapping out their ideas. They then began transferring their thinking from the map into a paragraph of writing. As you look at Figure 9.5, you can see the initial ideas they offered, which Ms. Smith wrote on the whiteboard at the front of the class.

Here is a key: As you view the page of the partially created Thinking Maps and "hear" the language of the students as they generated both the maps and the classroom discourse that follows, consider that when students are suggesting a map to use, they have established a cognitive and metacognitive stance in relationship to the text. They are decoding the underlying cognitive patterns—or text structures—they see distributed across the linear progression of the story. You can hear *and* see the language of cognitive skills surfaced: *describing, comparing,* determining *cause.* Here is how the 1st graders organized their thinking about this book:

FIGURE 9.5

Students' Thinking Maps

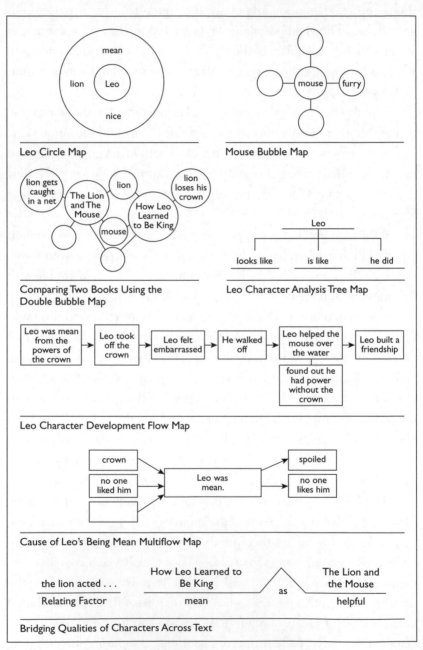

Leo Circle Map

Mouse Bubble Map

Comparing Two Books Using the
Double Bubble Map

Leo Character Analysis Tree Map

Leo Character Development Flow Map

Cause of Leo's Being Mean Multiflow Map

Bridging Qualities of Characters Across Text

Source: Reprinted by permission © 2004 Corwin.

Erin: You could use the circle map . . . put the topic in the middle and all ideas that you get in your mind from that topic, you write down in the circle . . . Leo . . . details about Leo . . . he was mean and he was nice.

Megan: A bubble map about a mouse. You say a word about what the mouse is, like furry . . . describing words.

Billy: We could do a double bubble. We could compare *How Leo Learned to Be King* and *The Lion and the Mouse* . . . they both have a lion and a mouse.

Mark: A tree map. I am thinking of . . . about Leo . . . what he looks like . . . and, um, I think, and what he is like . . . and what he did

Thomas: You could organize it with a bridge map. In *The Lion and the Mouse*, the lion was mean to the mouse, but in *How Leo Learned to Be King*, the lion was nice to the mouse by helping him get over the river.

Alexis: You could use a flow map. First he was mean. Then when they took off the crown he, like, got a little embarrassed. He walked away, he got surprised, because he met a mouse. And at the end he helped the mouse and *they became friendship*.

Regan: Multiflow . . . what caused him to be mean. The crown made . . . the crown could have caused him to be mean.

Erin: No one liked him. They took away . . . they didn't want him to be their king.

Shawn: We've got a lot of maps, don't we?

Teacher: That makes me think . . .

Shawn: . . . that we are like 2nd graders! [Laughter by all]

From the point of view of research on reading comprehension, here is an excerpt of our analysis of what we saw during this classroom observation:

[A] closer look shows that students have changed how they are understanding texts: They are surfacing dynamic patterns of content from the linear landscape, the wall of text. The range of structures bound within the line-by-line text becomes unveiled in the form of mental maps. They are changing the form, transforming text maps. (Piercy & Hyerle, 2004, p. 65)

Given this example of 1st graders' fluency with Thinking Maps, let's step back and consider how the Habits of Mind are intimately connected to fundamental cognitive skills and facilitated through the use of Thinking Maps.

Reflecting

Gathering data through all senses arises from a fundamental interplay between the "senses" of the body and of the mind trying to "make sense" of the data. As a Habit of Mind, openness to all sensory experiences is heightened by our capacities to organize and reflect on the range of senses. When students are offered a cognitive map and *specific language* as conscious filters for their primary sources of information (their senses), then their capacity for valuing information is enhanced and their descriptive language grows. In this classroom, when Megan says she could use a bubble map for describing the mouse as "furry," she is beginning to cluster together and reflect on the unique qualities she perceives as important. She is aware that the bubble map is defined by the cognitive process of *describing* qualities of things based on all the senses and that she and her classmates will attempt to use adjectives to describe the qualities. This tool helps learners *gather* perceptions in a map and then expand their attention by seeking a range of different types of descriptors using all of their senses. Within the Thinking Maps model, the definition of the cognitive skill of "describing" is clarified for students: descriptors are sensory, logical, or emotional (aesthetic). For example, describing the mouse as "white" would be a sensory description, "fat" would be a logical description (based more on measurement of what one considers "fatness"), and "beautiful" is an aesthetic or emotive description (based on the eye of the beholder).

Students learn to draw upon this fundamental definition embedded in the bubble map to describe sensory information across disciplines, such as *properties* in science, *attributes* in math, *character traits* in the study of literature, *societal/cultural traits* in the social sciences. Having a visual tool in hand to gather the sensory information supports students in *reflecting* on how they are seeing the interrelationships of different kinds of information from their senses—the sounds, tastes, smells, and textures as well as the visual information. Learners become aware that often this information is not "factual" just because they sense it, but that their sensory perceptions are framed by the context of the investigation and their own prior knowledge.

When Megan suggested using the bubble map, she, like all the other students, was asking a question of herself and her peers: How could we each describe this mouse? Each of the eight Thinking Maps, respectively, is thus a reflective question connected to a thinking skill and opens wide the doors to the maps of a child's mind. By giving students these tools, the essential questions that teachers ask students on a day-to-day basis in classrooms become *student* centered, based on well-defined cognitive skills as patterns:

Map and Thinking Skill	Essential Question
1. Circle map for defining	How am I defining this idea in context?
2. Bubble map for describing	How am I describing this thing?
3. Double bubble map for comparing	How are these alike and different?
4. Tree map for categorizing	How do I group these things together?
5. Brace map for part/whole	How do the physical parts fit together to form a whole object?
6. Flow map for sequencing	How do I see this sequence of events?
7. Multiflow map for cause-effect reasoning	How did these causes lead to this event and what were the effects?
8. Bridge map for analogies	How do these ideas transfer to other ideas?

Early in the process of learning Thinking Maps, teachers and students become aware that these essential questions and combinations of questions are foundations for learning content-specific knowledge and building academic vocabulary. Students become aware that the questions that they ask of themselves, or that are asked of them at the end of chapters in textbooks and on tests, often require multiple steps of thinking. The language of Thinking Maps then becomes a framework for decoding the cognitive processes embedded in text or in a given task, giving students an independent way of organizing, interpreting, reflecting upon, and generating their own problem-posing questions about learning.

As students move from novice to expert use of Thinking Maps, a metacognitive stance develops from gathering data from their senses and questioning how they are perceiving and mapping the information. The Thinking Maps thus offer a space for "displayed *metacognition*" as each fundamental cognitive skill is surfaced visually by the learners in order to see their own representation of a pattern of information. As students *see* how they are thinking in maps, what is immediately apparent is the spatial edge of their knowledge base (comparable to what we do when we look at a road map that shows only a part of a city). They also see the open mental spaces within the configuration of the maps and may think about their thinking: What is it that I don't know?

As shown in the example of 1st graders thinking about Leo the lion, students already have basic definitions for cognition, from which they can develop deeper metacognitive responses. In most classrooms, from kindergarten to college, few students could actually name and define their fundamental human cognitive skills, and far fewer would know how to activate these skills and transfer them across disciplines. A question that is apparent from the discussion in the first part of this chapter is this: When *cognitive* skills are not clearly identified and developed over multiple years, how can we expect students to become *meta*cognitive?

Memory plays a central role in cognition *and* reflection. Because the brain can hold only limited information in short-term memory, Thinking Maps offer an external place to hold information while simultaneously enabling learners to internally reflect on the holistic patterns of their thinking in real time. They don't have to "think back" and remember in their mind, but only look down at a representation of the thinking they created from a blank page. As 1st grade students, Billy has the ability to re-*view* and "re-*vision*" his double bubble map comparison of two books (text-to-text analysis), while Regan can view her thinking of the multiple causes and effects for Leo becoming a "mean" leader. They both can then go back to reference the text for more information and clarification. Both children can also view how much information they have mapped, expand and reconfigure the maps, reflect on the validity of their claims, and spatially *see* what they don't know.

Within the Thinking Maps language, the capacity to reflect on our thinking using our senses, questioning, and metacognitive behaviors is at one level supported through the eight interrelated tools. There is an additional metalevel to the language that comes out of the field of frame semantics (Lakoff & Johnson, 1980) and is defined by the common phrase from the field of critical thinking: *frame of reference*. Although not shown in the 1st grade example, a central dimension of the Thinking Maps language is the use of a rectangular frame that is hand drawn by students around any one of the maps. The metacognitive frame is used by stepping back from the map or maps being created and asking these reflective questions: What is influencing how you are thinking? What experiences and beliefs are influencing how you are seeing this information? Where are your sources? How are you approaching this problem? If this is what you know, what is unknown to you? The metacognitive frame is an essential tool for use in the areas of interpretation of texts, current events, cultural awareness, conflict resolution, and for any topic that surfaces multiple perspectives.

For example, when Regan was analyzing the causes and effects for Leo being "mean," the teacher could have added a rectangular frame around the multiflow map and asked Regan and the other children, "When in your life have you felt like you were acting mean? What caused you to be mean?" The students could then have used this frame of reference to connect themselves to the literary character for deeper, personal, more meaningful interpretation of the text.

Ultimately, Thinking Maps provide a language for collaborative cognition and deeper listening to oneself and others. The cliché "I see what you mean" gets expanded to include *how* others are seeing *what* they mean. The visual representation on the page or whiteboard becomes the mental work space between students and teachers so that one may listen and then see the holism of another person's thinking.

The capacity to listen to, to visualize, and to reflect on one's own thinking—metacognition—is deeply related to the lifelong behavior of being able to listen with empathy to others. Listening to oneself may be even more difficult for some than listening closely to the ideas of others. The maps, along with the metacognitive frame, engage deeper discourse and listening in learners of all ages, for often is it very difficult to follow the auditory sequence of ideas and much easier to "see" the holism of meanings as they are drawn out from a blank page. Seeing the evolving Thinking Maps developed by others through a common language engages a quality of reflectiveness, as one begins to see the collaborative overlapping patterns of thinking beyond the mind's eye.

Attending

A second cluster of Habits of Mind that seem closely related are in the area of "attending" over time to tasks that require patience and often analytic, detailed thinking. If students do not develop the internal capacity to stay with a problem, an assignment, or a project that may extend over minutes, hours, days, and weeks, they will be seduced by the instant gratification offered by a visual media–saturated world that often honors the immediacy of quick sound bites and visual bits over close attention to quality thinking.

As students like the 1st graders in the example develop a novice-level use of Thinking Maps, they each have eight distinct pathways for getting started in *posing questions* and *persisting* toward a solution to a problem. The students could initially decide on a single pattern for thinking about the story and then map out alternative options for pursuing the interpretation of the text. As mentioned earlier, what is not revealed in the snippets of classroom interaction is that, after her students had created the maps, Ms. Smith then asked them to return to their desks and independently choose one or several of the maps to use. They individually mapped out their thinking and then began to write a paragraph about the story. The maps then became the movable mental workspace for shifting from classroom discussion, to prewriting, to a final product.

The complete 60-minute videotape of classroom work shows many students raising their stretched hands to get the attention of the teacher, jumping with answers to offer, but not with what Benjamin Bloom called "one shot," impulsive thinking. They knew they were responding not with one answer that was either right or wrong, but with an expectation that they would offer their ideas within a broader map and pattern of thoughts. In this way, Thinking Maps have a built-in "wait time" (Rowe, 1974) that establishes in classrooms a way of managing the impulsivity not only of the students but of teachers as well. It is evident on the videotape that Ms. Smith seemed ready to move on at times, but the maps offered an efficient and effective process for moving to final reflections without prematurely moving to the writing process. With alternative maps always available, with strategic use of multiple maps, and with the reflection time built into the process of constructing the maps by hand on paper, whiteboard, or computer, classroom participants are able to see beyond the blurted answer and have a visual record they can use for reflecting on their systematic processes.

Developing the habits of *persisting* and *managing impulsivity* created an environment in which a deeper level of analytical thinking was required of students in this classroom. The student examples shown are only the starting point for accurately pulling more information from the text, organizing the ideas in meaningful patterns, and then being able to *communicate the ideas with clarity and precision*. Each Thinking Map begins with a graphic primitive, such as the flow map that Alexis offered for sequencing the plot of the story. She detailed the sequence of the story by starting with one box and an arrow and extending to six boxes: from Leo becoming mean after becoming king to ultimately "becoming friendship" with the mouse. Alexis is showing a capacity to accurately display the events of the story, which is easily checked against the text by Alexis herself, her peers, and the teacher.

By the time students had returned to their desks and mapped out their thinking for a piece of writing, they had expanded and clarified their thinking. When we take into account short-term memory capacity, having a visual record along with a verbal explanation gives students and teachers a way of adding more information in a structured way. The visual form allows for clarity of expression because students can clearly see the reasoning that they are doing and present this to classmates and their teacher as a clear view of how they have put information together.

The example used to this point has been with literature at a 1st grade level. This can be compared with a 40-page Thinking Maps document created by a high school student from the Chicago area. All the teachers and students at Niles North High School had been trained in Thinking Maps and Thinking Maps software, so this student used the Thinking Maps software for mapping out a whole biology text, chapter to chapter. For each chapter she decided which map or maps best reflected the key concepts and information of the text. With accuracy and great clarity, for example, she showed types of cells using a tree map, a detailed causal feedback system in the blood cycle using a flow map, and dozens of intricately interrelated parts of a muscle using a brace map. What the 1st grade students were doing with Leo the lion for the interpretation of literature was mirrored by this student at an advanced, precollege level of sophistication. In both examples, the precision of language and the clarity of the thinking are apparent, demonstrating that the maps enable students at any level to attend to long-term tasks requiring *persistence, managed impulsivity*, and most of all, *accuracy*.

Generating

One of the common theoretical and practical dimensions of the Habits of Mind and the Thinking Maps models is that both rely on the *interdependency* of, respectively, 16 dispositions and 8 cognitive skills. This is evident when we see how the analytical behaviors of *persisting, managing impulsivity, striving for accuracy*, and *thinking and communicating with precision and clarity* need to be in balanced development with more generative dispositions such as *flexibility, creativity*, and *finding humor and wonderment* in the approach to problems. Both models directly honor and support the interdependence of analytical and creative thinking, rather than seeing them as dichotomous.

The Habits of Mind concerned with analytic accuracy and precision are intimately connected to learners' abilities to be flexible and creatively generate ideas. Costa and Kallick (2004) state that "flexible people are the ones with the most control" (p. 22), because they are able to shift their thinking and retain key information without losing their focus. Looking back at the 1st grade maps, ask yourself: "Is this creative or analytical thinking?" It is both, I suggest, because students are expanding rich patterns of ideas in multiple, linear, and nonlinear ways across the page. There is an inherent structure in the language of Thinking Maps that is generative, enabling students to always start with a blank sheet of paper and draw out their thinking. Students do not need preformed templates, as is the case with so many graphic organizers. One of the barriers to thinking found in most graphic organizers is that students may be given templates and be required to stay inside the boxes, thus limiting their capacities to be flexible and creative.

Several of the Thinking Maps, such as the circle map, are often perceived as directly supporting creative, imaginative thinking. First-grader Erin understands the map and its purpose when she says that she could use a circle map for Leo by putting "the topic in the middle and all ideas that you get in your mind from that topic, you write in the circle." Often we ask students to draw the "frame" around the circle map so that they begin the metacognitive process of linking the creation of ideas to their own experiences and prior knowledge. This challenges students to think about what in their frame of reference may be constraining a more flexible, creative approach to a topic or a problem, which often causes a deeper, expansive ripple effect of flexible thinking. By placing the concentric circles in a frame, students are actually mirroring an ancient visual tool of the East, called a *mandala*, used for reflecting on one's daily life surrounded by deities symbolically representing different ways of being in the world. Carl Jung used this mandala form regularly as he creatively reflected on his own shifts of mind and heart each morning. He also used mandalas with his patients to help them open their mind while centering their thinking and feelings.

In a more subtle way, Thinking Maps also support open, flexible thinking as a pathway to humor and wonderment. I once opened a fortune cookie after a Chinese meal to read this saying: "Life is a tragedy for those who feel, a comedy for those who think." Although we want empathic learners, we also want creative problem solvers living at the edge of their knowledge and finding the discrepancies when they reflect on the state of the world with its ambiguities, contradictions, and absurdities. At the end of the 1st grade classroom conversation, everyone shared in the laughter when Shawn verbally cut off his teacher. Shawn said, "We've got a lot of maps, don't we?" and the teacher began to respond by saying, "That makes me think—"; then Shawn cut her off, saying, "That we are like 2nd graders!" We all laughed, I believe, because Shawn could see that he and his classmates had gone beyond themselves: he could *see* the class as highly productive thinkers, and he responded with awe and with an obvious enjoyment of learning.

Great comedians usually have a personal, social, or political critique or a unique perspective on the world that shows the incongruity of self-evident truths drawn from the foibles of being human. The teachers I remember are those who could surface absurdities, generate meaningful humor out of the context of classroom content teaching, and engage students in a playful discourse filled with dry humor. Sometimes we can unveil a certain idea that opens a student's mind to perceiving the world in a different way. Once, with a high school class in California, I engaged the students in seeking out the central metaphors in their own writing through the use of a multilevel bridge map that I called a "World Map" for generating metaphorical understandings in common language (Hyerle, 1996). This led one student to walk up to me afterward and state in an awestruck manner, "I never understood that language works like this." The awe and wonderment was about this student understanding the analogical bridge between thought and language that can be mapped out and seen.

Projecting

Shawn was projecting himself beyond the moment, seeing himself not just as a 1st grader, but as a 2nd grader and a continuous learner. This ability to project beyond the moment may be the catalyst for animating the Habits of Mind. If a student does not hold a vision of being a continuous learner, then even the idea of developing the Habits of Mind may seem irrelevant. The students in this classroom showed that they could project themselves as confident learners by applying past knowledge to this new text, taking risks with their thinking as they mapped it out, and working interdependently as a group to discover different ways of working with the text.

We can only learn in the moment from the accumulated past information and knowledge that reside within the schemas and frames we hold in our memory. The Piagetian concepts of accommodation and assimilation rely on an understanding that we each have life experiences saved as rich, deep schemata in the recesses of the brain that are animated and transformed by the mind. Students' abilities to apply past knowledge are dependent upon them holding onto the ideas in long-term memory in a way that can be called up to consciousness in order to be applied to present learning. Because students are often asked to conceptualize and remember ideas in a linear form (auditory, written, and numeric), their knowledge may not be deeply connected, and thus neural networks are holding onto information through mindless rote and repetition. Students end up playing the game of school: they memorize information for the Friday test, and it is then lost.

Thinking Maps help to transform information into knowledge that then supports students in applying new information and knowledge in novel situations. The double bubble map and the bridge map were both used by these students to, respectively, compare a book they had read in the past to the present book, and to create an analogical bridge between how different characters acted in the two books. Looking closer at this situation we can see that the 1st grade students have a rudimentary use of Thinking Maps; but with each year of using these tools, they will begin to fluidly and dynamically transfer these cognitive skills and maps into novel situations, remembering different ways of applying isolated maps and also remembering how they used different combinations of the maps to understand a text.

The foundation of knowledge and the fundamental language for learning that students gain through Thinking Maps also offer a platform for risk taking. Because they know that they have eight pathways for patterning their ideas, students gain support in moving beyond their existing experiences and knowledge to discover new territories of content knowledge and thinking. One of the greatest barriers to risk taking is the expectation for "right" answers, inside and outside classrooms. So many students, and teachers, are driven to find the one right answer; yet even if there is one "right" answer in a given task, it is still found within a pattern of information. Openness to thinking as risk taking does not mean that students play out on the edge of their ideas without an understanding of taking responsible risks. The Thinking Maps models offer both dynamism and structure, enabling students to risk playing out their ideas about, for example, *How Leo Learned to Be King*, while also acknowledging that there are useful structures through which they can take risks.

This dynamism and this visual structure of the language make these tools public in form, thus facilitating group interdependence. Once individual students learn to use the maps, cooperative learning is elevated to a new level because groups now have a way to see thinking, communicate evolving thoughts, and synthesize ideas into new maps that facilitate the integration of ideas into conceptual understandings. It is quite evident in this example that these 1st grade students have a common language that they use with confidence and fluency and for clarity of communication. So often in collaborative groups there is a dominant voice or a strongly stated belief that can hold sway over other people. We have found that Thinking Maps give all learners silent visual pathways for showing classmates and teachers their thinking even if they cannot or do not share their ideas verbally.

In this example, students moved from a classroom discussion to individual work with the text. Often teachers will use the technique of think, pair, share (McTighe & Lyman, 2001) with Thinking Maps: individual students show their thinking by using one or multiple maps, pair up with a peer to talk through their ideas, and then share their maps within the structure of a cooperative group. In the cooperative group, they can effectively and often efficiently rethink, reorganize, and synthesize the individual Thinking Maps into a rich complex of new ideas. The maps created in the cooperative group may then be shared with the whole class by posting them on the wall for a gallery walk, sending them around the room in carousel fashion, or presenting them via a media presentation (using Thinking Maps software or simply on an overhead projector).

The students have a common language for thinking and communicating, but so do the teachers as members of a faculty and of larger learning communities. The use of Thinking Maps as a language for lifelong learning is instilled when all are involved. The interdependent nature of the tools enables participants from across learning communities—classrooms, grade levels, whole schools, feeder patterns, and whole districts—to think interdependently and to use a common language for learning and leadership. Over the past five years, our work with Thinking Maps has shifted from the primary focus on improving instruction and learning, to leadership and learning applications across whole schools. The maps are now used to support grade-level teams in curriculum planning and alignment, school leadership teams in decision making, whole-school faculties in effective and efficient meeting facilitation, and for mentoring and coaching (Alper & Hyerle, 2006). The use of Thinking Maps by students, teachers, and administrators across classrooms and whole schools clearly represents to students that this language for thinking is for lifelong learning.

Endnote

Near the end of a two-day leadership seminar through which leadership teams from different schools and school districts learned how to use Thinking Maps for problem posing, problem solving, and decision making, a superintendent and her team presented their work using several Thinking Maps to study the problem of the high school dropout rate in their region. The team showed how they used a circle map for defining the problem in context, and the frame for creatively generating ideas and for reflecting on the stakeholders who were influencing their thinking. This thinking drew them toward the use of a multiflow map for identifying the interdependent short- and long-term causes and effects of high school students dropping out of the learning process. They then transformed information from the two maps into a tree map for analytically organizing the ideas and inductively developing possible solutions. They used several other maps, but ended up using a flow map for detailing a multifaceted plan for dropout prevention.

Of course, this collaborative group was quite happy about the thinking they had developed together and how, during their presentation, the rest of the participants could see their ideas through a common visual language. After the presentations by the entire team, the facilitators of the seminar showed the videotape of the 1st grade students, showing how they used Thinking Maps to think about and interpret *How Leo Learned to Be King*. It was in that moment that these lifelong educators deeply understood how a simple language for generating eight cognitive patterns could be used to develop ideas and also to join closely together as a group of thinkers. Both groups—an adult team of educators and a classroom of 1st graders—were questioning and reflective, persistent and accurate, flexible and creative, and working interdependently as leaders and learners within an unbroken flow of continuous learning.

References

Alper, L., & Hyerle, D. (2006). *Thinking maps: Leading with a new language.* Raleigh, NC: Innovatative Sciences.

Bloom, B. S. (Ed.). (1956). *Taxonomy of educational objectives. Handbook I: Cognitive domain.* New York: McKay.

Buzan, T. (1994). *Use both sides of your brain.* London: Dutton.

Costa, A. (1991). Foreword. In J. Clark, *Patterns of thinking.* New York: Allyn & Bacon.

Costa, A., & Kallick, B. (2004). *Assessment strategies for self-directed learning.* Thousand Oaks, CA: Corwin.

Darling-Hammond, L. (1997). *The right to learn.* San Francisco, CA: Jossey-Bass.

Hyerle, D. (1996). *Visual tools for constructing knowledge.* Alexandria, VA: ASCD.

Hyerle, D. (2000). *A field guide to using visual tools.* Alexandria, VA: ASCD.

Hyerle, D. (Ed.). (2004). *Student successes with Thinking Maps®.* Thousand Oaks, CA: Corwin.

Lakoff, G., & Johnson, M. (1980). *Metaphors we live by.* Chicago: University of Chicago Press.

McTighe, J., & Lyman, F. T., Jr. (2001). Cueing thinking in the classroom: The promise of theory-embedded tools. In A. Costa (Ed.), *Developing minds: A resource book for teaching thinking* (pp. 384–392). Alexandria, VA: ASCD.

Novak, J., & Gowin, R. (1984). *Learning how to learn.* New York: Cambridge University Press.

Piercy, T. D., & Hyerle, D. (2004). Maps for the road to reading comprehension: Bridging reading text structures to writing prompts. In D. Hyerle (Ed.), *Student successes with Thinking Maps®* (pp. 63–74). Thousand Oaks, CA: Corwin.

Rowe, M. (1974). Wait time and rewards as instructional variables: Their influence on language, logic and fate control. *Journal of Research in Science Teaching, 11,* 81–94.

Thinking Maps®: Technology for learning [Software]. (1998; 2007). Cary, NC: Thinking Maps.

Part III

Assessing and Reporting
on Habits of Mind

*A goal of education is to assist growth toward greater complexity
and integration and to assist in the process of self-organization—
to modify individuals' capacity to modify themselves.*

—Reuven Feuerstein

So, how might we know students are getting better at the Habits of Mind? Part III, Assessing and Reporting on Habits of Mind, provides a framework as well as many strategies for collecting evidence of students' increasing capacities and propensities for the Habits of Mind. The most important persons collecting and reflecting on that evidence are the students themselves. One of the great powers of the Habits of Mind is that they provide many opportunities for students to set goals for themselves, to monitor their own performance, to reflect, to self-evaluate, and to self-modify.

In Chapter 10 we describe indicators of growth in each of the Habits of Mind. Teachers need to be alert, observing how students perform over time as they confront problems and tackle challenging, discrepant events. Teachers need to listen closely to students' comments and collect anecdotes as a record of students' deepening and broadening of their understanding of the Habits of Mind, leading to eventual internalization of the habits. Our goal is to see students use the habits as an internal compass to guide decisions, thoughts, and actions.

Chapter 11 provides a wide range of assessment strategies and techniques. We suggest that students help to develop these assessment tools and the description of criteria for improving performance. Not surprisingly, students learn more when they are involved in constructing and conducting their own assessments.

It is often said that one learns through experience. We think otherwise. We believe that people learn by *reflecting* on their experiences. Chapter 12 provides a range of strategies, prompts, and examples of ways teachers can invite students not only to be reflective, but also to learn to value reflection. In our busy, stress-filled lives, taking the time to reflect is often a rarity. We believe that learning is enhanced with "mindfulness." This means reflection *for* action, reflection *in* action, and reflection *on* action.

In Chapter 13, Steve Seidel presents a powerful integration of the use of the Habits of Mind as teachers study student work. In addition to using a specific protocol to facilitate the careful study of student work, he guides the conversation with such habits as questioning and posing problems and responding with wonderment and awe. He describes a carefully facilitated environment in which teachers learn to trust one another and, especially, to trust their "wondering."

Chapter 14 focuses on communicating to others about students' maturity from initial awareness toward their increasing skillfulness in, propensity for, valuing of, and adoption of the Habits of Mind. Parents and the community, other teachers, and students themselves become the "audience" for acknowledging and celebrating milestones in their journey.

—*Arthur L. Costa and Bena Kallick*

10

Defining Indicators
of Achievement

Arthur L. Costa and Bena Kallick

> How much do students really love to learn, to persist, to passion-
> ately attack a problem or a task? . . . to watch some of their prized
> ideas explode and to start anew? . . . to go beyond being merely
> dutiful or long-winded? Let us assess such things.
>
> —*Grant Wiggins*

We are more likely to observe indicators of achievement if we first take the
time to specifically describe the kinds of evidence that would confirm that
students are acquiring the Habits of Mind. What would we see them
doing? What would we hear them saying? How would they be feeling?
This chapter contains general descriptions of indicators that show students are acquiring, applying, and internalizing the Habits of Mind. We
provide some samples of observable indicators for some of the habits.
Because these indicators will vary according to students' abilities, grade
levels, subject matter, culture, and developmental levels, we encourage
you, along with your colleagues, to round out the list by generating additional indicators for your students in your own school and community.

The Habits of Mind truly take on meaning when they are defined in
the context of day-to-day classroom life. Thus, teachers will want to consider indicators for themselves first, then expand their consideration to

include students, colleagues, parents, and perhaps even other community members. The habits should be described in terms of the content being taught, and they should be explained within the context of a particular classroom's characteristics. Although the habits need to be considered within these parameters, we suggest using the general indicators presented in the following sections as starting points to decide what to look for when using the feedback and assessment strategies described in Chapter 11.

Persisting

> Be like a postage stamp: Stick to one thing until you get there.
>
> —*Margaret Carty*

Persistent students have systematic methods for analyzing a problem. They know how to begin, what steps must be performed, and what data need to be generated and collected. They also know when they must reject their theory or idea so they can try another.

Students demonstrate growth in persistence when they increase their use of alternative problem-solving strategies. We see them collect evidence to indicate that a problem-solving strategy is working. If the strategy isn't working, they back up and try another (see Figure 5.1).

Students who have developed this Habit of Mind know how to draw upon a variety of resources. They ask others to clarify and to provide data. They consult books, dictionaries, databases, and online resources. Sometimes they go back to clarify a task or to analyze the directions.

Students who persist draw on previous experiences and apply that knowledge to solve the current problem. Thus, these students also demonstrate another Habit of Mind often linked to persistence: applying past knowledge to new situations. Many teachers find that several Habits of Mind naturally cluster together like this. As you consider indicators for a particular habit, you may also want to consider other habits linked to it.

Notice how the indicators that we have described here might fit into a checklist such as this:

- Demonstrates systematic methods of analyzing problems.
- Distinguishes between ideas that work and those that do not.

- Considers many alternatives when solving a problem.
- Continuously clarifies the task while monitoring performance.

We have provided this example—and one for the next habit, managing impulsivity—to demonstrate how to turn these indicators into checklists. You and other members of your staff or team may want to continue to develop such checklists for your assessment practices for the other Habits of Mind. (For more on checklists, see also p. 199 in Chapter 11.)

Managing Impulsivity

It is easier to suppress the first desire than to satisfy all that follow it.

Benjamin Franklin

As students become less impulsive, we observe them clarifying goals, planning a strategy for solving a problem, exploring alternative problem-solving strategies, and debating consequences of their actions before they begin. They consider before erasing, and they pay attention to the results of their trial-and-error efforts so they avoid making haphazard responses.

When students have developed the habit of managing impulsivity, they are engaged with problem solving, and they pay close attention to what is occurring during a lesson or other classroom activity. They note what works as they solve a problem, and they redirect their strategies by developing a plan. They learn how to use wait time to their advantage. They also develop strategies for participating in activities, such as jotting down notes in a discussion so that they can remember the points they want to make when it's their turn to speak.

As a checklist, the indicators might appear like this:

- Uses wait time as an opportunity to think through a problem.
- Attends to results of trial-and-error efforts to determine a course of action.
- Pays attention to what is working.
- Uses strategies for self-management such as note taking.

Listening with Understanding and Empathy

> If there is any secret of success, it lies in the ability to get the other person's point of view and see things from his angle as well as from your own.
>
> —*Henry Ford*

We know students are improving their listening skills when they set aside their own value judgments, prejudices, and autobiographical stories to devote their mental energies to attending to another person. They demonstrate their understanding and empathy for another person's idea by paraphrasing it accurately, building upon it, clarifying it, or giving an example of it. We know students are listening to and internalizing others' ideas and feelings when we hear them say statements like these:

- "Peter's idea is . . . , but Sarah's idea is . . . ."
- "Let's try Shelley's idea and see if it works."
- "Let me show you how Elena solved the problem, and then I'll show you how I solved it."

After paraphrasing another person's idea, a student may probe, clarify, or pose questions that extend the idea further: "I'm not sure I understand. Can you explain what you mean by . . . ?" Empathy may be demonstrated by taking another's view or perspective: "I can see why Danielle views it that way. If I were her, I'd want the same thing." Empathy for another person's feelings or emotions is also demonstrated when the student labels those emotions or feelings:

- "You're *upset* because . . . ."
- "You're *confused* about . . . ."
- "You sure were *happy* about . . . ."

Thinking Flexibly

> When one door is shut, another one opens.
>
> —*Miguel de Cervantes*

As students become more flexible in their thinking, they move from an ego-centered view to an allocentric view—they are able to see things from others' perspectives. We hear them considering, expressing, or paraphrasing other people's points of view or rationales. They state several ways of solving the same problem, and they evaluate the merits and consequences of two or more alternate courses of action. When making decisions, they often use words and phrases such as "however," "on the other hand," "if you look at it another way," or "John's idea is . . . , but Mary's idea is . . . ."

Students who have developed this Habit of Mind become systems thinkers. They analyze and scrutinize parts, but they also shift their perspective to the big picture, noting broader relationships, patterns, and interactions.

Students who are flexible thinkers generate many ideas. During a brainstorming session, their participation is usually fluent and productive. They are reluctant to see closure to group work. We hear them say, "Let's think of more ideas before we decide which one we want to use!"

Thinking About Thinking (Metacognition)

I thank the Lord for the brain He put in my head. Occasionally, I love to just stand to one side and watch how it works.

—*Richard Bolles*

We can determine if students are becoming more aware of their own thinking when we give them the opportunity to describe what goes on in their heads as they think. Students who have succeeded with this habit can list the steps for how they will solve a problem, and they can tell you where they are in the sequence of those steps. They trace the pathways and blind alleys they took on the road to a problem's solution. They describe what data are lacking, and they also describe their plans for producing the missing data.

Students who have developed this habit are articulate about their reasoning processes. When asked to explain their answer to a problem, they give the solution and then describe the reasoning process that brought them to their conclusion. They also use proper cognitive terminology to describe their mental processes:

- "I have a *theory* that . . . ."
- "I'm *conducting an experiment*."
- "The *sequence of steps* in my *strategy* was first to . . . , and then I . . . ."

Students who are skillful in their ability to think about their own thinking

- Are aware of the kind of thinking they are engaged in.
- Can describe how they engaged in this type of thinking.
- Evaluate whether the way they engaged in the thinking approach was effective.
- Plan how they will engage in the same type of thinking the next time it is needed (Swartz, Costa, Beyer, Kallick, & Reagan, 2007).

Striving for Accuracy

Measure a thousand times and cut once.

—*Turkish proverb*

As students mature in this Habit of Mind, we observe them taking greater care with their work. They check their projects, assignments, and tests again and again, asking others ("critical friends") for feedback and correction. They establish standards of excellence, and they attempt to meet—and even exceed—those standards.

These students set higher and higher standards as they attempt to excel beyond a previous record. They express dissatisfaction with incomplete or sloppy work, and they request opportunities to improve upon their work. They also demonstrate a lack of complacency with the status quo.

Questioning and Posing Problems

Quality questions create a quality life. Successful people ask better questions, and as a result, they get better answers.

—*Anthony Robbins*

Over time, we want to observe a shift from the teacher asking questions and posing problems toward the students asking questions and finding problems for themselves. Students become more alert in recognizing discrepancies and phenomena in their environment and more inclined to inquire into their causes. They demonstrate increased skillfulness in approaching problems strategically, with greater interest and challenge. They enjoy and seek opportunities for learning from solving problems (Barell, 2003).

Children pose questions naturally. They ask questions out of curiosity, intrigue, or interest. Yet with appropriate instruction—and time for reflection—children begin to ask questions more strategically. Trial lawyers use interrogation strategies with witnesses to build their cases. Scientists pose a series of questions to gather data to prove or disprove a theory. So, too, students begin to formulate questioning strategies and to link a sequence of questions to test hypotheses, guide data searches, clarify outcomes, or illuminate fallacious reasoning.

Maneuvering through the complexities of a task requires a conceptual framework from which questions can be formulated. Thus, strategic questioning implies that students hold a mental map in their head. For example, planning a trip requires questions about schedules, time lines, alternative destinations, arrivals, departures, and locations. Planning a science experiment requires similar kinds of questions about the task at hand: needed tools and supplies, possible strategies, the order of steps in the experiment, and evidence that the experiment has reached its conclusion.

Students' questions gain greater flair, power, and complexity with time and practice. They expand their range and repertoire of question types. They know how to design questions to gather data; make inferences; guide experimentation; and create, apply, and draw conclusions (see the section in Chapter 8 on developing students' skillfulness in questioning). Eventually, they can explain the function of a question and, when asked to explain their work, state the reason that they are asking a particular question.

Students soon see how the significance and power of good questioning can lead them to better understanding. Their class participation shows evidence of questions about the authority of a work, an author's point of view, the possible need for more data, or a provocative part to be examined. Their questions also stimulate others' thinking, raising even more classroom questions.

Applying Past Knowledge to New Situations

Learning is the ability to make sense out of something you observe based on your past experience and being able to take that observation and associate it with meaning.

—Ruth and Art Winter

Students who have developed this Habit of Mind can abstract meaning from one experience and apply it to a new one. We know students are growing in this ability when we hear them make statements like "This reminds me of . . ." or "This is just like the time when we . . . !" We also see evidence of this ability when students explain what they are doing now with analogies about or references to previous experiences. We see them call upon their store of knowledge and experience to support theories that explain a situation or to outline a process to solve a new challenge.

We definitely know students are transferring their knowledge to new situations when parents and other teachers report how a student's thinking has changed at home or in other classes. For example, parents may report increased interest in school. They may see their child better plan the use of time and money. Or they may report increased organization of the child's room, books, and desk at home. At school, a social studies or an industrial arts teacher may describe how a student used a problem-solving strategy that originally was learned in science or math class.

Thinking and Communicating with Clarity and Precision

A word to the wise is not sufficient if it doesn't make sense.

—James Thurber

As students acquire more exact language for describing their work, they begin to recognize concepts, identify key attributes, distinguish similarities and differences, and make more thorough and rational decisions. If value judgments are made, students spontaneously offer the criteria on which the judgments were based. When comparing, they describe the attributes and significance of their comparisons. They state the reasons behind their generalizations, and they voluntarily provide data to support their conclusions.

Students who have developed this habit use the correct names for objects, ideas, and processes. When universal labels are unavailable, they use analogies such as "That's crescent shaped" or "It's like a bow tie." They speak in complete sentences, voluntarily provide supporting evidence for their ideas, elaborate, clarify, and define their terminology. Overall, their speech becomes more concise, descriptive, and coherent.

Gathering Data Through All Senses

It is not easy to describe the sea without the mouth.

—*Kokyu*

Students who have developed this habit feel free to engage and explore all their senses. When they are confronted with a problem, they suggest strategies for gathering data or for solving the problem that incorporate a variety of senses: visualizing, building a model, feeling textures, acting out or dancing to a poem or a work of prose, listening to and visualizing recurring cycles and patterns, or moving to the rhythms. They seek ways to engage all the senses, wanting to hold, touch, feel, taste, smell, and experience objects and events.

These students' enriched written and oral language displays an ever-increasing range of sensory metaphors: kinesthetic, auditory, visual, gustatory, and olfactory. They experiment with vivid, sensuous, and evocative descriptions and alliterations, describing "a waterfall of problems," "atonal music slapping my ears," or "gardenias: the gods' belief in aromatherapy."

Creating, Imagining, Innovating

Originality is simply a pair of fresh eyes.

—*Thomas Wentworth Higginson*

We know students are creating, imagining, and innovating when we see them deliberately and voluntarily use strategies for stimulating, generating, and releasing inventive ideas for a new task. They expand the possibility of creative insight by preparing their minds with much knowledge about a subject. Then, they generate options and possibilities.

When students who have developed this habit face an impasse, they deliberately widen the scope of their search with techniques such as brainstorming, mind mapping, synectics, or metaphorical thinking. They search for theories, explanations, and frameworks that have generative potentials, that lead to further meanings. They pursue promising theories, and they constantly hunt for nubs and kernels of viable ideas. They explore options, think of possibilities, generate strategies, and explore consequences (Perkins, 1995).

Responding with Wonderment and Awe

> The real mark of the creative person is that the unforeseen problem is a joy and not a curse.
>
> —*Norman H. Mackworth*

Students who respond with wonderment and awe display an attitude that says "I can" and "I enjoy." These students seek out problems to solve for themselves and to submit to others. They make up problems to solve on their own, and they request them from others. These students solve problems with increasing independence, without the teacher's help or intervention. We hear their growing autonomy in statements such as "Don't tell me the answer! I can figure it out by myself!"

Students who have developed this habit are curious, and they derive pleasure from thinking. Their environment attracts their inquiry as their senses capture the rhythm, patterns, shapes, colors, and harmonies around them. They will stand transfixed by the beauty of a sunset, study with fascination the geometrics of a spider web, or be charmed by the opening of a spring bud. They can't help but exclaim their exuberance: "Wow!" "Cool!" "Awesome!" "All right!"

Students who have developed this habit also display compassionate behavior toward other life forms. These students understand the need to protect the environment. They respect the roles and values of other human beings, and they perceive the delicate worth, uniqueness, and relationships of everything and everyone they encounter.

Taking Responsible Risks

> There are risks and costs to action. But they are far less than the long-range risks of comfortable inaction.
>
> —*John F. Kennedy*

Although students learn to manage their impulsivity, at the same time they also begin to show evidence of taking more risks in their work. Maybe they write dialogue for the first time in their stories. Perhaps they use humor to make a particular point, or they throw out an idea in a discussion without qualifying it by saying, "I might be wrong about this . . . " or "I know this may not be what is called for, but . . . ."

Students who are practicing responsible risk taking show a willingness to try out new strategies, techniques, and ideas. They explore new art media, wanting to experiment with different effects. They are willing to test a new hypothesis, even when they feel skeptical. In a group, they often can be heard saying things like "Let's try it!" or "What's the worst thing that can happen if we try? We'll only learn from it!"

Finding Humor

I'd rather be a failure at something I enjoy than be a success at something I hate.

—George Burns

As students develop this habit, they learn to distinguish between clowning around and using humor to increase their own or a group's productivity. They learn not to take themselves too seriously. They joke about errors they have made, poke fun at themselves, and seek the humor and absurdity in situations that seem to warrant it.

Students who have developed this habit are often observed using humor to relieve a group's tension. They know the difference between using humor antagonistically and using humor to raise their own and others' spirits. They generate stories, metaphors, and puns. They are also quick to laugh and collect humorous stories to delight others.

Thinking Interdependently

Community is . . . a dynamic set of relationships in which a synergistic, self-regulating whole is created out of the combination of individual parts into a cohesive, identifiable, unified form.

—Center for the Study of Community, Santa Fe, New Mexico

Students who think interdependently set aside their own ego needs to serve others. They devote their energies to enhancing the group's resourcefulness. They put others before themselves, and they derive satisfaction when others excel and are recognized.

As work increases in abstraction and complexity, we are pressed to find its meaning through what Lev Vygotsky calls "social construction" of knowledge. Students show evidence of increased interdependence in group work and discussions when they focus on analysis, synthesis, and evaluation. Their language reflects their desire to understand how others are thinking and to keep making sense out of the problem or text. They offer interpretations and hypotheses to the group, and at the same time, they build on other people's ideas. They often can be heard saying, "When I see this, it makes me think this is what is happening. What do you think?"

Students showing evidence of this habit monitor the equality of group participation. They show concern for all members of the group, and they are aware of classmates who are isolated or excluded from the work. We hear them say things like "We haven't heard from Rick yet" or "Tess hasn't had a chance to speak." They help each other learn to ensure that all members of the group contribute to the task and succeed. Students demonstrating this habit not only contribute to but also learn from the group: "You really helped me see . . ." or "Thanks for showing me how to . . . ."

Remaining Open to Continuous Learning

> The value of the average conversation could be enormously improved by the constant use of four simple words: "I do not know."
>
> —André Maurois

Although it is human to defend our biases, beliefs, actions, and knowledge, it is also human to transcend the protective instinct by tapping into the courage to learn and change. For students who have developed this habit, the encounters, events, and circumstances of life in school and community become invitations to improve themselves by remaining open to continuous learning. As Ethyl Barrymore observed, "It's what you learn after you know it all that counts."

Students who have developed this Habit of Mind use feedback. They always assume that there is more to learn. We see them ask the next set of questions after a conclusion, ask for peer feedback, and seek new resources to modify their knowledge. They realize that to get anywhere always implies a further journey to the next place. They understand that expertise is not knowing everything but knowing the next, more sophisticated level of the work. As each level of knowledge is achieved, a whole new set of questions emerges (see also pp. 194–196).

These students are willing to let go of the need for the safety of "rightness" to claim the uncertainty of new investigations and knowledge. They strive to learn and are dissatisfied with mere judgments. They demonstrate a willingness to risk the potential of a lesser grade for the possibility of a greater challenge. They are resourceful, and they use the resourcefulness of others. They are proud to admit that they don't know an answer or a solution, and they are intrigued by the potential for further inquiry. We hear them say things like, "That's an interesting idea. How could we find out more about it?"

In Summary

There is great value in making the Habits of Mind explicit with indicators that guide us in observing growth and improvement. As we develop a common language for describing the Habits of Mind, we bring attention to a developmental growth students experience as they become aware of what the habits mean, learn to build their capacity for becoming more skillful in using the habits, value the benefits of the habits as they work more productively, and make a commitment to using the habits. Ultimately, students internalize the habits as a way of being. Assessment provides a measure of that developmental growth and, with explicit language, provides a cognitive map for continuous growth and learning (see Chapter 4).

References

Barell, J. (2003). *Developing more curious minds*. Alexandria, VA: ASCD.

Perkins, D. (1995). Insight in minds and genes. In J. J. Sternberg & J. E. Davidson (Eds.), *The nature of insight* (pp. 495–533). Cambridge, MA: MIT Press.

Swartz, R., Costa, A., Beyer, B., Kallick, B., & Reagan, R. (2007). *Thinking-based learning: Activating students' potential*. Norwood, MA: Christopher Gordon.

11

Assessing Habits of Mind

Arthur L. Costa and Bena Kallick

What gets measured gets done. Measurement is the heart of any
improvement process. It must begin at the outset of the program,
be visible, and done by the natural work group itself.

—*Tom Peters*

When educators are serious about helping students develop the Habits of
Mind, they find ways to make those habits integral to instruction, assessment, and feedback. There is a distinction between assessments *of* learning and assessments *for* learning (Stiggins, Arter, Chappuis, & Chappuis,
2004). On one hand, an assessment *of* learning is a summative assessment. The results are provided, and students move on to the next topic for
learning. Typical assessments of learning include final exams, benchmark
tests, and state tests. Their purpose is to judge learning, and the audience
for the results includes individuals other than the students. On the other
hand, assessments *for* learning are used to guide feedback and coaching
for students. Often referred to as formative assessments, they are designed
for students to know how they are maturing and developing toward a
higher and more skillful level of performance and excellence (Armstrong,
2006). The feedback and coaching are valued as a significant part of classroom instruction, providing the indicators and evidence on which more

objective judgments can be made. Assessment without feedback merely serves as judgment. Feedback is the part of assessment that enables us to make sense of judgment and improve our work. Educators must consciously create school cultures that require both feedback and assessment. This chapter considers different ways to achieve this goal.

Guiding Assumptions

The following assumptions support a feedback and assessment system that promotes students' use of the Habits of Mind:

- Data energize learning.
- Students must set and meet goals.
- Schools must become learning organizations.
- Assessment requires self-regulation.

Data Energize Learning

Students learn and grow when they have the opportunity to consider external and internal data. External data include feedback from teacher evaluations and test results. They also include "coaching" information from peers and teachers.

Many students are familiar with various types of external data, but they are less conversant with the credibility of their internal data. The term *internal data* describes information a student processes from feedback as well as self-evaluation and reflection. Students need opportunities to self-evaluate and generate these kinds of data. They must learn how to compare their current performance with previous performances, and they must learn how to analyze their performance in terms of benchmarks for effective performance.

Remember that neither external nor internal data are useful for learning unless feedback is frequent and stated in constructive terms. Feedback given too long after an assessment or a learning event won't influence a student in the same way as data offered almost immediately. Also, students find it more helpful to hear constructive comments on their work. They need (and want!) to hear what they can do, not just what they cannot do.

Students Must Set and Meet Goals

Students need to participate in the goal-setting process. It has always seemed puzzling that students are expected to reach goals that others have set for them. Michael Jordan, an extraordinary athlete, has stated, "You have to expect things of yourself before you can do them." The key to a self-directed and self-modifying learner is the ability to set meaningful goals and to find ways of knowing whether those goals have been met and to what standard. Students must participate in the goal-setting process and create the work plans that will help them fulfill the requirements of the stated goals.

As part of the process, students and teachers should agree on documentation methods so that students not only are aware of their goals but also can monitor and celebrate their successes. As they monitor their goals, they can modify their strategies if they are not moving toward success.

Schools Must Become Learning Organizations

At first glance, this assumption seems somewhat obvious, but the thought behind it bears restating: Schools must become the kinds of learning organizations where every participant is continuously growing and learning. Assessment won't be valued unless it is a part of every person's work in the organization.

Such integration means that when data energize learning, teachers will use data as catalysts for learning about students, students will use data as sources for improving their work, and boards of education will use data to create opportunities for professional development. When we expect students to participate in setting and meeting goals, we consider all of us to be students of teaching and learning. Every member of a school community recognizes the significance of setting goals that benchmark growth and learning. And every member learns how to celebrate the successes that lead the organization to greater learning and improvement.

Assessment Requires Self-Regulation

All programs—and the individuals working in them—must become self-managing, self-monitoring, and self-modifying (Costa & Kallick, 2004). This process of assessment and feedback ultimately leads to learners who are self-assessing. Self-knowledge is the first step in this kind of self-assessment.

Much of the work of self-evaluation is developed through metacognitive processes using the habit of thinking about your thinking. Students need to be able to answer questions such as these:

- What is the best environment for your learning?
- Where do you choose to study?
- Where do you choose to work creatively?
- How do you work with others?
- What is your preferred learning mode (e.g., visual or kinesthetic)?
- What do you consider to be your talents or strengths (e.g., arts, oral presentations, persuasive arguments)?
- Where do your interests lie?
- How do you use criteria to determine whether your work is good?
- Do you check for accuracy and precision?
- Are you persistent as you develop your work?

Many teachers ask students to regularly reflect on questions such as these. The self-assessment data generated by these questions promote students' learning and growth. The data also provide useful information for teachers as they facilitate learning.

Self-knowledge builds on internal and external reflections and observations. Feedback from teachers is a rich source of external data. Teachers can give evaluative feedback about thinking by focusing on a variety of questions:

- What is the student's disposition or attitude toward learning?
- How does the student think about assessing information?
- What information does the student consider important?
- How does the student use a reasoning process to think about the information being gathered?
- How does the student use strategies to solve problems?
- How does the student communicate the results of the student's learning?
- What is evidenced in the student's performance as the student applies this learning to new situations?

Learning Through Feedback Spirals

You can never step into the river of time twice.

—Heroclitus

Feedback improves your learning as it makes you go above and beyond.
—Student from Glenora Elementary School, Edmonton, Alberta, Canada

Feedback spirals are an important way that organizations can achieve self-regulation. These spirals depend on a variety of information for their success. In some cases, individuals make changes after consciously observing their own feelings, attitudes, and skills. Some spirals depend on the observations of outsiders (such as "critical friends"). In other cases, those directly involved in change collect specific kinds of evidence about what is happening in the organization's environment. Once these data are analyzed, interpreted, and internalized, individuals modify their actions to more closely achieve the organization's goals. Thus, individuals—and the organization—are continually self-learning, self-renewing, and self-modifying.

Figure 11.1 shows how components of a feedback spiral may be diagrammed as a recursive, cyclical pathway. Here we describe each element along the spiral:

• *Clarify goals and purposes.* What is the purpose for what you are doing? What beliefs or values does it reflect? What outcomes would you expect as a result of your actions?

• *Plan.* What actions would you take to achieve the desired outcomes? How would you set up an experiment to test your ideas? What evidence would you collect to help inform you about the results of your actions? What would you look for as indicators that your outcomes were or were not achieved? How will you leave the door open for other discoveries and possibilities that were not built into the original design? What process will you put in place that will help you describe what actually happened?

• *Take action/experiment.* Execute the plan.

• *Assess/gather evidence.* Implement the assessment strategy.

FIGURE 11.1
Continuous Growth Through Feedback Spirals

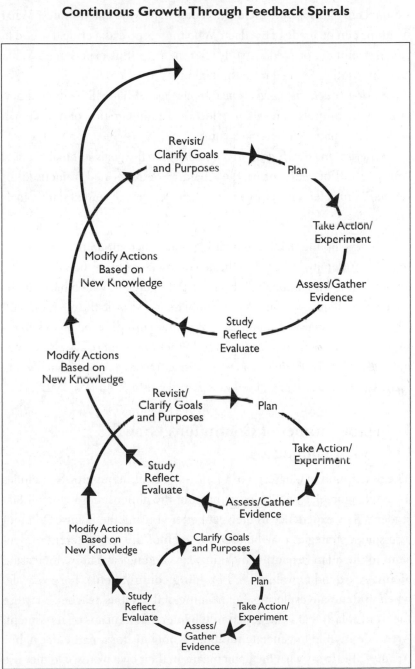

Source: Costa and Kallick, 1995, p. 27.

• *Study, reflect, evaluate.* Whether this is an individual or an organizational change, how are the results congruent with stated values? What meaning can be made of the data? Who might serve as a critical friend to coach, facilitate, or mediate your learning from this experience? What have individuals learned from this action?

• *Modify actions based on new knowledge.* What will be done differently in the future as a result of reflection and integration of new knowledge? Is this plan worth trying again?

• *Revisit and clarify goals and purposes.* Do the goals still make sense? Are they still of value, or do they need to be redefined, refocused, or refined? This element returns to the first step in the spiral: clarify goals and purposes.

To develop the habit of remaining open to continuous learning, the school community gathers data through conscious observation of feelings, attitudes, and skills; through observation and interviews with others; and by collecting evidence showing the effects of their efforts on the environment. These data are analyzed, interpreted, and internalized. Based on this analysis, the organization or individuals modify actions to more closely achieve the goals. Thus, individuals and the organization become continually self-learning, self-renewing, and self-modifying (Costa & Kallick, 1995).

Using the Journey of Continuous Growth to Guide Planning

The description in Chapter 4 of a journey of continuous growth includes a chart (Figure 4.1) that helps to map out the dimensions of growth that students may experience as they get better at using the habits. Different assessment strategies may be used for each of the five different dimensions in the chart (exploring meanings, expanding capacities, increasing alertness, extending values, and building commitment). For example, when students are exploring the meaning of the habits, teachers may use the word splash that is suggested in Chapter 7 as a means of assessment. Are students able to generate multiple synonyms for a particular habit? Are they able to say what the habit means in their own words? Do they use the language of the habit in their journals?

FIGURE 11.2

An Assessment Continuum for the Dimensions of Growth

Dimensions	I'm there.	I'm getting there.	I really need to work on this.
Exploring Meaning			
Expanding Capacities			
Increasing Alertness			
Extending Values			
Building Commitment			

As students are becoming more alert to the habits, are they able to find the "mindful language" that is embedded in assignments, tasks, or tests? For example, can they highlight the mental activity that is called for when the linguistic cue is "Analyze this problem"? Are they alert to the Habit of Mind they need to engage as they think about the problem?

This chapter presents various strategies that teachers can use to assess student growth in developing the habits and that students can use to self-assess. Teachers can use the continuum in Figure 11.2 to record the development of the class as a whole in the five dimensions, and students may use the continuum to record their self-assessment along the dimensions of growth.

Measuring Dispositions

The Habits of Mind define what is meant by being "smart." Many classroom teachers have searched for ways to make those attributes visible to students and observers. A first step in this process is helping students to recognize when and where they can most effectively apply the habits and setting goals accordingly.

Goal Setting

Goal setting provides the opportunity for students to consider what it is they want to accomplish and how they will do so. It is important to encourage students to think big and then act small—one chunk at a time. When goal setting is a priority, goals are set at multiple levels: school, classroom, and individual student. Many people use the acronym

"SMART" to help with the goal-setting process. The acronym is defined as follows:

> Specific—For a goal to be meaningful, it must be specific. A goal such as "I would like to read the whole dictionary" would be too global. Rather, the goal might be "I would like to be able to read the first section of the children's dictionary in the next month."
>
> Measurable—The goal must be able to be measured. Criteria and methods for measurement must be clarified at the outset.
>
> Attainable—The students must be realistic about achieving the goal. Often the most important consideration is time management. Will the student have enough time to accomplish what is set forth?
>
> Realistic—Is it realistic to expect that the student will, for example, read sections of the children's dictionary? Some questions arise. Is enough time provided for achievement? Is the goal one that will move the student forward in the given context of learning?
>
> Timely—Will all that is set forth be accomplished in a timely fashion? Too often we set goals that can't be accomplished in the time frame provided.

At the Skokie Intermediate School in Winnetka, Illinois, students are required to set academic and behavioral goals that are defined through the Habits of Mind. They follow this format:

Goal: (How do I intend to improve my learning habits? Which Habits of Mind do I need to attend to?) _____

_____

Evidence: (How will I know that I am improving? What strategy will I use to benchmark my use of the Habits of Mind?) _____

_____

Goal setting is an important way to help students become more metacognitive. They learn to use the feedback spiral to mark and celebrate their growth in learning.

Checklists

It is important for students to know what to look for as they target their goals for improvement. Checklists help to develop a set of indicators that can guide many strategies for assessing growth. (In Chapter 10 we provided a set of indicators that might serve as the basis for two such checklists.) In some classrooms, teachers have students develop these lists. In other instances, groups of teachers gather and develop indicators that they then bring to the students so that students can provide examples and definitions about what these indicators might look like and sound like in the classroom. If these indicators are to provide data for assessing growth in the use of the Habits of Mind in a school, they must be agreed upon so that information about progress is consistent Figure 11.3 shows an example from Sunrise Valley Elementary School in Fairfax County, Virginia. Representative teachers from each grade worked together to develop the set of indicators to use as a checklist for the habit of listening with understanding and empathy. Teachers assess students by using this

FIGURE 11.3

Teacher-Developed Indicators for a Habit of Mind

Habit: Listening with Understanding and Empathy	
Demonstrating Understanding	**Showing Empathy**
• Making connections between what you say and what the person directly before you (and before that person) has said. • Asking relevant questions. • Agreeing to disagree and justifying your answer with reference to the text. • "I was thinking . . ." • Paraphrasing. • Asking clarifying questions. • Using feeling words to show you understand: "I understand," "I feel sad." • Using hand signals—signing, thumbs up, and thumbs down.	• Showing that you're listening with eye contact. • Showing that you're listening by nodding or shaking your head. • Allowing only one voice at a time. • Turning body toward the group and the speaker.

checklist and looking for evidence of when students are showing these actions. Students self-assess using the format shown in Figure 11.4.

The checklist in Figure 11.3 is one example from a school that has focused assessment on only a few of the habits. Similar checklists can be developed for any of the habits. Often schools have a schoolwide checklist for all teachers to use with students, as well as a class-based checklist for each particular class. The idea is to focus on one or two habits that the entire school agrees students should be working on. Teachers and students then identify one or two more habits that may be needed for the students in a particular classroom. As students begin to collect data about their behavior over time, they may create a graph to track their progress. They will find it helpful to receive feedback from their peers and their teacher in addition to their own assessment of how they are doing. Students can keep a folder with the results from their checklists, each carefully dated. When reporting time comes, students can create a bar graph of each behavior and see a profile of how frequently ("often," "sometimes," "not yet") they are using the behaviors and reflect upon the graphs in order to set goals for the next quarter or semester.

As students become more familiar with the process of observing these behaviors in their own work, they often shift to a checklist for the group with whom they are working. At this point, they are asking, "How are *we* doing?" The same checklist can apply for either individual or group evaluation. Once students feel comfortable assessing themselves, the teacher might ask them to rate themselves and the others in their group. Students can then compare ratings and see how accurately they perceive themselves. The teacher might also rate the students and give specific examples of how they are demonstrating the positive behaviors of a particular habit.

Keeping an inventory such as a checklist during class interactions, when solving problems, and after interacting with others can help individuals and groups gather valuable data for self-reflection and planning for learning as they begin to self-monitor more effectively. A class meeting might start with a facilitator seeking criteria from the class as a reminder of how to work succussfully as a group.

During group work or a class discussion, students can monitor their own behavior and be aware of each other's performance. Before the end

FIGURE 11.4

Student Self-Assessment Form for a Habit of Mind

Name: _____

Listening with Understanding and Empathy

Learning Outcomes for Demonstrating Understanding	Evidence	Not Yet, But I Will Try	Date
• Making connections between what you say and what the person directly before you (and before that person) has said.			
• Asking relevant questions.			
• Agreeing to disagree and justifying your answer with reference to the text.			
• "Your idea made me think of . . ."			
• Paraphrasing.			
• Asking clarifying questions.			
• Using feeling words to show you understand: "I understand," "I feel sad."			
• Using hand signals—signing, thumbs up, and thumbs down.			
Learning Outcomes for Showing Empathy	**Evidence**	**Not Yet, But I Will Try**	**Date**
• Showing that you're listening with eye contact.			
• Showing that you're listening by nodding or shaking your head.			
• Allowing only one voice at a time.			
• Turning body toward the group and the speaker.			

of the work, the teacher can ask the students to reflect on the group inter-action and to describe how the criteria were or were not met. Students can explore their feelings and discuss indicators of how the team is working more synergistically together. Teachers may pose metacognitive questions such as these:

- What decisions did you make about when and how to participate?
- What metacognitive strategies did you use to monitor your own communicative competencies?
- What were some of the effects of your decisions for you and others in your group?
- As you anticipate future team meetings, what commitments might you make to strengthen the groups' productivity?
- What signals will you look for in the future to alert you to the need for these communicative competencies?

Rubrics

Scoring rubrics are another way to assess the Habits of Mind. These rubrics also promote self-evaluation when students help develop them. Each category should be sufficiently clear so that students can learn from the feedback about their behavior and see ways to improve.

Figures 11.5 through 11.9 are examples of rubrics for several Habits of Mind and for group cooperation. They were developed by educators at Tamalpais Elementary School in Mill Valley, California. After the rubrics were developed, the teachers discussed them with their students, adding to and refining them so that students understood the expectations. The developmental continuum in these rubrics (from novice to expert) derives from Tech Paths for Math (Kallick & Wilson, 1997).

Portfolios

Keeping track is a matter of reflective review and summarizing in which there is both discrimination and record of the significant fea-tures of a developing experience. . . . It is the heart of intellectual organization and of the disciplined mind.

—*John Dewey,* Experience and Education

FIGURE 11.5

Rubric for Thinking About Thinking (Metacognition)

Level of Work	Criteria
Expert	Describes in detail the steps of thinking when solving a problem or doing other kinds of mental tasks. Explains in detail how thinking about thinking helps improve work and how it helps to develop a better learner. Describes a plan before starting to solve a problem. Monitors steps in the plan or strategy. Reflects on the efficiency of the problem-solving strategy.
Practitioner	Describes one's thinking while solving a problem or doing other kinds of mental tasks. Explains how thinking about thinking helps learning and helps to improve work.
Apprentice	Includes only sparse or incomplete information when describing how one is thinking and solving a problem or doing other kinds of mental tasks. Sees only small benefits gained from thinking about thinking and learning.
Novice	Is confused about the relationship between thinking and problem solving. Sees no relationship between thinking and learning. Is unable to describe thinking when problem solving.

Source: Tamalpais Elementary School, Mill Valley, California. Based on Marzano, Pickering, and McTighe, 1993.

FIGURE 11.6

Rubric for Persisting

Level of Work	Criteria
Expert	Does not give up no matter how difficult it is to find the answers to solutions. Evaluates the use of a variety of strategies to stay on task.
Practitioner	Does not give up when trying to find the answers or solutions. Stays on task.
Apprentice	Tries to complete tasks when the answers or solutions are not readily available, but gives up when task is too difficult. Gets off task easily.
Novice	Gives up easily and quickly on difficult tasks.

Source: Tamalpais Elementary School, Mill Valley, California. Based on Marzano, Pickering, and McTighe, 1993.

FIGURE 11.7

Rubrics for Managing Impulsivity

Level of Work	Criteria
Expert	Sets clear goals and describes each step to be taken to achieve the goals. Schedules each step and monitors progress.
Practitioner	Sets clear goals and describes some of the steps needed to achieve the goals. Also sequences some of the steps.
Apprentice	Begins to work with unclear goals. Describes only a few of the steps needed to achieve the goals. Becomes distracted from schedule.
Novice	Begins to work in random fashion. Is unclear about the goals or is unable to state the goals or outcomes or steps in achieving the goals.

Level of Work	Criteria
Expert	Evaluates a situation carefully and seeks advice from other sources to decide whether more information is needed before acting. Looks for sources of information that might help and studies them to find important information.
Practitioner	Evaluates a situation to decide if more information is needed before acting. Searches for information if needed.
Apprentice	Evaluates a situation quickly to decide if more information is needed before acting. Searches for only the most obvious information.
Novice	Acts with inadequate or incomplete information and shows little inclination to gather further data to inform decisions.

Source: Tamalpais Elementary School, Mill Valley, California. Based on Marzano, Pickering, and McTighe, 1993.

FIGURE 11.8

Rubric for Thinking Flexibly

Level of Work	Criteria	
	In Repertoire	**In Perspective**
Expert	Uses time and resources creatively to find as many ways as possible to look at a situation. Evaluates these many ways to see how useful they might be. Expresses appreciation for others' points of view. Changes mind and incorporates others' points of view in own thinking.	Consistently explores as many alternatives as time and resources will allow and analyzes how the identified alternatives will affect outcomes. The alternatives illustrate extremely diverse but highly useful ways of looking at situations.
Practitioner	Finds a variety of ways to look at a situation and evaluates how useful they are. Describes some ways others' points of view are found to be new and different from own perspective.	Consistently generates alternative ways of approaching tasks and analyzes how the alternatives will affect those tasks. Some alternatives show originality in the approach to the tasks.
Apprentice	Describes different ways of looking at a situation from own perspective.	Sporadically generates alternative ways of approaching tasks and analyzes how the alternatives will affect those tasks. Some alternatives show originality in the approach to the tasks.
Novice	Looks at a situation in only one way, and that way often is one's own. Looks no further even when it is clear that doing so would be helpful.	Rarely generates alternative ways of approaching tasks. The few alternatives lack originality.

Source: Tamalpais Elementary School, Mill Valley, California. Based on Marzano, Pickering, and McTighe, 1993.

FIGURE 11.9

Rubric for Group Cooperation

Level of Work	Group Criteria
4	Demonstrates interdependence. Shows contributions from all members. Shows indicators of cooperation and working together, compromising, and staying on task. Welcomes disagreements as learning opportunities. Completes task with accuracy and within time limits. Listens to others' points of view. Shows evidence of paraphrasing, clarifying, and empathizing.
3	Reaches agreements through arguing and debate. Shows evidence of some paraphrasing and clarifying. Sometimes strays from task. Shows evidence of some members remaining silent or refraining from participating.
2	Demonstrates some off-task behavior. Rushes to complete task in the most expedient way because of time limits. Argues or encourages members to get task over with.
1	Demonstrates little on-task behavior. Argues and shows disinterest.
0	Shows chaos. Does not complete task. Engages in put-downs. Reduces group size because of members leaving. Complains about having to participate in task.

Source: Tamalpais Elementary School, Mill Valley, California.

Many teachers use the Habits of Mind as a way to organize students' portfolios. For example, the portfolio can be sectioned with folders, each labeled with a Habit of Mind. Students choose work based on their best example of whatever habit they're focusing on at the time. They place the work in the portfolio in the appropriate file, and they reflect on why they chose that particular piece and what it should say to the reader of the portfolio.

Students can coach one another through peer conferences as they build these portfolios. One teacher we know asks students to read the work in a student's portfolio and help the student reflect on why that student chose a particular piece.

When portfolios are developed around the Habits of Mind, the habits are transdisciplinary. This approach answers the question many teachers face about how to have one portfolio that can work across all subjects.

"This poem has no beginning" was the first line of a poem in the portfolio of Tracy from Southampton Public Schools in Southampton, New York. When asked why she wanted to include this poem in her portfolio, she replied, "I want to be able to describe my process for developing a piece of writing." She then described how she often takes a walk through the woods by a stream, returns to her room, clears her desk, plays music, and starts to write. In the case of this particular poem, she still was not feeling inspired. She sat with pen in hand and finally wrote, "This poem has no beginning," and the writing just seemed to flow from there.

Tracy was trying to describe what some might call incubation—that time when one is developing an idea, either consciously or preconsciously. Through work with her teacher, she came to understand the significance of making that process of development conscious, explicit, or what we refer to as metacognitive. Tracy entered this piece as an example of how she had grown as a writer and how aware she was of her process for moving an idea from incubation to reality.

Amy, a 6th grade student in Mamaroneck Public Schools in Mamaroneck, New York, was asked to choose a piece of writing for her portfolio that demonstrated her development as a problem solver. The teacher was surprised by her choice, but she better understood when she read the following reflection:

> This piece was written after my grandfather died. I was so sad that he died, and I did not know how to rid myself of the sadness. We went on a class trip, and I took photos of where we were. I placed those photos around my bed and laid on my bed for hours looking at the photos and thinking about my grandfather. Finally, I got up and wrote this piece. It shows how I was able to solve my problem of sadness through writing.

In this reflection, Amy clearly shows evidence of her disposition for problem solving and drawing from previous experiences to reflect on her learning.

When classroom communities require that students use portfolios to build narratives of their own learning, and when they focus on the opportunities for student reflection as Tracy's and Amy's teachers did, the Habits of Mind are a powerful frame to guide them through their work. Teachers and students often ask, "What goes into a portfolio?" A better question is "What will be the frame or structure of the portfolio?"

In Kathleen Reilly's 10th and 12th grade English classes at Edgemont High School in Edgemont, New York, the students' portfolios are framed with the Habits of Mind. Each student has a list of the habits permanently fixed to the inside of the portfolio cover. Students also work with checklists that help them look for the Habits of Mind in their work.

Their work with the habits begins with the teacher's response to individual essays on the specific terms of *persistence*, *precision*, and *accuracy*. In the space at the bottom of a checklist, students are asked to choose which of those Habits of Mind they think will help them write better essays.

Later in the school year, students are pushed further in their reflections about essays. They must ask peers to assume the role of coach. For example, 10th grader Sam tells Michael that Michael's essay illustrates his flexibility in thinking when he "uses many metaphors for the journey: development, emotional progression, humility." Sam also notes how Michael's precision of language shows in his "good use of synonyms." After he reads Sam's reflection, Michael notes that he can improve his essay "by listening to others—taking fellow students' advice to heart." He adds that he will get better at this writing stuff when he "applies metacognition, . . . trying to understand how I came to my thesis and prove it."

In Reilly's class, stretching the Habits of Mind to serve as a structural frame for character analysis was a natural outgrowth of earlier work. Students could not resist writing about character strengths and weaknesses. Working with 10th graders on *Huckleberry Finn*, Reilly created portfolio assignments that asked direct questions about the students' thinking patterns, the intellectual and emotional choices of the literary characters, and the way the students thought about their essays. Overall, the Habits of Mind provided a sensitive structure for the portfolio. Students easily adapted to the list, and they made connections to specific instances in the novel as well as to their own lives. Here are some questions Reilly asked about the novel:

- What specific Habits of Mind are apparent in this character? Cite scenes where you recognize the Habits of Mind.
  - How could this character have behaved more intelligently?
  - What possible alternative strategies could this character have used to solve problems?

Reilly uses a reflection/response form to give students the choice of character to think about. Although many chose to analyze Huck, Tom, or Jim, others were drawn to negative characters: Pap, the King, and the Duke. Just the task of "thinking about thinking" initiated conversations about Twain's intention in creating characters to educate and challenge Huck.

Specifically, although Huck was unanimously credited with possessing persistence and creativity, students sharply criticized him for his lack of flexibility in thinking about Jim, for not listening to others, and for not reflecting. As John put it, "One of Huck's major problems is his . . . trouble seeing Jim and all blacks outside of the prejudices existing in society. Huck needs to think outside this mind-set."

Centering on an analysis of the King, Tina found his major faults were in "being overly impulsive. . . . He started schemes without thinking."

Another question pushed students to think about their own process of arriving at conclusions about characters. Beverly wrote, "I tried to put myself in his shoes, to think about how I would react." Tina wrote, "I thought about each habit and tried to apply it to the King. . . . [If] I wasn't sure, I tried to apply each trait to a real-life example to see how the King would react." By the end of the year, students went back through their portfolio and saw how easily they talked about literature in terms of the Habits of Mind.

Although Reilly teaches English, she asked students to include in their portfolios writing examples from other classes. What followed were discussions of audiences, the styles and expectations of other disciplines, and the ways that a powerful voice can be heard in every piece of writing. The examples gave insight into the possibilities of using the Habits of

Mind as a transdisciplinary frame with students completing a portfolio representing their work in several subjects.

Portfolios can help us continuously re-create the narrative of our own learning. All the failures and misfires are in a portfolio, sitting right next to the triumphs and breakthroughs. Peers cheer the growth they see, the power of words selected, and the essays they wish they had written. Students delight in their changes, cherish the praise, and work even harder to produce an admirable product. Beyond the chronological history of work produced, the portfolio reveals a deeper layer where the patterns of work tell a personal story of a student's learning. The Habits of Mind serve as a powerful framework for this work.

Performances

Teachers become increasingly aware of the significance of the Habits of Mind when students prepare presentations of their work. These performances require orchestration and a great deal of social thinking. Students can receive feedback about the Habits of Mind during three parts of the performance:

- When they are planning for a performance.
- When they are in the process of working on the performance.
- When they are presenting their work to an audience.

During Planning

In an example of incorporating the habits into the planning phase, a science teacher presents a challenge to his students. They must work together to create a persuasive presentation to the class about a solution to a particular ecological problem. He asks the students to choose one habit they feel especially strong in and one that they need to work on. They then plan how they will work to develop the habits through the actions they take. Next they develop a list of indicators as a group: What will a habit look like when we see it happening? They agree to keep records of when they observe the use of a habit. What is important about this process is that they plan to pay attention to the Habits of Mind *before* they begin their work.

During the Process

Record-keeping forms are useful for students to document their observations about the Habits of Mind. In one high school class, students keep a log of their process during project development. Group members rotate responsibility for log entries for each day that they are working together. They reflect on the following questions:

- What did we learn today?
- What did we notice about the way the group is working?
- What did the group and group member do to contribute to the group's success?
- What might we do to be more effective as a group?
- Which Habits of Mind would help us to be more productive?

During the Presentation

During a presentation, students are required to focus on striving for accuracy; thinking and communicating with clarity and precision; creating, imagining, innovating; questioning and posing problems; and thinking about thinking (metacognition). The audience is asked to pay attention to the accuracy of the information. They also take note of the use of proper terminology. Figure 11.10 shows an example of a rubric developed by educators in the Mamaroneck Public Schools for judging the quality of a 6th grade exhibition.

In a book by Wasley, Hempel, and Clark (1997), the authors discuss the gains that students have made as a result of developing exhibitions:

> We saw young people like Tommy, Sean, and Hakim discover topics of interest and develop them over time so that they build legitimate skills, recognized by adults and other students—recognition they would not have easily obtained had the school not changed its requirements. We saw evidence that students understood important concepts thoroughly and could apply them in new circumstances: math in building boats, data gathering and analysis in forecasting weather, electronics in wiring car radios. We noted gains that were embedded in students' abilities to work

FIGURE 11.10

Rubric for Personal Exhibit Assessment

6th Grade Exhibition

Presenter's Name: _____

Scorer's Name: _____

Date of Presentation: _____

Scoring Criteria	Clear 3	Moderate 2	Not Quite 1
Through this exhibit, the creator demonstrates the following:			
That she/he is a successful PROBLEM SOLVER			
1. Defines the problem.			
2. Brainstorms/thinks of possible solutions.			
3. Persists to find a solution.			
4. Takes action.			
That she/he is a thorough RESEARCHER			
5. Raises questions/chooses topics to research.			
6. Knows where to look for information.			
7. Uses a variety of sources.			
8. Takes time to be thoughtful.			
9. Organizes the data.			
10. Checks for accuracy of information.			
That she/he is an effective COMMUNICATOR			
11. Uses his/her own voice (words) to express ideas.			
12. Uses feedback to strengthen his/her work.			
13. Final product communicates in an organized and meaningful way to the audience—ideas are clear and easily understood.			
Her/His PLAQUES			
14. Reflect on strategies and process.			
15. SHOW GROWTH in all areas.			
Please write further comments below. Your words are very important!			

Source: Central Elementary School, Mamaroneck, New York.

on a particular topic over time. They demonstrated persistence—an important ability in nearly all walks of life. Tanya, whose parents were recovering addicts, ran the data over and over again in order to make sure her findings were correct, and then she ran them again with a new set of variables. We saw papers, videos, speeches that were rehearsed and nearly errorless, because students had developed a consciousness of audience and correctness. (p. 201)

Anecdotal Records

As teachers strive to be constantly alert to students' demonstration of the Habits of Mind, they document student work. The most significant part of this strategy is to be systematic about record keeping. One teacher found that she was able to observe all the children in her class when she designed a special notebook. She tabbed each section with a student's name and used sticky notes to jot down information when students demonstrated various Habits of Mind. When she wanted to write narrative comments about students at the end of the first marking period, she had a good pool of data from which to draw.

Parents and caregivers can also be asked to record students' growth. Many teachers send a copy of the Habits of Mind home and ask parents to notice when the child is using the behaviors. When conference time comes, the parents share their observations with the teacher. Figure 11.11 shows a tool that educators in Maple Valley, Washington, use to encourage parents to track how students demonstrate thinking behaviors. Parents also receive a two-page guide explaining how they can strengthen students' thinking behaviors.

Besides documenting performances, teachers are also alert to students' comments before, during, and after learning activities, projects, and assignments. Students often reveal their awareness, understanding, and application of the Habits of Mind as they plan for and reflect on their work. Here are student comments about the Habits of Mind collected by Michele Swanson at Sir Francis Drake High School in San Anselmo, California:

• *Persisting.* "In the last project when I couldn't have been more stressed, I wanted to quit and walk away, but no matter how much I wanted to give up because I had no idea what I was doing or how it was

FIGURE 11.11

12 Ways Your Child or Student Shows Growth in Thinking Skills

This is a parent/teacher tool for rating a student's home/school thinking behaviors at the beginning and end of a school year. It should identify student strengths and weaknesses and promote some parent/teacher "team" goal setting to help the student develop more successful thinking strategies.

Mark each behavior using N = Not Yet; S = Sometimes; F = Frequently

During the _____ school year, I notice that

Name: _____ Age: _____ does the following:

Parent		Teacher		Behavior
Fall	Spring	Fall	Spring	
1.				Keeps trying; does not give up easily.
2.				Shows less impulsivity; thinks more before answering a question.
3.				Listens to others with understanding and empathy.
4.				States several ways to solve a problem (shows flexibility in thinking).
5.				Puts into words how he/she solved a problem; is aware of his/her own thinking.
6.				Checks for accuracy and precision; checks completed work without being asked.
7.				Asks questions; wants to find out new information.
8.				Uses knowledge already learned in new situations; can solve problems in everyday living like using allowance, taking messages, going to the store, and practicing safety.
9.				Uses words more carefully to describe feelings, wants, and other things.
10.				Uses touch, taste, smell, sound, and sight to learn. Enjoys music, art, experimenting, and active play.
11.				Enjoys making and doing original things; likes to show individuality in thought and dress.
12.				Enjoys problem solving, curiosity, wonderment, and inquisitiveness.

Source: Tahoma School District, Maple Valley, Washington.

going to be done, no matter how much I wanted to throw the Makita because it wasn't working, no matter how much responsibility I was forced to take on, I stuck with it until the end, always knowing (hoping) it would turn out great."

• *Listening with understanding and empathy.* "Listening before pre-judging someone's contribution makes sense. Being patient helps. I was surprised at the great ideas and how much everyone added."

• *Finding humor.* "Getting to know these people can really impact your life and your work very positively, so you always have to keep a light and open heart, and humor can aid in this." Also, "Humor keeps people relaxed and much more comfortable even while working on serious subject matter."

• *Thinking about thinking (metacognition).* "I sometimes have to talk to myself and tell myself to work harder, or to stop slacking." Also, "They give us time to think about everything—all of our actions and work and that is something that really helps. Not many kids get that; it's so neat."

• *Thinking interdependently.* "It's not about what you want or somebody else does. It's about working as a team to get the job done." Also, "At first, I was not a good group worker because I felt controlling and perfectionist. I had to step back and examine my thinking and adjust to be cooperative and open. I changed the way I thought about my role in the group process."

• *Questioning and posing problems.* "Asking the right questions is very helpful in order to learn how to use the equipment effectively."

• *Applying past knowledge to new situations.* "Every time I finished a project, I was able to enter the next one with more knowledge of the group process. Also, with each project I became more technologically advanced, which helped me add value to the group."

• *Striving for accuracy.* "Our venue was four minutes long. After every four minutes, I had to move everything back to the original spot in one minute. Every single little thing had to be perfect."

Interviews

Oprah Winfrey, Mike Wallace, and Barbara Walters are all master interviewers. They have the capacity to place the most timid person at ease by creating trust and rapport, and they have developed the skills to lead the most reticent guest to reveal that person's deepest emotions and secrets. Teachers, too, can use interviews to lead students to share their reflections about the Habits of Mind. Here are some examples of interview questions:

- As you reflect on this semester's work, which of the Habits of Mind were you most aware of in your own learnings?
- Which Habit of Mind will you focus your energies on as you begin our next project?
- What insights have you gained as a result of employing these Habits of Mind?
- As you think about your future, how might these Habits of Mind be used as a guide in your life?

Interviews provide teachers with opportunities to model the habits of listening with understanding and empathy, thinking and communicating with clarity and precision, and questioning and posing problems. Teaching students to conduct interviews provides situations in which they must also practice these Habits of Mind. The ultimate purpose of interviewing, though, is to lead students to another powerful strategy: the self-interview.

Journals and Logs

Consciousness about the Habits of Mind often begins with journal entries designed to help students focus on how they are developing. Learning logs and journals are a way to integrate content, process, personal feelings, and the Habits of Mind. They are especially powerful in engaging metacognition and helping students to draw forth previous knowledge.

Before or directly after a unit, a project, or an area of study, invite students to make entries in their logs or journals. Short, frequent bursts of writing are sometimes more productive than infrequent, longer assignments. Teachers, too, can join in the writing process by reflecting on their teaching, analyzing learners' learning, preserving anecdotes about the class interactions, and projecting ideas for how they might approach a unit of study differently in the future.

Sometimes students will complain, "I don't know what to write." To stimulate thinking, post questioning stems on a chart or in the front of the log or journals. Consider these sentence starters to help students use the Habits of Mind as a way of documenting their learning:

- One thing that surprised me today was . . . .
- I felt particularly flexible when I . . . .
- I used my senses to . . . .
- As I think about how I went about solving the problem, I . . . .
- A question I want to pursue is . . . .
- When I checked my work, I found . . . .
- Because I listened carefully, I learned . . . .

You can collect specific log entries from time to time, read through them, and share written comments with students. This practice helps build stronger relationships with the learners and provides a useful way to informally assess how well they are doing and how their conscious use of the Habits of Mind is developing.

Add annotated journal or log entries to portfolios. Invite students to choose an entry from the beginning, middle, and end of the learning period. These entries can be included in a final portfolio along with the student's reflections and synthesis connecting the entries or general comments about learning over time (Lipton, 1997).

In Summary

Not all of the Habits of Mind are assessed using the same techniques. After deciding which habits you wish to focus on in your school and classroom, you can use the matrix in Figure 11.12 to plan for a balance of assessment strategies for collecting data related to those habits.

This chapter has emphasized the importance of shifting the paradigm of assessment. Instead of being external and critical, without sufficient feedback for change, assessments should be descriptive, should provide a good road map for the further development of skillful thinking, and should encourage the student to take responsibility for following that roadmap. The power of the assessment-learning spiral can be dramatically enhanced by including opportunities for students to self-assess, with teacher guidance, during the course of regular instruction. Infusing the Habits of Mind into instruction dramatically enhances both content

FIGURE 11.12

Planning Matrix for Collecting Evidence

Habit of Mind	Type of Assessment							
	Checklist	Portfolio	Rubric	Interview	Anecdotal	Performance	Exhibition	Journal
1. Persisting								
2. Managing impulsivity								
3. Listening with understanding and empathy								
4. Thinking flexibly								
5. Thinking about thinking (metacognition)								
6. Striving for accuracy								
7. Questioning and posing problems								
8. Applying past knowledge to new situations								

FIGURE 11.12—(*continued*,

Planning Matrix for Collecting Evidence

Habit of Mind	Type of Assessment								
	Checklist	Portfolio	Rubric	Interview	Anecdotal	Performance	Exhibition	Journal
9. Thinking and communicating with clarity and precision								
10. Gathering data through all senses								
11. Creating, imagining, innovating								
12. Responding with wonderment and awe								
13. Taking responsible risks								
14. Finding humor								
15. Thinking interdependently								
16. Remaining open to continuous learning								

learning and the development of skillful thinking abilities (Swartz, Costa, Beyer, Kallick, & Reagan, 2007). But the habits can also help students develop skill at *assessing their own abilities* in ways that direct them to become continuous learners throughout their lifetime.

References

Armstrong, T. (2006). *The best schools: How human development research should inform educational practice*. Alexandria, VA: ASCD.

Costa, A., & Kallick, B. (1995). *Assessment in the learning organization: Shifting the paradigm*. Alexandria, VA: ASCD.

Costa, A., & Kallick, B. (2004). *Assessment strategies for self-directed learning*. Thousand Oaks, CA: Corwin.

Kallick, B., & Wilson, J. (1997). *Tech paths for math: An assessment management system for your classroom*. Amherst, MA: Technology Pathways.

Lipton, L. (1997). *50 ways to literacy*. Arlington Heights, IL: SkyLight Publishers.

Stiggins, R., Arter, J., Chappuis, J., & Chappuis, S. (2004). *Classroom assessment for student learning*. Portland, OR: Assessment Training Institute.

Swartz, R., Costa, A., Beyer, B., Kallick, B., & Reagan, R. (2007). *Thinking-based learning*. Norwood, MA: Christopher Gordon.

Wasley, P., Hempel, R., & Clark, R. (1997). *Kids and school reform*. San Francisco: Jossey-Bass.

12

Learning Through Reflection

Arthur L. Costa and Bena Kallick

A defining condition of being human is that we have to understand
the meaning of our experience.

—*Jack Mezirow*

Most of us go through life viewing our experiences as isolated, unrelated events. We also view these happenings simply as the experiences they are, not as opportunities for learning. Psychologists refer to this type of life-view as an "episodic grasp of reality" (Feuerstein, Rand, Hoffman, & Miller, 1980), and it is not a habit we want to pass along to children. Instead, we want students to get into the habit of linking and constructing meaning from their experiences. Such work requires reflection.

Reflection has many facets. For example, reflecting on work enhances its meaning. Reflecting on experiences encourages insight and complex learning. We foster our own growth when we control our learning, so some reflection is best done alone. Reflection is also enhanced, however, when we ponder our learning with others.

Reflection involves linking a current experience to previous learnings (a process called *scaffolding*). Reflection also involves drawing forth cognitive and emotional information from several sources: visual, auditory, kinesthetic, and tactile. To reflect, we must act upon and process the information, synthesizing and evaluating the data. In the end, reflecting also means applying what we've learned to contexts beyond the original situations in which we learned something.

Valuing Reflection

> The art of teaching is the art of assisting discovery.
>
> —*Mark Van Doren*

Teachers who promote reflective classrooms ensure that students are fully engaged in the process of making meaning. They organize instruction so that students are the producers, not just the consumers, of knowledge. To best guide children in the habits of reflection, these teachers approach their role as that of "facilitator of meaning making."

In the role of facilitator, the teacher acts as an intermediary between the learner and the learning, guiding each student to approach the learning activity in a strategic way. The teacher helps each student monitor individual progress, construct meaning from the content learned *and* from the process of learning it, and apply the learnings to other contexts and settings. Learning becomes a continual process of *engaging* the mind that *transforms* the mind.

Unfortunately, educators don't often ask students to reflect on their learning. Thus, when students *are* asked to reflect on an assignment, they are caught in a dilemma: "What am I supposed to do? How do I 'reflect'? I've already completed this assignment! Why do I have to think about it anymore?"

In response to our questions, students who are inexperienced with reflection offer simple answers such as "This was an easy assignment!" or "I really enjoyed doing this assignment." If we want students to get in the habit of reflecting deeply on their work—and if we want them to use Habits of Mind such as applying past knowledge to new situations, thinking about thinking (metacognition), and remaining open to continuous learning—we must teach them strategies to derive rich meaning from their experiences.

Setting the Tone for Reflection

Most classrooms can be categorized in one of two ways: active and a bit noisy, with students engaged in hands-on work; or teacher oriented, with students paying attention to a presentation or quietly working on individual tasks. Each of these teaching environments sets a tone and an expectation. For example, when students work actively in groups, we ask them to use their "six-inch" voices. When we ask them to attend to the teacher, we also request that they turn their "eyes front." When they work individually at their desks, we ask them not to bother other learners.

Teachers must signal a shift in tone when they ask students to reflect on their learning. Reflective teachers help students understand that the students will now look back rather than move forward. They will take a break from what they have been doing, step away from their work, and ask themselves, "What have I (or we) learned from doing this activity?" Some teachers use music to signal the change in thinking. Others ask for silent thinking before students write about a lesson, an assignment, or other classroom task.

In the reflective classroom, teachers invite students to make meaning from their experiences overtly in written and oral form. They take the time to invite students to reflect on their learnings, to compare intended with actual outcomes, to evaluate their metacognitive strategies, to analyze and draw causal relationships, and to synthesize meanings and apply their learnings to new and novel situations. Students know they will not "fail" or make a "mistake," as those terms are generally defined. Instead, reflective students know they can produce personal insight and learn from *all* their experiences.

Guiding Student Reflection

To be reflective means to mentally wander through where we have been and to try to make some sense out of it. Most classrooms are oriented more to the present and the future than to the past. Such an orientation means that students (and teachers) find it easier to discard what has happened and to move on without taking stock of the seemingly isolated experiences of the past.

Teachers use many strategies to guide students through a period of reflection. We offer several here: discussions, interviews, questioning, and logs and journals.

Discussions

Sometimes, encouraging reflection is as simple as inviting students to think about their thinking. Students realize meaning making is an important goal when reflection becomes the topic of discussion. For example, conduct discussions about students' problem-solving processes. Invite students to share their metacognition, reveal their intentions, detail their strategies for solving a problem, describe their mental maps for monitoring their problem-solving process, and reflect on the strategy to determine its adequacy. During these kinds of rich discussions, students learn how to listen to and explore the implications of each other's metacognitive strategies. The kind of listening required during such discussions also builds the Habits of Mind related to empathy, flexibility, and persistence.

Interviews

Interviews are another way to lead students to share reflections about their learning and their growth in the Habits of Mind. A teacher can interview a student, or students can interview classmates. Set aside time at the end of a learning sequence—a lesson, a unit, a school day, or a school year—to question each other about what has been learned. Guide students to look for ways they can apply their learnings to future settings. Interviews also provide teachers and students with opportunities to model and practice a variety of habits: listening with understanding and empathy, thinking and communicating with clarity and precision, and questioning and posing problems.

Questioning

Well-designed questions—supported by a classroom atmosphere grounded in trust—will invite students to reveal their insights, understandings, and applications of their learnings and the Habits of Mind. Here are possible questions to pose with each student:

• As you reflect on this semester's work, which of the Habits of Mind were you most aware of in your own learnings?

• What metacognitive strategies did you use to monitor your perform-ance of the Habits of Mind?

• Which Habit of Mind will you focus on as you begin our next project?

• What insights have you gained as a result of employing these Habits of Mind?

• As you think about your future, how might these Habits of Mind be used as a guide in your life?

Logs and Journals

Logs and journals are another tool for student reflection. Periodically ask students to reread their journals, comparing what they knew at the beginning of a learning sequence with what they know now. Ask them to select significant learnings, envision how they could apply these learn-ings to future situations, and commit to an action plan to consciously modify their behaviors.

Modeling Reflection

Students need to encounter reflective role models. Many teachers find such models in novels in which the characters take a reflective stance as they consider their actions. A variety of novels and films use the design ele-ment of reflection as the way to tell a story. For example, in Marcel Proust's *Swann's Way*, the main character is affected by the smell of a "petite madeleine" that reminds him of his past. Proust uses this device to dig into the character's past. In Mem Fox's *Wilfrid Gordon McDonald Partridge*, Wilfrid discovers that life's meaning can come from the retrieval of powerful memories. The memories truly are given meaning, however, through making them explicit to someone else.

Although fictional role modeling is useful, students also need to see adults—parents, teachers, and administrators—reflect on their practice. Perhaps you can offer an example from your own work. We offer here an excerpt from Bena Kallick's journal reflecting on a workshop session. She sent her reflection to the workshop participants. Here's the excerpt:

To: The third-year teachers and mentors
From: Bena Kallick
Re: Yesterday's session

Reflecting on the day, I am still mad at myself for not listening more closely to your needs for the afternoon session. I wanted to share some of my thoughts with you.

First, I find that I can use the Habits of Mind as one lens for reflection. As I reconsidered yesterday, there were four habits that I focused on: listening with understanding and empathy, thinking flexibly, managing impulsivity, and remaining open to continuous learning.

Listening with understanding and empathy. One of the strengths in my work is my capacity to stay immersed in the work of others. I need to be able to listen to the surface text of the work, pay attention to the subtext of the individual (the context of the classroom, the personality of the teacher, the intentions and values that are expressed as the person presents the work), and make certain that my comments and critique are in tune with the person who I hope will be able to make use of them. I felt that our group was tuned to the work that was presented and that I was able to model that level of listening. As a result, I think that the presenters were able to listen to their own work more deeply.

The other half of my listening, however, was not as attuned. Patricia tried to suggest that we make time for you to share your own work in the afternoon, but because I lunched with Michelle and was involved with some of the issues and problems she was working on, I lost some of my perspective on where the group was. As a result, I jumped in with the plan to look at the possibility for "brand x" rubrics. Although I cast the afternoon for the possibility of your working on your own rubrics, I observed that almost everyone either worked on the general rubric (with energy and commitment) or started to do their own work for the classroom. I thought that most people were using the time productively, and so I did not listen carefully to Patricia's concerns. I should have lunched with Patricia and David, talked through what was in my head for the afternoon, and listened at that time for their read of the group and its needs.

Thinking flexibly. I always pride myself on the degree to which I am willing to shift plans and respond to the group's immediate needs. That strength, however, can also become a weakness—and I think that happened yesterday. When Dan suggested that we move to developing outcomes that would work across the disciplines, I immediately went there without checking with the group. Maybe that happened because the question is of intellectual interest to me right now and I also wanted to work on it. I have been struggling with how to develop a rubric that would be sufficiently rigorous and, at the same time, descriptive enough to provide a set of criteria for students that would show them what was expected regardless of subject. Clear criteria would address a question such as "Why do we need to write properly if I am in a science class?" To me, these criteria are a significant part of building a learning culture. I was exploring using the criteria in relation to the Habits of Mind—I will develop this thought more fully in a moment.

Managing impulsivity. Well, this is where the habits intersect and sometimes feel contradictory. I moved very quickly with Dan's suggestion. I would say that I did not manage my impulsivity. Can you be both flexible and manage your impulsivity at the same time? I think the way to do that is to check your moves. I should have done so with the group instead of assuming I knew where to go. Had I managed my impulsive act through a quick check on the afternoon agenda, we might have gone down the same path, or a different one, and at least made the decision together.

Remaining open to continuous learning. I started thinking about Evonne Goolagong. (She's a really great tennis player. What I always admired about her was her grace, agility, and enormous flexibility. She had all the strokes, and often what got in her way of winning was that she did not make the right choice of stroke for the occasion.) I think I am at a point in my career where I have many choices in my repertoire for each teaching situation. Sometimes I do not take the time to think through which is the right choice for the occasion. I am finding it easy to excuse impulsive behavior by thinking of it as flexible behavior. Because I am an "in the moment" teacher, I need to pay attention to this more than I have been recently. I am grateful to you yesterday for reminding me of the importance of this dynamic in order for me to continue to be the teacher I imagine I would like to be!

After this particular reflection, Kallick worked with the teachers to design their next session to better meet everyone's needs. Sharing parts of the reflection brought them to another level of understanding as they worked together in a learning community. Reflection can bring the same spirit of community to your classroom, too.

Students also learn much when they see examples of reflection from other students' journals. You might want to cull a variety of examples to share. Here is a reflection from a group journal written by students from the Communications Academy at Sir Francis Drake High School in San Anselmo, California:

> Today our group spent most of the time reading articles and the ballot info pamphlet. We have all participated and have been open and informative. Our goal seems to be execution of the actual set of criteria for our project. . . .
>
> We are passing around our wonderful journal to write down what we want to do or improve on for ourselves. I want to work on reading. I find myself reading enough to slide by but not enough to be fully educated in the subject. It takes a lot of time, so I need to find some of that, too. I want to be able to answer the questions I have asked with precision and accuracy. My stretch goal would be to do everything assigned to me completed and on time. If I start to slack off, just kick me back into place. . . .
>
> I want to be more patient. I also feel I talk a lot and don't mean to. I want to try to listen with understanding and empathy.

The students at University Heights School in New York City are required to reflect on the Habits of Mind they have adopted when they present their portfolios to a panel of judges. The following excerpt is a reflection from one student:

> Through "Thinking Critically and Questioning," we investigate questions, myths, and even proven knowledge. From that we gain intelligence (learning from proof, not opinion) and experiences to find what we believe to be the truth. . . .
>
> I learned the importance of an education. Ignorance is a weakness. It fogs the mind and blurs the human eye. Only knowledge can clear our visions of this weakening lack of thought. . . .
>
> I learned the value of our pride. In my opinion, those who were forced to serve without pay were not slaves. They were captives to slaves of greed.
>
> Now that I have this strengthened knowledge, I must apply it to my life. But the success of that assignment can only be judged by me. Only I know what is happiness and beauty in this mind and it will take me an entire lifetime to apply what I have learned to my existence.

Developmental Issues

The work of educators at Croton Elementary School in Croton-on-Hudson, New York, shows how the quality of students' reflections changes as children develop their reading and writing skills. When kindergartners were asked to reflect orally, they gave rich descriptions of their work. But as they developed their writing ability and were encouraged to write their own reflections, the reflections became less descriptive. This change puzzled the teachers until they realized that students are more concerned about spelling, punctuation, and other aspects of editing when they first learn to write. Because students do not have a great deal of fluency with their writing, they are more limited in what they describe.

In contrast, when meeting with the teacher, the kindergartners elaborated on what they wrote about their work. And once students became more fluent with their writing skills, they were able to represent their reflective thoughts more easily.

Teaching Students How to Reflect

Initially the students at Croton Elementary often offered stereotypical comments such as "This was fun!" or "I chose this piece of work because it is my best." Teachers realized that they needed to spend time teaching students how to reflect. They asked students, "What does a reflection look like when it really tells you something about the experience?" After considerable discussion—and after considering models of reflection from students and published authors—the students began to understand what was called for. Reflection was not a time for testimonials about how good or bad the experience was. Instead, reflection was the time to consider what was learned from the experience. Reflection was a time to describe what students saw in their own work that changed, needed to change, or might need to be described so another person might understand its meaning.

Figure 12.1 shows how teachers characterized student work as students acquired the capacity for reflection. The teachers then summarized key statements that students made about their work when asked the question "What would I change to make my work better?" Students from kindergarten through 2nd grade made comments such as these:

- I would add to the picture.
- I would use what I know to show more in the picture.
- I would add what is missing.
- I would be more careful.

Students in 3rd and 4th grade made comments like these:

- I would correct.
- I would proofread.
- I would pay attention to conventions.
- I would extend more.
- I would stay to the subject.

FIGURE 12.1

Students' Stages of Reflection

Kindergarten
Describes what is drawn.

Focuses on drawing.

Comments on realism.

Shows interest (what student really loves).

Mentions use of color.

Mentions use of letters.

Pays attention to what letters spell.

1st Grade
Focuses on conventions.

Wants papers to have a neat appearance.

Talks about what was liked in drawing.

2nd Grade
Focuses on details.

Focuses on colors.

Shows development of an idea.

Relates to content of story (how student feels about the content of what was written).

3rd–5th Grade (Learning-to-Read Stage)
Responds in depth to dictation.

Starts to write by self.

Teachers used these phrases to describe 3rd and 4th grade students' writing as the teachers reflected upon it:

- Uses humor.
- Talks about genre or type of writing.
- Attends to style (uses dialogue).
- Describes well enough for a reader to picture what was written.
- Focuses on script.
- Focuses on description.
- Offers information.
- Is interesting.

- Works hard.
- Is exciting.
- Attends to the reader.
- Is clear.
- Does not drag writing out.
- Uses descriptive words.

Through this experience, the teachers realized that the questions they asked might limit students' responses. They reminded themselves that the purpose of reflection is threefold:

- To help students become more aware of their writing—what makes writing work and what does not.
- To help students take more responsibility for their writing—to know that writing must be understood by an audience and to learn how to anticipate a reader's response through self-evaluation.
- To see growth in writing over the school year and to be able to talk about that growth with students' parents.

Teachers emphasized to students that the purpose of reflection was not to develop a carefully crafted piece of writing, but to develop the capacity for metacognition.

Sentence Stems

Sentence stems can stimulate reflections. Use them in conferences (where reflection can be modeled), or put them on a sheet for students who choose writing to jump-start their reflections. Here are examples of possible sentence stems:

- I selected this piece of writing because . . . .
- What really surprised me about this piece of writing was . . . .
- When I look at my other pieces of writing, this piece is different because . . . .
- What makes this piece of writing strong is my use of . . . .
- Here is one example from my writing to show you what I mean.
- What I want to really work on to make my writing better for a reader is . . . .

Student Choices

Students may prefer simply to describe what is going on in the writing in their own way. When students set their goals, they will use their reflections as a basis for directing their learning journey. Students might collect work throughout the year as part of a portfolio process. Every quarter they can review the work in their collection folders and choose one or two pieces to enter into their portfolio. When they make those choices, they can take the opportunity to reflect on the reasons for their choices and to set goals for their next quarter's work.

Building the Voices of Reflection

The ultimate intent of teaching reflection is to get students into the habit of reflecting on their own actions and constructing meaning from those experiences. When they develop the Habits of Mind related to reflection, they will hear both an internal and an external voice of reflection.

Internal Voice

The internal voice of reflection is self-knowledge. Self-knowledge is difficult to describe in detail, but we can define it as both *what* and *how* we are thinking. Self-knowledge includes ways of thinking that may not be visible to us consciously. Given our culture, students have difficulty realizing that they need to engage in "self-talk." To help students develop the internal voice of reflection, they can be asked to do the following:

• Write a letter to themselves detailing what they learned from an experience.

• Send themselves a letter of advice, reminding themselves of what to look out for the next time they do something.

• Interview themselves.

• Make a list of connections they see between their work and others' work. Include peers' work along with work that has been studied in the classroom.

• Record the steps they go through to solve a problem. Guide them to comment on how useful those steps were.

External Voice

Students hear an external voice of reflection in others' comments, suggestions, assessments, evaluations, and feedback. External sharing of reflections is important because this kind of reflection multiplies the learning for each individual. As students review the learning events that have taken place, they give their learning new meaning. The opportunity to share often validates a student's internal conversation. Here are suggestions for helping students develop the capacity for sharing their reflections:

• Sit in a circle. Ask each person to share one reflection on the day's activities.

• Organize small-group reflections in which students share their thoughts. Then ask a reporter to present those thoughts to the whole class.

• Invite students to share problem-solving strategies. Ask them to focus on how many different ways they can effectively solve a problem.

• Ask students to share at least one example in which they observed their group using the Habits of Mind.

During these classroom experiences, teachers have an opportunity to model the Habits of Mind themselves. They can show evidence of good listening skills, probe for clarity and understanding, ask thoughtful questions, and share metacognitive thinking. Through experience and continuous modeling, the class begins to learn how to use the Habits of Mind in reflective conversations, which strengthens the transfer to the internal voice of reflection.

Documenting Reflections

Many teachers document reflective conversations as a way of assessing progress with the Habits of Mind. For example, as mentioned in Chapter 11, some teachers create a notebook tabbed with each student's name. They also keep sticky labels close at hand. When a student makes a significant comment that shows evidence of using a Habit of Mind, the teacher jots down the key words from the comment on a label and sticks the label on the tabbed page for that student. This record provides a rich source of information for a conference or a student report.

You might also consider reading student journals and noting how student reflections are developing. Keep a record for each student with notes about whether the student has moved from superficial to in-depth reflections. Indicators of in-depth reflections include making specific reference to the learning event, providing examples and elaboration, making connections to other learning, and discussing modifications based on insights from this experience.

Developing the Habits of Mind related to continuous growth and improvement requires the capacity to be self-reflective. As students reflect on their learning, they gain important assessment information about how they perceive the efficacy of their thinking.

> Many of us grow up thinking of mistakes as bad, viewing errors as evidence of fundamental incapacity. This negative thinking pattern can create a self-fulfilling prophecy, which undermines the learning process. To maximize our learning it is essential to ask: "How can we get the most from every mistake we make?"
>
> —Michael Gelb and Tony Buzan

Reference

Feuerstein, R., Rand, Y., Hoffman, M., & Miller, R. (1980). *Instrumental enrichment: An intervention program for cognitive modifiability*. Baltimore, MD: University Park Press.

13

Wondering to Be Done

Steve Seidel

I remember meditating on these attached objects. . . . (feet and hands, especially, but also chest, knees, stomach) . . . looking at them, touching them, feeling them from the outside and from the inside, wondering about them because there was wondering to be done, not because there were answers to be found.

—*Jane Smiley,* A Thousand Acres

Several years ago, I spent three months conducting a series of workshops with 10 teachers from Fuller Elementary School in Gloucester, Massachusetts. When the final session was over, I began a long period of wondering about the value of the work we'd just completed.[1] Our work had gone well in so many ways. We enjoyed ourselves and remained engaged with our task. Final evaluations were strongly positive, pointing to many lessons and benefits for the participating teachers.

So why did I doubt?

Our workshops were conducted in five sessions. Four lasted four hours; the final session was a two-hour reflection. The task was to explore

Adapted by permission of the publisher from Allen, D. (Ed.), *Assessing student learning: From grading to understanding* (New York: Teachers College Press, © 1998 by Teachers College, Columbia University. All rights reserved), pp. 21–39. Adaptation first appeared in Costa & Kallick 2000, © 2000 ASCD.

the benefits and difficulties of working with a protocol for examining children's work, called *collaborative assessment conferences*. This protocol had been designed by my colleagues at Harvard Project Zero and myself during our work in the Pittsburgh Public Schools on Arts Propel (Seidel, 1998). Each participating teacher shared a piece of writing from a K–5 student, and we followed the conference structure to consider the student's work.

The conference protocol called for extensive examination and description of each work. Over the three months, we read and talked about 10 pieces of student writing. What a luxurious experience! Four hours at a time just to look at and talk about student work! There were no placement decisions to make, no scores to decide on, no remedial plans to hammer out. It was a situation so out of character from the way professional time is usually spent in most schools that virtually everyone participating was, at times, ill at ease

Still, our work progressed, and in time, some interesting things began to happen. Reflecting on the first conference, Julie noted the effect of considering student work collaboratively: "It made me see a lot more than I would just sitting alone. And the more you looked, the more you saw." These comments seemed true to me; I had noticed that the teachers' first hesitant observations led slowly but surely into a sequence of more and more specific descriptions. It wasn't until the sessions were completed that the consequences of this phenomenon became clearer to me.

As I reviewed the workshops, I noticed certain patterns in our conversations. The more the teachers looked at a piece of student writing, the more they recognized the complexity of the child's effort and accomplishments. As they grappled with the complexity of the work, they became even more interested in the child who created it. The more interested they became in the child, the more they wanted to meet and talk with the child. They generated questions that only the young author could answer. The teachers deeply wanted those answers, and they wanted to get to know the child, too.

With all these positive outcomes, why did I still wonder about the value of our experiences? Perhaps it was because I kept hearing one of the workshop teachers, Elizabeth, asking how our work would translate into something positive for her students. Liz raised this question several times in the course of the meetings, both orally and in her written reflections, and I always felt inadequate trying to answer her. I didn't know if sitting together for so many hours talking about specific pieces of writing would translate into something positive for her students. What meaning would these teachers make of the workshops, and what would they take back to their classrooms?

I did notice that as the sessions progressed, Liz became very involved with our discussions. At one point, she wrote about one effect these sessions were having on her:

> [It may be] off the subject, but I'm aware of how alive I feel when I am part of a conversation [or] discussion about *language*—I like to be reminded about possibilities and options—offering the child options—seeing possibilities in writing. There doesn't have to be a definitive answer—*so* different from when I *was* a student. [emphasis in original]

Liz seemed torn between her sense of responsibility to her students and her enjoyment of our work. She deeply believed that if she was not in class with students, she should be doing something that clearly would benefit them. In retrospect, I suspect that in the high-stakes, outcome-based world of education and professional development, I heard Liz's very real and very serious question—"How will my students benefit from this?"—and felt insecure about what I really believed. Though I shared my thoughts with that group, I was not confident.

I've spent the last several years engaging many more teachers in regular sessions devoted to collaboratively looking at pieces of student work. I better understand the value of that activity and the protocol we use. In short, I've come to believe that the protocol encourages a sense of wonder: about children, writing, teaching, curriculum, assessment, and more. And, like Jane Smiley's narrator in *A Thousand Acres*, I've found value in wondering because "there was wondering to be done, not because there were answers to be found."

The Protocol Steps

The collaborative assessment conference protocol has a series of distinct sections and basic guidelines. Briefly, the protocol follows this structure:

1. *Read the text.* In silence, everyone reads a student text that has been brought to the session by a participant who has agreed to be the "presenting" teacher for the conference.

2. *Observe and describe.* The presenting teacher remains silent. All other participants discuss the work, and they focus first, as strictly as possible, on a description of the piece.

3. *Raise questions.* Description is followed by articulation of questions about the text, the author, or the context of the writing.

4. *What is the child working on?* The readers speculate on what they think the child was working on as the child created the text.

5. *The presenting teacher responds.* Throughout the discussion so far, the presenting teacher has been silent. At this point, the presenting teacher adds personal observations about the text, answering as many questions as possible.

6. *Teaching moves and pedagogical responses.* Together, the readers and presenting teacher consider possible teaching moves to encourage and challenge the writer.

7. *Reflection.* When all this conversation is complete, the entire group, including the facilitator, reflects on the conference. They consider its satisfactions, frustrations, and confusions as well as ways to improve the next conference.

In addition to prescribing when the presenting teacher should listen and speak, the protocol has two major guidelines or rules. First, participants are asked to withhold their judgments of the work under consideration. This restraint includes expressions of taste ("I like [or don't like] ___ about the work") or of quality ("This is [or isn't] good"). Second, in the initial phases of the conference, as little information as possible is revealed about the writer and the context of the writing (such as assignment, grade, gender, or materials provided). These guidelines make collaborative assessment conferences quite different from most forms of assessment regularly practiced by teachers.

Furthermore, most teachers rarely experience any form of structured and regular professional conversations about specific pieces of children's work. It is hardly ever part of regular staff discussion, inservice programs, or most teacher training courses. In this light, the Gloucester workshops, focused and structured as they were, were an extraordinary professional experience for these teachers. Without making specific claims for their value, it is reasonable to suggest that the focus and structure of these workshops were a radical departure from the ordinary.

A Conference in Action

Following is an account of the discussion around one piece of student work we considered during the Gloucester workshops and the first from a 1st grade classroom. This was the eighth piece of student work we had discussed together. The text is briefer than a full transcript, but it does represent the flow and focus of the session.

After we settled in, Julie and Pam handed out copies of "May Is" for everyone to read. Before continuing with this chapter, stop and read "May Is" in Figure 13.1. Reading this work carefully before going any further will help you understand the discussion that follows. (You might even want to read the work aloud.) Julie had agreed to take the role of the facilitator for this conference, and Pam was the presenting teacher. Julie gave people several minutes to read and reread the text and to consider the picture. After Julie called for observations and descriptions, it didn't take long for the teachers to raise the issue of punctuation in the piece or, more correctly, the lack of punctuation.

The teachers noted the ambiguity of the author's meaning. Ellen said, "To me, it [the text] is a child brainstorming the world going on around them or feelings about the month of May, which is 'bees in flowers' and 'birds in the sky.'"

Alyce jumped in, "Or 'sky dogs walking flowers'! That's what I see."

Cherylann was the first to point to the lack of punctuation: "I don't see any punctuation, and I see an interesting choice of word placement that sometimes doesn't reflect whether the child has sentence structure, such as the whole idea of 'butterflies dancing in the sky dogs walking flowers. . . .' or is it 'dogs walking. flowers that are blue and red.' There isn't a real finite way of knowing where things stop and start."

FIGURE 13.1

"May Is"

Throughout this conference, the issue of no punctuation, and the subsequent ambiguity of the phrasing in the piece, came up time and again, through and around observations, as part of questions and speculations. We talked about the relationship of the text to the picture and the process through which this work came to be. We commented on the child's spelling and raised questions about the ending. (The child appears to have written and erased "thats the end" after "two lips" in Line 4. This erasure cannot be seen in this book, but it's evident on the original work.) There was extensive discussion about whether or not this was a poem. But the dominant concern was over how to read the meaning of these words and phrases without any punctuation to guide the way. Here is the discussion:

> *Annette*: I want to know why the writer stopped at "two lips."
> It seems like there should be more to this. Unless . . .
> *Cherylann*: Maybe the dogs are blue and red.
> *Annette*: The dogs are walking flowers that are blue and red tulips.

A short time later, Margaret came back to the final phrases of the piece:

> *Margaret*: I have a meaning question. Is it "flowers that are blue and red, tulips" or "flowers that are blue and red tulips"? And if you put an exclamation point on it, it would make a meaning to the whole poem.
> *Annette*: If you are interpreting it by the picture, it looks like she is saying "flowers that are red and blue" and "tulips" is another thought.
> *Liz*: Is the tulip made of red and blue?
> *Annette*: No, it's purple.

Later, someone questioned how the child could mean "in the sky dogs walking flowers," and Cherylann offered that it made sense to her. Upon reading those lines, she had imagined looking up at a sky full of clouds and seeing "dogs walking flowers" in the ever-changing cloud formations. Alyce wanted to see "all of us put in the punctuation we think should go in here. We'd come up with seven or nine different pieces."

Because Julie seemed to be handling the role of the facilitator quite comfortably, I decided I could participate in this conference as a reader. I had been quiet for some time, but in examining the poem, I made a discovery that startled me. I had noted earlier that the child had written "thats the end" in Line 4 after "two lips" and then erased it. Somehow, this observation, and my own confusion over why this child had broken the lines where she did, led me to count the syllables in each line.

"I noticed [something]. . . ," I said. "I did this quickly counting on my fingers. There are four lines. I didn't have to use my fingers for that, but there are 10 syllables in Lines 1, 3, and 4, if you count 'thats the end', which the writer has taken out, and 11 [syllables] in Line 2."

This observation was striking to others as well, and it immediately raised questions about whether the number of syllables was an accident or intentional. What implications did the syllables have for whether or not this was a poem? Could this young child have actually counted the syllables? Could she have known that syllabification is an established way many poets determine where to break the lines of their poems? Could she have "invented" this poetic form? Or was this syllabification simply an accident? As usual, we reached no clear conclusions. The discussion proceeded and explored questions about the nature of the assignment. (Could the child have been told to go outside and observe nature on a recent May day?) The group jumped back and forth between observations and thoughts about the feeling of the piece and its structural components (e.g., punctuation, line breaks, and use of conjunctions).

Finally, it was Pam's turn to speak, and she was quick to note that in September this child was writing complete sentences with punctuation. "As a matter of fact, the poetry piece I had her do before last time was much more sentence oriented. Less free flowing. It was interesting to me that she broke out of that mold." Julie asked Pam to say more about this. "She was very much into a prose mold. Here's my complete thought, and this is the ending. This strikes me as atypical of her work."

Pam added that "two lips" was, indeed, meant to be tulips, and that the last line should be read as "flowers that are red and blue [pause] tulips." Pam reported that she had heard the writer read this poem aloud, and her reading of the final line made clear where the pause should be.

Teaching Moves and Responses

After considerable conversation about the child and her relationship to this piece of work, to writing in general, and to Pam, Julie decided it was time to move on to a discussion of teaching moves and responses. I include here a significant portion of the transcript of that part of the conference because it touches on so many issues that seem central to where the group had come by this point, our next-to-last session:

Julie: Pam, what did you do or might you do in relation to this?

Pam: With this particular piece of work, I'm not sure, because where it wasn't an assignment [it was done during free-choice time], I don't know that she should touch it. Perhaps I'd have her work on commas.

Steve: To me the question is to think back to, What did I say? What was my response?

Pam: Thinking back, I wonder if she wanted to share it with the class. I could go back and offer her a chance to do that.

Nancy: I would think the very last thing you would want to do is punctuate [this piece].

Pam: No. I don't want to touch this. But I do want to talk about the use of commas in future work. No, I wouldn't touch this.

Liz: You might show her some poetry and how it is put in lines. She might want to put this in more standard form of poetic lines.

Steve: Except I think . . .

Liz: It might help with the meaning. There is still some confusion for me.

Cherylann: But the various meanings were really interesting.

Liz: Well, what is the problem then? The value is in the meaning for us, or is the value in the meaning they want to have?

Steve: Well, would that be a response? To say, hey, I can read this in two different ways. I can read this and it means "dogs walking flowers" and that makes me laugh or as "dogs walking [pause] flowers that are blue." Just to let her know that when you write poetry this way it has an ambiguity that is playful.

Liz: I like that approach better than the way . . . my approach was more clinical.

In the midst of this interchange, Liz posed a question that I take as central to this whole enterprise. In essence, she asked, "Whose meaning matters? The writer's or the reader's?" During discussion of a piece called "Beautiful Butterfly" in our third session, Cherylann had talked about the writer's voice and the reader's voice. She named the issue but didn't really push the question. The problem was complicated for these teachers. If the job of a writing teacher is to help children communicate clearly and effectively what they mean to say, how might the teacher attend to both the child's intent and the meaning the teacher makes from the text? This question is further complicated by recognizing the remarkable variety of meanings that could be drawn from a single text.

In retrospect, it is no surprise that Liz raised this question when we were talking about teaching moves. Just a bit later, Margaret picked up on this issue of multiple meanings: "If you are to read it aloud and say there are lots of ways of looking at this, it opens up for a writer a different way of looking at their work. It would be interesting to see if the child saw other ways."

Talking About the Conversation

The last steps in the protocol are to conclude the discussion of teaching moves, thank the presenting teacher for sharing the work with the group, and make sure everyone is prepared to move from talking about the work in question to talking about the conversation about the work. Julie felt it was time to move on. She checked with the group, and getting consent, she moved into the reflection on the conference.

"All I can say is, whatever you are doing, you are doing a great job because when she [Pam's student, Jessica] left me at the end of last year, she couldn't do this. Bits of it, maybe, but not all of this. So I applaud you," said Alyce, starting off the reflection.

Pam took a turn to talk about her experience of the discussion. Frustration was the first thing she expressed: "That was really hard not to talk, and I felt a lot of time was wasted on 'tulips.' If I could have just said, 'This is how she meant it!' The tulip conversation was OK that it went that way, but at the time it seemed like wasted time. And I just wanted to say, 'flowers that are red and blue [pause] tulips!' And get on to the next thing!"

Pam's comments were followed by some silence, so Julie asked if there were any other thoughts about the process. I felt obliged to defend, or at least explain, why I tolerate and even encourage the kind of "wasted time" Pam described. I had talked before about this kind of conference as a practice, something that might be done regularly as a part of keeping one's clinical eye focused and keen.

"You are practicing your ability to wonder about children's work," I said. "It is an exercise in living with the idea that there isn't one right answer and [in] entertaining the [multiple] possibilities. I think there is some value in that even if, in the end, you tell us what the child meant and we accept that."

Annette responded by commenting on how the child's reason for writing might affect the way the teacher chooses to respond to the ambiguity or lack of clarity in the writing. The rest of the conversation picked up and pursued these themes:

> *Cherylann:* But in terms of the process, if Pam had clarified the question and we'd never had the conversation about what to say to that child about the ambiguity . . . . And what I take away from this conversation is that the next time a child comes to me with a poem, I may say, "Hey, this is really ambiguous. Did you mean that? Do you mean it to be this way?" Talking about the process, if you had clarified it beforehand, we never would have discussed the issue of ambiguity.
>
> *Margaret:* I agree. And I think one of the most wonderful things you can say to a child about their work is, "I thought about this. And in my thinking I can see all different kinds of meanings." And that ambiguity is part of the richness. That it can mean one thing to the person who wrote it and something equally rich and equally meaningful to someone else. Isn't that wonderful? That kind of richness of experience.
>
> *Steve:* Why do you think that's wonderful?
>
> *Margaret:* I think that's wonderful because it is telling the person that wrote it that there are more things in heaven and earth than they can see. Something that they have written has

more meanings than they meant. It also has meanings for others that might be different. Their experience has made it one meaning, and my experience has made it another meaning. And that's not to say that my meaning is right. A piece is very rich when there are lots of meanings. Language is very flexible.

Cherylann: But it also carries into other forms. Right now I'm concentrating on the science fair. If a child came up with ambiguous language in that, there would be a problem. Sometimes ambiguity is appropriate and fine, but not in science writing. Sometimes you need concise, precise language.

Julie: What I think is important about going back to the child and saying that "I've been thinking about your work" is the message that "You matter to me. And your work matters, and you are on my mind and you exist in my mind when you are not with me."

Liz: "And I respect you. . . ."

Julie: "And I respect you enough to think about you or your problem or your work. . . ."

Margaret: That's why I think your immediate reaction may just be, "Oh, that's very interesting." But if you come back with, "There are a lot of meanings here, and I wonder what you meant. . . ."

Liz: It shows you are really interested in their learning.

I have included this rather lengthy account of a collaborative assessment conference to provide an example of how questions emerge in the course of these conversations and the way in which a genuine interest in the child writer can grow from examining the meaning of the text. Questions, in this case, are both an expression of interest and a means by which to explore one's curiosity.

Where Do Questions Come From?

Questions come from becoming curious about something that has engaged our attention. It is a curious phenomenon that we often have difficulty staying interested in things about which we believe we know everything—or nothing at all. To become engaged with something, it helps to have some, but not too much, familiarity with the subject. Like works of art, the things children make can be highly engaging. They can captivate, confuse, charm, and alarm us. But if we think we know everything about children, their work, or a particular child, we won't watch with such care. The protocol is a trick, then, to focus attention and encourage engagement.

Questions come from engagement and from having our perceptions challenged. I believe three elements of the collaborative assessment conference protocol combine to encourage engagement:

- Withholding context.
- Withholding judgments.
- Hearing your colleagues describe what they see on the page (and in turn saying what you see).

Withholding Context

Perhaps the most fundamental beliefs underlying collaborative assessment conferences are that (1) the work children produce is worthy of serious consideration and analysis, and (2) in that work we can see much about children and their interactions with the environments in which they produced the work (the classroom, school, family, and community). Most readers, given information about a child and her context for producing a piece of writing, will view that child's work through the lens of that information; they won't let a picture of the child emerge from the work itself. Teachers often adjust their expectations of work based on their associations to the bits of information they have about a child (usually things like age, gender, grouping in school, neighborhood, native language, and socioeconomic background).

Nothing is surprising about such interpretation. Taking small clues about people and making assumptions about who they are is one way in which we all negotiate our way through a complex world. The problem for teachers is that our associations often mislead us, and they might actually blind us to important aspects of a child's character and learning.

In describing group examinations of children's writing at the Bread Loaf School of English, Armstrong (1992) addressed the effect of knowing the context of the writing on a reader's investigation of the text:

So we begin by immersing ourselves in the text. It doesn't always pay at first to know too much about the child who wrote it or the circumstances of its composition. As Geoff Keith said in our class the other day, the trouble with concentrating on the child rather than the story is that "it allows you to marginalize the text." . . . All the time we're trying to concentrate our whole attention on the significance of the words on the page. (p. 3)

One of the central goals of this protocol is to encourage direct engagement between teachers and student texts with little context about the child or the assignment. As one of the Gloucester teachers said, we were focusing on "the actual writing itself." Of course, much of this contextual information is revealed in the course of the conference, but the initial reading and discussion are conducted in as decontextualized a fashion as possible. In general, everyone knows the presenting teacher and what grade she teaches, so there are strong clues about the context of the work that cannot be hidden.

In every one of these workshops, the challenge of looking at children's work in this decontextualized manner was considered confusing, difficult, and frustrating. Liz questioned this practice a number of times. In the third session, she declared, "I find so much energy goes to figuring out who the child is, and that feels very artificial. I mean, when do we ever read work without knowing who the child is?"

On this occasion, I responded, "Well, certainly, in your classroom, you always know who the child is. So why do I do that?" But then, instead of offering a direct answer, I asked another question: "Is there anything gained in *not knowing* the identity of the child when you first encounter the work?"

A bit later, Liz came back to this issue: "To me the essence of writing is to make an 'I am' statement. The person—and this came up last week—the person's voice and the energy in the writing are an 'I am' statement. And that's part of why some kids have trouble with writing, and then to totally deny the identity of the person . . . ."

This criticism seemed to me a rather harsh description of the protocol. I responded, "Well, the question, Liz, is that if the child is really present in the work, are we really denying them or are we just looking for them in a particular way within the work?"

Responding to this interchange, Annette offered her perspective: "I felt a lot like Liz, that a lot of valuable time was wasted because we didn't know the identity of the child, because we were almost making up reasons for things that would be completely simplified if we just knew who it was. And yet, especially when I was choosing some of the other work, I was really glad that people wouldn't know who the child was because I really wanted to hear a real reaction to the writing and not to the personality of the child. I don't even know how to explain why, but some of the selections I picked, if people knew who the writer was, there would be a strong reaction because the children's personalities are so strong. But I think there are some really interesting pieces of writing there just to respond to. And it really does provide more objectivity and insight."

Withholding Judgments

In collaborative assessment conferences, teachers are asked explicitly to keep their opinions of the work to themselves. The structure leaves essentially no room for statements about personal taste (likes and dislikes), judgments of quality ("This was really good!"), or judgments about developmental level ("This is excellent for a kindergartner!"). As facilitator, I often chose to allow some judgmental statements, especially in the first conferences. I simply didn't want to cut people off as they did what is habitual: make quick judgments. As participants came to see reasons for withholding judgments in these conferences, I became more diligent in stopping people when they made judgmental comments.

This practice is wholly different from scoring sessions in which pieces or collections of student work are judged in relation to a set of criteria by teams of independent readers. True, scorings by independent readers are also largely decontextualized, although the prompt, or assignment, is known to the scorer. Little information may be provided about the writer or the circumstance of the writing, but the purpose and premise of the reading are entirely different from the collaborative assessment conferences. In scoring sessions, readers are making judgments immediately and, in most cases, without benefit of conversation with other readers. They usually can, but are not required to, provide evidence from the texts for their judgments.

In collaborative assessment conferences, the purpose of the reading is to investigate the meaning of the writing and the child's intent (what the child was trying to say and do in the piece), to bring the reader closer to the child through becoming familiar with the text. This purpose presents difficulties for many participants. Meaning is subjective, and a teacher's grasp of a child's intent is speculative. Sometimes there is considerable evidence, and other times there is very little. In these sessions, teachers' concerns about the subjective nature of this practice were almost as constant as those about the decontextualized readings of the works.

These two aspects of the protocol—the decontextualized nature of our readings and the nonjudgmental character of the discussion—are based on a belief that seemed to be deeply unsettling for most of the teachers. Simply put, in relation to children's writing, there are no absolute or right answers about meaning or quality. Not only that, the structure of the conference demands more questions than answers. The structure encourages speculations based on evidence, and it requires thinking about how to teach writing based on reasonable but uncertain ideas about what children are working on and interested in.

To some people, finding a compelling question is a more important moment in the learning process than finding an answer. Although that belief is not at the heart of our educational system, it is at the heart of this collaborative assessment practice. This belief seemed to be quite disconcerting for many of the participants, but I also suspect that all the questions were deeply exciting to the teachers. Margaret was the most vocal about the delight she felt at times in this work. At the end of the final session, she spoke about how these meetings had "made me very humble." The repeated process of thinking she knew what was going on in a piece of work, and then hearing something surprising from one of her colleagues that made her rethink her whole interpretation, delighted her.

"[I would] think, 'Well, this and this and this,' and somebody would come along and say something that would open up a whole new world for me," she said. She suggested that simply looking at a work with a colleague "and saying, 'What do you see?' and 'This is what I see!' [would be] immensely fruitful."

I came to understand that this kind of careful examination of "the actual work itself" can be a bit like stepping through Alice's looking glass. At first, the room seems familiar, but further exploration reveals remarkable surprises. Looking at students' work not only allowed us to see the child presented in a unique fashion but also provided unique views of the classroom with its complex of materials, ideas, pedagogy, and approaches to writing.

Questions Raised

Raising questions about the work did not seem especially difficult for the Gloucester teachers. In all the conferences, they raised at least a half dozen questions, and most conferences generated many more. At least two significant kinds of questions came up in these sessions. The first were questions that one could ask of any piece of student writing, and they concerned the context of the work (e.g., age and gender of the author and whether the child worked alone or received help). The second kind of questions were those that could only be asked of a particular piece of writing. They grew more directly out of the specific description of a particular piece.

The specificity of questions raised may well be an indication of the depth of engagement the readers have had with the text. The deeper the reading (which I take to be an indicator of the rigor and success of the descriptive process), the more text-specific the questions. In the discussion of "May Is," for example, participants asked many text-specific questions. One that intrigued a number of us had to do with why the child erased "thats the end" from the last line.

Further analysis of all the other questions that emerged in the course of the 10 conferences revealed that they fell into three major categories: teaching, curriculum, and assessment; the nature of writing in different genres; and children as writers. These categories are significant because they provide insight into both the participants' concerns and interests and what aspects of a child's work can and are likely to be explored through using the protocol. In working with numerous other groups of teachers and the protocol, I've found these categories to be consistently useful for parsing the questions raised. What I find significant about these categories is that they represent a range of concerns that cover many aspects of serious professional development in the realm of teaching writing. In other words, through collaborative assessment conferences, teachers are likely to articulate issues and concerns that are both important to them and significant to the field.

The first category encompasses questions about teaching, curriculum, and assessment. In the conversation about "May Is," for example, participants talked at length about the relationship between the lack of punctuation and the meaning communicated in the poem. This discussion gave rise to questions about when and how to approach the problem of teaching punctuation. Should Jessica's poem be corrected for punctuation? Can punctuation be discussed in the context of exploring what meaning Jessica wants to communicate? What could Pam do to help Jessica as a writer at this point? These kinds of questions may come up at any time in the conference, but they are most likely to emerge during the discussion of teaching moves. Other questions in this category explore the relationship between the assignment and what the child hands in. In particular, these questions address how children make sense of teachers' instructions and what kinds of assignments encourage creativity and expressiveness.

The second category is questions about writing in particular genres. Given the nature of the pieces we read, most of our questions centered around story writing, poetry, and writing with illustrations. Through the discussions of several poems, many questions emerged about the nature of poetry. What makes a poem a poem? Can a piece of writing be a poem simply because a child declares it to be a poem? These are obviously important questions, and although there may be no absolute answers to them, how deeply a teacher has considered them and their complexity will have significance for how the teacher structures an assignment and responds to students' writings.

The final category of questions raised in these sessions concerned children as writers and sought a developmental perspective. Here are three of the many questions I noted from the 10 conferences:

1. Do children imagine an audience when they are writing? If so, what audiences do they imagine? Peers? Teachers? Parents? Others?

2. How is a child's writing influenced by the things the child has read or has been read? Are those influences observable?

3. Is there a point in a young child's development as a writer when the child begins to desire standards, criteria, or rules for good writing?

Taken together, these kinds of questions represent a sample of sincere and genuine teacher concerns. If noted and pursued, they could easily provide the basis for compelling professional discourse.

Wonder (the Verb)

An interesting paradox emerges in considering the meaning of *wonder*. My dictionary offers two definitions of *wonder* as a verb:

> 1. a. To have a feeling of awe or admiration; marvel. b. To have a feeling of surprise.
> 2. To be filled with curiosity or doubt. (*American Heritage Dictionary*, 1993)

It is with both of these meanings in mind that I identify the act of wondering as a goal of participation in the protocol. Both have been discussed in this chapter. The poem itself inspired admiration, and we marveled at the complexity of the images and meanings in the text. We further admired Jessica's seriousness and playfulness as a writer and an illustrator. Jessica's efforts reminded us of the challenge of becoming a writer. This is a goal we ask all our students to accept and embrace, but also one that takes years and enormous persistence to achieve.

We were also filled with surprise and doubt. Did Jessica intend this ambiguity? Were our own interpretations of the text reasonable? Why did others read this poem so differently from the way I read it? What, as a writing teacher, can I or should I do to help this child at this point in her development?

The combination of awe and doubt is a particularly potent mixture. Both have a way of opening us up to learning. We become engaged with the object of our awe—the text or the child or, usually, both. We become humble because of the complexity of the challenge of becoming a writer and the desire and seriousness of the child that leads the child to accept the challenge. We are also humbled by the uncertainty we feel as teachers, for we also face a remarkable challenge. We doubt our own capacities to meet the challenge, but we are inspired by our students.

The paradox I find in my dictionary's definition of *wonder* as a verb is that I believe "to wonder" is not always as passive as this definition suggests. Wondering is not simply being filled, and it is not always spontaneous or magical. Wondering can be an active effort, to "be filled." For example, we travel great distances to be filled with wonder in museums and in nature. We also seek wonder in the plant on the windowsill, and we find wonder among the children in the classroom. Wondering takes time, attention, and effort. It is not unlike prayer.

Liz's Question—Again

I left the last session of the Gloucester workshops with considerable uncertainty that Liz or I or the others had an answer to Liz's question. She wanted to know how her students, or any of the children in the school, would benefit from their teachers taking hours at a time to leave the classroom, sit in a room together, and talk about single pieces of student work. This question sat on my shoulder during the countless hours I've studied the transcripts of those sessions. I wanted to see if any clues to Liz's question could be found in what actually transpired during those sessions. In time, I found some clues.

Let's return to a piece of the conversation shared earlier in this chapter. Julie, Liz, and Margaret were reflecting about the conference for "May Is":

> *Julie:* What I think is important about going back to the child and saying that "I've been thinking about your work" is the message that "You matter to me. And your work matters and you are on my mind and you exist in my mind when you are not with me."
>
> *Liz:* "And I respect you. . . ."
>
> *Julie:* "And I respect you enough to think about you or your problem or your work. . . ."

Margaret: That's why I think your immediate reaction may just be "Oh, that's very interesting." But if you come back with, "There are a lot of meanings here, and I wonder what you meant. . . ."

Liz: It shows you are really interested in their learning.

Why is this conversation so important? If teaching and learning are an interaction, surely the feelings between teacher and student will determine much about the success of that interaction. Arguably, respect is the critical feeling for a mutually beneficial relationship. But it cannot be respect built entirely on role or some other general quality ("authority figure" or "older person"). The stresses of classroom life are too great to sustain respect built on such an abstract foundation. Respect must rest solidly on the particulars of the specific people involved. Teacher and student must come to know, appreciate, and respect the passions, curiosities, experiences, efforts, and accomplishments of each other. This type of respect doesn't happen quickly. When it develops, it builds, I suspect, from genuine interest in each other as individuals. That interest has to come from some interaction that makes one take notice of another.

Talking about respecting children and their work seems easy. Many of us in education do this kind of talking all the time. I worry, though, that we often like the idea of respecting children more than we actually experience the feeling deeply enough to inform and guide our behavior. I worry because so much of what I've seen in schools—from the condition of buildings and learning materials to many of the daily interactions between adults and children—seems to disregard and disrespect the very seriousness of intent and complexity of thought that we saw demonstrated over and over in the 10 texts we examined. Real respect is not a simple thing to build. I suspect it rests best on particulars, and it sits poorly on generalities.

Over three months, these 10 teachers left their classrooms to sit around a table and read and discuss children's writing. In our 18 hours together in the superintendent's meeting room and the school library, our examinations of these texts followed the pattern established by the protocol. We started by looking, and we dwelled on what we saw. As we looked more, we saw more, and in turn, we became more interested. Interest kept us looking, and as even more was revealed to us, we became amazed. Through all this time, we deepened our appreciation of the complexity of the tasks undertaken by these children and the significance of their accomplishments. In short, we felt respect.

Our work made us want to meet these children, to get to know them, to ask them our questions and hear their answers, to tell them what confused us and delighted us and made us wonder. We wanted to learn from them and to help them in their learning. We wanted to look at the work of other children, too.

Much was unresolved when the last session was completed. Significant questions had been raised but not answered. Few of the teachers knew yet how this work would really influence their teaching. None knew if they would ever use the protocol again or sit with colleagues in similar sessions. Still, when we left the table at the end of our last session together, this looking and wonder and respect made a fine foundation, I thought, for going back into the classroom the next morning.

References

American Heritage Dictionary. (1993). New York: Dell.

Armstrong, M. (1992). Children's stories as literature: An interview with Michael Armstrong. *Bread Loaf News*, 5(1), 2–4.

Costa, A., & Kallick, B. (Eds.). (2000). *Assessing and reporting on habits of mind*. Alexandria, VA: ASCD.

Seidel, S. (1998). Learning from looking. In N. Lyons (Ed.), *With portfolio in hand: Validating the new teacher professionalism* (pp. 69–89). New York: Teachers College Press.

Smiley, J. (1991). *A thousand acres*. New York: Knopf.

14

Reporting Growth
in Habits of Mind

Arthur L. Costa and Bena Kallick

Useful communication must always be in the language of the
receiver.

—*Edward de Bono*

We are all familiar with report cards that assign letter or number grades for
academic progress. However, do you remember the days when report
cards also included a grade for conduct? Schools have always deemed it
important to report students' academic progress and how students conduct themselves as citizens of the school, but most schools never convey
how students conduct themselves as *learners*. The Habits of Mind are an
excellent framework for explicitly describing the behaviors expected of
all learners. This chapter describes a variety of ways for reporting students'
growth as learners.

Traditionally, parents, administrators, and members of the board of
education are the most significant audiences for reporting. Teachers report
to parents and to building-level administrators. Administrators report to
the board of education. The board reports to the community. Many
schools are expanding this concept of reporting to develop Habits of Mind
related to continuous improvement and learning. In these schools,
students report to parents or board members. Parents report to teachers.

Students, teachers, parents, administrators, board members, and community members all come to share a sense of responsibility for learning and accounting for progress.

Reporting to Parents

Because the main concern in reporting is communication, schools need to design reporting systems that are easily understood by those receiving the information. Although educators want to report everything that they believe parents must know about a child's progress, good intentions and important information sometimes get lost in a fog of educational jargon. For that reason, parents should help design reporting systems.

Some design groups include parents; others rely on parent surveys, interviews, or focus groups. For example, Margo Montague, an educator in the Bellingham Public Schools in Bellingham, Washington, developed a report card through a process of teacher design, parent response, and final revisions. A committee of teachers developed a set of items they believed were significant to each child's cognitive development. With the help of a consultant, they presented these items to parent focus groups. The parents were asked to interpret the meaning of each item, and the focus group leader noted parents' confusion about any item. The teacher group revised the reporting process, using the focus group's comments as a basis. In the end, they arrived at a report card that had significant meaning for teachers and parents. (This process is described more fully in Chapter 6 of *Assessment in the Learning Organization*, Costa & Kallick, 1995.)

The John Lyman Elementary School in Middlefield, Connecticut, used a similar process to develop its report card. After careful consideration by teachers and parent groups, they developed a report card that uses the rubric shown in Figure 14.1.

Figure 14.2 is part of the Lyman school report card. This figure shows how teachers report data on 4th graders' growth in work habits, which are listed under Habits of Mind linked to citizenship. Lyman educators have also developed detailed rubrics that describe students' level of performance on these work habits. Figure 14.3 contains the 4th grade rubric for two of those habits: (1) makes appropriate choices to complete tasks and

FIGURE 14.1

Rubric for School Report Card

4 = Exemplary
Initiates extensions independently.
Reflects on own learning.
Makes connections across disciplines.

3 = Proficient
Works independently.
Seeks help when needed.
Applies acquired skills consistently.

2 = Developing
Works on familiar tasks with growing independence.
Begins to acquire repertoire of skills.

I = Emerging
Depends on adult or peer assistance.
Has limited skills.

Source: John Lyman Elementary School, Middlefield, Connecticut.

FIGURE 14.2

Excerpt from 4th Grade Report Card

Citizenship * Work Habits	Nov.	March	June
Makes appropriate choices to complete tasks and meet goals (seat choice, use of time).			
Shows thoroughness in work.			
Work is neat and legible.			
Makes smooth transitions.			
Takes responsibility for actions.			
Communicates needs, concerns, feelings, and opinions.			
Works cooperatively and productively with a variety of peers.			
Makes positive contributions to the school community (study buddy, school chores, school boards, senate, assembly).			

Source: John Lyman Elementary School, Middlefield, Connecticut.

FIGURE 14.3

4th Grade Rubric for Two Work Habits

Work Habits for Citizenship

Makes appropriate choices to complete tasks and meet goals [persisting, managing impulsivity].

4   Works efficiently enough to allow for self-initiated extensions. Sets new goals as goals are reached.

3   Makes appropriate choices to complete tasks and meet goals. Can plan his/her week.

2   Sometimes makes appropriate choices to complete tasks and meet goals.

1   Rarely makes appropriate choices to complete tasks and meet goals.

Shows thoroughness in work [striving for accuracy, thinking and communicating with clarity and precision].

4   Exceeds grade-level expectations for the amount of reflection and effort used to complete work.

3   Takes sufficient time to do his/her best with all assignments. Shows concern for completeness of work. Willing to go back and improve work when asked.

2   Sometimes takes sufficient time to do his/her best with all assignments. Sometimes shows concern for completeness of work. Sometimes is willing to go back and improve work when asked.

1   Rarely takes sufficient time to do his/her best with all assignments. Rarely shows concern for completeness of work. Rarely is willing to go back and improve work when asked.

Source: John Lyman Elementary School, Middlefield, Connecticut.

meet goals (persisting, managing impulsivity) and (2) shows thoroughness in work (striving for accuracy, thinking and communicating with clarity and precision).

At the Marcy Open School in Minneapolis, Minnesota, parents, teachers, and children consider progress in both academic subjects and the Habits of Mind. One page of the school's progress report lists each

FIGURE 14.4

Excerpt from School Report Card

Marcy Open School 20__

Student/Parent/Teacher

Progress Evaluation for _____ Grade: _____

Teacher: _____

Mark each behavior using N = Not Yet; D = Developing; O = Often

This year, I notice that _____ does the following:

	Teacher		Parent/Child	
	Winter	Spring	Winter	Spring
1. Keeps on trying; does not give up easily.				
2. Thinks out possibilities before answering a question.				
3. Listens to others with understanding and care.				

Source: Marcy Open School, Minneapolis, Minnesota.

Habit of Mind with a brief description. Another area lists whether or not a habit was a "personal goal area" for the student that particular grading period. In another set of columns, the teacher indicates whether the student is using a habit rarely, developing it, or consistently applying it. A section of Marcy Open School's report card also allows parents to note their children's work on the habits (see Figure 14.4). Having the teacher report and the parent report side by side allows the child to see how the two compare. In addition, the parent and the teacher work with the student to set goals for the next quarter.

The Tahoma School District in Maple Valley, Washington, is another example of a district that seeks parent input on the Habits of Mind. Parents report to teachers about their child's progress by describing specific examples of how their child is exhibiting the Habits of Mind at home. See Figure 11.11, p. 214, for a blank report.

Putting Students at the Center

Because students are at the center of all reporting, it makes sense that they should become a part of the reporting procedure. Many schools now are conscious of the need to help students learn how to self-evaluate, and they include students in the reporting process. Children are part of parent conferences, they write narratives for their parents on their report cards, and they grade themselves as a part of the report card.

Including students in a conference provides them with another rich opportunity to practice their Habits of Mind. They must be reflective and metacognitive, and they must check for accuracy and precision. As they organize their learning, they also make sense of their learning. They set goals for themselves that foster the habit of remaining open to continuous learning.

Teachers who conduct student-led conferences usually write letters to parents offering them the option of attending the conference with their child or not. Most parents opt to attend the conference with the child. Sometimes, parents want a few minutes alone with the teacher, too. The teacher then offers activities to keep the student occupied during the private conversation.

At the elementary level, some teachers conduct four conferences simultaneously in the classroom. The teacher sets up activities such as these:

- Student shares portfolio.
- Student solves a problem that is on the board.
- Student describes the student's present work in the classroom.
- Student, parents, and teacher reflect on student's work and set goals for the next quarter of work.

The teacher is able to spend 15 minutes with each student and parent group; students spend one hour with their parents. For example, four student-parent groups would be scheduled in the conference at the same time, rotating through the four activities. Student A would be sharing his portfolio with his parents; Student B would be solving a problem on the board in a demonstration to her parents; Student C would be describing her work in the classroom to her parents; and Student D and his parents and the teacher would be reflecting and setting goals.

Whatever the format, students prepare for these conferences in many different ways. In the Charlevoix-Emmet Intermediate School District in Petosky, Michigan, students use an organizer to reflect on their learning and prepare for the conference. They group their activities under three main headings: (1) procedures and things to do before conference, (2) procedures and things to do at conference, and (3) portfolio checklist. Other organizer sheets help students specifically summarize the academic objectives they worked on, the things they think they did well, and the things they want their parents to notice about their work. The organizer also offers a space for parents to write comments after they have seen the child's work.

Writing Narratives

In a classroom we visited in Scarsdale, New York, the teacher asks her students to write a narrative on their report card regarding their progress. The students describe their learning and how they might improve it. They also give specific examples of work in which they have shown the most persistence. Throughout their description, they discuss how they use the Habits of Mind to discipline their work.

Narratives encourage students to be self-reflective before they see the commentary the teacher has made. This type of writing also provides an opportunity for students to measure their self-perception against the teacher's perception and, if there is a difference, to talk about any misperceptions.

Sometimes teachers write a narrative rather than simply report academic progress with a number or letter grade. Susan Martinez at John Lyman Elementary School in Middlefield, Connecticut, wrote this progress report about a 2nd grader in her class:

Math Development

Myra picks up new mathematical concepts quickly and is able to apply the new knowledge immediately to solve problems. She has been working on activities involving sorting, graphing, estimating (both quantity and volume), and place value. She has also been doing a lot of group problem solving. She is able to generate multiple solutions to a problem and can usually explain in words how she arrived at her solution. She is developing efficient strategies for doing mental computations. She enjoys a mathematical challenge and is willing to struggle with a problem when the answer is not immediately apparent.

Reporting to the Board and the Community

Schools must also report progress with the Habits of Mind to the board of education and the community. Although most communities consider the Habits of Mind to be important, they don't often take the time to reflect on the habits' meaning and to notice improvement. If board members are already working on their own behavior—acting as role models for students and using the Habits of Mind to guide their work and communication—then they have a deeper appreciation for the assessments that are brought before them.

Many schools provide a profile of student progress with the Habits of Mind that are based on checklists and self-evaluation profiles. For example, the rubrics shown in Figures 11.5 through 11.9 in Chapter 11 can be used to track students over time. A graph will show progress and areas where students still need work.

Students can also make presentations reflecting their understanding of the habits. Through the preparation and presentation, they become living models of using the habits. Community events are an important opportunity for students to showcase how they use the Habits of Mind. They can participate in planning, implementing, and evaluating events.

For example, back-to-school night is a prime event at which students can show their understanding of the Habits of Mind through examples of their classroom work that demonstrate the habits. Students who are keeping electronic portfolios often have examples of their use of the habits as they work with a team to solve a problem. Parents, board members, and community representatives are thrilled to see actual video clips showing students thinking interdependently, listening with understanding and empathy, and questioning and posing problems.

Schools can invite board members to hear students speak to parents about their study of the Habits of Mind. At Meadowview Elementary School in Eau Claire, Wisconsin, teams of 6th grade students used their public speaking skills to deliver a presentation on the Habits of Mind to the city council. (City council members commented that they became self-analytical about their own behaviors as a result.)

Although the Habits of Mind don't readily translate into numbers, they can easily be observed in the context of daily life. Board members will need to get used to trusting their own observations rather than looking for quantifiable measurements of the habits' success. Board members should be able to find examples of students' progress with the habits from students' employers, parents, and students themselves as they demonstrate the use of the habits on public occasions.

Eventually, educators, students, parents, and community members will begin to see the influence of the Habits of Mind in the community at large. For example, Zelda's Tip Top Café in Adrian, Michigan, displays a large poster listing the Habits of Mind. The restaurant owner, impressed by the use of the Habits of Mind in the schools, decided to use the same list as a guide for her employees. Each week, the coworkers agree to focus on a particular habit, and they practice the behaviors as they serve customers. Children who eat in that restaurant are reinforced by the visible attention to the same behaviors they are learning in school.

Promoting Self-Evaluation

Ultimately, the most enduring legacy of evaluation is the habit of self-assessment. When students internalize a sense of what constitutes high-quality work, they will work toward that goal without prompting.

Ask students to assess their own work against carefully crafted rubrics that define different levels of performance. (See Chapter 11 for several sample rubrics.) Many teachers ask students to fill out a self-assessment survey a few times during the school year. Then, students create a graph of their progress. They can use this information to report to their parents in a conference or as an addendum to their report card. Teachers can easily create a simple survey that asks students to rate their development in use of all the Habits of Mind on a continuum from "not using yet but I'm learning" to "I usually try to behave this way." The inventory in Appendix D contains sample statements from a survey created by Steve Huffman at Sacred Hearts Academy in Honolulu, Hawaii.

Another strategy is to ask students to complete a "self-report" for next year's teacher. Many teachers ask their students to write a letter to or create a CD for the teacher they'll have the following year. In Eau Claire, Wisconsin, students send to next year's teacher a description of themselves. Here is an excerpt from one student's work:

> I am a hands-on, auditory, and visual learner. But the two methods of learning I prefer to use the most are auditory and visual. When I do math, I like to have the problem in front of me so I can keep looking it over as many times as I want until I get the answer. . . . In social studies, I am an auditory learner. . . .
>
> When I work in class I like to work with a partner . . . because you get a chance to have two different opinions so you become flexible in your thinking. . . .
>
> When I work in a group, my strength is contributing a lot because I am not shy. That's why I think the habit of mind that I use the most is risk taking. My weakness when I work in groups is that I give in quickly in order to move on. The habit of mind that I would like to concentrate working on the most is metacognition because it lets you think about how you do things.

Celebrating Progress

Don't forget the importance of celebrating students' achievements, too. Most schools have trophy cases for sports, and they offer a variety of honors and awards for high grades. Why not offer awards for students who exhibit the Habits of Mind? Many schools offer certificates, buttons, ribbons, and even bumper stickers for outstanding use of the Habits of Mind. There are myriad possibilities for celebrating students' achievement and signaling the community's belief that the Habits of Mind are worth striving for (see Chaper 15).

Reporting students' work on the habits honors progress, identifies areas for growth, and celebrates the strengthening of the entire school community. A school will celebrate and reward what it values. As the Habits of Mind become valued, so, too, will their achievement be recognized.

References

Costa, A. (2008). *The school as a home for the mind.* Thousand Oaks, CA: Corwin.

Costa, A., & Kallick, B. (1995). *Assessment in the learning organization: Shifting the paradigm.* Alexandria, VA: ASCD.

Part IV

Leading Schools with Habits of Mind

Management is about arranging and telling. Leadership is about nurturing and enhancing.

—Thomas J. Peters

Having worked with numerous schools and school districts over the past decade, we have found that one element in successful implementation of the Habits of Mind is the support for the habits by leadership personnel. Often the school principal holds this role. Sometimes, however, a teacher, department facilitator, librarian, counselor, or vice principal is given this opportunity. Some of the functions and responsibilities of this person are the following:

• Making presentations to staffs, parents, and the public about what the Habits of Mind are, how to teach them, their importance, and their place in the school curriculum.

• Advocating the values and benefits of the Habits of Mind, encouraging others to employ them in their own lives and careers, and recognizing performance in others.

• Coaching teachers, administrators, and parents in the use and value of the Habits of Mind.

• Designing action research and encouraging data collection about the effects of the Habits of Mind on students and staff.

- Facilitating group discussions about student work, protocols, data-driven dialogue, literacy circles, and other events and processes related to the Habits of Mind.
- Creating electronic and face-to-face networks of people using or interested in the Habits of Mind.
- Suggesting teaching strategies, ways to get started, ways to communicate with parents, ways to assess students, and ways to work with the community on the Habits of Mind.
- Modeling the Habits of Mind.

Chapter 15, "Creating a Culture of Mindfulness," presents the idea that teachers will more likely teach for intellectual growth, interdependent thinking, problem solving, and creativity if they are in an intellectually challenging, collaborative, and creative environment themselves. This chapter describes some of the conditions that signal to staff, students, and community that thinking and the Habits of Mind are valued in the school.

Chapter 16, "Habits of Mind for the Systems-Savvy Leader," by Jennifer Abrams, suggests that leadership is the key to success in school change. Skillful leaders must know how to employ the Habits of Mind to work within a system—politically and charismatically—to achieve change and to build a program that may diverge from traditional practices.

Chapter 17, "Leading Is a Habit of Mind," by Bill Sommers and Diane Zimmerman, demonstrates how the Habits of Mind are incorporated into what leaders know, do, and feel. The Habits of Mind and leadership might be congruent with each other. Modeling is essential!

—Arthur L. Costa and Bena Kallick

15

Creating a Culture of Mindfulness

Arthur L. Costa and Bena Kallick

Celebrate what you want to see more of.

—*Tom Peters*

Visitors to the town of Pugwash in Nova Scotia, Canada, are greeted with this sign: "Welcome to PUGWASH, Home of the Thinkers." The city obviously is proud that it was the site of the first Pugwash Conference in 1957, which brought together 22 influential scientists to discuss the threat of thermonuclear weapons. Since then, a variety of scholars and government leaders have met at Pugwash Conferences around the world to consider issues related to armed conflict and global problems. The Pugwash Conferences and Joseph Rotblat, one of the group's founders, were awarded the 1995 Nobel Peace Prize.

"Home of the Thinkers" sends a bold message about what the community of Pugwash values. Their welcome sign could easily recognize the city's beautiful seaside setting, its summertime Gathering of the Clans celebration, or its deep historical ties. Instead, Pugwash calls itself "Home of the Thinkers."

Many schools proclaim that they value the Habits of Mind. By themselves, however, proclamations are empty. Schools can't just say they value the Habits of Mind and expect success. The habits must be lived and practiced by every individual in the learning organization, and they must be institutionalized throughout the entire system. If schools truly value the Habits of Mind, they must also deliberately construct themselves as homes for the mind.

In this chapter we draw upon our work with numerous schools around the world, as well as on the years of research and the theories of numerous leaders in the field of school improvement and transformation (see, e.g., Frymier, 1987; Fullan, 1993; Garmston & Wellman, 2009; Hargreaves & Fink, 2006; Louis, Marks, & Kruse, 1996; Marzano, Waters, & McNulty, 2005; Senge, 1990; Sergiovani, 2004). The sections that follow discuss some of the factors that contribute to a "culture of mindfulness" in which the Habits of Mind can develop and thrive, to the benefit of staff and students. Of course, the greatest benefits accrue when practices and processes are managed well, provided with adequate time and financial resources, and sustained over an extended period of time.

Infusing the Habits of Mind into the Culture of the School

If the Habits of Mind are to become schoolwide goals, the school must have a climate that supports the basic idea that the habits are necessary. Efforts to infuse the Habits of Mind into the school curriculum and instructional program will prove futile unless the school environment signals to the staff, the students, and the community that the development of the intellect and interdependent thinking are the school's basic values. Making the Habits of Mind a reality in schools and classrooms requires more than merely acquainting staff members with the habits and recognizing the habits in students' performances.

Many factors influence teachers' thinking as they make daily decisions about curriculum and instruction. These include their own culture; their knowledge of the content being taught; state, district, and local standards of learning; the tests used for student assessment; their own cognitive and learning styles; their knowledge about their students; and their professional values and beliefs about education. All of these influence their judgments about when to teach what to whom.

Less obvious but vastly more persuasive influences on teacher thought are the norms, policies, and culture of the school setting. Hidden but powerful cues emanate from the school environment. Teachers will more likely teach for thinking, creativity, and interdependence if they are in an intellectually stimulating, creative, and cooperative environment themselves. (See the Waikiki story in Chapter 21.)

Shared Vision and Common Purposes

Teamwork is the ability to work together toward a common vision. The ability to direct individual accomplishment toward organizational objectives. It is the fuel that allows common people to accomplish uncommon results.

—Andrew Carnegie

Schools that have implemented the Habits of Mind have found that one of the most powerful benefits has been the transformation of staff by uniting around a shared vision and common purposes. The Habits of Mind provide such unity in at least four ways. First, they provide an agreed-upon set of attributes and characteristics of the graduates of the school—the "end products" of years of instruction. Second, they apply to all disciplines and are basic to all content areas. It takes persistence, for example, to become a skilled athlete, musician, artist, craftsman, mathematician, or scientist. Therefore, members of diverse and sometimes disparate departments in a secondary school can come together to explore ways that each, in its own way, can contribute to and enhance the learning of the Habits of Mind. In an elementary school, grade-level groups can identify which Habits of Mind might be emphasized at developmental levels and gather evidence of student progress. Third, the Habits of Mind provide a common terminology. Administrators, teachers, students, support staff, and parents share meaning, find examples, and recognize the use of (and sometimes the lack of) the Habits of Mind in students and in themselves. Fourth, staff members use the Habits of Mind to converse about or diagnose individual students' needs and make individual learning plans accordingly.

Furthermore, the Habits of Mind are as beneficial to the adults in the school as they are to students. No one ever "achieves" the Habits of Mind. They are developmental tasks in which individuals continue to grow and learn throughout their lives.

Signals, Recognitions, Celebrations, and Rituals

To ensure that all members of the school community value the Habits of Mind, the school must clearly convey its vision of itself as a place for learning. For example, Encinal High School in Alameda, California, states its vision this way:

> Encinal High School is a home for the active mind—a coopera-
> tive community promoting knowledge, self-understanding,
> mutual respect, global understanding, adaptability to change,
> and a love for lifelong learning.

Enhancing intelligent behavior is explicitly stated in this school's philosophy and mission. District goals, policies, and practices are constantly scrutinized for their consistency with and contribution to that philosophy. The school district aligns its procedures for continuing to study, refine, and improve practices so that the school grows toward more intelligent application of the Habits of Mind.

Students, staff, and parents will better understand the importance of the Habits of Mind if mottos, slogans, and mission statements identify *thinking* as a purpose of education. For example, "Thought Is Taught at Huntington Beach High" is emblazoned on one school's note pads, and "Make Thinking Happen" is printed on the stationery of another. "Lincoln Schools Are Thought-Full Schools" is the motto painted on one district's delivery trucks for the entire community to see. In the Auburn School District in Washington State, the newsletter of the district's "thinking skills" network is titled "The Rational Enquirer." The superintendent distributes bookmarks reminding the community that thinking is the schools' goal. The motto of the Patti Welder Middle School in Galveston, Texas, is "Panthers 'Paws' to Think." The staff of the Bleyl Junior High School in the Cypress Fairbanks School District in Houston, Texas, refer to themselves as the "United Mind Workers."

In many schools, student-made posters and other items serve as reminders of the attitudes and habits that the school promotes. At Furr High School in Houston, Texas, and at Waikiki School in Honolulu, the

Habits of Mind are plainly exhibited on the walls, in the corridors, and along the stairways. (See Chapters 20 and 21 for accounts of each of these schools, respectively.) Each class at Waikiki School develops a logo and a slogan for the "mindful" school. The school votes on which should be selected as the logo and slogan for the year and then has them imprinted on T-shirts. "We're Training Our Brains" is the motto on buttons proudly produced, sold, and worn by the special education students at Jamestown Elementary School in Pennsylvania. Many schools send home calendars, awards, reminders, and newsletters informing parents and others of the school's intent and ways that they can engage children's intellect.

Leadership

Some people think that it is holding on that makes one strong. Sometimes it is letting go.

—*Sylvia Robinson*

Shared identity and beliefs provide direction for an organization without the control that is often characterized as uniformity. Instead, the organization has a pervasive consistency about what is important, which allows for a high degree of individuality to be expressed. The leaders of such organizations must infuse, articulate, and weave the Habits of Mind into the vision, values, and purposes—the very fiber of the organization — and they must live the habits. In most schools that have succeeded in implementing the Habits of Mind, someone volunteers or is chosen to be a "cheerleader" for the habits. It might be an administrator, a department chair, a mentor teacher, a resource teacher, or other staff member. Preferably it is a team of such staff members. The individual or team assumes such responsibilities as coaching staff members in lesson design, communicating with parents, orienting new staff members, conducting action research, collecting archives of lessons infused with the Habits of Mind, organizing and providing professional development, gathering and organizing instructional materials, leading literature circles, facilitating Habits of Mind discussion groups, and contributing to the school's Web site.

Their work and their effectiveness will, of course, depend on the school's or the district's administrative leadership. As described in Chapter 20 of this book, school leaders view themselves as role models and mediators of the staff's and students' intellectual capacities. They know that the level of teachers' intellectual development has a direct relationship to student behavior and student performance. Teachers who function at higher levels intellectually produce students who function at higher levels intellectually. Characteristic of these teachers include their ability to empathize, to symbolize experience, and to act in accordance with a disciplined commitment to the Habits of Mind. In the classroom they employ a greater range of instructional strategies, elicit more conceptual responses from students, and produce high-achieving students who are more cooperative and involved in their work. Successful teachers are mindful teachers, and they stimulate their students to be mindful as well. Outside the classroom they model the kinds of skillful thinking and intellectual behaviors they are teaching students in the classroom. School leaders facilitate building such environments.

A leader's role, therefore, is to constantly protect, monitor, and enhance the continual learning and refining of the Habits of Mind so that the habits not only are increasingly internalized by students, but also become valued and internalized by the staff. Staff members should increasingly

- Be aware of and recognize the Habits of Mind in themselves and others.
- Value the Habits of Mind as an internal compass to guide actions, thoughts, and decisions.
- Be skillful and capable in performing the Habits of Mind.
- Apply the Habits of Mind in an ever-expanding range and variety of settings.
- Be committed to monitoring, reflecting on, evaluating, and improving use of the Habits of Mind.
- Be spontaneous and habitual in the use of the Habits of Mind.

(Chapter 4 describes this "journey" of continuous growth in the Habits of Mind in detail.)

Classroom Interaction

School leaders stay in touch with instruction in the classroom. Knowing that the teachers have been learning about teaching the Habits of Mind, they observe and they facilitate peers' observations of each other with these indicators in mind:

• Is there evidence that the nature of the work is sufficiently generative so that the Habits of Mind are required?

• Are the students clear about which Habit of Mind they are engaged with?

• Are opportunities provided for students to reflect on their use of the Habits of Mind?

• Is there evidence in the classroom environment that suggests that the Habits of Mind are valued?

Observers might want to check with students to see how they perceive the habits. Based on those observations, a leadership group might organize faculty meetings and dialogue groups to share their observations about practice and to encourage questions, concerns, learnings, modifications, and next steps.

Group Norms Through Dialogue

David Perkins (2003) suggests that an organization functions and grows through conversations and the quality of the conversations determines how smart the organization is. Leaders ensure that the Habits of Mind become group norms. At the beginning of a staff or department meeting, for example, they might provide a moment for centering—changing the tone of the group by using techniques such as silent meditation, breathing exercises, or brain-compatible music. Many authors believe that music helps to synthesize brain activity as auditory input is directly associated with memory, feelings, and mood. Music carries meaning and the brain's response is shown in right hemisphere activity. Such responses to music include imagination, creativity, and personality development. For more information on how music supports learning, see Jensen, 1996; Sousa, 2001; and Wolfe, 2001. School leaders may then invite the group to focus on one or several of the habits; for example, "As we examine our agenda today and the problem we are focused on, which of the Habits of Mind might be most important for us to employ?" The group generates several suggestions; for example, "We need to listen to each other, remain open to continuous learning, question and pose problems, persist, and—most certainly—find humor." The leader can then invite them to pay attention to themselves to see which they are employing.

Toward the end of the meeting, the group can take some time to reflect on how the Habits of Mind served them. Individuals can be asked to share their observations of themselves, to reflect on which Habits of Mind they used or should have used, and to make a commitment for improving their own use of one or more of the habits. Members can comment on what effects the use of the habits had on group productivity and, as they consider future meetings, which ones they might want to focus on again (Costa & Kallick, 1995).

Coaching

Roger Evered and James Selman (1989) suggest the importance of leaders' fostering a culture that values coaching as a key element: "The current management culture, with its focus on controlling behavior, needs to be replaced by a management culture in which skillful coaching creates the climate, environment, and context that empowers employees and teams to generate results" (p. 16). Coaching is one of the most powerful means to overcome the extreme isolation that teachers experience (Costa & Garmston, 2002; Ellison & Hayes, 2006). Coaching is an intellectual activity that requires use of the Habits of Mind. Coaching, it has been found, produces intellectual growth for a variety of reasons:

• *Coaching enhances instructional thought.* The act of teaching is, itself, an intellectual process. Jackson (1968) found that teachers make more than 1,300 decisions a day. The behaviors observed in the classroom are artifacts of decisions that teachers make before, during, and after instruction. The purpose of coaching, therefore, is to modify teachers' capacities to modify themselves—to plan, monitor, and reflect upon their instructional decision making, perceptions, and intellectual functions.

Coaching provides a rich experience for teachers to think about their thinking (Costa & Garmston, 2002).

• *Coaching supports continuous learning.* As continuous learners, teachers who desire to improve their craft seek coaching, and they benefit from being coached. Skillful artists, athletes, musicians, dancers—including Sasha Cohen, Yo-Yo Ma, Mikhail Baryshnikov, Michelle Kwan, Tiger Woods, and Jackie Joyner-Kersey—never lose their need for coaching. Likewise, in education, to continually perfect their craft, teachers profit from coaching as well. Good schools are in the habit of remaining open to continuous learning.

• *Coaching supports effective teamwork.* Welding together the individual efforts of team members into a well-organized and efficient unit requires the persistence and stamina of an expert coach. This concerted effort, however, does not "just happen." It takes someone—a conductor—who "knows the score" to provide the synergy. It takes time, persistence, practice, and coaching to develop a winning athletic team, a celebrated symphony orchestra, or a learning organization. Building on teamwork develops the muscle of thinking interdependently.

• *Coaching enables educational innovations to achieve their full impact.* Joyce and Showers (1988) found that efforts to bring about changes in classroom practice are fruitless unless the teacher is coached in the use of the innovation. Only when the component of coaching was added was the innovation internalized, valued, and transferred to classroom use.

• *Coaching enhances the intellectual capacities of teachers, which, in turn, produces greater intellectual achievements in students* (Costa & Garmston, 2002). Vygotsky (1978) provides a strong theoretical support for coaching as a means of intellectual growth:

> Every function in . . . cultural development appears twice: first, on the social level, and later on the individual level; first between people (inter-psychological), and then inside (intra-psychological). This applies equally to voluntary attention, to logical memory, and to the formation of concepts. *All the higher functions originate as actual relationships between individuals.* (p. 57, emphasis added)

It is through social interaction that new concepts and intellectual behaviors are formed and grown.

Thinking Interdependently

> Success depends, above all, upon people. Build relationships, teams, partnerships—and motivate people to contribute. Cultivate leadership, creativity, excellence. Listen; seek new ideas and advice.
>
> —*Ruth Scott*

Intellectually effective people seem able to "be at home" in multiple areas of functioning. They move flexibly from one style to another as the situation demands it. They have an uncanny ability to gather data through their senses. They "read" contextual cues from the situation or the environment as to what is needed, and then they draw forth from their vast repertoire those skills and capacities needed to function most effectively in that setting.

Leaders realize that humans grow intellectually through resolving differences, achieving consensus, and stretching to accommodate dissonance. They realize there is a greater possibility for making connections, stimulating creativity, and growing the capacity for complex problem solving when such differences are bridged. Interdependent learning communities are built not by obscuring diversity but by valuing the friction those differences bring and resolving those differences in an atmosphere of trust and reciprocity.

School leaders bring the teaching staff together to function as a learning community to make changes that could improve the functioning of the school even though the leaders themselves may have strong ideas on the subject. Forward-thinking leaders deliberately bring together people of different political and religious persuasions, cultures, genders, cognitive styles, belief systems, modality preferences, and intelligences to work together on issues and problems. They structure groups composed of representatives from different schools, diverse departments, various community groups, and different grade levels to envision, to describe learning outcomes, to plan curriculum, to plan staff development activities, and to allocate resources.

Three practices that school leaders can support as ways to encourage interdependent thinking and build learning communities among staff members are (1) lesson study, (2) joint study of student work, and (3) book study.

Lesson study is a practice that has been adapted from Japanese education (Langer, Colton, & Goff, 2003; Stigler & Hiebert, 1999). The following example of lesson study comes from an elementary school that uses the practice. Teachers followed this procedure:

1. Teachers identify a curricular area that students have difficulty understanding. (In this example, 5th and 6th grade teachers chose "generating questions and managing impulsivity in problem solving" as the habits they were looking for; "place value" was the content.)

2. Teachers meet together at the grade level and develop a lesson plan (in this case, to teach place value). They script the lesson and consider all of the options. They consider the students, the need for differentiated instruction, and some of the variables they can anticipate. They make certain that the lesson is teaching for thinking, and they experiment with some of the strategies presented in this book or in other readings and research.

3. One of the teachers teaches the lesson, and as many teachers as can observe the lesson do so. The observers take good notes on their observations. Because they all planned the lesson, they are able to focus more easily on students than on the teacher. They are expected to observe student learning.

4. Teachers come back to discuss their observations. Once again, because they were all the lesson designers, critique is easier. They talk about what worked and what did not work. They revise the lesson in light of what they observed.

5. Another teacher tries the lesson with an additional observation.

6. They reflect once again and enter the lesson in their database of lessons that have been tried, honed, and successfully taught.

This highly focused and shared responsibility for designing, teaching, and reflecting on student learning is a powerful tool for building collaboration and professionalism.

Studying student work is another way to encourage reflection on practice. There are many protocols that are used for this purpose (McDonald, Mohr, Dichter, & McDonald, 2003). The essence of the practice is to bring examples of student work to the group for the group's input as to whether the work reflects the identified learning outcomes. For example, the group might want to study whether students are showing evidence of skillful decision making or of metacognition in their work. They might study the responses that students have described in their writing or on a student-produced video to determine whether the student is becoming more skillful in one or more Habits of Mind.

Book study is key. The staff is encouraged to study books that deal with teaching and other realms of education. Much like the close study of text that they expect from their students, the teachers read deeply, delving into the text of their books chapter by chapter, seeking applications in the dailiness of their teaching.

Highly successful educators discuss student progress with their colleagues and share ideas with each other. They believe that collegial discussions centered on teaching and learning have more impact on their practices than formal administrative observations and evaluations (Bello, 2004). Each of these practices helps to build a thoughtful (sensitive and caring) and thought-full (full of thought) environment that supports the importance of skillful thinking.

Continual Learning

Autopoesis: (Greek) Self-production. The characteristic of living systems to continuously renew themselves and to regulate this process in such a way that the integrity of their structure is maintained. It is a natural process which supports the quest for structure, process renewal and integrity.

—*Margaret Wheatley and Myron Kellner-Rogers (1996)*

Senge (1990) emphasizes that a learning organization challenges existing mental models. Intellectual growth is found in disequilibrium, not balance. Out of chaos, order is built, learning takes place, new understandings are forged, new connections are bridged, and organizations come to function more consistently with their mission, vision, and goals.

School leaders, in an atmosphere of trust, challenge existing practices, assumptions, policies, and traditional ways of delivering curriculum. Leaders search for problems whose answers are not known. They encourage experimentation, action research, and data production. This implies that an atmosphere of choice, risk taking, and inquiry exists. Data are generated without fear that they will be used as a basis for evaluating success or failure. Creativity will more likely grow in a low-risk atmosphere.

Leaders empower teachers to develop an internalized locus of control. They appreciate the possibilities of efforts toward continual growth that marshal the motivations and unleash the talents of those who work directly with children day after day.

Leaders help the teaching staff to design strategies for collecting data (Lipton & Wellman, 2004) and to use the assessment data to guide, inform, and reflect on practice. Staff members learn how to design feedback spirals, including finding multiple ways of gathering data, establishing criteria for judgment, and working together to develop their common understanding and the reliability of observations and reporting of results.

Pollinating and Sustaining

School leaders spread the word by helping other schools understand the Habits of Mind. Ideally, all the primary, elementary, and middle schools that feed into a particular secondary school should be focused on the Habits of Mind. This consistency provides a seamless, continuous, integrated, and articulated series of learning experiences for students. We fully realize that the Habits of Mind are not "habituated" in one lesson, one term, or one year. It takes numerous recurring encounters with the habits for students to understand that they are basic to all learning, at all levels, and in all subject areas.

Modeling

Leaders increasingly value and employ the Habits of Mind themselves. They draw forth the habits when confronted with decision-making and problem-solving situations that require complex, careful thought. They verbalize their own thinking in order to model metacognitive reflection with the staff. As continual learners they seek suggestions about how to think through issues they face together. In short, they practice the Habits of Mind openly in designing strategies for achieving the vision of their school as a home for the mind (Costa, 2007). See also Appendix B.

Parents and Community

Because parents are children's first teachers, it is much more likely that students will learn the Habits of Mind if they are modeled, recognized, and reinforced at home as well as in school. Many schools have included the Habits of Mind in their reports of progress. In parent-student-teacher conferences, for example, students lead the discussion and share indicators of their growth in the Habits of Mind by providing evidence and artifacts of their questioning, metacognition, flexibility of thinking, persistence, listening to others' points of view, and creativity.

Parents, too, look for ways in which their children are transferring intellectual growth from the classroom to family and home situations. In Waikiki School, for example, parents of kindergartners watch for indicators of caring behaviors at home and report such incidents to the teacher.

Some schools and school districts have created parent handbooks with the intent of having families practice the Habits of Mind at home. In this excerpt from a handbook for parents in Eau Claire, Wisconsin, the Habits of Mind have been translated into language parents can easily relate to:

Skills for a Lifetime: What's It About?
Do your family members . . .

- explore the consequences of their actions before they decide to do something?
- try to see things from other people's point of view?
- tackle problems and try to figure things out for themselves?
- talk together about situations, asking questions and listening to each other?
- speak up (in a courteous way) for what they believe is right, even when it's not popular?
- realize that they can't believe everything they hear, read, or see on television?
- work hard, and not give up on tough problems, puzzles, homework, jobs?

- examine assumptions on taken-for-granted ideas?
- develop a "plan of action" before they launch into a project?

Some districts hold orientation meetings for parents new to the school's learning community. Lisa Davis-Miraglia, formerly of Westorchard School in Chappaqua, New York, gives us a powerful example of how she reaches parents at the beginning of the school year and how she keeps the momentum of teaching the Habits of Mind connected to the world beyond the school walls:

> Every September our school holds Open House Night to introduce parents to the teachers and to the overall curriculum for the year. I've always found it quite difficult to give an overview of the entire curriculum in the hour allotted. So, a few years ago I asked myself what I truly wanted each student to leave my class knowing and able to do. The bottom line for me was that I didn't want a curriculum-driven class. I was going for depth not breadth. I wanted to work on the child's being the responsible learner, and I wanted my students to walk out of my class as "lifelong learners." My next problem was how to convey the concept of life-long learner to the parents.
>
> We start the night by brainstorming a list of characteristics they thought employers wanted employees to know or be able to do upon employment. Invariably, almost every skill that the U.S. Dept. of Labor issued in 1990 is on our brainstormed list and more. For example, the following were found on both lists:
>
>> To be able to work cooperatively or as part of a team
>> To be able to solve a problem in more than one way
>> To be able to communicate effectively
>> To be able to access, analyze, synthesize and utilize information
>
> I then go on to talk about Signs of Intelligent Life or Habits of Mind. I then explain that I will teach these Habits of Mind using the curriculum as my vehicle. The following is how I first explicitly teach the skills I am looking for so that when they occur naturally the students and parents are aware of them on a conscious level.

After we've been in school for a few months and have gotten to know each other better, I introduce my students formally to the Habits of Mind. We talk about what they mean, and then we decide which ones we should work on as a class.

Invariably, someone asks why we don't work on all the habits. This comment leads to a discussion about goals and biting off more than we can chew. We agree to focus on six Habits of Mind by having each table select one. We also agree to post the remaining habits so that when someone exhibits a habit, he can still be recognized. I chose Metacognition because that rarely gets chosen and I think it is an important habit to foster. We also decided not to choose habits that we felt we were already pretty good at, such as Sense of Humor.

The Habits of Mind selected this year include: Decreasing Impulsivity, Persistence, Flexibility in Thinking, Risk Taking, Metacognition, and Transference. Each group then develops a definition that we can all understand—"in kids' language"—designs a symbol, and identifies an example and puts it on a poster. The posters are hung around the room and buttons are made with the symbols on them. When someone recognizes a child using the behavior, he or she gets a button for the person who used the behavior and one for himself or herself for identifying it. The excitement is incredible for the first few weeks, and the kids sometimes purposefully do or say something to get recognized. However, after the novelty wears off, the process becomes much more natural and less intrusive. It's phenomenal to hear a child from another class ask his peer why she got the button and to hear the explanation: "I used flexibility in my thinking today when I solved a problem in more than one way." The child gets recognized for her thinking again outside of the classroom.

It is important for kids to know why we teach what we do and where they will need this later in life. Therefore, each child interviews two people about their use of Habits of Mind in their daily life.

Children interview parents, siblings, the principal, custodians, even a taxi cab driver in NYC! The cab driver's examples were funny and concrete enough so the kids really understood the meaning of these habits. For example, when asked if he ever had to "decrease his impulsivity," he responded, "Oh, yeah, every time some kid decides to run across the street when the sign says, Don't Walk, or when the car next to me decides to cut me off and I want to curse him out, but I can't because I have an old lady in the back seat." When asked about being flexible in his thinking, he replied, "I have to know where all the parades, traffic jams, and construction are so that I can think of the fastest route for my customer. I can't just go the same way to Grand Central Station every day. I have to be able to get there using many different routes." The cabbie went on to give examples of risk taking (every time he picks up a person), transference, and persistence. The child interviewing noted that the cabbie was also using metacognition or thinking about his thinking.

Some schools conduct parent education meetings to discuss and practice such skills as listening with understanding and empathy, striving for accuracy, and thinking and communicating with clarity and precision. Strategies are practiced and suggestions are given for knowing how to deal with children who need to manage their impulsivity.

In many cases, when parents become aware of the Habits of Mind, they find them useful not only in their homes but in their businesses as well. As mentioned in Chapter 14, patrons entering Zelda's Tip Top Café in Adrian, Michigan, see the list of the Habits of Mind in a framed poster on the wall. The staff focuses on one or more of the habits each week. We've received reports of increased sales when sales staff are acquainted with and employ the Habits of Mind. Certainly listening with understanding and empathy, using clear and precise language, and managing impulsivity endear a prospective buyer to any salesperson.

Some schools have invited business people from the community to discuss with students how the Habits of Mind are used in their careers as architects, scientists, entrepreneurs, salespeople, nurses, truck drivers, or mechanics. When secondary students apprentice in a workplace, they often are asked to observe their own use of the habits as well as how the habits are used by the workers. In some instances, employers are asked to provide feedback to the students based on the Habits of Mind.

At the Turning Point Learning Center in Emporia, Kansas, middle-grade students create a series of public service announcements that are broadcast on television and in the school. The intent is to acquaint the populace of the region with the Habits of Mind. Students, of course, translate them into "teen-speak."

Building an Action Research Agenda

As schools decide to embrace the Habits of Mind, leadership teams or the entire faculty may design action research projects to capture indicators of their effects. Typically they start with a question such as this: What interests you about the effects of Habits of Mind? The staff then generates a list of possible effects, such as these:

- Impact on students.
- Achievement/test scores.
- Self-directedness.
- Discipline referrals.
- Grades.
- Study habits.
- Personal life.
- Relationships with peers.
- Relationships with family life.
  members.
- Attendance.
- Dropout rates.
- Graduation rates.
- Others.
- Impact in the classroom:
  ○ Instructional strategies.
  ○ Lesson design.
- Impact on staff as a whole.
- Impact on individual staff members professionally.
- Impact on teacher's personal
- Impact on the school culture.
- Impact on family/community.

The staff also discusses and decides how such information can best be collected (e.g., through interviews, questionnaires, surveys, or journals), who the data sources are, and over what period of time the information should be collected (Edwards, 2007).

School leaders encourage and manage the collection of artifacts indicating growth in the Habits of Mind, including such items as exemplary student work, model lesson plans, newsletters, and videotaped lessons and interviews. This collection is often organized into a school portfolio the public can view.

In Summary

The development of the Habits of Mind as goals of education is not just kid stuff. Education will achieve an intellectual focus when the school becomes an intellectually stimulating environment—a home for the mind for all who dwell there; when all the schools' inhabitants realize that freeing human intellectual potential is the goal of education; when staff members strive to get better at it themselves; and when they use their energies to enhance the intellectual skills and Habits of Mind of others. Educational leaders constantly monitor the "intellectual ecology" of the school. Their chief purpose is to ensure that thinking, creativity, and interdependence will become neither endangered nor (worse) extinct.

> If your vision statement sounds like motherhood and apple pie and is somewhat embarrassing, you're on the right track. You bet the farm.
>
> —*Peter Block*

References

Bello, N. (2004). *Reflective analysis of student work: Improving teaching through collaboration*. Thousand Oaks, CA: Corwin.

Block, P. (1987). *The empowered manager*. San Francisco: Jossey-Bass.

Costa, A. (2007). *The school as a home for the mind*. Thousand Oaks, CA: Corwin.

Costa, A., & Garmston, R. (2002). *Cognitive coaching: A foundation for the renaissance school*. Norwood, MA: Christopher Gordon.

Costa, A., & Kallick, B. (1995). *Assessment in the learning organization*. Alexandria, VA: ASCD.

Edwards, J. (2007). *Designing an action research agenda*. Denver, CO: Center for Cognitive Coaching.

Ellison, J., & Hayes, C. (2006). *Effective school leadership: Developing principals through cognitive coaching*. Norwood, MA: Christopher Gordon.

Evered, R., & Selman, J. (1989). Coaching and the art of management. *Organizational Dynamics, 18*, 16–32.

Frymier, J. (1987, September). Bureaucracy and the neutering of teachers. *Phi Delta Kappan, 69*(1), 9–14.

Fullan, M. (1993). *Change forces.* New York: Falmer.

Garmston, R., & Wellman, B. (2009). *Adaptive schools.* Norwood, MA: Christopher Gordon.

Hargreaves, A., & Fink, D. (2006). *Sustainable leadership.* San Francisco: Jossey-Bass.

Jackson, P. (1968). *Life in classrooms.* New York: Holt Rinehart Winston.

Jensen, E. (1996). *Brain-based learning.* Del Mar, CA: Turning Point Publishing.

Joyce, B., & Showers, B. (1988). *Student achievement through staff development.* New York: Longmans.

Land, G., & Jarman, B. (1992). *Break-point and beyond: Mastering the future today.* New York: Harper.

Langer, G., Colton, A., & Goff, L. (2003). *Collaborative analysis of student work: Improving teaching and learning.* Alexandria, VA: ASCD.

Lipton, L., & Wellman, B. (2004). *Data-driven dialogue.* Sherman, CT: Miravia.

Louis, K., Marks, H., & Kruse, S. (1996). Teachers' professional community in restructuring schools. *American Educational Research Journal, 33*(4), 757–798.

Marzano, R., Waters, T., & McNulty, B. (2005). *School leadership that works.* Alexandria, VA. ASCD.

McDonald, J., Mohr, N., Dichter, A., & McDonald, E. (2003). *The power of protocols.* New York: Teachers College Press.

Perkins, D. (2003). *King Arthur's round table.* New York: Wiley.

Senge, P. (1990). *The fifth discipline.* New York: Doubleday.

Sergiovanni, T. (2004). *The lifeworld of leadership: Creating culture, community, and personal meaning in our schools.* San Francisco: Jossey-Bass.

Sousa, D. A. (2001). *How the brain learns.* Thousand Oaks, CA: Corwin.

Stigler, J., & Hiebert, J. (1999). *The teaching gap: Best ideas from the world's teachers for improving education in the classroom.* New York: Free Press.

Vygotsky, L. (1978). *Mind in society: The development of higher psychological processes.* Cambridge, MA: Harvard University Press.

Wheatley, M. J., & Kellner-Rogers, M. (1996). *A simpler way.* San Francisco: Berrett-Koehler.

Wolfe, P. (2001). *Brain matters: Translating research into classroom practice.* Alexandria, VA: ASCD.

16

Habits of Mind for
the Systems-Savvy Leader

Jennifer Abrams

When I began to work outside the classroom as a teacher on special assignment, I was excited about the opportunity to create and facilitate learning communities, to work one-on-one with new teachers, and to design and offer trainings to supervisors and my colleagues. I was eager to be with team members who were trying to live up to their roles as teacher-leaders, to be agents of change in the schools, to work on reforms that focused on student learning.

My key learning in the first years of doing work outside the classroom was this: I had a credential in how to work with children through the subject I was teaching; I did not have a credential in how to work with adults. My teacher credential program didn't instruct me on how to work effectively with the other professionals in my school and district. Although some administrative credential programs might offer courses that focus specifically on human resources protocols and communication processes, coaches, directors, instructional supervisors, and other teacher leaders might not have taken those courses and, as a result, need to hone these skills to work more effectively with a variety of adults.

Being able to work well with adults is one of the keys to changing schools for the better. As Rick DuFour and Bob Eaker, two strong proponents for professional learning communities, state, "The most promising strategy for sustained, substantive school improvement is building the capacity of school personnel to function as a professional learning community" (DuFour & Eaker, 2004 p. xi). However, teachers often don't feel they see things change "for the better when they come together to work with each other." As a result, they become ever more cautious about stepping outside their classrooms yet again. Dennis Sparks (2005), the former executive director of the National Staff Development Council, writes of the "resignation and dependency" that teachers often feel in the face of change. The pervasive feeling among many educators is that "nothing is going to change" and that "the principal should do something" (p. ix) instead of taking action themselves. Researchers from DuFour and Eaker to Fullan and Schmoker say adults working with one another will make the difference in student achievement. "The professional learning community model is a powerful way of working together that profoundly affects the practices of schooling. But initiating and sustaining the concept requires hard work. It requires the school staff to . . . work collaboratively on matters related to learning" (DuFour, 2004, p. 11). And to do that hard work we need to "begin the process of shifting from resignation to possibility and from dependency to a sense of personal power" (Sparks, 2005, p. ix).

So what dispositions, skills, and knowledge must a teacher-leader have to create that shift from resignation to possibility? What do we need to learn in order to become effective collaborative colleagues and powerful agents of change in schools? What do we need to know and be able to do? One piece of essential learning on the way to becoming a systems-savvy leader is to put the Habits of Mind into action in everyday adult-to-adult interactions. Conscientiously cultivating and embodying the Habits of Mind can help us to become the resourceful, adept, systems-savvy leaders we need in our classrooms and in our schools.

The Meaning of "Systems Savvy"

What does it mean to be "systems savvy"? Let's start with a description of systems-savvy leaders. Systems-savvy leaders lead from a place that is not solely self-referential or self-serving but is instead systems-aware and service-oriented. They strive to make change from a student-focused and other-focused center. They move through an aggressive learning agenda that results in their learning the skills and capabilities needed to further the goals of the school for the benefit of the students. They have a philosophical orientation to an organization that makes them both an integral part of the institution and, at the same time, able to see it from the outside. They make an effort to use their intrapersonal, interpersonal, group, and contextual intelligence simultaneously.

Along with this identity driving their behavior, systems-savvy leaders have a sense of responsibility for moving initiatives through and taking action—action that does right by the school and all students. And to move things forward, they become politically intelligent. They don't think about the word *politics* with distaste. They don't ignore the leanings of the various stakeholders in the organization. Being systems-savvy, they feel obligated to understand all points of view. And in the best sense, these politically literate, systems-savvy leaders use their understanding of all the sides in a debate to move forward initiatives that will best benefit students, not just themselves.

As we teach students literacy skills—how to understand the facts in a story, how to predict what will happen next, how to question the motivations and actions of characters, how to read for context clues, and how to summarize—we, too, need to be systems literate. Our schools are narratives written by us, and so we need to be systems literate about our contexts. There are formal and informal structures to understand, procedures to follow or redesign, dynamics between individuals to appreciate, cultural symbols to understand, awarenesses to cultivate. All of these aspects of a school or a district are essential understandings for a leader who wants not only to fit into an organization, but also to move one forward. Systems-savvy leaders act from an identity that says, "I can make a difference and I want to work with others to do so." They learn about the culture of their school in order to make their contributions meaningful and relevant to those who work with them.

How Do the Habits of Mind Fit In?

Organizational literacy and "on the ground" knowledge of a given school are just a start in being a systems-savvy leader. Systems-savvy leaders acquire certain skill sets, capabilities, and Habits of Mind to assist them in the work they want to do.

The Habits of Mind we have been cultivating in our students need to be the habits we learn ourselves. In our contexts, in our schools, honing our Habits of Mind can help us better navigate the systems we work in, help us change the discourse we speak with, and open us to be even more effective leaders. All of us can continue to develop these intelligent behaviors throughout our lifetimes. So on this, our professional path, the Habits of Mind are an integral component in our own development as systems-savvy leaders (Costa & Kallick, 2000).

The five Habits of Mind discussed here are not exhaustive, by any means. Working on integrating a greater awareness of all 16 habits is the ultimate goal for the systems-savvy leader. The five highlighted here—persisting, managing impulsivity, listening with understanding and empathy, communicating with precision and accuracy, and thinking interdependently—are most fundamental in beginning the work of becoming more systems savvy.

Persisting

Change requires lots of time, courage, patience, and endurance. Successfully implementing a new school reform, a curriculum change, or a new program requires a knowledge of the change process, implementation dips, people's reasons for resistance to change, and an ability to use positive self-talk.

Let's consider an example of teachers at a high school who find that cheating is on the rise in all grade levels. They begin to talk about possible reasons for the increase. They agree they need a multipronged approach, prioritize their action steps, and propose a solution. They go to the administration to get some support for the initiative. They hit a roadblock. They go to the site council to share their views, but addressing cheating isn't a school goal for the year. They keep talking. They talk to members of their departments and find out what others are thinking. They refine their strategy. They keep talking. They talk to colleagues in the lunchroom. They talk it up at staff meetings. They write. They learn from one another about which processes have been effective and which ideas and communication strategies have not. And eventually they get a bit of time on the agenda at the next staff meeting to propose some suggestions for what can be done to stop cheating.

Step by step. Learning who the right people are, the right words, the right timing. These teachers embody the verb *persist*. It all begins with the keen yet painful understanding that persistence is a must for anyone who wants to promote good systemic change in an organization. Persistence means being aware of and acknowledging reality, anticipating resistance, and expecting, from the outset, the need for support. Like marathon runners who have cheerleaders on the sidelines, drinks to sustain them, and an understanding that walls will be hit, systems-savvy leaders know the art of persistence. Persistence is the first habit to be cultivated by a systems-savvy leader who wants to make change.

Politically literate leaders who persist ask questions such as these:

• Who do I have on my support team?
• Am I dealing with reality in a way that moves us forward, or am I getting hooked on other people's resistance to the change?
• Do I know where we are in the journey? Where we are in terms of the change process?
• Do I know what needs to happen at each stage?
• What do I know about what I need to do when the going gets tough?

Managing Impulsivity

We have all been there: sitting in a brainstorming session when someone shouts out, "That won't work!" Or perhaps receiving an e-mail from a parent on a night when you aren't at your best and promptly but carelessly sending off a response, only to say to yourself the following morning, "Oops!" Or how about hearing an announcement at a staff meeting and then hearing yourself audibly sigh in discontent as the principal looks your way. Sound familiar?

Managing impulsivity extends far beyond teaching the students in your elementary classroom to not shout out their answers and to raise their hands instead. It is a skill of self-management and self-monitoring that serves the systems-savvy leader well (Costa & Kallick, 2000).

We teach students to make sure they understand all the directions before starting an assignment, but in our own professional lives we don't read the memo in full and then we complain about the action needed. We moan and groan immediately about a hire or a change in policy without learning about the rationale behind it. We immediately jump to a negative judgment of a proposed program (such as block scheduling or teaming) without thinking through either the pros or cons. We admit to ourselves that some of our responses just weren't "ready for takeoff."

And getting things ready for takeoff is key when we want to make a successful change as a systems-savvy leader. Managing impulsivity for adults takes many forms; it's not just stopping the occasional "blurt out" in a meeting. It's paying attention to body language during meetings or interactions—to the eye rolling, the slumped shoulders, and the audible gasps. It's waiting 24 hours to respond to a memo, a proposal, an e-mail, or a comment. It's noticing when a teacher is ready to begin teaching a class and choosing not to interrupt her as she is closing the door. It's not bringing up a major emotion-laden point with a teacher five minutes before school begins. It's practicing responses that respect both ourselves and our colleagues when we are caught in a pinch—such as saying, "I always give myself 24 hours to think about a new proposal" or "This is complex and has many facets to it; I'd like to take a bit of time to think this through before I give my perspective."

Managing impulsivity isn't a problem for everyone. For some on the systems-savvy path, the key will be to manage *passivity*. Some educators know they never speak up. They wait until it is too late, when the decision has been made and the schedule finalized, and then they are hurt and frustrated but say nothing because they didn't say anything at the onset. They perceive those who come to a meeting and steamroll through the agenda as pushy and intense. They fear they never have the right words at the right time and always wonder how someone else can marshal the right phrases at the perfect moment while they are bumbling around looking for a sentence stem and worrying about stuttering. Managing passivity is as much of a challenge in becoming an agent of change as managing impulsivity. Learning how to advocate, not just inquire, can increase feelings of empowerment. Practicing with colleagues and getting more skilled at what to say and when to say it will help the more passive systems-savvy leader learn how to speak up before the pressure is on. Finding a voice could be the boost needed to feel more in control. Systems-savvy leaders who manage their impulsivity ask questions such as these:

- Is this a good time to take a risk and pose a challenge?
- What is the intensity of this need? Does it need to be handled now, or can it wait?
- Am I in the right frame of mind to say something, or will I become too emotional?
- If I speak up, who or what else will this affect? What is the ripple effect?
- If I bring this issue up, do I have an action plan thought out? Can I support the individual through the changes I would like to see made? Do I have a game plan in mind?
- Can I say what I want to say and still project acceptance of my colleague?
- If I do bring up the concern, is there enough time to really deal with it, or will it just cause problems?

Systems-savvy leaders who manage their passivity ask questions such as these:

- How important is it for the students or other staff that I bring this up?
- Is what is going on in the classroom physically unsafe, academically unsound, or emotionally damaging to students or colleagues?
- What might happen if I didn't have the conversation?
- What am I trying to accomplish? *And*, if I speak up, will it move me toward or away from that goal?
- No matter the outcome, is this something I have to say because I have to say it?
- Does my silence lead my colleague to think I agree with his perspective or behavior? Is that OK?

One of the most important skills to cultivate is the ability to separate action from reaction. Thinking first and then speaking with confidence is a Habit of Mind essential to becoming systems-savvy.

Listening with Understanding and Empathy

Those of us who work in schools are always rushing. When are we not? The phrase "Do you have a minute?" is commonplace. And yet we all know most interactions require more than 60 seconds. The systems-savvy leader might be accustomed to fixing things, putting out fires, solving problems, and being the crisis-control person in the office. That orientation can get things done in the short run—for now. But somehow that problem resurfaces in another form just a few days later. How does this happen? Systems-savvy people know there is the tip and there is the iceberg, and if we want to make change, dealing with 1 percent of the story won't do it. Those who are systems savvy know that listening with understanding and empathy is one way to make change stick and to help those who work with them to become more self-directed and resourceful. They understand the comment "Silence is never more golden than when you hold it long enough to get all the facts and feelings before you speak."

Consider this example. A new teacher comes to a colleague to discuss her feelings of being overwhelmed. She is dealing with too many pressures outside the school day—a new relationship and a family illness. On top of those challenges, she faces the management of the various courses she is teaching and the moving to and from the many different rooms she works in each day. What does this teacher want from her colleague in terms of an ear? The layers of listening required in this situation are many. And yet most of us start with the "positional" ear—the one that hears with our own role in the forefront. The principal might empathize and be a cheerleader, presuming it is just a new teacher's moment of panic and nothing more. He has been around for decades and has heard many teachers speak of being overwhelmed at the start of the school year. An assistant principal in charge of facilities may listen to the scenario and immediately think, "If I get her into one room, all might be OK." A department chair might listen and begin to feel overwhelmed herself, saying, "This is going to be hard for me if she keeps crying and acting this way. When will the parents begin to call?"

An immediate and most instinctive way to listen could be through the filters of role. Starting from an immediate, first-person professional perspective might be the "default position," but listening with understanding and empathy in the identity of a systems-savvy leader requires *several* ears and the ability to know the filters. It requires the skill to hear for the "micro" in the moment and then, when the time is right and the information is thoroughly understood, to think for the "macro" implications next.

In this example, the systems-savvy leader thinks about the teacher first. How is this person doing? What exactly is her challenge? What supports does she need? Can those resources be found to support her?

When the problem is understood at the personal level, the next step can be to think about the repercussions of this dilemma, taking into account the considerations of the school. What if things cannot be resolved? What if she needs to take a leave? Who needs to be notified? What are the next steps? How will this affect the students, the department, and the school? What can be done in the meantime?

According to Kupersmith and Hoy (1989), one of the key reasons a leader is trusted is because the leader is a person first and a role second. Learning and remembering to paraphrase, summarizing, and being *in* relationship with a colleague on a *personal* level, not just a *positional* level, is key to getting the job done well.

Why don't leaders like to listen? Some people don't like silence because of a fear of losing control of the conversation. Accustomed to being fix-it people who provide solutions and offer suggestions, they may see silence or the voice of the other person taking up air space as an indication that they aren't in control of the situation. Actually, the opposite is true. Listening with the goal of understanding and empathy helps the politically literate assist colleagues in solving problems and thinking up new solutions; it provides them an ear and then ultimately facilitates their becoming more self-directed—which is an ultimate goal of the systems-savvy leader.

Systems-savvy leaders listen and ask questions such as these:

• Can I sit still and focus on the other person completely? What would help me do so?

• Do I practice paraphrasing? Acknowledging the feeling and content of the communication being offered to me?

• Do I practice not telling my story? Not giving advice? Not providing solutions?

• Do I know when I am listening and when I am thinking about what I need to do as a principal, a coordinator, or a supervisor? Can I separate my thinking and set that aside?

• Knowing that the personal can come before the positional in many situations, do I know when those times are and ways that I can show this "shift" to the person who is talking to me?

Communicating with Precision and Accuracy

We all know the saying "It isn't what you say; it's how you say it"—the tone, the wording, the timing, the pacing, the intent behind the message. The systems-savvy leader knows that precision and accuracy in all communications are essential.

A contemporary example of the importance of communicating accurately is e-mail. E-mail is terrific because it can help us to communicate at any hour and to anyone; but no doubt we all know a number of possible communication snafus common to the medium: the e-mail that doesn't start with a "Hello" or end with a "Thank you" and gives off an air of rudeness; the message that is written in one long paragraph and consequently results in the recipient overlooking precious information; the e-mail that says simply, "Come see me Monday morning" and causes a new teacher needless distress all weekend as she contemplates what the meeting will be about; or the dismissive, hurriedly written e-mail that says, "We gave that position to your colleague, John," leaving the recipient far more hurt than he would have been had a face-to-face encounter taken place. All of these moments remind us that the ability to communicate with precision and accuracy is indispensable to a systems-savvy leader.

As we roll out new initiatives, awareness of our audience and forethought in communication are also vital. If we don't think ahead of time, we can put ourselves further behind in just a few sentences. Case in point: In furthering an agenda related to closing the achievement gap, the director of staff development has changed the job description for the new teacher coaching position to include more work on equity. The training has been put on the schedule, and it is mandatory. The trainer assertively states, "We are doing this." The coaches, accustomed for years to doing work a certain way, feel resistance and communicate it in many ways.

Some shut down. Others defensively argue against the requirement. They leave the first meeting uncomfortable and spend 30 minutes in the parking lot processing their anger around the new requirements.

And yet the work needs to happen. It will require more effort by the coach who doesn't feel comfortable with the new obligations. The coach might not have the knowledge and skills to do the work. She might not believe in the purpose of the new work. It might not align with her sense of what the job is about. But it still needs to be done. The systems-savvy leader knows that although it would be possible to simply describe the new job in terms of its discrete tasks, it wouldn't be appropriate. Given that the coaches are hesitant about the work and feeling threatened by the new parts of the job, merely sending out a memo or communicating the new directives via e-mail would be negligent. The systems-savvy leader anticipates the need to choose words carefully, to set the tone deliberately, and to empathically acknowledge in conversation the uncomfortable change from current practice to what needs to be done in the future. The systems-savvy leader listens and speaks clearly. The resistance is still present, but far less than if the words are ill considered and improvised. Systems-savvy leaders plan for precision.

Consider another example. A new director of a K–5 school has been urged to start walk-throughs at her school. She thinks about this new initiative carefully. Supervisors have conducted few observations up until now, and teachers have appreciated the resulting autonomy. The head of the school suggests rolling out the initiative by announcing it during the staff meeting among all the other business items for the week. The systems-savvy director decides there is more to it than just stating the facts. She thinks to herself, "I must lay the groundwork for teachers, over time, and communicate to them what we mean by classroom observation, what it accomplishes, how teachers can develop professionally through observation, how we can make it nonthreatening, how other professionals offer up their work for others to watch, and how, as members of a profession right along with medicine and law, we can do the same." The director decides how she wants to share this with the teachers before she steps into anyone's domain, creates more frustration, or increases discomfort. Otherwise the intent of a program will never be accomplished.

It isn't just *what* the systems-savvy leader says; it's *how* and *when* and so much more.

Systems-savvy communicators think through questions such as these:

• What words are truthful and accurate and can be heard by the listener without increasing defensiveness or anxiety?

• What "trigger words" will put listeners on edge and inhibit their ability to listen to the message?

• When I say what I want to say, what else might I need to say in order to be as clear and supportive as I can be?

• What medium is most appropriate for the communication?

Thinking Interdependently

Because teachers are now asked to work together more often in professional learning communities, we need to ask ourselves how effectively we "play well with others." Most likely, this behavior wasn't a key factor in most teachers' decision to become a teacher. We got into the profession to work with children or adolescents, not adults. And that has been what we have done. Traditionally, teachers were asked to spend their time away from students making decisions about curriculum, instruction, and assessment solo, behind closed doors.

Now, more of us do business around such things as common assessments and grade-level teaming. It is said that one of the most important skills to have is an ability to think in concert with others (Costa & Kallick, 2000). Do we have the skills to do so? Do we know how to advocate and inquire? Do we know how to dialogue and discuss? Systems-savvy leaders are self-aware. They know that thinking with others reveals points of view they couldn't come up with alone. They know that their knowledge increases if they are open to what the group has to say.

When first beginning to do action research or putting an idea in front of a school staff to see how it is received, it is scary to imagine what data will come back. Will others offer feedback in forms that shouldn't be heard? Will others dismiss the concept as not doable? The systems-savvy leader knows that the key to change lies in learning how to think with others, to advocate thoughtfully, and to inquire with empathy.

In *Schools That Learn*, Senge and others (2000) speak of the need to learn how to be an effective group member, to learn to state one's assumptions aloud ("Here's what I think"), to describe one's reasoning ("Here is why I arrived at this conclusion"), and to ask for others' perspectives ("You might think differently; what are your thoughts?").

Some educators might consider advocating for an idea to be a type of confrontation, and they might feel uncomfortable at the thought of not being liked or appearing mean. Systems-savvy leaders look at thinking interdependently as an opportunity to share a perspective and be passionate, but they anticipate that others will have their say as well. Systems-savvy leaders will want to know others' views because they understand that more knowledge helps bring about buy-in and can lead to a sense of ownership from all the stakeholders in a given school.

Systems-savvy leaders know that one change is actually many changes. Although we normally think of interdependent thinking as something that happens during team meetings or among members of decision-making bodies, this Habit of Mind also shows up during everyday interactions with assistants, secretaries, and associates who support the work of the school. Systems-savvy leaders think interdependently from step one of a process that uses this type of support; they constantly think about the ripple effect of their actions. They know that acting *independently* can cause others to feel unseen or unappreciated.

Consider this example. Let's say someone needs to change the location and date of a training for 60 new teachers in order to accommodate a previously scheduled meeting that was inadvertently overlooked (an interdependent moment gone awry). As we think through how to correct this error, witness how a lack of interdependent thinking can cause additional problems. The ripple effect might occur like this:

• Sending announcements of a date change puts more on an assistant's plate. The need to communicate the change quickly adds more stress to the plate, in the form of "This must get out now!"

• Once the announcement is delivered to the 60 participants, they must rethink day care arrangements, change car pool plans, and possibly switch previously scheduled meetings.

• Rooms might already be booked, so the location of the session might need to be changed, which might lead to possible adjustments in necessary equipment.

• Those who were presenting might not be able to join because of previous commitments, thus requiring a restructuring of the format of the session.

This example involves only a 24-hour date change of a 90-minute meeting. It is *not* program restructuring, rearranging teaming formulations, or a major school reform movement that would need to take place over a number of months or years.

Systems-savvy leaders who think interdependently also take into consideration the feelings around the content of the meeting. They don't immediately assume the meeting has no emotional overtones to it. They don't presume that there is nothing heated to discuss or that any type of change isn't a "big deal."

The systems-savvy leader thinks about how many times this type of thing happens to the assistant who needs to do the quickstep to manage the change; how many times the worker at the meeting location needs to hurry through a room set up in one place and rush over to assist with the new arrangement; how many times this can happen without damaging positive relationships with those who help behind the scenes.

A systems-savvy leader extrapolates from this small, short-term example to the needed and much bigger changes ahead. Systems-savvy leaders ask the questions, "What is the ripple effect of my action? What will be affected?"

Systems-savvy leaders who are interdependent thinkers also ask questions such as these:

• Am I aware of my assumptions and values, and do I know when they are getting in the way of moving forward with my colleagues?

• Am I able to stand outside myself and see how I might be having an impact on others or be seen by others?

• If I am hearing another perspective, do I listen to it and react appropriately, changing behavior if necessary?

• Am I open to doing things in a way other than my way?

• Am I open to hearing all perspectives? And when hearing all perspectives, do I honor them or shut down?

• If concepts come up at a meeting or staff session that are uncomfortable or confusing, do I manage my anxiety in a way that is appropriate?

• Do I want to work in a group and show that interest by exhibiting appropriate body language?

• When communicating with other adults, do I ask for other perspectives? Do I seek to understand the other points of view?

• Do I manage my impulsivity or interrupt often, inserting my point of view at times when others want to be heard?

• Do I use positive presuppositions when coming together with a given group—presuming positive intent and potential?

• Am I aware that I am not allowing equitable participation by talking too much at meetings or talking too little and not contributing?

What's at Stake

When we assume new leadership positions, we have great aspirations. We bring new energy, new insight, and a ton of passion. And then reality hits, and the work is more than anticipated. As Terry Pearce (2000) says, "There are many people who think they want to be matadors, only to find themselves in the ring with 2,000 pounds of bull bearing down on them, and then discover that what they really wanted was to wear tight pants and hear the crowd roar." This is when the Habits of Mind come into play.

Working to make change in schools is a meaningful way to make a life. It is what children need us to do on their behalf. Cultivating the Habits of Mind helps us do our work in the most day-to-day and visionary ways. Systems-savvy leaders have agendas they want to pursue, and one of them is their own learning—asking themselves which Habits of Mind will help them accomplish their goals. Cultivating the habits of persisting, managing impulsivity, listening with understanding and empathy, communicating with precision and accuracy, and thinking interdependently is imperative for our efforts to help schools to become places that thrive. Harriet Lerner (2001) says

Our conversations invent us. Through our speech and our silence, we become smaller or larger selves. Through our speech and our silence, we diminish or enhance the other person, and we narrow or expand the possibilities between us. How we use our voice determines the quality of our relationships, who we are in the world, and what the world can be and might become. Clearly, a lot is at stake here. (p. 239)

Systems-savvy leaders know this in their hearts and their heads and use the Habits of Mind with heart, thought, and intention. The education of all our students is at stake.

References

Costa, A., & Kallick, B. (Eds.). (2000). *Discovering and exploring habits of mind.* Alexandria, VA: ASCD.

DuFour, R. (2004, May). What is a "professional learning community?" *Educational Leadership, 61*(8), pp. 6–11.

DuFour, R., & Eaker, R. (1998). *Professional learning communities at work: Best practices for enhancing student achievement.* Bloomington, IN: National Educational Service.

Kupersmith, W., & Hoy, W. (1989). *The concept of trust: An empirical assessment.* Presentation at the annual meeting of the American Educational Research Association, New Orleans, LA.

Lerner, H. (2001). *The dance of connection: How to talk to someone when you're mad, hurt, scared, frustrated, insulted, betrayed or desperate.* New York: Harper Collins.

Pearce, T. (2000, April 30). Leadership coaching . . . A contact sport. *San Francisco Examiner.*

Senge, P., Cambron-McCabe, N., Lucas, T., Smith, B., Dutton, J., & Kleiner, A. (2000). *Schools that learn: A fifth discipline handbook for educators, parents and everyone who cares about education.* New York: Currency.

Sparks, D. (2005). *Leading for results.* Thousand Oaks, CA: Corwin.

17

Leading Is a Habit of Mind

William A. Sommers and Diane P. Zimmerman

People often ask us, "How do you teach leadership?" We think a better question is "How do you learn leadership?" Noel Tichy (1997), in his book *The Leadership Engine*, proposes that leaders have two main responsibilities: first, to be the head learner; and second, to develop other leaders. We believe that we develop leaders by managing internal and external resources to bring out the best in each person. In addition, we lead by inspiring others toward common visions—for both how we work together and what we believe about that work.

The Call to Leadership

As we reflect on our teaching experiences, we realize that we were unconsciously on a path to leadership. We experimented with trial and error; we did what worked. Every day felt like a new adventure looking for *innovative* solutions to the puzzles embodied in our students. We asked *questions* and took *responsible risks* to solve the riddles of learning; we *reflected on our thinking* and actions and continued to learn from experience. We look back and *laugh* at some of our trials and tribulations; naiveté invited us to experiment through *questioning and posing problems* in our bid for elegant solutions. We now know we are positive deviants; we are always optimizing solutions with the existing surroundings. It didn't seem to matter what

307

kind of school, what the level of diversity or socioeconomic standing, or what kind of administration we worked with in the organization. Others said, "Where did you learn that? We need to know that," and we found ourselves in front of peers teaching them what we knew. Teaching peers required that we learn to *think* and *communicate with clarity and precision*. We did not necessarily name the Habits of Mind at that time, but we are aware that the habits were clearly evidenced in the way we worked.

It was fun, exciting, and daunting. Neither of us had aspirations to seek many of the jobs we took—including the highest-level jobs in our systems; sometimes, we think these jobs found us, because they were a next logical step for us as teacher-leaders. Yet, being a superintendent or the president of a national organization is not an easy feat. Crediting fate as our sole guide would be dishonest; we arrived at these destinations through *persistence*, determination, diligence, and hard work. However, we were always willing to reflect on what we did, willingly took feedback from those we trusted, and learned from experience. We found that we cultivated Habits of Mind that helped us focus, commit, and stay passionate about our work. Most important, when leaders embody these habits, others emulate creating a culture that adopts these mental attitudes. This short essay tries to answer the question: How do you learn to be a leader and what is the significance of the Habits of Mind as a part of that learning?

This is not a how-to manual, but rather an exploration of how these habits helped us be competent, confident, and more successful as leaders. The frame of the Habits of Mind makes cognitive processes concrete, bringing *clarity and precision to our thinking* and actions, and thereby providing opportunities to learn and grow.

The Habits of Mind are pervasive enough to cover the territory; they allow us to set a rich context for our leadership discoveries and they continue to provide ongoing knowledge, skills, and applications in our leadership roles. By adopting the Habits of Mind as a thinking frame, leaders widen their repertoire of possible actions and foster *flexibility* in response. Having only one or two response sets for difficult problems limits a leader's influence and ability to find resolution. When leaders learn to stay *flexible*, they increase their personal and professional efficacy by being able to imagine possibilities and *innovate* along the way. That ability, in turn, expands a leader's sphere of influence. The Habits of Mind are fractal in that by adopting one, others tend to emerge on their own as part of the larger pattern. For example, by *thinking flexibly* we also find *creative* options. In addition, *thinking flexibly* requires that we *listen to others with understanding and empathy*. As leaders, *thinking about our thinking* is key to our success and helps us build healthy organizations that foster excellence.

Opportunists—Seeking Every Opportunity

As a way to explore these cognitive processes, we offer vignettes from our own careers as educators. We hope these vignettes will help you clarify how you might cultivate your own thinking and actions—and find ways to be a leader who makes the difference that matters. Each leader must learn to connect his or her own dots; here we describe how we connected our dots. In retrospect, we know that our leadership has created legacies in both the people and the organizations that have transcended our tenure.

One of the many traits we have in common is that we are both opportunists. By this we mean, when we get a mind-set, we seek every opportunity to get to our destination. Some might call it stubborn, others *persistent*; we say it is also about focus so that we can seek every opportunity that brings us closer to our goals.

A story comes to mind about when Bill became a principal in an urban school where the dropout rate was 275 out of 2,000 students. When Bill asked why it was so high, the response was "It is always that way." Here was an opportunity to confront an issue that was assumed to be unsolvable. By staying focused on the task, bringing in other staff who wanted to make a difference, and engaging the students to be part of the solutions, he emboldened his staff to seek every opportunity to keep students in school and was able to cut the dropout rate in half in one year.

Looking back on the process, he *questioned* the belief that nothing could be done; he worked to establish *clarity* about intentions, and he *listened* to students, staff, and parents. He *created* a small learning community that stayed focused on this group of students and that was *persistent* despite the odds. In the succeeding years, Bill and his team continued to learn and make necessary changes to keep more students in school.

Focus—Paying Attention to What Matters

To distinguish tenacity from rigidity, we emphasize the importance of focus. Focus provides a way to *think about our thinking,* to gain *clarity,* and to foster *persistence* when the going gets tough. Focus allows us to stay true to our values and *flexible* in our actions. In addition, with focus we learn to ignore what does not further our mission. When considering a new venture, we ask how does the new agenda further or distract from the current focus? Which is more important: A focus on students who are having difficulty learning, or the creation of another after-school activity? Both are important; however, leaders must keep the focus on what is most important and place less emphasis on issues that detract. As leaders, we create focal points of concentration to sustain the mental energy needed to *persist* and accomplish our collective dreams.

However, ignoring certain things does not mean that we make unilateral decisions and shut out others' viewpoints. We know that *persistence* is a productive Habit of Mind. When others persist, it reminds us to take a step back and *listen* by asking, does this person speak singly or for a silent group? Sometimes through *questioning and posing problems* we have gained *clarity,* and the resistors have found avenues for embracing the mission. Better yet, sometimes resistance creates an opportunity in which the focus or mission is expanded to include the new information or to *apply past knowledge to a new situation.* Finding opportunities for group synergy is a pinnacle moment in leadership. It makes the hours spent exploring and thinking as a group worth the time. By asking a group to help us think about ideas in relation to our focus, the group grows in its collective ability to think in terms of the Habits of Mind. More often than not, people learn from their own travels down the various leadership paths and *thinking about their thinking* on that journey. As we heard Judy Arin-Krupp (1982) say, "Adults don't learn from the experience, they learn from processing the experience." We never want to rob someone of his or her own learning or reflection, yet we maintain that leaders are the keepers of the focus.

Distributing Leadership—Mining for Group Gold

As opportunists, we continuously mine for group gold. By this we mean that we *listen* deeply to those we work with so that we can learn about both the person and the person's ideas. Buckingham and Coffman (1999), in their book *First Break All the Rules*, write about building on people's strengths rather than focusing on and trying to improve their weaknesses. We know that *managing impulsivity, thinking and communicating with clarity and precision, taking responsible risks*, and *finding humor* increase group efficacy. These Habits of Mind build enthusiasm and energy; strengthen relationships; help identify assets, strengths, and talents; and create possibilities that help us rise to the challenge.

In her job as superintendent, Diane seeks opportunities to amplify the positive and to explore values and beliefs that need examining. Each time she entered a new school system, she searched for a collective vision for that system. She found that if she was patient, the vision emerged. We both believe that one of the most frequent causes of missed opportunities in organizations is the fact that we do not *listen to others with understanding and empathy*. By *listening* to those with whom we work, we find understandings that *create* pathways we did not know existed. Diane is reminded of a time when the group had jumped to conclusions without *thinking about their thinking*, and the quietest member said in a soft voice, "Is there any room here for another opinion?" It was so quiet that we almost missed it. With this one question, the entire group started to talk, and it turned out we did not have as much agreement as was assumed. Diane reflects, if we had moved forward, the solution would not have worked because we had limited buy-in. By *questioning and posing problems*, we found a more elegant set of responses and a more enduring consensus.

All too often the U.S. school culture tends to focus on the deficits. We are suggesting that we reframe the question using an asset frame: "What resources can we bring to this problem so that it is the best problem we have ever had?" When we have a commitment to the welfare of others, we must enroll others in the solution side of the problem solving and provide opportunities that encourage *innovation, clarity, precision and accuracy*, and professional learning. Professional learning paired with a commitment to Habits of Mind creates group gold.

Beware of Quick Fixes

We believe that the metaphor of a firefighter aptly describes the day-to-day job of a principal. Although principals and superintendents strive to be instructional leaders, more often than not they end up managing tasks and demands. Because of the increasing demands from our schools, every time staff members, students, district personnel, parents, or community members want something, school leaders tend to try to quickly solve the problem. With heightened accountability for student learning, demands for rapid-fire solutions have increased. No Child Left Behind has placed responsibility for student learning in our hands—which is a good thing; however, we are also noticing a rush to quick fixes such as listing standards on chalkboards or creating pacing guides. When schools move rapidly to the quick fix, they inadvertently move away from fostering the Habits of Mind. When firefighters are faced with a roaring fire, there is no time to think; they must depend on using past knowledge to respond immediately. Is this what we want for our schools? We think not.

So, how do we get from firefighter to education leader? Goethe said, "The things that matter most should never be at the mercy of things that matter least." Learning for students and adults is our most important job. That means principals and superintendents must keep the focus on learning as the priority and not be pulled away at every request. An example would be having a classroom observation scheduled and then being faced with a parent who comes into the office to complain about parking at the band concert. Which is more important? Leaders need routines, ways to assure the parent that you will get back to them while keeping the focus on that all-encompassing job—improving student learning.

In a system that rewards the quick fix, it takes tremendous focus for leaders to *manage their impulsivity* and not solve every problem immediately and to *persist* in staying focused on what matters most. Principals and superintendents must *think creatively, imagine* other possibilities for solving problems, and *innovate* when possible. Einstein said, "You cannot solve problems at the same level of thinking that created them." We believe he was right. When we need to slow down or reframe our thinking, we seek other professionals who have served as our coaches or friendly critics.

There is a positive side to firefighting. Larry Cuban (1985) states that you have to put out fires quickly, you have to work on fire prevention, and sometimes you have to know when to start a fire. Good advice. Responding quickly can save precious time, money, and energy. Paradoxically, taking *responsible risks* by starting a fire or two can put new energy into the system.

Habits of Mind—The Embedded Vision

An old adage says: If you don't know where you are going, any road will do. We have found that whether it is we as leaders, staff we are working with in schools, parents who have a problem, or a community member with a concern, the impact we have is directly related to helping the other person create a vision for what they want. Susan Scott (2002), in her book *Fierce Conversations*, says people usually have absolute clarity about what they don't want. Our challenge as leaders is to help others define, with *precision and accuracy*, what they do want. Without being clear about the goal and what success looks like, sounds like, and feels like, we are less likely to reach our goals. So leaders help others define what they want and how to get there. When we help others see what could be—by *persisting; thinking about our thinking; applying past knowledge to new situations; creating, imagining, innovating*; and *responding with wonderment and awe*—we develop inspiration and aspiration that challenges and promotes breakthrough thinking and actions.

Finally, leaders must remember that setbacks can be opportunities. When managed well, setbacks promote new standards of performance by posing mistakes as opportunities for learning. Instead of focusing on failure, we emphasize feedback and expect others to grow and learn from experience. The judicious use of feedback can reframe a problem, clarify the desired results, and provide pathways for making needed adjustments. Richard Farson and Ralph Keyes (2002) wrote a book about the idea that the one who makes the most mistakes wins. Mistakes are feedback. Learning is not making the same mistake twice but learning from it. As Eleanor Roosevelt said, "Failure is not getting knocked down; failure is not getting up." This is the essence of *persistence*.

Keeping Hope Alive

Our careers have taken us far. For us, the Habits of Mind have provided ways to stay resilient and to maintain hope for the public schools. We believe one of the greatest needs of leaders is to keep hope alive (Sommers, 2007); we conclude with an acrostic using the word hope.

H is for *humility*—remaining open to continuous learning. If we are not humble enough to say we don't know or that there might be a better way, we tend to think we have the answer. As Robert Pascale (1990) has said, "Nothing fails like success." When we are successful, we stop looking for more right answers. As leaders, we must remain humble.

O is for *options*. Options—the products of *thinking flexibly, listening, creating*—can help people and organizations develop. Looking for more options to learn, teach, and lead can move people and organizations to higher levels of performance. *Creativity* increases options for people. As our world increases in complexity, leaders will need more and more creativity.

P is for *persistence*. We persist when we have the passion for learning and performance. Impatience with systems means that we both continue to battle with our *impulsivity*. After a staff meeting, a former colleague of Bill's gave him a note with "TTT" written on it. She told Bill that no matter how much he wanted something, "Things take time." We still get impatient, and we remind ourselves to go slow to go fast.

E is for *everyone*—*thinking interdependently* and remembering that we are not lone rangers. There are always others who want the same results. There are always others willing to help. We have to widen our vision to include others. Our work should not be done by one person, one thing at a time.

We know we have problems in education, and because it is a human endeavor, we always will. We also believe we have solutions, many that we have not thought of yet. So our pearls of wisdom are these: keep on thinking, keep modeling the Habits of Mind, and keep on leading and learning. Isn't that what developing other leaders is all about? Isn't that what students deserve?

References

Arin-Krupp, J. (1982). "Motivating experienced staff," workshop, Minneapolis, MN.

Buckingham, M., & Coffman, C. (1999). *First break all the rules*. New York: Simon & Schuster.

Cuban, L. (1985, September). Conflict and leadership in the superintendency. *Phi Delta Kappan, 67*(1), 28–30.

Farson, R., & Keyes, R. (2002). *Whoever makes the most mistakes wins*. New York: Free Press.

Pascale, R. (1990). *Managing on the edge*. New York: Simon & Schuster.

Scott, S. (2002). *Fierce conversations*. New York: Penguin Putnam.

Sommers, W. (2007). Our kids deserve your best. *Journal of Staff Development, 28*(1), 7.

Tichy, N. (1997). *The leadership engine*. New York: HarperCollins.

Part V

Learning from Mindful Schools

The most powerful form of learning, the most sophisticated form of staff development, comes not from listening to the good works of others but from sharing what we know with others . . . . By reflecting on what we do, by giving it coherence, and by sharing and articulating our craft knowledge, we make meaning, we learn.

—*Roland Barth*

The chapters in this section provide a more personal lens through which to view the work related to the Habits of Mind. In each instance, the authors describe their journey as it affected themselves, the people with whom they work interdependently, and the schools that have flourished as a result of focusing on the habits. As you read each chapter, you will see that each author addressed the challenges he or she faced in a different way: there is no *one* best way. We hope that these case studies will illuminate some possibilities for your own work.

In Chapter 18, Mary (Valorie) Hargett and Margaret Evans Gayle present research from the state of North Carolina that is intriguing in several ways: it illuminates the impact of the Habits of Mind, it shows that the Habits can be learned easily by underprivileged children in primary grades, and it demonstrates what can happen if teachers, over time, work together to teach and continually reinforce the habits. Of significance is the research design, which might serve others in assessing the impact of the Habits of Mind on their students, staff, and community. The research and the experience of learning were so convincing that the school district has now developed districtwide plans to adopt and implement the Habits of Mind.

In Chapter 19, Curt Schnorr and Thommie DePinto Piercy share their experiences in "starting from scratch" to build a vision and to bring to fruition a school where the Habits of Mind are valued, taught, and lived.

Chapters 20, 21, and 22 are success stories. Bertie Simmons, principal of Furr High School in Houston, Texas, describes the journey of her school as it went from being one of the lowest-performing high schools in the Houston Independent School District to one of high achievement and excellence. Then, Bonnie Tabor and other staff members describe their experiences in the Waikiki School in Honolulu, Hawaii. They paint a picture of one of the longest-known implementations of the Habits of Mind—more than 17 years. Such persistence has allowed the Habits of Mind to seep into every nook and cranny of the school, creating a unique and "mindful" culture. For the staff, the Habits of Mind are "in their bones." In Chapter 22, Nancy Skerritt and her colleagues from the Tahoma School District in Maple Valley, Washington, describe their work to bring a continuous growth plan for the Habits of Mind into a K–12 school district.

These success stories describe the beneficial impact of what can happen to students, staff, and the community when the Habits of Mind become their shared vision.

—*Arthur L. Costa and Bena Kallick*

18

Habits of Mind in North Carolina: Increasing Intellectual Capacity of Disadvantaged Students

Mary P. Hargett and Margaret Evans Gayle

Within the first week of opening the 2005 school year at Thomasville Primary School in Thomasville, North Carolina, kindergarteners were learning about managing their impulsivity and were able to articulate in complete sentences what that meant. One young child said that managing impulsivity meant "not taking other students' books and materials, not touching them when they are working, not taking their snacks, and not interrupting them when they are talking." The teacher asked her "why managing her impulsivity was important," and she said, "It will hurt their learning."

In spring 2006 at this same school, 1st and 2nd graders were debating which of the two Renaissance painters, Leonardo or Michelangelo, was more persistent with completing his work and which one was the most creative. The two debaters and the moderator had furnished their own costumes for the debate and were serious about the task at hand. Their classmates, at the end of the debate, asked provocative questions of the two debaters and a lively discussion was evident. Each audience member used a rubric to evaluate which debater made the most points. At the end of this activity, students were in learning style centers practicing the theories and techniques that Leonardo and Michelangelo developed and are now considered to be indicative of Renaissance paintings. The students were studying pulleys, measurements, painting techniques, and da Vinci's "Vitruvian Man," all relating to the curriculum unit.

The learning strategies used were developed by teachers trained in Bright IDEA (Interest Development Early Abilities) to implement a concept-based curriculum unit on exploration, using the latest research on best practices and integrating the Habits of Mind as an important part of the unit.

Rationale for Project Bright IDEA

In 1996, the North Carolina General Assembly enacted legislation to give local school districts more flexibility in developing and implementing academically gifted programs for minority and economically disadvantaged students. In 1997, Article 9B of the North Carolina General Statutes stated, "Outstanding abilities are present in students from all cultural groups, across all economic strata, and in all areas of human endeavor." As written into law, this article provides the underlying assumption for developing research-based nurturing programs for all children to have access to more rigorous and challenging curriculum and provides the foundation for building and restructuring pedagogies that promote concept-based, qualitatively differentiated curriculum including instructional delivery and comprehensive balanced assessments. These in-depth approaches have been developed to serve as a K–2 transformational model for all students with Habits of Mind. The question is that when students are presented with complex problems for which there are no immediate answers, what habits do they employ to navigate the world of vast information and create meaningful solutions? The habits become the sustaining framework of the heart and mind for adapting and changing students' dispositions when required to operate successfully in a globally competitive world.

Based on the data from the pilot project, Bright IDEA 1 and the Bright IDEA 2 research, underrepresented student populations are performing at higher levels than many teachers believed possible. These populations include those children, regardless of race or ethnic group, who may have language patterns and limited English experiences, cultural backgrounds, economic disadvantages, and/or educational disadvantages, disabilities, or differences that make it difficult for them to demonstrate their potential on traditional identification measures of talented and gifted.

The Changing Nature of Giftedness

Giftedness may be considered a set of qualities or "potentials" that can be recognized and developed in children, not a mere label assigned to a lucky few (Dunn, Dunn, & Treffinger, 1992). Based on this understanding and acceptance of the nature of giftedness, the conceptual frameworks for Bright IDEA center on the supportive work regarding the development or nurturing of intelligences and intelligent behaviors (HOM) in all children. Transforming the traditional perspective of fixed and unchangeable intelligence into a 21st century research-based perspective that intelligence is flexible and subject to great changes both up and down, depending on kinds of stimulation the brain receives from its environment, is one of the most powerful liberating forces to influence the restructuring of education, schools, and society (Costa, 2000).

Howard Gardner believes that there are many ways of knowing, learning, and expressing knowledge, and these intelligences can be nurtured in all human beings (Gardner, 1993). He believes with proper mediation and experience, everyone (beginning in the earliest stages of childhood and throughout life) continues to develop the intelligences, thus improving the quality of one's life. Therefore, a new definition of intelligence centered on robust habits of mind (intelligent behaviors) that defines specific thinking processes and knowledge structures is needed so that through a person's efforts, intelligence and performance grow incrementally (Costa & Kallick, 2000). Students can be taught cognitive strategies and effort-based beliefs through habits of mind. The curriculum must associate higher-order learning that requires students to pose questions, accept challenges, find solutions not immediately apparent, explain concepts, justify their reasoning, and seek knowledge. In that way, students are held accountable for the development of intelligent behaviors.

Project Bright IDEA 2 was designed as a transformational model by nurturing the potential and developing talent in students in regular K–2 classrooms and with a major goal to change the dispositions of teachers to have high expectations for all students. This model required a partnership among teachers, instructional specialists, principals, and parents to work on the goals together and to be consistent with implementing the research-based strategies.

Bright IDEA was implemented as an integrated approach to transforming the classroom for kindergarteners, 1st and 2nd graders into a vibrant community of learners and problem solvers. This unique K–2 research model, funded by the Javits Program of the United States Department of Education, was designed and implemented by the North Carolina Department of Public Instruction and the American Association for Gifted Children at Duke University. The model was used as a response to a legislative mandate to increase the number of gifted children from underserved populations into challenging academically and intellectually gifted programs. Based on the success of Project Bright IDEA 1, a pilot intervention program (2001–2004) for closing the achievement gap, Project Bright IDEA 2 (2004–2009) was awarded the Javits grant to offer the program to more schools and to research the effects on gifted programs from nurturing the potential of students in regular classrooms from underserved populations.

Teachers and principals from the designated schools have all been trained and are in the full implementation phase of learning new ways of teaching gifted strategies and the Habits of Mind, through a concept-based curriculum, to all of the K–2 children in the research project.

Bright IDEA Goals

The project has four goals: (1) to increase the number of gifted students from underserved populations via changing the dispositions and capacity of regular classroom teachers to wisely use curricula tailored to teaching those students; (2) to study the extent to which such strategies increase the number of 3rd grade students from underrepresented populations who enroll in gifted programs; (3) to advance the quality of these students' metacognitive and cognitive skills; and (4) to create a research-based multidimensional, preidentification model for gifted intelligent behaviors based on Costa and Kallick's Habits of Mind (2000) and on Frasier's Traits, Attributes, and Behaviors (Frasier, 2003–2004).

Beginning in kindergarten and tailoring gifted methodologies for regular classroom teachers to use with all children, Bright IDEA 2 is built on the most advanced research and best practices and focuses on empowering regular classroom teachers, principals, and curriculum specialists, through training and mentoring, to become curriculum architects for the future. They are trained to design interdisciplinary, concept-based curriculum units consistent with state standards, infused with Building Thinking Skills (Parks & Black, 2004) and Gifted Intelligent Behaviors, and to change their classroom environments to meet the learning styles of all children. Students are challenged to use the full range of their talents and intellectual abilities as they address authentic and complex academic tasks. The program builds upon and extends the North Carolina Standard Course of Study through rigorous concept-based integrated tasks and a research-based thinking skills program. The teachers and principals create scholarly environments that engage students actively and consistently in sophisticated investigations of materials and texts, and in learning activities that require them to understand and apply critical and creative processes that are quite advanced for K–2 students. Students are engaged in centers that provide task rotations through four major learning styles (Silver, Strong, & Perini, 2000) and multiple intelligences (Gardner, 1993).

Professional Development

The professional development component built upon and extended the work of Mary Frasier's Talents, Attributes, and Behaviors and the Habits of Mind that have been adapted into Gifted Intelligent Behaviors that can be observed and documented on each child in Bright IDEA 2 classes. The first phase of training focused on integrating the state standards with Building Thinking Skills (Parks & Black, 2004), Bloom's revised taxonomy, Marzano's new taxonomy (Marzano & Kendall, 2007), mathematics research (Olive & Sheffield, 2003), and Stage 1 of Understanding by Design (McTighe & Wiggins, 2004). After the initial training, participants were prepared to write a concept-based interdisciplinary unit based on a Bright IDEA design template. The units were developed and written during a five-day summer institute under the leadership of the design team and learning styles trainer, Dan Moirao. As a result of the training and the practice in the classroom, the project has produced 135 concept-based integrated curriculum units. These units provide for rigor and high-quality differentiated instruction for the population of diverse students. The units were taught and revised, and some were selected for publication and dissemination at the end of the funding period.

The Habits of Mind are not taught in isolation but infused into their curriculum units with a focus on the habits or gifted intelligent behaviors being part of successful work and problem-solving attributes that all children need to know to be able to succeed in school, in work, and in life. Children seem to love learning the big vocabulary words that describe the habits and demonstrating that they know what they mean. Teachers demonstrate their own creativity with the Habits of Mind through conceptually designed learning tasks, which incorporate multiple intelligences that students use to demonstrate their understandings on topics within the standard course of study and beyond. Their teaching strategies with Habits of Mind lead to high-level discussions using essential questions to get children to think and reflect on their answers with their peers. High-level multicultural literature and nonfiction books provide the background for all of the interdisciplinary units. These scholarly environments are engaging students actively and consistently in sophisticated investigations of materials, texts, and learning activities that require them to understand and apply advanced critical and creative processes.

Research Questions and Data. The goals help structure the research questions for evaluating the project and for determining the potential for using the model across the state and the nation. The major questions:

1. What are the dispositions of teachers toward children from diverse groups?

2. Can Bright IDEA increase the number of underserved children identified for gifted programs?

3. What effects will Bright IDEA have on the metacognitive levels of children? Can we measure their levels? Can we teach intelligent behaviors that show individual student progress?

4. Can the effect on students be linked to changing the dispositions of teachers?

To answer these questions we are collecting student data from all three cohorts from the North Carolina K–2 Assessments, from a math problem-based questionnaire, and from preassessments and postassessments of the Habits of Mind. Reading levels are determined from the K–2 Assessment, the math questionnaire was designed to specifically help evaluate the metacognitive levels of students, and special units with rubrics were created to assess the progress toward acquiring Habits of Mind. Out of these assessments of the curriculum units, Habits of Mind are observed in students and scored on rubrics for each behavior and reported as progress toward independent learning and potential for gifted programs.

The professional development model that includes national, state, and local trainers has been required for all participants and is providing the data on the impact of the training on principals' and teachers' dispositions and their practices. An Educator Disposition Questionnaire was administered prior to training and at the end of the 20 days of training, in addition to several evaluation instruments for professional development activities and individual interview sessions.

A Buddy System Observational Tool was created as an adaptation of the Japanese lesson plan study approach, to assist the teachers and principals as they observe each other's classrooms and build a consensus for developing the environment for the Bright IDEA classroom. This tool helps to demonstrate how a Bright IDEA classroom deviates from a typical classroom and promotes teachers' continual improvement of the learning environment as they become more adept at teaching their units and managing their classrooms.

The Bright IDEA design is unique as it focuses on how teacher learning and the application of new pedagogical knowledge affect the quality of students' metacognitive and cognitive skills. Intensive professional development during the first year and a follow-up, on-site training component begin the transformation of each teacher's disposition. The research group includes three cohorts of participants from 11 school districts with two or three schools in each district. The total participants who have completed training in the Bright IDEA research-based practices include 168 K–2 classroom teachers, 28 principals, 11 coordinators for gifted programs, and 30 instructional specialists and lead gifted teachers.

These classrooms are beginning to represent true communities of learning that encourage both students and teachers to be risk takers engaged in experimental, investigative, and open-ended learning processes. Children and teachers in these unique inquiry-based learning communities are using their existing knowledge while striving to create new knowledge. Students are accepting greater responsibility for developing and applying a deep understanding of significant concepts, generalizations, essential questions, and skills and procedures to problem finding and problem solving for which there are no predetermined limits. Students are beginning the journey of lifelong learners and thinkers, capable of independent reasoning, with the potential to be identified for gifted programs and to succeed in more challenging courses.

The Bright IDEA Transformation

The Bright IDEA transformational pilot and research models integrate the Habits of Mind and Mary Frasier's Ten Core Attributes of Giftedness through a thinking skills curriculum that builds upon and extends the North Carolina Standard Course of Study with children's multicultural literature to enrich learning and provide support for the diversity, second languages, and emotional needs of the students. Criteria for observing and nurturing students' potential have been developed from Habits of Mind with a major focus on Frasier's Ten Core Attributes of Giftedness that are seen across all cultural groups. These HOM or gifted intelligent behaviors as defined by Frasier help teachers to develop all students' abilities in the areas of communication, motivation, interest, memory, humor, problem solving, imagination, inquiry, insight, and reasoning. In collaboration with the design team, teachers developed two-dimensional rubrics for each intelligent behavior that define five possible developmental levels, thus allowing teachers and parents to identify potentially gifted behaviors. These intelligent behaviors were integrated within the teacher's daily instruction that provides students opportunities to increase their ability of working toward more thoughtful, intelligent action or Habits of Mind (Costa & Kallick, 2000).

Teachers prepare awareness sessions for parents on how to nurture children's Gifted Intelligent Behaviors (GIBs) at home. These sessions provide critical information to help parents understand the importance of practicing these behaviors for their children's success in school, work, and life.

The mission of Project Bright IDEA 1 and 2 was to increase the potential for the number of children from underrepresented populations to be placed into gifted and higher-level programs and to close the gap among all populations of students. All students showed significant gains on state assessments across all subgroups of the populations, indicating that the gap among subgroups was closed. North Carolina headcount data will continue to be evaluated to determine how many children are placed in higher-level or gifted programs over the next few years.

The preassessment and postassessment on the intelligent behaviors were based on a five scale rubric: (1) readiness; (2) emergent; (3) progressing; (4) early independent; and (5) independent.

Multicultural literature units were field tested during Project Bright IDEA 1 and were revised for Bright IDEA 2 participants to teach and collect data on the children's progress toward becoming independent learners on selected behaviors that are taught in each of the units. The preassessment and postassessment units are taught and children observed in each of the designated research classrooms.

What Was the Impact on Children?   In addition to integrating a thinking skills program into the North Carolina Standard Course of Study, we fostered students' abilities in developing five cognitive skills critical for success in achievement and testing: (1) describing; (2) finding similarities and differences; (3) sequencing; (4) classifying; and (5) forming analogies. This program has been excellent for helping students develop vocabulary. Outcomes for the children included: improved vocabulary development; clarified thinking processes integral to content learning; improved observation and description skills; improved interaction with peers; demonstrated growth on literacy, mathematics, and writing assessments; and improved conceptualization of mathematics, social studies, and science.

What Was the Impact on Teachers?   Outcomes for teachers included the following: integrated the HOM/GIBs throughout the North Carolina

Course of Study with concept-based instruction and a thinking skills program; incorporated Marzano's new taxonomy of educational objectives and the revised Bloom's taxonomy into the course of study; developed multicultural literature units that were concept-based with the integration of HOMs and GIBs; changed the classroom environment to include the teaching of thinking skills and providing for all learning styles; developed new rubrics and tools for observing gifted intelligent behaviors and talents; applied new mental models and strategies for children to connect knowledge; involved parents in understanding the model and how they could help their children at home; developed a deep understanding of how children learn; and designed and implemented concept-based curriculum to teach integrated knowledge.

Data Collection

If funded for the entire five years, student data will be collected on approximately 4,500 Bright IDEA kids and 4,500 standard program kids. Across the three cohorts, research-based staff development has been administered to 250 professionals in 11 school districts and data are still being collected on the effect of training on teachers' dispositions and their practices. Data are being collected on the changes in the educators' dispositions over time. A separate instrument on the attitudes of the participants toward the staff development and the transformational model will provide data on factors related to change and stress.

As a result of the training and their practice in the classroom, the project will produce approximately 135 concept-based integrated curriculum units, with rubrics for assessing the GIBs as integrated with HOM. These units will provide for rigor and differentiated instruction for the high population of diverse students.

Findings from Project Bright IDEA 1

The findings of Project Bright IDEA 1 demonstrate three key aspects of the success of the program: (1) the ongoing commitment from the state education agency, local school districts, and the American Association for Gifted Children to promote success in the academically and intellectually gifted (AIG) programs for underrepresented populations; (2) that teacher training in concept-based instruction can promote student achievement and teacher expectation; and (3) that in preliminary findings, Bright IDEA 2 is increasing the number of children identified for gifted programs and is changing the dispositions of teachers to have higher expectations for all of the children they teach.

The Future

Project Bright IDEA goes against the grain of some approaches that stress tight scripting of lessons, limited teacher flexibility, and an emphasis on memorization and test preparation. Bright IDEA works within normal classroom constraints and does not extend the school day or school year or include extra tutoring or other special services. The strategies are designed to work with all content areas in kindergarten through 2nd grade and to succeed with all children. This approach could possibly revolutionize the way gifted students are identified. If all teachers, especially K–2 teachers, are trained to recognize gifted intelligent behaviors and how to grow these behaviors, the research supports that gifted and advanced classes will reflect the diversity of student populations. A challenge for gifted education is to reexamine elementary identification programs to include a systemic way of identifying, nurturing, and monitoring the growth of gifted intelligent behaviors in all children beginning the first day in kindergarten and continuing through high school. The infrastructure created by Art Costa and Bena Kallick with the Habits of Mind has provided the "how" to create this component in gifted education programs.

One of our teachers told the story of an African child, adopted and brought to her kindergarten class as soon as she arrived in the United States. She had been raised in an orphanage and had never worn clothes, had no language or social skills, had not been held, and had never seen the outside world. By spring this child was speaking English and reading and writing stories that would certainly identify her as gifted. The teacher said that the child may have done well in any class, but she felt that the Bright IDEA class made the difference in her level of achievement and her ability to reach her early potential.

Ron Tzur, a mathematics university professor and evaluator of Bright IDEA 2, said, "The two core notions behind Bright IDEA are that every kid has talent and that intelligence can be nurtured and the teacher's role is to nurture it. Bright IDEA tailors gifted methodologies for regular classroom teachers to use with all children. This raises the performance of gifted and regular children and has led to the extraordinary results achieved by Bright IDEA. We look forward to continuing the controlled research methodology over the course of the grant to get a better understanding of these issues."

At Thomasville Primary School, the demonstration site for Project Bright IDEA 2, Phyllis Lupton, former principal and director of Project Bright Tomorrow, said, "Bright IDEA works with every child. It nurtures every child. It makes every child reach a higher level of expectation and achievement. In most cases, Bright IDEA students' test scores increased by 50 to 100 percent. But as good as the test data are, the important thing is that the students are becoming—and staying—excited about learning. They are becoming lifelong learners."

Mary Watson, director of Exceptional Children, North Carolina Department of Public Instruction, stated, "Bright IDEA shows a new, exciting, and highly productive path for education in this country. Education and political leaders may have to broaden their thinking and policies now that we have demonstrated a more natural and far more effective classroom approach than is the norm today."

Lessons Learned with Habits of Mind and Gifted Intelligent Behaviors

The heart and mind of both the pilot project, Bright IDEA 1, and the research project, Bright IDEA 2, is the instructional infusion of the Habits of Mind/Gifted Intelligent Behaviors in every aspect of teaching and learning. In both Bright IDEA programs, teachers consistently report amazing results of children's higher-level vocabulary and deeper understanding of concepts and applications of the intelligent behaviors with their real-world experiences. Children from very impoverished environments have been quick to use the vocabulary of GIB at the most unusual and unexpected moments in their classroom activities. Parents have even reported their children making connections within their family experiences and the intelligent behaviors. Sometimes children counsel their parents about their intelligent behaviors! As teachers witness the growth of their students' understanding of the intelligent behaviors, the teachers' own understanding deepens with the students' internalization. This deeper understanding is reflected with the consistent infusion of the intelligent behaviors in

Socratic questioning and discussions, performance-based tasks, and assessments designed by the teacher.

When everything has been taught and said in the education of students, what are children embracing that will empower them to be successful, productive reflective learners in the 21st century when exposed to a problem or issue whose answers are not immediately available? Do children have a toolbox of successful habits or intelligent behaviors in which to guide them in the decision-making or problem-solving process when presented with complex ambiguous content? Or do they have obsolete or isolated facts with little understanding?

Until the data have all been collected and a final report is written that outlines the measurable outcomes, we are truly amazed at the reception of Bright IDEA training and practices that we are hearing from teachers and principals. Their bottom line is what they have seen in the behaviors, attitudes, and achievement levels of their students. The component they love the most to teach and observe that the students love to use the most is the Gifted Intelligent Behaviors as integrated with HOM. The training by Art Costa and Bena Kallick on the Habits of Mind has been the highlight of the professional development component for all of the participants. Because of the success of the HOM Bright IDEA training, North Carolina has designed a Leadership Academy for Habits of Mind and has trained the first cohort of mentors selected from the participants in Bright IDEA 2 and will conduct a second group of mentors during the next year. The academy will have a group of 70 mentors who can provide the leadership and training for HOM in their districts and beyond.

In Summary

Project Bright IDEA has integrated several research-based practices and designed high-quality curriculum and an engaging environment to prepare students for 21st century skills and learning behaviors for a lifetime. The design was based on the assumption that learning and teaching need to be organic, integrated, and based on big ideas, concepts, intelligent behaviors, and real-world experiences. It is important that all students are taught a rigorous curriculum. It is difficult to assess which components of the program have the most impact on student achievement; it may take all of them to help students have what they need, not only to be successful in work and life, but to be able to take a test successfully. The North Carolina story is still being written.

References

Alexander, I. (1990). *Personology, method and content in personality assessment and psychobiography*. Durham, NC: Duke University Press.

Anderson, L., & Krathwohl, D. (2001). *A taxonomy for learning, teaching and assessing: A revision of Bloom's taxonomy of educational objectives*. New York: Longman.

Costa, A. (Ed.). (2001). *Developing minds. A resource book for teaching thinking*, (3rd ed.). Alexandria, VA: ASCD.

Costa, A., & Kallick, B. (Eds.). (2000a). *Activating and engaging habits of mind*. Alexandria, VA: ASCD.

Costa, A., & Kallick, B. (Eds.). (2000b). *Assessing and reporting habits of mind*. Alexandria, VA: ASCD.

Costa, A., & Kallick, B. (Eds.). (2000c). *Discovering and exploring habits of mind*. Alexandria, VA: ASCD.

Costa, A., & Kallick, B. (Eds.). (2000d). *Integrating and sustaining habits of mind*. Alexandria, VA: ASCD.

Darity, W., Jr., Tyson, K., & Castellino, D. (2001, May). *Increasing opportunity to learn via access to rigorous courses and programs: One strategy for closing the achievement gap for at-risk and ethnic minority students*. Report prepared for the North Carolina Department of Public Instruction.

Dunn, R. S., Dunn, K. J., & Treffinger, D. (1992). *Bringing out the giftedness in your child: Nurturing every child's unique strengths, talents, and potential*. New York: Wiley.

Gardner, H. (1993). *Multiple intelligences: The theory in practice*. New York: Basic Books.

Marzano, R. J. (2001). *Designing a new taxonomy of educational objectives*. Thousand Oaks, CA: Corwin.

Marzano, R. J. (2004). *Building background knowledge for academic achievement*. Alexandria, VA: ASCD.

Marzano, R. J., & Kendall, J. S. (2007). *The new taxonomy of educational objectives* (2nd ed.) Thousand Oaks, CA: Corwin.

McTighe, J., & Wiggins, G. (2004). *Understanding by design professional development workbook*. Alexandria, VA: ASCD.

Parks, S., & Black, H. (2004). *Building thinking skills program, K–1 and 2–3*. Ventures Thinking.

Sheffield, L. J. (2003). *Extending the challenge in mathematics*. Thousand Oaks, CA: Corwin.

Silver, H. F., Strong, R. W., & Perini, M. J. (2000). *So each may learn: Integrating learning styles and multiple intelligences*. Alexandria, VA: ASCD.

Smutny, J. F., & von Fremd, S. E. (2004). *Differentiating for the young child*. Thousand Oaks, CA: Corwin.

19

Bringing a Vision to Life

Curtis Schnorr and Thommie DePinto Piercy

Several years ago, Friendship Valley Elementary School in Westminster, Maryland, was just a partially completed shell. The new building obviously lacked a physical core at that point, but the school lacked a spiritual core, too. The building had been assigned a principal but no staff members or students. As construction crews shaped the outward appearance of Friendship Valley, the principal, and eventually the staff, needed to create a vision for why Friendship Valley had been built and what the school would achieve once students walked through its doors.

Senge (1990) says that in its simplest form, a vision answers the question "What do we want to create?" (p. 206). He believes a vision generates a sense of commonality that permeates the organization. Wheatley (1992) describes a vision as organizational clarity about purpose and direction. Where would Friendship Valley finds its clarity, purpose, and direction?

The search ended soon after a presentation by Arthur Costa on "Creating Schools as Homes for the Mind." Staff members read *The School as a Home for the Mind* (Costa, 2007) several times, and they identified key features of a home for the mind. As construction crews finished building the physical shell of Friendship Valley, staff members enthusiastically took up the work of constructing a home for the mind inside the new school's classrooms, offices, and halls.

Refining the Vision

The precepts of a home for the mind are simply stated, but they hold a powerful message. Many of Friendship Valley's new staff members found they shared these beliefs. These professionals had reached a crossroads in their careers, and they wanted a new direction for their work. The vision of a home for the mind sparked a deep sense of purposefulness for them, and they drew tremendous energy from that vision.

Staff members were encouraged to examine what they had done in their professional lives to this point and how they might do their work differently. All teachers received copies of *The School as a Home for the Mind*, which includes a chapter titled "The Search for Intelligent Life" (Costa, 2007, pp. 19–31). Costa's work provided a framework for inquiry and dialogue as staff members considered two important questions: (1) What do you really want Friendship Valley to be? and (2) What will students and staff look like in this school?

As staff members answered these questions, their focus kept returning to the Habits of Mind (which are described as "intelligent behaviors" in *The School as a Home for the Mind*). The habits supported all that these professionals believed in, and they saw that the habits clearly would benefit staff members *and* students. Thus, the Habits of Mind became a vital building block in Friendship Valley's home for the mind. The Habits of Mind created a common language of enthusiasm, hope, and commitment. Staff members soon believed the habits were a wonderful vehicle for taking the school's vision off the wall and into the classrooms and community of Friendship Valley.

Transforming the Vision into Culture and Practice

From the beginning of their work, Friendship Valley's administrators promoted a culture that fostered trust and intellectual curiosity, embraced conflict and diversity, encouraged collaboration and cooperation, and reveled in caring and celebrating. This culture could not have been developed without the Habits of Mind. The habits were institutionalized into the school's culture and practice through four avenues: distributed leadership, open and honest dialogue, cognitive coaching, and staff development.

Distributed Leadership

Creating a safe learning environment and helping others succeed are key elements of a leader's role. Administrators established several important norms that encouraged faculty members to take increased responsibility for decision making. Each norm reinforced one or more of the Habits of Mind. As a result of following the norms, committees and teams became more dynamic and successful, and staff members took the initiative for problem solving. Here are the norms:

• Membership on the School Improvement Team (SIT), which is the central nervous system of the school, was open to all staff members. Because everyone had the opportunity to be included in policy-level decision making, all staff members felt empowered. This norm encouraged the habits of thinking flexibly; listening with understanding and empathy; and creating, imagining, innovating.

• Grade-level, team facilitator positions were open to all faculty members. This decision called upon the habits of thinking flexibly, taking responsible risks, and thinking interdependently.

• Schedules and schoolwide policies were open to suggestions for change. Administrators drew on the habits of applying past knowledge to new situations and questioning and posing problems.

• Teachers created the school handbook, and staff members—not administrators—drafted school policies. Carrying out this norm required the habits of listening with understanding and empathy, questioning and posing problems, remaining open to continuous learning, and taking responsible risks.

Open and Honest Dialogue

"Roundtable dialogues" furthered the development of trust among staff members. These voluntary roundtables focused on relevant topics and provided a context for lively discussion. The roundtables also supported staff development and offered an opportunity to practice open, honest dialogue. Professional use of several Habits of Mind evolved through these roundtables: persisting, questioning and posing problems, listening with understanding and empathy, and managing impulsivity.

The roundtables began when a faculty member suggested that staff members discuss a relevant topic and a related article, such as Costa and Garmston's (1998) "Maturing Outcomes." The article was distributed for staff members to read before the roundtable. As they prepared for the meeting, participants privately chose one Habit of Mind to focus on during the discussion.

To start a roundtable meeting, the facilitator posed an open-ended question to spark the group's discussion. Staff members were encouraged to openly and honestly share insights, humor, support, or reservations about the topic at hand. Teachers often remained in the media center after the roundtable to continue their dialogue with colleagues rather than linger in the parking lot. Participants left the roundtables with much more than knowledge about a topic. They gained trust in their colleagues, and they fostered collegiality with other staff members.

Cognitive Coaching

To teach students the Habits of Mind, teachers themselves must practice in an intellectually stimulating environment. Cognitive coaching fostered this kind of environment, and this approach became a cornerstone for enhancing teachers' intellectual capacities.

As part of the coaching process, each teacher scheduled a planning conference with an administrator. Then the teacher completed a planning conference sheet that included provocative questions to spark ideas. The planning conference was held before a classroom observation. Classroom observation provided the opportunity for collecting data about the teaching behaviors and the student learning discussed in the planning conference. A reflecting conference was held after the observation to allow teachers the opportunity to share impressions of the lesson, data, and future planning.

Teachers monitored their own behaviors and progress toward their goals. As they proceeded from the planning stage to implementing their lessons to reflecting on their learning, they found that the processes of cognitive coaching reinforced the Habits of Mind. For example, as one teacher coached another, the teacher might focus on listening with understanding and empathy. Or, the teacher might guide the person being coached to think flexibly about the lesson being planned. When another coach shared data, that person might use the habit of thinking and communicating with clarity and precision. Finally, the entire coaching conference could be a model for practicing the habit of remaining open to continuous learning.

Staff Development

At Friendship Valley, teachers are viewed as leaders committed to achieving the school's vision inside their classrooms. Teachers were encouraged to accept greater responsibility for student achievement. They truly were invested in this effort because they helped determine school improvement outcomes, identified strategies to drive the outcomes, exercised professional judgment about curriculum content, and were responsible for instructional decisions. Administrators furthered this atmosphere in five specific ways. They

- Encouraged collaboration among grade levels by establishing common staff development strategies and resources.
- Supported teacher experimentation and autonomy; they defined "failures" as opportunities to learn.
- Modeled and supported professional behaviors related to caring, optimism, humor, and friendliness.
- Minimized the threat of risk taking.
- Encouraged solving school problems through effective communication and group decision making.

Eventually, all staff development initiatives were selected with an eye toward how they could further the school's work with the Habits of Mind. This staff development occurred in stages. For example, administrators first provided staff members with a foundation in the Habits of Mind through articles, texts, and videos. The habits were reinforced with large wall charts, small desktop models, and samples of instruction that integrated the Habits of Mind.

Risk taking was supported with the help of Toni Worsham, director of the Maryland Center for Thinking Studies at Coppin State College in Baltimore, Maryland. Her site visits were followed with informal, after-school sessions where she and faculty members discussed techniques for instructional decision making and delivery. Having a professional consultant support the vision through workshops, classroom visits, and a graduate course provided the momentum to continue risk taking.

The next stage of staff development provided direction in using visual tools for thinking. Staff members initially used Frank Lyman's question/response cueing strategy (McTighe & Lyman, 1991). Lyman's question/response cues are graphic representations of seven different types of thought. These cues enable teachers to provide instruction on different types of thought, and the cues offer students a vehicle to comprehend texts at higher levels of thinking. Lyman's classroom visits supported teachers in their instructional decisions. After-school sessions allowed time to question and ponder future instructional directions.

David Hyerle introduced the staff to Thinking Maps®, visual tools that collect and organize thought into visual patterns (Hyerle, 1995). Students used the maps to construct, discuss, and assess their thinking. Such work created a subtle shift in communication, which could be seen everywhere: in students' thinking displayed in the hallways, during small-group literature discussions, and during the faculty's school improvement meetings. (See also Chapter 9.)

Professional development included numerous full-day visits by a variety of presenters who stayed for after-school faculty gatherings to explore topics in depth. This on-site professional development proved so successful that it evolved into a staff development norm for the school.

Each type of staff development contributed to specific learnings by the faculty. The combined staff development deepened understanding of the Habits of Mind. Ultimately, developing professional capacities with the Habits of Mind resulted in students using the habits. Student use in turn resulted in improved student achievement and community involvement.

Influencing Students and Community

Schools need community support. From the moment Friendship Valley opened, staff members worked to share their energy and excitement about the new school and its unique approach. Even before the building opened, a teacher created a videotape depicting the distinctive elements of Friendship Valley and showing how the school would serve students and the community. This video was shown to students and community groups months before the school opened. In most cases the presentation was the viewers' first encounter with the precepts of a home for the mind and the Habits of Mind.

Staff members believed everyone in the school community had to understand these precepts. Teachers and administrators used newsletters, parent information nights, and student displays to further their message about the Habits of Mind. In time, students became the most powerful messengers about the habits. Parents saw that their children were excited about learning. From the first day, staff members at Friendship Valley worked to create what Perkins (1992) calls "a climate that fosters an energetic culture of thoughtful teaching and learning" (p. 112). This climate sparked students' enthusiasm about the power of thinking and learning.

Staff members used every opportunity to emphasize their commitment to the Habits of Mind. Before the first open house, they hung posters about the Habits of Mind throughout the hallways. On the first day of school, students took home messages about the Habits of Mind. Staff members wrote newspaper articles about the habits. Office referrals underscored the Habits of Mind. Students weren't simply disciplined; they were asked to problem solve using Habits of Mind that would serve them better if a similar situation arose again. The school's message was clear, consistent, and simple: The Habits of Mind can be used in every facet of staff members' and students' daily lives, both in and out of school.

Looking for Results

Although the staff and administration were determined to stay the course with the Habits of Mind, they understood that they had to show results, too. At first, results were seen in ways that couldn't be quantified. Students began to question more intelligently through using precise language. They treated others with empathy and respect, as evidenced by their decreased impulsivity and how they truly listened to what others had to say. Students began to enjoy problem solving, and they spent more time seeking solutions when an answer was not readily apparent. Creativity was on display throughout the classrooms and hallways in art projects, extended learning projects, physical activity, and music. Students talked about how they used the Habits of Mind at home, and they even described how their parents sometimes failed to use the habits!

Although these results were satisfying and important, staff members understood that the true judgment would come from the school's results on state-mandated tests. Results from the first year yielded scores that were above state and county averages in all areas. Performance on these tests improved yearly. Ultimate recognition came from the state of Maryland in the form of a performance award for significant academic progress.

Friendship Valley Elementary School has come a long way since those first days when it was nothing more than a physical shell. Tour the building now and you'll see a vibrant home for the mind supported by the Habits of Mind. In kindergarten, students manage their impulsivity and use clear and precise language as they describe the flight of butterflies. In 1st grade, students enjoy problem solving as they graph the letters of their name. A 2nd grade math lesson begins with the teacher referring students to the directions on the board; he also reminds the children to turn on their Habits of Mind related to listening.

Third graders use all their senses as they watch their egg-crate parachutes float from the roof of the building. Fourth graders use creativity and prior knowledge in the wax museum they've created. Fifth graders use persistence and flexibility in their thinking during a unit on the Negro Baseball League. No classroom or office is untouched by the Habits of Mind: art, music, gym, media center, reading, speech and language, special education, and guidance counselor.

In the late spring of each year, teachers and other staff members gather to reflect on the current school year and plan for the next year. They always ask themselves several key questions: What impact have we made on student instruction and the development of a thinking school? What will we continue to value and respect as educators and a school? What has worked and allowed our school to be successful? In the years since Friendship Valley initially embraced the Habits of Mind, staff members have continued to remodel and recharge their home for the mind in various ways under new leadership.

References

Costa, A. (2007). *The school as a home for the mind*. Thousand Oaks, CA: Corwin.

Costa, A., & Garmston, R. (1998). "Maturing outcomes." Unpublished manuscript.

Hyerle, D. (1995). *Thinking Maps® tools for learning*. Cary, NC: Innovative Sciences.

McTighe, J., & Lyman, F., Jr. (1991). Cueing thinking in the classroom: The promise of theory-embedded tools. In A. Costa (Ed.), *Developing minds: A resource book for teaching thinking* (Rev. ed., Vol. 1, pp. 243–250). Alexandria, VA: ASCD.

Perkins, D. (1992). *Smart schools*. New York: Free Press.

Senge, P. (1990). *The fifth discipline*. New York: Doubleday.

Wheatley, M. (1992). *Leadership and the new science: Learning about organizations from an orderly universe*. San Francisco: Berrett-Koehler.

20

A "Throwaway" School No More

Bertie Simmons

I should have known what to expect when I was asked to come out of retirement to become the principal of a troubled high school in Houston, Texas. After all, I served as district superintendent from 1969 to 1982, and E. L. Furr High School had been one of my schools. Still, I had been retired five years, and although it is common knowledge that the cogs of change move slowly in education, in some respects, things can change at breakneck speed. Such had been the case at Furr High School.

I awoke feeling exhilarated the first day I was to report to Furr, only to be faced with a fierce thunderstorm as I made my way to the school. Sharp daggers of lightning crackled across the sky like huge buzz saws out of control. Each light show was followed by an eardrum-shattering boom of thunder that then rumbled off into the distance, leaving me terrified. I slowed to a pace that angered other drivers on the ship channel bridge, and they honked loudly at me as they slap-washed my car with grimy water. This trip was a foretaste of what I was to experience at Furr High School.

The Furr that I encountered this time had little resemblance to the school I had known five years earlier. Minorities had moved into the areas feeding the school, and whites had mostly scampered to the suburbs, taking with them their fancy hairdos. Nineteen buses transported the students from 11 competing neighborhoods, and gang fights were an accepted phenomenon as the 11 identified gangs battled for respect. Academic achievement was pushed to the rear as administrators struggled to control student behavior. Accepted classroom etiquette included students sitting on top of the desks and tables while eating, drinking soft drinks, and laughing loudly as acoustic and electric signals emanated from a multitude of boom-boxes and bounced off vibrating walls.

Student attendance was the lowest in the district, and standardized test scores were among the lowest. Teacher apathy was at an all-time high. The school, located on the far eastern boundary of the school district, was identified by the students as a "throwaway" school; school personnel yelled and cursed each other and the students. There was little evidence of teaching and learning except in the magnet hall, where students were actively engaged in meaningful high-level instruction. The regular school with its low expectations and the well ordered magnet school screamed of the haves and the have-nots located on the same campus of E. L. Furr High School.

Concerned parents were demanding a change and were more than willing to assist in any way possible. They requested teachers who believed in the students and who cared about the students' futures. They wanted their students to be required to behave in an appropriate manner and to be instructed in a way that would ensure they were college-ready. They wanted the school personnel to behave as professionals and to set an example for the students. "We are looking for a miracle worker. We are looking for someone who cares about our kids and who can either change the folks who are presently here or hire all new people who can get the job done. This kind of school would not be tolerated on the other side of town. We hope you are that miracle worker," they articulated, with hope in their eyes and voices.

I had intended to remain at Furr for only three months, until a new principal could be identified to replace the one who had recently retired. Near the end of my three-month tenure, the superintendent requested that I continue as principal through the following school year. Although I had deep concerns about taking on that responsibility at the age of 66,

I finally agreed to assume the role in the hopes of making a difference in the lives of the students and a few teachers who were struggling to provide a quality education for them.

I knew the first thing we had to change was the culture of the school. This meant changing the behavior not only of the students but also of teachers who were floundering hopelessly in a bottomless pit of apathy. I was well aware of the enormousness of the task and that I would need all the help I could muster. It was then that the superintendent requested that I attend a conference in Park City, Utah, where Heidi Hayes Jacobs was presenting her work on curriculum mapping.

I was reluctant to agree to attend the conference because I was aware that Park City was known primarily as a site of the Winter Olympics and as a ski area. I had recently lost a 16-year-old granddaughter in a snow skiing accident, and she had, in fact, been my motivation for accepting the principal position at Furr. Her expressed desire had been to make the world a better place for all people, and I thought by going to Furr, I might be able to do that in her stead. I was not sure I was emotionally ready for a ski area.

I agreed to attend the conference but found it difficult to concentrate on the sessions I attended, and I decided to leave early and return to Houston. I would attend one more session and then depart. It so happened that session was being conducted by Bena Kallick. When she mentioned cognitive coaching and Art Costa, my interest was sparked and I listened intently because I had used Costa's work as a superintendent five years earlier. Then she discussed the work the two of them were doing with the Habits of Mind, and I was completely enthralled. I knew I had found the help I needed to change the culture at E. L. Furr High School.

Bena agreed to come to Houston to assist me, and we began a long and enduring relationship as we worked to transform the school into a professional learning community. Staff and students worked on the Habits of Mind to become better, more productive human beings. The entire school environment was saturated with the habits. They became an integral part of the curriculum; they were painted in bold, colorful letters on the walls of the school; books on the habits were purchased, and staff participated in book studies; Bena and Art and Marian Leibowitz conducted workshops; teachers began to discuss the habits with the students during advocacy period, and building administrators conducted workshops. Slowly, the culture began to change. Teachers became more civil to each other and to the students. In 2002 after one huge gang fight, instead of sending 42 gang members to an alternative school, I called them together and discussed their behavior and how they might use the habits to stop the violence and bring peace to the campus and to their daily lives. I promised a trip to New York City to see Ground Zero if we had no more gang fights for an entire year. The gang members kept their promise, and I kept mine.

I should not have been surprised by the reaction when I sought assistance from the district to fund a trip to New York City for a group of gang members. "I would keep this very quiet," I was told by individuals within the school district. "People are going to think you are crazy for making such a request." I began to hear rumblings from the teachers that I was rewarding bad behavior and that it was clear that I was a student advocate, not a teacher advocate. This was the first time that it had occurred to me that someone would think that those two positions were mutually exclusive. Still, I practiced the Habits of Mind and persevered. As the end of the year and the time for the field trip approached, the students had kept their word and we had had no gang fights. I had not been able to raise funds to cover the expenses for the trip. I was about to decide that I should encourage the students to have a "baby" gang fight so I could save face. Suddenly, I began to receive checks from all over the country, congratulating me for my efforts and wishing to contribute. Art Costa, Bena Kallick, and Marian Leibowitz had spread the word, and before I knew it, I had received sufficient funding for 32 gang members to take the trip to New York City.

One of the highlights of the trip occurred when a street gang, obviously identifying us as "gangstas," attempted to pick a fight with the Furr students. Alfredo, a burly gang leader with a long, curly ponytail, approached me and whispered, "Miss, get us out of here before we get into a gang fight right in the middle of New York City! We are trying to practice managing impulsivity, but this is a new skill for us and I don't know how long we can hold out." We got out of there fast and enjoyed the remainder of the trip, including visits to the United Nations building, a Broadway play, Ground Zero, and other tourist sites, without incident. The trip was highly successful and changed the lives of those gang members who participated. Three years later, we had not had a gang fight on campus.

Changing adult behavior was significantly more difficult for me than changing student behavior. The district professional development department had received funds from Texaco/Chevron for innovative leadership development experiences for teachers and administrators. We were fortunate to be selected to participate in this program. We took 25 Furr teachers to Estes Park, Colorado, for a seven-day "Thinking Expedition" led by Rolf Smith of Strategic Innovation. During those seven days, we identified the "summit" of our Furr "mountain," and we spent long hours developing plans for reaching the peak. We formed teams based on our strengths and personality types and climbed Old Man Mountain, celebrating our accomplishment before descending in the dark. Rock climbing provided an opportunity to build trust and was symbolic of the challenges we faced as we worked to establish community on our way to the Furr summit.

While in Colorado, we visited the Eagle Rock School—a school for students who did not fit into the mainstream. One of their practices that we brought back to Furr was a weekly "gathering" at which students and teachers voluntarily meet to share ideas and talents. Even today, students and teachers continue to gather each Friday morning to celebrate accomplishments and to exchange ideas and talents.

After returning to Furr from Colorado, a selected group of teachers met to develop a statement of philosophy and core values of the school. Later we shared it with the Furr school community and signed a covenant to follow the document as we went about our daily duties. I was surprised at the outcome of their work and how enthusiastically parents, students, and school staff signed the covenant. Apparently our hours spent on the Habits of Mind had taken root. It had happened so gradually and naturally that no one had noticed. Building a culture to support this set of beliefs had become a way of life at the school and in the community; it continues today.

Teachers are using the Habits of Mind as an integral part of their instruction as they work to polish and sharpen their own use of the habits. Students are becoming more aware of the importance of the habits, and it is not unusual to hear them making such remarks as "Remember, we must persevere." Many students keep notebooks in which they reflect on and make notes about experiences in which they have been required to use the Habits of Mind to solve problems or accomplish tasks. These notebooks are full of examples demonstrating how the habits have been internalized and practiced on a daily basis at school, on the job, and at home. This profound awareness will serve the students well as they continue their journey through the world.

I believe it is important that school principals be a part of any learning activity they require of teachers. The habit I chose to continuously seek to improve was managing impulsivity. It is becoming increasingly more difficult, given the many unreasonable demands on the schools from outside the school community, where compliance overshadows competence and caring. Still, my awareness of the habits serves as a guide and enables me to find humor in absurd situations and to persevere.

Study and practice of the Habits of Mind have developed a high level of self-awareness, skills, and attitudes within the school community, leading to a deep and abiding capacity for trust and better understanding among the community members. Furr is a "throwaway" school no more! E. L. Furr High School is a school of compassionate, creative, productive, and responsible individuals who work together in a joyful, collaborative environment to provide the best education possible for all students. It is truly a professional learning community in the highest sense and a vibrant place of teaching and learning. Hector, a student, said it best when he remarked, "Miss, Furr feels like a real school." We are all committed to keeping it "real."

21

The Mindful Culture of Waikiki Elementary School

Bonnie Tabor, Sandra Brace, Matt Lawrence, and Arnold Latti

We introduce this chapter with a teacher's comments:

> Waikiki School confused me at first. I showed up expecting an average public elementary school, but this is not what I found. Before even entering the school office I noticed signs and slogans everywhere about thinking, about intelligence, and about joy. The office had "Mindfulness" displayed everywhere. The staff was smiling, laughing, helpful, and relaxed even though there was a lot going on. There was a sense of community, of excitement but order; and as the day progressed I saw this in the classroom, the teachers room, and even on the playground. The school had a great "feeling" about it—a feeling that I learned later has been created by a commitment to *thinking*.
>
> As a reading teacher, later as the music and dance teacher, and finally full-time in the special education department, I have worked with every student in the school, have been in every classroom, and have seen the benefits of the "mindful" focus across the board. I was amazed by the students' abilities to take risks and their ability to decrease their impulsivity even during

high-energy activities. They had a little slogan to "STAR" their behavior that they knew meant Stop, Think, Apply mindfulness, and then Respond. But it was their sheer enjoyment of what they were doing that delighted me most and best demonstrates the benefit of the mindful school. Happy kids learn more, retain more, and are more willing to share knowledge. Overall the students did an outstanding job learning the music and dance material, remembering concepts, and demonstrating improvement in skills as measured by their performances, which were excellent. All performance standards were met, and exceeded, with exuberance. The primary benefit for the students, in the end, was their success.

A good example of the benefits of the mindful school for students and teachers happened while I was assisting the 6th grade teacher during a language arts lesson. I walked in to find the class and teacher in mid-discussion on the floor, in a circle. Something very serious had happened—someone had been shoved pretty hard. The teacher guided the students in sharing one by one how the incident made them feel, steering them away from names and specifics. They passed a plush Scooby-Doo [stuffed animal] and waited quietly while everyone shared; some students spoke at length, some just a sentence, but all were heard. The teacher then drew their attention to the mindful behaviors that applied to the incident and asked the students to select one and explain how they would have applied this behavior to the situation. The students then shared their ideas. As it turned out, the consequences for the participants in the situation were grave, but the focus was on the collective construction of alternative behaviors for similar situations in the future. Blame was diffused, and understanding provided learning for all. I was amazed by this process, and especially that 6th graders were capable of it. I learned that the students practiced this circle thinking tool regularly, and had since the 1st grade.

Demographics

Waikiki School serves 391 students from kindergarten through grade 6. More than 50 percent of the students live outside the school's boundaries and attend by choice. Its draw may be its unique curriculum, which couples instruction in the Hawaii State Content Standards with instruction in the Habits of Mind. Using research to identify behaviors associated with effective adults, we emphasize the explicit teaching of these behaviors to all students in the school. The infusion of this model within standards-based instruction defines the strength of Waikiki School.

In 2007–08, 40 percent of the students qualified for the free/reduced lunch program, 38 percent for English Language Learner (ELL) assistance, and 10 percent for special education services; and 40 percent lived in single-parent homes. Despite the intensity of student needs, our school continues to exceed all national and state standards, making consistent yearly gains. Waikiki has been recognized as a Hawaii Distinguished School, attaining adequate yearly progress (AYP) each year since the inception of this award. We have consistently been rated in "Good Standing—Unconditional" under the No Child Left Behind Act and have consistently made the state's Stanford Achievement Test Honor Roll. Waikiki advanced to become a Blue Ribbon School by 1995 and a National Blue Ribbon recipient in 2007. In a survey of Hawaii's best schools in *Honolulu Magazine*'s May 2008 issue, Waikiki School was given an A+ based on test scores and desirability, and was ranked fifth of 258 schools.

In the Beginning

Mindfulness was not adopted at the Waikiki School to promote a good feeling. On the contrary, it was brought in to help students with their thinking skills in order to raise scores on statewide testing and to improve academics schoolwide. The school believed that the best way to develop students' thinking skills was to have students use those skills every day and to think about thinking every day.

Waikiki School's evolution to being a mindful school began in 1991 with the adoption of the school's vision, mission, and belief statements.

Vision:

Waikiki School is a safe, vibrant, nurturing environment that encourages lifelong learning. We believe that lifelong learning is a desire for continuous growth which results in responsible, competent, and confident individuals. Implicit in this vision is nurturing learning of the heart and mind through collaboration, thoughtfulness, and direct instruction in thinking.

Mission Statements:
- We encourage our school and community to work together.
- We provide a strong foundation that respects the contributions and uniqueness of each individual.
- We work together to develop positive self-esteem, well-being, and desire for active lifelong learning.

Belief Statements: To be an environment where . . .
- Instead of seeking power we seek to empower others.
- Instead of controlling people we seek to enhance creativity and free the intellect.
- Instead of uniformity of practice we seek to evolve a collective vision of excellence.

When the school began to implement mindful school practices, it was driven by this ambitious goal: To develop, implement, and reflect upon strategies to assess impact of the use of the Habits of Mind on . . .

- Student achievement.
- Teachers' professional growth.
- Staff collaboration.
- The school as a learning organization.

The school conducted a series of workshops for staff and parents beginning in 1991. As a result of these inservice sessions, the staff adopted the Habits of Mind, which have been integrated into the curriculum in the years since and have become the expected norm throughout the school, permeating the Waikiki School culture. Over the years, other staff development experiences have extended and enriched the staff's understanding of curriculum integration, authentic assessment, direct teaching of thinking skills, concept development, cognitive coaching, the Philosophy for Children program, collaborative learning, and thematic unit planning. The skills learned in these workshops continue to be used in the classrooms, at staff meetings, and at parent workshops. Other activities that supported Waikiki School's focus included visits to "mindful schools" on the U.S. mainland, a parent–child interaction workshop to inform parents of thinking and problem-solving processes, and a slide show presentation that communicated the vision, goals, and programs of the school.

School T-shirts, note pads, and stationery with the mindful school logo helped to spread the school's philosophy. The PTA initiated an annual Mindful School T-shirt Contest, inviting students in kindergarten through 6th grade to enter their unique designs depicting "mindfulness and thoughtfulness." Classes voted on which design should be adopted for that year.

Although the Habits of Mind are emphasized every year, the staff focuses also on the development and implementation of "cooperation and caring for others." In addition to classroom and whole-school activities, all classes formed inter-grade level "cooperation and caring" classroom teams that planned and participated in a variety of learning activities. At the same time, the faculty was developing a "cooperation and caring" assessment tool, which would later be finalized by the student council and used by the student body to self-assess their own growth with this Habit of Mind. This became an ongoing emphasis and has become an integral component of our mindful initiatives.

The Mindful School Culture

Staff members of the Waikiki School assert that they have created more than a friendly school climate. Rather, they view themselves as participants in a distinct and definable school culture. *Culture* can be defined as the attitudes, beliefs, values, language, traditions, customs, and social norms of a group of people that are reproducible for new members (Waxman, Tharp, & Hilberg, 2004). A *school culture* is the historically transmitted patterns of meaning that include the norms, values, beliefs, ceremonies, rituals, traditions, and myths understood, perhaps in varying degrees, by members of the school community (Stolp, 1994). The following sections describe how these values are exhibited and sustained at Waikiki School.

A Common Language

At Waikiki School, the Habits of Mind are prominently displayed in the office, on bulletin boards, in the cafeteria, on the ceiling of the main walkway, and in every classroom. Children learn age-appropriate definitions and applications for these behaviors beginning in kindergarten. On the playground the habits are used as a reference for analyzing choices, especially in situations requiring discipline. Habits of Mind are also integrated into daily classroom assignments and discussions; they are part of the active vocabulary of the mindful school culture.

Values and Beliefs

Along with their common language of "intelligent behavior," the values and beliefs of the Waikiki School community embody the characteristics of the mindful school culture. The most significant value of our school culture is that of becoming and nurturing a "community of thinkers." This community highly values and uses practices inherent in collaboration, involvement, and learning within a cooperative environment.

Focus on the Whole Child

Enrichment classes in physical education, Japanese language, Hawaiian language and culture, and technology are provided weekly to all students. Grants provide residencies for artists who work with students. Partnerships with the University of Hawaii provide weekly philosophy lessons and the assistance of student teachers. Enrichment academies provide extended-day opportunities in gymnastics, robotics, rocketry, French, and more. Extended-day tutoring and homework assistance provide help for Title I recipients, limited English speakers, and others. An after-school program provides childcare for working parents. Adult education partnerships provide classes in English instruction for ELL parents. During lunch recess, student clubs in photography, drama, and watercolor painting are available. Community volunteers provide extra love and support as "lunch pals." Student council, peer mediation, and gradewide and schoolwide community service projects extend learning beyond classroom walls. A Comprehensive Student Support System provides an additional array of services. A Primary School Adjustment Project with a contracted psychiatrist, a school-based behavioral health specialist, a school counselor, and counseling interns provide individualized intervention services as needs arise.

Orientation and Professional Development

When new teachers join the school, senior members of the faculty introduce them to the language, values, and beliefs of the school culture in whole- and small-group discussions, with staff members collaboratively assigned to convey the language of intelligent behavior. To provide context for the instruction, staff members draw upon their own experiences that relate to the concepts inherent in "mindful behavior." Furthermore, the staff leaders give assistance where needed, helping new teachers assimilate into the Waikiki School culture each semester through additional staff development experiences.

Staff Meetings

The school's cultural value of collaboration is transmitted and practiced through staff meetings. All major school decisions are brought before the school's faculty for input and approval. During the decision-making process, the principal asks questions such as "Is there anyone who can't live with that?" If someone cannot, discussion continues or the matter is dropped altogether. One year the school was offered Title I status and money, both of which the principal admitted wanting. The staff gathered in a circle, and each member (about 30 teachers) shared thoughts and feelings. Many staff members were uncomfortable with the change, so the principal informed the district superintendent that the school was not interested in the offer. For one new teacher present at the meeting, the experience was a powerful example of how the Waikiki School staff members practice and live their values.

Concept Attainment

The main vehicle for conveying the language of a mindful school to students is "concept attainment." The purpose of the process is for students to make meaning out of a Habit of Mind, or intelligent behavior. The process begins with one intelligent behavior (for example, listening with understanding and empathy) written in a bubble. The teacher then asks students for examples of a child listening with understanding and empathy, and of a child not doing so. This request puts the instruction in context, as children's names or actual events are used in both the example and the counter-example. Students then are encouraged to come up with attributes of the intelligent behavior, testing each one against the examples. Students may say listening with understanding and empathy is "nice," "polite," "thoughtful," "respectful," "courteous," and so forth. The class then divides into small groups for a collaborative activity in which each group takes the class-generated information and comes up with one generalization or definition of the concept. The process concludes with a presentation of definitions and a vote for the one that will be displayed in the room. This process is taught to new teachers for the purpose of transmitting the school's language to all students year after year.

Philosophy for Children

The cultural value and focus of "creating a community of thinkers" is transmitted from teacher to student through a program called Philosophy for Children. Dr. Thomas Jackson, who heads the program in Hawaii, and his graduate students work closely with several schools to train teachers in the thinking tools offered in their program.

The program has a language of its own. For example, there are "magic words," which serve the purpose of class management. Any student can say "POPAAT" to remind everyone, "Please, one person at a time." "PSL" stands for "please speak louder," which students say when they can't hear their classmates. The magic words empower students to help keep the conversation on topic and within accepted boundaries. The program also includes a "tool kit" to help students with their thinking. It includes words such as *assume, inference, true, reason, example, counterexample*, and the question "What do you mean by that?"

Students sit in a circle with the teacher, pose a philosophical question, and attempt to make meaning out of it under structure provided by magic words and the tool kit. Students talk when they are passed a "talking stick" or a "community ball." Nearly all classrooms participate in some form of Philosophy for Children, making each classroom a community of thinkers.

Cooperation and Paired Classes

At Waikiki School every class is paired with another class at a different grade level. Twice per quarter, those classes get together to promote the cultural value of learning through cooperation. For example, last year a class of 3rd graders took their science and social studies reports to the kindergarten classroom, paired up with kindergarteners, and read their reports to them. The 3rd graders were encouraged to solicit questions and engage in further discussion about the topic after the reading was over. The pairing allows both grades to engage in language development as the older students assist the younger ones.

Student Council

The Waikiki School Student Council promotes the school's cultural value of involvement through schoolwide activities. The council designs two rubrics per year for self-assessment of intelligent behavior, and it organizes recycling and clean-up days grounded in the intelligent behavior of "cooperation and caring." Several teachers are actively involved in the student council meetings, posing questions to nurture dialogue that assists the executive board in making meaning out of their pursuits. The question "What does this have to do with mindfulness?" is often asked to refocus the students on the school's cultural values. Ultimately, though, it is the student council that decides upon and executes the mindful school activity.

Mindful Mediators

Every year a group of students is chosen to be trained as playground conflict mediators. A trained faculty member teaches those students how to use the Habits of Mind to help children in conflict talk out their problems. The mediators keep records of every conflict, which have reduced in number since the program's inception. The mindful school's common language empowers children to make meaning out of a problem and take action toward solving it.

Mindful Assemblies and Open Houses

One method for transmitting culture to parents and guardians is through quarterly "mindful assemblies." The focus of the assemblies is to give awards to those students exhibiting intelligent behavior. An older student sets up the awards and presents a context for the concepts for the parents by giving a definition and an example of what that Habit of Mind means.

A second opportunity to set a context for what it means to be a student or a parent in a mindful school happens yearly, at the fall quarter open house. It begins with the principal welcoming all parents, guardians, and community members and describing the school's culture to them. In recent years, a video about the mindful school has been shown as well. Parents then go to each of their children's classrooms, where they can see the Habits of Mind integrated into their child's reading, writing, social studies, science, and math work. Students are encouraged to explain their assignments to their parents.

Community Council

Administrators, teachers, parents, and community members are all represented at quarterly school Community Council meetings. The values of cooperation and collaboration are evident at these gatherings where people who were previously considered outsiders (including parents, neighboring businesses and business owners, extended family members, community organizations) are educated in the language, values, and beliefs of a mindful school and are now a voice in the decision-making processes related to the school. Information sharing takes place mostly through dialogue as the council attempts to make meaning out of complex problems. The process has enabled our school to maintain its vision, by integrating state and federal mandates into the Mindful School structure. Regardless of outside pressure, we remind ourselves in the Community Council that learning to use and continually improve our mindful behavior is our purpose of education.

What Are the Benefits?

Mindfulness provides the school culture with a unique kind of safety. A consistent ideology and framework is applied to every situation, issue, and problem. All decisions are based on good thinking and a shared understanding that mindfulness is the goal. Everybody's feelings are respected, and everyone participates in the process of education using mindfulness as a primary tool. This in turn produces consistent policies and consequences. The resulting security provides a concrete sense of safety—an essential component in the students' self-esteem and a contributor to their willingness to take risks as part of the learning process.

Mindfulness creates a spirit of equality that benefits the entire school culture as well. Students (as well as faculty, staff, and administrators) are clear about what is expected of them (mindfulness). They feel secure that they will always be listened to with empathy, and all attempts will be made to understand their perspective on an issue, even if they are in the wrong. In a sense, no one gets "everything they want" at the mindful school, but *everyone* gets *some* of what they want. Cooperative learning, peer mentoring, and peer mediation reinforce this daily at the Waikiki School.

Mindfulness also provides a learning environment in which students know that their diversity will be respected, acknowledged, and celebrated. This attitude benefits the students and their families by supporting self-esteem and cultural identity. The community benefits from diverse cultural exchange, and a sense of pride promotes community involvement and responsibility.

Mindfulness promotes good communication. Its very nature is diplomatic. Flexibility and a willingness to consider options open up many possibilities for interesting connections, alternative scheduling, and the necessary pruning to weed out practices that just aren't working within the school. The school benefits from a flowing process that is constantly self-assessing and striving to improve itself. If it needs to change, it can.

Everyone who encounters the mindful school is empowered by it, because mindfulness creates standards of behavior and expectations that nurture growth. At the Waikiki School, there is peace on the playground. Student work covers the colorful bulletin boards that line the halls. The campus is clean and attractive. And students and staff at Waikiki School experience a lot of joy in the education process. The award-winning cafe-teria provides wonderful lunches daily. Laughter rolls out of the teacher lunchroom. Community volunteers come regularly to work with the students. Faculty, staff, and administrators are willing to do whatever it takes as project deadlines approach or emergencies come up. Teachers participate in many social activities together, and the principal has something positive and empowering to say to the faculty at every meeting. The focus is mindfulness, and the result is a rich environment for learning and growth — for everyone.

A learning environment that fosters flexibility in thinking is of great benefit to special education students with learning disabilities, and it satisfies the social ideal of equal and appropriate education for all. Flexible thinking and caring, respect for diversity, and empathic listening benefit students with special needs by providing education that recognizes them, supports them, guides them to their strengths, celebrates their contributions to the school culture, and strengthens their self-esteem. An exemplary case involves a student who had been to five schools before she entered Waikiki School as a 3rd grader with a diagnosis of disruptive disorder and emotional disturbance. Instruction in the mindful behaviors, a language and clear reasons for appropriate behavior, and being heard with empathy and addressed as an individual in a climate of compassion have turned this student around. She has been able to learn, to complete all state testing, to meet standards, and to experience success in many areas of her education. Her need for one to one support was reduced by 40 percent in two years, and she is making consistent gains. Most important, she is a happier person. She wants to come to school. She does her homework immediately after school in the resource room. She is willing to work on her issues, and she is learning how to regulate her behavior through mindfulness.

One student who recently began middle school reported that she is at the top of her special education language arts class. "Even the 8th graders are lower," she confided happily, "and we're going to be reading *Esperanza!*" She was talking about a children's novel that was read and adapted into a play. She had played the part of Esperanza in the production. "I will be able to help everybody" she said proudly. "My writing will be the best."

Waikiki has created an engaging schoolwide curriculum that sparks an authentic interest in academics among all students—including special education students. These programs (which the special education department follows with modification and supplementation) encourage creativity, problem solving, learning that is relevant, and originality. The special education student has a place in the mindful school and feels included and celebrated. Special education students are willing to take risks despite their disabilities, knowing the outcome will be protected by mindfulness. In this environment, the special education students at Waikiki have created plays, films, and videos and presented them to the rest of the school. They have taken risks and have been the "stars" in front of their peers. And they know how to be mindful—a skill that will be invaluable as they navigate the complexities of their lives. In this way the school culture benefits from the unique gifts of the special education students and their unique contribution to the joyful expansion of consciousness that is the by-product and, perhaps, the greatest benefit of the mindful school.

In Summary

In addition to the tests they take at school, Waikiki School students are prepared to perform well on the tests of life. Teachers and staff don't simply teach values; rather, they seek to model the behaviors they want to see their students develop. Teachers are encouraged to be individuals in the classroom and to exercise their strengths and creativity. In a sense the whole school is on the same page, but every page is wonderfully different.

This school culture results in a dynamic learning community in which all participants are challenged to become ever more mindful, ever more thoughtful learners to support the collective efforts of the school. The synergy that results from this unification of purpose promotes an environment that both honors and challenges the intellect of all. By caring for and learning from one another, all members of the learning community (teachers, community members, parents, students, and staff) are encouraged to grow and to integrate their learnings into daily practice. The adventure implicit in lifelong learning becomes a reality.

Waikiki School is the most functional of educational environments. It is evident that the school is deeply committed to doing whatever it takes to become an ever more effective "mindful" learning community where compassion, competence, and harmony of the heart and mind are nurtured. We believe, and the data clearly show, our efforts are working. We intend to continue to provide the finest in cutting-edge education for our community, producing graduates well prepared to become productive, ethical participants in the world of tomorrow.

References

Stolp, S. (1994, June). Leadership for school culture. *ERIC Digest*, 91. (ED370198).

Waxman, H. C., Tharp, R. G., & Hilberg, R. S. (Eds.). (2004). *Observational research in U.S. classrooms: New approaches for understanding cultural and linguistic diversity*. Cambridge: Cambridge University Press.

22

Integrating the Habits of Mind: A District Perspective

Nancy Skerritt, Emilie Hard, and Kristin Edlund

When you start on your journey, pray that the road is long, full of
adventure, full of knowledge.

—*C. P. Cavafy*, The Journey to Ithaca

Seeking full implementation of the Habits of Mind has defined our journey of almost two decades in the Tahoma School District in Washington
State. We are committed to a curriculum designed to prepare our students for living and working in the 21st century. Our journey officially
began when we adopted a set of outcomes in 1990 that captured the district's learning goals for our students. These include becoming self-
directed learners, collaborative workers, community contributors, quality
producers, effective communicators, and complex thinkers. We realized
at the time that to achieve the outcomes, students would need to acquire
thinking skills and Habits of Mind rather than a specific body of content.
Our ambition was to provide opportunities to learn the outcomes at each
grade level and in every content area.

At the heart of our foundational work was the identification of a specific thinking skills curriculum. This curriculum consists of 20 thinking
skills and the Habits of Mind, which we originally described as "thinking

behaviors." During the 2006 school year, we convened a committee of parents and district educators to review our district's student profile and to update the learning goals to reflect current thinking regarding 21st century skills. The committee reaffirmed our belief in the original six outcomes and our emphasis on developing thinking skills and Habits of Mind by revising the indicators for each of our district outcomes (see Figure 22.1). The new language is even more congruent with the Habits of Mind, and we are restructuring our district leadership model to achieve full implementation.

What have we learned on our journey? What adventures have we encountered, and what are the next best steps to support our students? Three themes have emerged for us. The first is the importance of structures; the next is the power and influence of leadership; and the final theme is maintaining the persistence to stay the course.

The Importance of Structures: Nested Objectives

Our district adopted the model of nested objectives (Costa & Garmston, 1998) as a way to focus on process-based learning and to develop our curriculum units. This model incorporates thinking skills, Habits of Mind, and universal outcomes as curriculum goals. Students use content knowledge as a vehicle for developing thinking processes. We have created elementary curriculum units with clear outcomes and guiding questions that incorporate content, activities, themes, thinking skills, Habits of Mind, and our district outcomes and indicators. These units have provided our teachers with lessons that focus on process-based learning and not just knowledge acquisition. Figure 22.2 shows an overview of the unit on Puget Sound Communities.

We communicate the goals of each elementary unit through a parent letter that emphasizes the thinking skills, Habits of Mind, and district outcomes and indicators that are developed using social studies and science content (see Figure 22.3). Reading, writing, and communication skills are integrated with the content, and students participate in rich activities to internalize an understanding of the various learning objectives.

FIGURE 22.1

Tahoma School District Outcomes and Indicators

I. Self-Directed Learners
- Set goals
- Show persistence
- Make effective decisions
- Evaluate work
- Use time effectively
- Strive for improvement

II. Collaborative Workers
- Contribute to shared vision
- Demonstrate flexibility
- Show empathy and respect
- Listen actively
- Are accountable
- Build on other people's thinking

III. Effective Communicators
- Communicate with clarity and precision
- Deliver information effectively and in multiple formats
- Interact with globally diverse audiences
- Listen, interpret, and evaluate

IV. Community Contributors
- Consider global perspectives
- Demonstrate personal, social, and civic responsibility
- Respect and value diversity
- Enhance the environment
- Engage in community service

V. Quality Producers
- Develop and/or utilize criteria
- Aspire to exceed expectations
- Skillfully use tools, resources, and technology
- Demonstrate accuracy and precision
- Create aesthetically pleasing work

VI. Complex Thinkers
- Imagine, create, and innovate
- Recognize and appreciate humor
- Gather, filter, and synthesize information
- Access multiple problem-solving strategies
- Reflect on and apply past learning to new experiences
- Generate questions to deepen understanding
- Explore and take risks

Source: Tahoma School District No. 409, Tahoma, Washington. Copyright © Tahoma School District. Reprinted with permission.

Like all districts, we are responsible for our students achieving state standards, and we have integrated these standards with our thinking skills and Habits of Mind. The various learning objectives are nested within the units of study so that students learn skills, processes, and Habits of

FIGURE 22.2

Overview of a Curriculum Unit

Puget Sound Communities
Grade 3

Outcome and Guiding Questions
Students will explore the systems, cycles, and relationships that make up the Puget Sound Communities of Seattle and Maple Valley in order to practice the skills of Self-Directed Learners and Community Contributors working toward improving the quality of our local environment.

1. **What communities make up the Puget Sound?**

   - Puget Sound Region
   - Maple Valley Area
   - Map skills
   - Guided reading (See Guided Reading Unit supplement)
   - Introduction to problem solving

Apply **Attending, Risk Taking, Persistence,** and **Deliberativeness** thinking behaviors.

2. **What are the relationships, past and present, that are part of the Puget Sound communities?**

   - Relationships: History of Maple Valley/Black Diamond/Seattle
   - Interviewing
   - Writing a friendly letter
   - Complete sentences/sentence fluency/variety
   - Systems: Community systems in Maple Valley, past and present

Apply **Inferring, Sequencing,** and **Comparing/Contrasting** thinking skills.
Apply **Persistence, Risk Taking,** and **Deliberativeness** thinking behaviors.

3. **How can we contribute to preserving and protecting our local ecology while practicing the skills of Community Contributors?**

   - Cycles: salmon
   - Community Contributors: identify roles and methods
     - Interviews
     - Friendly letter
   - Community service project: Preserving and Protecting Our Salmon (**Community Contributor** outcome)
   - Local authors
   - Project Menu (**Self-Directed Learner** and **Quality Producer** outcome)

Apply **Problem Solving** thinking skill.
Apply **Deliberativeness, Persistence,** and **Risk Taking** thinking behaviors.

Source: Tahoma School District No. 409. Used with permission.

FIGURE 22.3

Letter to Parents

Dear Parents,

We are excited to be starting our year with the Puget Sound Communities integrated unit! Students will have the opportunity to learn about Maple Valley's history along with the history of Seattle. We will focus on the themes of Systems, Cycles, and Relationships as we explore the systems that make up our community of Maple Valley, learn about the salmon cycle, and explore the relationship of past to present in our study of local history. We will emphasize the district outcome of Community Contributor as we consider ways to improve our school and neighborhoods.

Our thinking skill focus will be problem solving. We will practice a strategy for this thinking skill with literature as we explore problems characters have in stories. Then we will use our strategy to look at the problems salmon face to survive. Students will learn that a problem is a situation that needs a resolution. "Something is happening that is not right. We have to try to fix it." They will apply a strategy we will learn. The strategy includes defining the problem as a question, inventing alternatives, critiquing the alternatives, and executing a plan.

In addition, we will reinforce the thinking behaviors of attending, risk taking, persistence, and deliberativeness. We will apply these behaviors to pioneer settlers in our area, to the salmon as they make their way upstream, and to community service projects that we will select as a class. We will also read the newspaper to see how local people use thinking behaviors to be good community contributors.

Throughout the unit, students will practice reading and writing skills. We will focus on inferring to better understand what we read and will write friendly letters to thank local people we interview as we learn more about our history. We will also learn basic map skills. Students will explore a variety of picture and chapter books to build an understanding of our three themes: Systems, Cycles, and Relationships.

We would welcome any ideas or materials that might enrich our study of the Puget Sound Communities and our salmon resource. Please feel free to contact me if you have materials to share with the class. Thank you so much!

Sincerely yours,

Mind while achieving the content goals important in each curricular area (see Figure 22.4).

We are fortunate in Washington State to have adopted a set of state standards that identify the core processes of the disciplines rather than focusing on a specific body of content for students to learn. These processes reinforce thinking skills and Habits of Mind. An example is the teaching of problem solving and reasoning in mathematics. Students apply the thinking skills of finding patterns, interpreting and organizing information, and forming conclusions while demonstrating persistence, drawing on past knowledge, and using metacognition to explain their reasoning. Each content area contains key concepts and skills that link to a subset of the thinking skills and Habits of Mind. Identifying the foundational skills and habits allows our teachers to apply these while focusing instruction on the core content of their disciplines.

Habits of Mind Lessons

In addition to the structure of our curriculum based on the model of nested objectives, we have created specific lessons to teach each of the 16 Habits of Mind in a systematic way. Students are introduced to the habits at the elementary level through the integrated units. At middle school, grades 6 and 7, students engage in a two-year curriculum that provides direct instruction in each Habit of Mind. Eight habits are taught at grade 6 and the other eight at grade 7 (see Figure 22.5).

Teachers use the 45-minute advisory period one day a week to provide a lesson in one of the habits. A specific Habit of Mind is the focus for two to four weeks at a time and is integrated into the curriculum where relevant and appropriate. The habits form the thread for building content connections and serve as a social skills program at the middle level. We believe that it is important to directly teach the habits in a formalized approach to ensure that all students have opportunities to reflect on the importance and meaning of each of the 16 Habits of Mind.

The lessons that we provide use picture books and hands on activities that encourage interaction and creativity. For example, students explore *listening with understanding and empathy* by reflecting on the qualities of the boy interviewer in the book *So What's It Like to Be a Cat?* The next

FIGURE 22.4

Nested Objectives for Unit on Puget Sound Communities

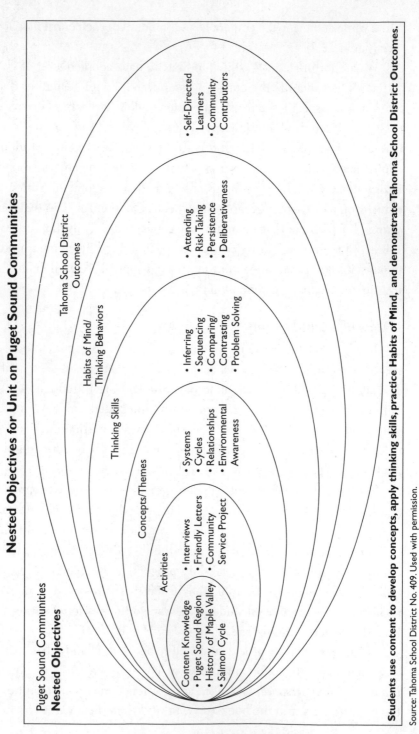

Puget Sound Communities
Nested Objectives

Tahoma School District
Outcomes

Habits of Mind/
Thinking Behaviors

Thinking Skills

Concepts/Themes

Activities

Content Knowlege
• Puget Sound Region
• History of Maple Valley
• Salmon Cycle

• Interviews
• Friendly Letters
• Community
  Service Project

• Systems
• Cycles
• Relationships
• Environmental
  Awareness

• Inferring
• Sequencing
• Comparing/
  Contrasting
• Problem Solving

• Attending
• Risk Taking
• Persistence
• Deliberativeness

• Self-Directed
  Learners
• Community
  Contributors

Students use content to develop concepts, apply thinking skills, practice Habits of Mind, and demonstrate Tahoma School District Outcomes.

Source: Tahoma School District No. 409. Used with permission.

FIGURE 22.5

Two-Year Curriculum for Teaching the Habits of Mind

**Tahoma School District
Habits of Mind**

Arthur L. Costa

Grade 6

Thinking Flexibly — Remains open to alternatives; sees many possibilities.

Managing Impulsivity — Thinks before acting; is deliberative.

Striving for Accuracy — Uses criteria to evaluate quality; demonstrates craftsmanship.

Gathering Data Through All Senses — Observes using all sensory pathways; engages the multiple intelligences.

Thinking About Thinking (Metacognition) — Puts into words his/her own thinking; self-reflects.

Thinking Interdependently — Builds on other people's thinking; works collaboratively.

Thinking and Communicating with Clarity and Precision — Uses words carefully; strives for specificity in language.

Finding Humor — Exhibits a whimsical approach to life.

Grade 7

Persisting — Keeps on trying; does not give up easily.

Applying Past Knowledge to New Situations — Learns from experience.

Questioning and Posing Problems — Asks questions; enjoys problem solving; is curious.

Creating, Imagining, Innovating — Enjoys making and doing original things; strives for fluency and elaboration.

Listening with Understanding and Empathy — Listens to others attentively and with sensitivity.

Taking Responsible Risks — Is willing to take on new challenges; is not afraid of making mistakes.

Responding with Wonderment and Awe — Enjoys problem solving; demonstrates curiosity.

Remaining Open to Continuous Learning — Strives for improvement; searches for new and better ways.

Source: Tahoma School District No. 409. Used with permission.

week, the students engage in a fast-paced paraphrasing activity called Relay Raps to practice the skills of active listeners. The students next explore the concept of empathy by reflecting on the character who leaves her home in the book *Goodbye, 382 Shin Dang Dong*. They display their understanding of empathy in a concept-definition map. Finally, they apply and practice the Habit of Mind by role-playing scenarios that require listening with understanding and empathy.

Students are encouraged to consider what the Habit of Mind looks like and sounds like when demonstrated. They think about the importance of the habit in relation to our district outcomes and indicators, and they personalize the habit as it reinforces interactions in their own lives. As students move into the junior and senior high schools, they have a common foundation for each of the 16 habits and are encouraged to apply them in their social interactions and academic work.

For example, teachers in our high school integrated programs identify specific Habits of Mind for emphasis in the curriculum. They link the habits to the district outcomes and indicators, and the students are very articulate regarding the value of the Habits of Mind as they think about their importance in their lives. When interviewed by visitors from Singapore regarding the Habits of Mind, one student summarized how the approach to learning is different in the Tahoma School District:

> I have been a student in the Tahoma School District my whole life, and recently I have been getting to know students who have transferred from other school districts. I realize that when we started to use the Habits of Mind, the teachers were showing that they really care about us and how we think and not just the curriculum. In other districts, the teachers just want to go over the basics about the topics. Here, the teachers help us to develop a bigger perspective and encourage independent thinking. They show us that they value our ideas.

Another student added, "I can see how I will use the Habits of Mind, not just in school but in life."

We believe that teaching the habits directly through lessons and then reinforcing them in our curriculum provides quality opportunities to learn these foundational behaviors. Our students could not achieve the district outcomes without learning the Habits of Mind. Our goal is to empower our students with lifelong behaviors that will support their personal and professional success, and we are confident that the Habits of Mind are creating thoughtful individuals who have a broader perspective on life.

Standards for Quality Teaching and Learning

Another important structure is our Standards for Quality Teaching and Learning document (see Figure 22.6). This document, included in our teaching contract, identifies expectations for Classroom Management, Classroom Environment, Lesson Planning and Design, Instructional and Classroom Teaching Practices, Assessment, and Professional Development and Responsibilities. Incorporated into the document is the commitment to developing and teaching units built on the structure of the nested objectives, providing instruction in thinking skills and Habits of Mind, and developing the processes of learning through best practices. Teachers are accountable by contract to demonstrating these teaching standards and are supported through a supervision model that includes coaching and consulting by building administrators and mentor teachers.

Structures in our curriculum provide a solid foundation for supporting our students in acquiring the Habits of Mind. Without formal structures, there is no guarantee that all students would have the opportunity to be introduced to each of the habits. Nor would students necessarily see how the habits support learning academic content and provide the foundation of our district outcomes. The outcomes, defined by the habits, are the key to making learning relevant to students' lives. We believe that the goals of education include acquiring the characteristics embodied in the Habits of Mind and that structures are essential to ensure opportunity to learn for all of our students.

The Power and Influence of Leadership

Leadership at both the school and district levels is crucial in order to fully implement a focus on the Habits of Mind. Emilie Hard, principal of Glacier Park Elementary School, has provided support and direction for implementing the Habits of Mind since the school opened in 2000. She has hosted numerous visitors from such faraway places as Singapore

FIGURE 22.6

**Tahoma School District Standards
for Quality Teaching and Learning**

MEETS STANDARDS	
CLASSROOM ENVIRONMENT	**INSTRUCTIONAL & CLASSROOM TEACHING PRACTICES**
Creates a classroom environment that is safe, inviting, respectful, and developmentally appropriate: • Provides for interactions that are consistently appropriate to student's culture, gender, and individual differences. • Reflects commitment to TSD Outcomes and Indicators. • Conveys enthusiasm for learning. • Uses technology to motivate and engage students in the learning.	Develops a repertoire of instructional and classroom teaching practices: • Uses a wide variety of active processing strategies to engage students in learning. • States learning objectives, gives clear directions, and consistently checks for understanding. • Mediates student thinking through questioning strategies, thinking skills, and Habits of Mind applications. • Differentiates instruction through 　○ Use of technology. 　○ Flexible grouping (e.g., cooperative learning, small groups, peer partners). 　○ Multiple intelligences. 　○ Monitoring and modifying instruction: content, skills, time. • Incorporates appropriate technology to improve learning.
CLASSROOM MANAGEMENT	**ASSESSMENT**
Creates classroom structures and communicates clear expectations in a manner that encourages appropriate behavior and promotes student learning: • Responds to behavior in a manner that is appropriate, successful, and demonstrates respect for student. • Establishes management practices that result in minimal loss of instructional time, such as 　○ Routines for handling materials and supplies. 　○ Smooth transitions with clear directions. • Uses technology for efficient access of classroom assignments and directions by students and parents.	Creates and utilizes multiple and appropriate assessment tools: • Aligns tools with lesson objectives to frequently monitor student learning and set future goals; tools include 　○ Rubrics, scales, checklists. 　○ Performance assessments. 　○ Objective tests. 　○ Portfolios. 　○ Student self-reflections and critiques. • Communicates clear assessment criteria and standards to students and families. • Uses data management systems to access and interpret data to make instructional decisions.

Source: Tahoma School District No. 409. Used with permission.

FIGURE 22.6   *(continued)*

Tahoma School District Standards
for Quality Teaching and Learning

LESSON PLANNING & DESIGN	PROFESSIONAL DEVELOPMENT & RESPONSIBILITIES
Consistently implements state and district adopted curriculums: • Uses curriculum documents (i.e., continuums, implementation guidelines, preferred visions, unit notebooks, etc.). • Designs lessons with clear objectives focusing on concepts, skills, and strategies (i.e., nested objectives and classroom 10). • Integrates curriculum through essential questions, key concepts/themes, thinking skills, Habits of Mind, and district outcomes. • Applies current research and best practices in delivery of instruction. • Incorporates reflection and assessment results in order to improve future lessons. • Intentionally plans for the appropriate use of technology to enhance learning.	Demonstrates continual commitment to professional growth and improved student learning: • Seeks out opportunities for staff development to enhance content knowledge and teaching skill. • Uses feedback for the purposes of self-reflection and goal setting. • Participates in development and support of the building site plan and district initiatives. • Accesses available resources and personnel to support students. • Assumes responsibility for parent communication in a professional and timely manner. Contributes as a member of a professional learning community: • Intentionally models TSD Outcomes and Indicators. • Practices effective communication skills (SPACE). • Presumes positive intent in working with students, families, and colleagues. • Employs a fully effective system for managing paperwork and timelines.

Source: Tahoma School District No. 409. Used with permission.

who wish to visit a school where the Habits of Mind truly help to define the school's culture. She has learned that when the whole school spotlights the Habits of Mind in consistent, regular ways, students acquire a deep understanding that enables the transfer of the habits to their learning in the classroom.

At the Building Level

At Glacier Park, one or two Habits of Mind are highlighted each month. The teachers have simplified the language for several of the habits to one-word descriptions. The habits are publicized in the school newsletter and teachers' communications with parents, featured in the weekly school announcements, and modeled in monthly assemblies. The Habits of Mind vocabulary is heard in students' conversations and seen in their writing. Teachers are committed to the value of the Habits of Mind and provide leadership in supporting full implementation. They reinforce the habits in the classroom curriculum and label the monthly habit when it is demonstrated by students in their classrooms.

Students eagerly anticipate the monthly assemblies because each Habit of Mind is reinforced with an original skit, song, or story. For example, 5th grade students helped the principal craft new lyrics for the song "Celebration" for the *elaboration* Habit of Mind, a component of *creating, imagining, and innovating*:

> E-la-bor-a-tion
> Come on!
> E-la-bor-a-tion
> Come on!
>
> Well there's some thinkin' going on right here
> Elaboration
> Adding on to other thoughts
> So bring your good ideas and your voice too
> We're gonna elaborate and learn a whole lot too
> Come on now
>
> Elaboration
> Let's all think and have a good time
> Elaboration
> We're gonna make our writing FINE!
>
> It's time to come together
> It's up to you . . . show your thinking
> Everyone at Glacier Park . . . come on!

Students performed the song, with dance moves, for the student body. Students were overheard enthusiastically singing about elaboration on the playground! The principal and the dean of students choose to be part of each skit that is performed so that they can clearly model the featured Habit of Mind. Time is provided for students to generate examples for using the habit during their school day and leisure time. The assemblies always begin and end with the school song, which also reinforces the district's outcomes and the school's mission of creating lifelong learners.

Teachers recognize students each month for outstanding demonstration of the highlighted Habit of Mind. Awards are presented, and students proudly wear ribbons that say "I use Habits of Mind at Glacier Park Elementary." Photographs of students who receive special recognition for modeling the Habits of Mind are displayed in the hallway, with every child represented at some point during the year. The message is this: "All of us can and do demonstrate the Habits of Mind, and this is valued at Glacier Park Elementary School."

Connecting literature with the Habits of Mind was a recent goal for the school. Staff members selected picture books that exemplify a particular Habit of Mind, and their photographs were taken with the books and made into posters for display. The posters are valuable reminders of how story characters display the attitudes and dispositions that we are striving to embody. Staff members take the lead in reinforcing the Habits of Mind, and they model the language and behaviors for the students.

As a result of the comprehensive schoolwide focus at Glacier Park, the students use the language of the Habits of Mind routinely and effortlessly. Positive student behaviors are the norm because the targets and expectations are clear. A culture of thoughtful, deliberate choices demonstrating Habits of Mind permeates the school environment. Glacier Park is not only a wonderful place for both children and adults; it is also one of the highest-performing schools in the state on the Washington State Assessment of Student Learning. More than 90 percent of the students are meeting the state reading standard, and more than 80 percent of the students are meeting the standard in math. We believe that students improve their ability to learn by demonstrating the Habits of Mind in their school environment.

At the District Level

At the district level, we are restructuring our leadership model to build a broad base of support for fully implementing our curriculum initiatives. Our principals are assuming more responsibility for monitoring the implementation of district curriculum, and we are fostering leadership skills among our teachers and principals through professional development institutes. Although we are pleased with our successes as measured by test data, anecdotal information, and various recognitions, we realize that there are pockets in our system where we do not yet have full implementation of our curriculum, including consistent development of the Habits of Mind. Responsibility is shifting from the central office to the schools for determining professional development initiatives. Our district mission statement is "Every Child, Every Classroom, Every Day: Quality Learning." Glacier Park's example helps us to understand the commitment needed for building leadership, in partnership with teacher leadership, to fully implement the Habits of Mind into the culture of a school.

Persistence to Stay the Course

In 1992 we were exploring different grade-level configurations at one of our four elementary schools. The planning team met with John Goodlad, author of *A Place Called School* (1984), to learn from his wisdom and insights into what makes a successful program. Goodlad's research on multiaged learning, one option under consideration, confirmed the academic and social benefits for students. However, he shared with us that in education, it can take 30 to 35 years for researched practices to become commonplace in classrooms.

Without persistence, the best ideas are short-lived. Parents want school to look and sound like their own experiences and have difficulty accepting changes. Even when their workplace looks dramatically different compared with years past, they want school curriculum and instructional practices to stay the same. To shift from a content-based curriculum to a process-based curriculum is challenging at best. Parents need to know that the students are still learning basic content and skills; however, parents also need to understand that the processes of learning, including the Habits of Mind, will serve students long after the content is forgotten.

Making these shifts takes time. Districts committed to incorporating the Habits of Mind into the curriculum are destined for a long and rich journey. Structures must be built, including units of study that integrate the Habits of Mind, specific lessons for teaching the Habits of Mind, and clear expectations for what is valued and expected in the classroom. Also, leadership at all levels must sponsor and guide the work. Finally, the commitment must be ongoing and model the habits of persistence, flexibility, and creativity. Our superintendent's goal is for us to feel confident in placing our own children in any classroom in our district, knowing that each child will receive the very best instruction and a consistent focus on the district outcomes. He keeps this goal clearly at the forefront as we proceed on our journey.

In *A Whole New Mind*, Daniel Pink (2006) tells us that we are entering the Conceptual Age, in which right-brained thinking will be valued more than logical reasoning skills because computers will increasingly perform the tasks once accomplished by skilled analytical workers. However, computers cannot create, understand relationships, and search for meaning, all of which are distinctly human goals. The Habits of Mind define what Pink and other futurists say will characterize successful people in the 21st century. If we want to provide our students with the new basic skills, then the Habits of Mind must be at the top of our list.

Our young people deserve preparation for work and for life that will empower them to succeed in an ever-changing world. We are at risk from environmental challenges, political unrest, and a myriad of social issues. How do we provide support for our children in these difficult times? We build a foundation on the Habits of Mind to educate caring, creative, and confident people who can address the unending challenges of a complex world.

References

Costa, A., & Garmston, R. (1998). Maturing outcomes. *Encounter: Education for Meaning and Social Justice, 11*(1) pp. 10–18.

Goodlad, J. (1984). *A place called school: Prospects for the future.* New York: McGraw-Hill

Pink, D. (2006). *A whole new mind.* New York: Riverhead Books.

The Tahoma School District Web page is at www.tahomasd.us. We invite you to explore the resources and information included at this site.

Appendix A:
Bringing Habits of Mind to Life

Here we present a variety of suggestions to further the journey of continuous growth toward internalization of the Habits of Mind. The suggestions demonstrate the use of the Habits of Mind in classrooms, schools, and communities. The list is grouped according to the dimensions that contribute to internalization of the Habits of Mind. Remember that the continuum is not sequential. For that reason, we do not list these in any order of priority. We encourage you to read through and consider each idea.

Some of these ideas may not work for your setting; others may be highly relevant. Your team, group, or staff may wish to rank each item according to the following scale:

- A = Already doing it.
- P = A good possibility.
- M = A must—implement immediately!
- U = Unlikely—it won't fly!

After ranking, develop an action plan to implement the Ms, appoint a subcommittee to study the Ps, and congratulate yourselves for already doing the As!

At the end of each dimension, you'll see that the list is purposefully incomplete. Encourage your staff members, students, and community members to brainstorm additions to fit your situation. Although you might be tempted to abandon the *Us*, save them for a later date. A school's circumstances constantly change, and today's *U* might be tomorrow's *P*.

Exploring Meanings

1. Develop a "code of ethics" based on the Habits of Mind. Distribute this code to every member of the school community. Display the code prominently, and encourage students and staff to refer to it often. All school policies should reflect this code of ethics.

2. Ensure that the school's recognition and reward systems are based on the Habits of Mind.

3. Watch for newspaper and magazine cartoons that illustrate one or more of the Habits of Mind. Display them in the school or classroom, and discuss them with students and staff.

4. Develop a school-year calendar designating one Habit of Mind to be emphasized per month or week. Suggest activities for parents and teachers to emphasize that habit.

5. At the conclusion of each faculty or team meeting, place Habits of Mind "fortunes" in the center of a table. Ask each participant to select a fortune and read it aloud. Here's an example: "Try to understand the other side's point of view. Try to understand other people's views even if you don't agree with them. Such work means giving them an opportunity to explain their concerns completely so that you can get a clear idea of what's bothering them."

6. Choose a personal motto or mission statement. Share this mission statement with others in the school community. Explain why you chose this motto or mission.

7. Interview students from several grade levels. Ask the following question: "What does it take to be successful in this school?" Compare what they report with the list of Habits of Mind.

8. Place a sign on the playground that suggests that students remember to use the Habits of Mind when they are playing with one another.

9. Place signs in the library or media center supporting use of the Habits of Mind.

10. Provide bookmarks that have the Habits of Mind printed on them.

11. Make bumper stickers that celebrate the school's dedication to the Habits of Mind.

12. Have students develop their own buttons to hand out as a reward when someone uses the Habits of Mind.

13. Create plays, poems, and dialogues in which the Habits of Mind are pertinent.

14. In colonial times, children made samplers with important mottoes and aphorisms. Create a needlepoint or cross-stitch project centered around the Habits of Mind.

15. Create a quilt using pieces of fabric with the Habits of Mind written on them.

16. Create rap songs for the Habits of Mind.

17. Invite students to create a blog around each of the Habits of Mind.

18. Develop a list of suggested readings and resources related to the Habits of Mind. Share this resource with parents.

19. Include a "Parents Corner" in the school newsletter where parents can share parenting tips, book titles, and "homework helps" that further the Habits of Mind.

20. Send a letter home to parents before the school year starts. Introduce yourself, your classroom, your enthusiasm, your expectations, and the Habits of Mind.

Expanding Capacities

21. Publicly recognize the Habits of Mind in the work of unsung heroes who keep the school running: custodians, repair staff, secretaries, cafeteria workers, and volunteers.

22. Use the language of the Habits of Mind in conversations with colleagues.

23. Admit your mistakes, and explain how you try to learn from them. Expect—and encourage—students and colleagues to do the same.

24. Institute a student-to-student tutoring program centered around the Habits of Mind.

25. Promote a schoolwide or intraclass service club. Part of the club's mission should be to infuse the Habits of Mind in the school, class, or community.

26. Discuss and demonstrate the Habits of Mind required to care for living creatures. Allow elementary students to take turns caring for class pets, or allow secondary students to care for lab animals in biology class. Also allow students to take the animals home over weekends and holidays.

27. Invite student volunteers to build a playground, pick up litter, plant trees, paint a mural, or remove graffiti. Before and after the event, discuss how the Habits of Mind play a part in accomplishing a task.

28. Invite students to take responsibility for maintaining and beautifying the school. For example, a class might "adopt a hallway," shelve misplaced library books, or plant flowers. Post signs identifying these special caretakers, and discuss the Habits of Mind required to accomplish these tasks.

29. When forming cooperative learning groups, review the Habits of Mind. Ask groups to select one habit to become the focus of group work. Toward the end of the work time, stop and reflect on how this Habit of Mind affected the group members' interactions. Such reflection will also require group members to name indicators that they are using the Habit of Mind.

30. Invite students to write thoughtful letters that include explanations of how they use the Habits of Mind. Examples are thank-you notes, letters to public officials, and letters to the editor.

31. Set up a buddy reading system between an older class and a younger class. Teach the older students Habits of Mind that will make their teaching experience successful.

32. Set up a metacognitive journal for the whole class in which students can record observations of the Habits of Mind.

33. Role-play a student-led conference, and emphasize which Habits of Mind students would use to describe their work to their parents.

34. Role-play a field trip, and emphasize which Habits of Mind would be used on the trip.

35. Ask students to create a way to communicate the Habits of Mind at back-to-school night.

Increasing Alertness

36. Establish the Habits of Mind as ground rules for discussions about all practices in the school.

37. Include discussions of the school's "ethos" in faculty meetings and workshops. How might the Habits of Mind become more apparent in the school's culture?

38. Encourage students and staff to discuss how class rules, school rules, and homework policies reflect and support the Habits of Mind.

39. When assessing staff development institutes, assess the degree to which the Habits of Mind were required for the work that was accomplished.

40. Start a school scrapbook with photos, news stories, and memorabilia reflecting the school's history and accomplishments with the Habits of Mind. Involve as many school members as possible in contributing to and maintaining the collection. Be sure to share the scrapbook with visitors and new families.

41. Describe to students how you use the Habits of Mind in community service, hobbies, avocations, or sports.

42. Hold a ceremony at the beginning and end of the school year to introduce, recognize, and emphasize the Habits of Mind.

43. Encourage students and staff to draw on the Habits of Mind to resolve and learn from school or class conflicts.

44. Ask students to investigate the significance of the school's traditions. Which traditions emphasize the Habits of Mind?

45. Build Habits of Mind related to empathy by inviting students to put themselves in the shoes of the people they are reading about or studying.

46. In classes, specifically address habits such as taking responsible risks, persisting, and striving for accuracy. Why are these habits essential to understanding? How are these habits applicable in class, in school, and in life?

47. Invite students to "adopt an elder" from the community. Arrange for students to visit, write letters to, read to, and explain the Habits of Mind to their adoptee.

48. Interview parents about how they use the Habits of Mind in their profession, job, or career. Which of the Habits of Mind make them successful in their work?

49. Set up a school-to-career program with an expectation that students will learn about the use of Habits of Mind in the workplace.

50. Ask students to discuss the use of Habits of Mind as they are working with technology.

51. Study television programs for examples of the Habits of Mind. Share this information with students, and ask them to do their own television study looking for the habits.

52. Select and watch movies to determine which Habits of Mind the main characters exemplify (e.g., *Babe* [listening with understanding and empathy]; *Chariots of Fire* [persisting]; *Saving Private Ryan* [taking responsible risks]; and *Apollo 13* [creating, imagining, innovating]).

53. Study great artists and consider how the Habits of Mind might have influenced their work.

54. Take advantage of school holidays (e.g., Presidents' Day, Martin Luther King Jr. Day, Labor Day, and Memorial Day) to explain why the Habits of Mind were important in the lives of those we celebrate.

55. Develop a bulletin board where teachers, administrators, and students can share awareness of, use of, and growth in the Habits of Mind.

56. Use the school newsletter to keep parents informed about students' use of the Habits of Mind. Include anecdotes about commendable student performance.

57. Create bulletin boards that focus on student work, with an analysis of how the Habits of Mind informed the work.

Extending Values

58. Pose the following question in a class or meeting: Can a person be "great" and "good" and still have character flaws?

59. Take a walk through your school with students, staff members, parents, or school officials. Ask them to interpret the school's values based only on their observations of the school environment and student and staff interactions. Where do they see strength in the Habits of Mind, and where do they see possible areas for improvement?

60. Develop a system of welcoming and orienting new students that emphasizes the Habits of Mind as the goals and values of your school. When a new student enrolls in the school, welcome the family as well.

61. Illustrate integrity. Let everyone in the school community see that you live your life with the same expectations of yourself that you place upon others for using the Habits of Mind.

62. Place a premium on good sporting behavior in physical education and sports programs. How are competing honorably and Habits of Mind related? How does participation in sports contribute to good Habits of Mind in life beyond sports?

63. Examine and reexamine the responsibilities of a citizen. What can students and staff do now to build the Habits of Mind of responsible citizenship?

64. Give students sufficient and timely feedback about their work using the Habits of Mind terminology.

65. During election years, encourage students to research candidates' positions, listen to debates, and participate in voter registration drives. Ask students to analyze the candidates' backgrounds and platforms in terms of the Habits of Mind.

66. Organize a visit to a meeting of the city council, board of supervisors, board of education, or other public decision-making body. Beforehand, share with these groups that students have been learning the Habits of Mind, and that they want to look for the habits in action in the meetings.

67. Ask students to prepare a report on a living public figure ("My Personal Hero"). The report should focus on how this individual embodies the Habits of Mind.

68. Use morning announcements, school and classroom bulletin boards, and the school newsletter to highlight student and faculty accomplishments that demonstrate the Habits of Mind.

69. During parent-teacher conferences, ask about parents' concerns. Model the habits of listening with understanding and empathy, and thinking and communicating with clarity and precision.

70. Use a variety of communications to tell parents how their children are using the Habits of Mind: personal notes, phone calls, personal visits, and classroom newsletters.

Building Commitment

71. Invite graduates to return and talk about their experiences with the Habits of Mind. Ask them to discuss which habits can help make transitions successful: from elementary school to middle school, from middle school to high school, or from high school to college or work.

72. Invite students to rate themselves on the self-assessment inventory found in Appendix D. Have them set a goal for themselves as to which of the habits they might wish to improve upon.

73. Invite students to choose a person in school, in history, or in their family (e.g., hero, coach, athlete, fictional character in a book, teacher, sibling, parent). Which of the Habits of Mind displayed by that person do the students most admire? Ask them to develop a plan to become more like the person of their choice.

74. Discuss with students which of the Habits of Mind are most needed in the school and community. Develop a series of "public service announcements" to be broadcast over the school's or community's TV network or radio.

75. Develop newspaper articles about the Habits of Mind and submit to the local newspaper.

76. Prepare a presentation to the local board of supervisors, city council, school board, or other adult governmental body. Encourage them to apply the Habits of Mind to their functions, decisions, and policies.

77. Examine school policies and practices to determine how the Habits of Mind might make them even more significant and valued.

78. Invite teachers to share with their students those Habits of Mind in which they are striving to improve. Have them ask students for feedback as to how they are doing and ways they might improve.

79. Invite students to translate the Habits of Mind into "teen-speak." Develop inspirational stories, plays, and essays using that terminology.

Appendix B:
Leading Schools
with Habits of Mind

1. Persisting

Leaders remain focused. They are committed to task completion. They never lose sight of their own and their organization's mission, vision, and purposes.

2. Managing Impulsivity

Leaders think before they act, remaining calm, thoughtful, and deliberative. Leaders often hold back before commenting, considering alternatives and exploring the consequences of their actions.

3. Listening with Understanding and Empathy

Leaders strive to understand their colleagues. They devote enormous mental energy to comprehending and empathizing with others' thoughts and ideas.

4. Thinking Flexibly

Leaders are adaptable. They can change perspectives, generate alternatives, consider options. They see the big picture and can analyze the parts. They are willing to acknowledge and respect others' points of view.

5. Thinking About Thinking (Metacognition)

Leaders are aware of their own thoughts, strategies, feelings, and actions and their effects on others. Leaders "talk" to themselves as they evaluate their plans, monitor their progress, and reflect on their actions, needs, and aspirations.

6. Striving for Accuracy

Leaders are truth seekers. They desire exactness, fidelity, and craftsmanship. Leaders do not accept mediocrity.

7. Questioning and Posing Problems

Leaders have intellectual curiosity, a need to discover and to test ideas. They regard problems as opportunities to grow and learn.

8. Applying Past Knowledge to New Situations

Leaders draw on their rich experiences, access prior knowledge, and transfer knowledge beyond the situation in which it is learned. They learn from their "mistakes."

9. Thinking and Communicating with Clarity and Precision

Leaders articulate their ideas clearly in both written and oral form. They check for understanding and monitor their own clarity of terms and expressions.

10. Gathering Data Through All Senses

Leaders have highly tuned observational skills. They continually collect information by listening, watching, moving, touching, tasting, smelling.

11. Creating, Imagining, Innovating

Leaders try to conceive problems differently, examining alternatives from many angles. They project themselves into diverse roles, use analogies, take risks, and push the boundaries of their own limits.

12. Responding with Wonderment and Awe

Leaders find the world fascinating and mysterious. They are intrigued by discrepancies, compelled to mastery, and have the energy to enjoy the journey.

13. Taking Responsible Risks

Leaders are courageous adventurers as they live on the edge of their competence. They dare to take calculated risks.

14. Finding Humor

Leaders have such high self-esteem that they do not take themselves too seriously. They are able to laugh at themselves and with others. They are capable of playfully interpreting everyday events.

15. Thinking Interdependently

Leaders recognize the benefits of participation in collaborative efforts. They seek reciprocal relationships, both contributing to and learning from interaction with others.

16. Remaining Open to Continuous Learning

Leaders resist complacency about their own knowledge. They have the humility to admit their weaknesses and display a sincere desire to continue to grow and learn.

Appendix C:
When Have Habits of Mind
Become Infused?

We are often asked, "How would you know when and if the Habits of Mind have been infused?" We usually respond by saying that we'd know it when there is a "harmony of heart and mind"; when the habits are mindfully infused throughout the curriculum, instructional practices, and assessment strategies; in the people and the culture of the school—so it is not just a Habits of Mind school but truly a "mindful school" dedicated to improving society. Furthermore, we believe infusion is a never-ending journey rather than a status to be achieved. It becomes a "way of being" rather than a "thing to do."

Note: This statement was composed and refined by an international group of educators during the 2007 Habits of Mind International Expo, held in Melbourne, Australia, and Auckland, New Zealand. They are James Anderson, Australian National Schools Network, Melbourne, Victoria, AU; Andrew Bills, Australian National Schools Network, Melbourne, Victoria, AU; Karen Boyes, Spectrum Education, Upper Hutt, NZ; Alan Cooper, Cooper Consultancy, Wanganui, NZ; Art Costa, California State University, Sacramento, California, USA; Faye Hauwai, The Learning Network, Auckland, NZ; and representatives from six schools: Phillip Moulds and Debra Creed from Brisbane Grammar School, Brisbane, Queensland, AU; Ross Kennedy and Trudy Francis from College Street Normal School, Palmerston North, NZ; Andrea Federico, Rasma Melderis, and Nicholas D'Aglas from Furlong Main Cluster Schools, St. Albans, Victoria, AU; Barry Musson, Matt Allen, and Martin O'Grady from Lindisfarne College, Hastings, Hawks Bay, NZ; Sharee Ineson and Noreen Melvin from Southlands Girls High School, Invercargill, Southland, NZ; John Melton, Sandra Brace, and Matt Lawrence from Waikiki School, Honolulu, Hawaii, USA.

Those are general statements. So let's "unpack" these ideas more fully to describe some indicators that the Habits of Mind truly are becoming invested, embedded, and infused into a mindful school:

All inhabitants of the school (staff, students, and parents) are increasingly . . .

• Spontaneously employing the language of the Habits of Mind.

• Aware of and recognizing the Habits of Mind in themselves and others.

• Valuing the Habits of Mind as a skillful internal compass to guide actions, thoughts, and decisions.

• Applying the Habits of Mind in an ever-expanding range and variety of settings.

• Becoming more skillful and capable in performing the Habits of Mind when confronting problems in a variety of settings.

• Committed to monitoring, reflecting on, evaluating, and improving the Habits of Mind.

• Unprompted in their habitual use of the Habits of Mind.

• Becoming influenced by the Habits of Mind in their daily behaviors, interactions, and learning.

Classroom Instruction

• Instruction focuses on alerting, experiencing, illuminating, practicing, valuing, reflecting upon, and evaluating the use of the Habits of Mind.

• The Habits of Mind are mindfully and meaningfully heard in the vocabulary of both students and teachers in their classroom interaction, in the cafeteria, on the playground, and at home.

• Lessons are planned to make the Habits of Mind explicit, as well as to create classroom conditions *for* the habits of mind and to teach *about* the habits of Mind.

• Instructional strategies are designed to directly teach, engage, monitor, and reflect on the Habits of Mind.

Curriculum Design

• Habits of Mind are woven through other curriculum initiatives and state-mandated programs.

• The curriculum is deliberately structured and planned to include the infusion of the Habits of Mind.

• Lessons and units are designed to infuse opportunities to use and to develop students' Habits of Mind.

• As students mature in their understanding of the Habits of Mind, the lessons also mature in sophistication and complexity.

• The Habits of Mind are stated as goals and outcomes of education.

• Students and staff collaboratively design assessments that guide students to self-evaluate and self-modify their skillfulness in the Habits of Mind.

• Students self-evaluate and self-modify their skillfulness in the Habits of Mind.

• The curriculum is designed to develop students' Habits of Mind on their journey toward internalization. Teachers and students plan, design, discuss, and evaluate curriculum designed to move students through each of the developmental dimensions of exploring meanings, expanding capacities, increasing alertness, extending values, and building commitment.

School Culture

• The Habits of Mind are recognized when they are performed; posters and slogans in the environment signal students and staff that the Habits of Mind are valued outcomes of the school.

• The Habits of Mind are reflected in the school's vision, mission statement, policies, norms, and group processes.

• School staffs model, monitor, manage, and modify their use of the Habits of Mind both individually and in group settings.

• Willingness and ability to support the school's focus on the Habits of Mind become part of the selection process for new staff and school leaders.

• The Habits of Mind are mindfully and meaningfully heard in the vocabulary of both administrators and teachers in their interaction, in the teachers lounge, and in faculty/staff meetings.

Parents and Community

- Parents are kept informed of their student's progress in the Habits of Mind.

- Parents new to the school are oriented to the Habits of Mind and become partners in modeling, acknowledging, and supporting the habits at home as well as at school.

- Awareness of the school's goals and activities is built throughout the community through such media as newsletters, community service announcements, television programming, Web sites, and business partnerships.

- Local businesses are informed and oriented about the Habits of Mind, and career days stress the habits.

- Parents reinforce and support the Habits of Mind at home.

- There is public recognition that the Habits of Mind are a central part of the school's life.

Action Research

- For longitudinal evidence of growth, data are collected over time to chronicle the impact that the Habits of Mind are having on students, individual staff members, school culture, and staff interaction.

- Artifacts of effectiveness, including best practices in lesson designs, student artifacts, newsletters, parent reactions and responses, vignettes, success stories, and other materials, are collected in archives.

- Staff members are motivated to study further, to add to their own knowledge base, and to contribute to the expanding reservoir of research on the effects of the Habits of Mind.

Pollinating and Sustaining

- Other nearby schools in the same cluster, schools to which students will advance, and business and governmental agencies are assisted in understanding HOM.

- Coaching and mentoring are provided to new staff members about HOM, their value, assessment, and instructional strategies.

- Because HOM are never mastered or fully understood, there is continual search for greater meaning, inquiry into their effects, gathering of further research, and striving for congruence.
- The staff strives to infuse HOM as norms of the school "the way we do things around here."

Leading Learning

- Leadership is distributed among staff members with responsibility for supporting and championing the Habits of Mind with staff and community.
- Leaders display their passion for and have long-range strategies for sustaining and achieving their vision of a mindful school built upon the Habits of Mind.
- Leadership is sustained with a system of succession.
- Resources of time, opportunities, and finances are provided to support achievement of the school's vision.
- Leaders model the Habits of Mind in their own interactions and behaviors.

Appendix D:
Inventories and Checklists

Rate Your Habits of Mind

Now that you know what the Habits of Mind are, read the following questions and rate yourself on a scale of 1 to 10 by circling the appropriate number. Provide evidence to support your rating. Be honest, but don't be too hard on yourself. Habits of Mind can be learned and practiced. The more you practice, the more intelligent you will become in your use of the Habits of Mind.

1. I am a persistent person. If I don't succeed on the first try, I keep trying until I do succeed.

Not yet, but
I'm learning.   — 1 — 2 — 3 — 4 — 5 — 6 — 7 — 8 — 9 — 10 —   I usually
behave this way.

Evidence:

Note: Appreciation is expressed to Steve Huffman, a teacher at Culver Middle School in Culver, Oregon, for developing this inventory and for giving permission to reprint it here.

2. I manage my impulses and am willing to delay gratification to attain long-term goals.

Not yet, but
I'm learning.   — 1 — 2 — 3 — 4 — 5 — 6 — 7 — 8 — 9 — 10 —   I usually
behave this way.

Evidence:

3. I listen to others with understanding and empathy.

Not yet, but
I'm learning.   — 1 — 2 — 3 — 4 — 5 — 6 — 7 — 8 — 9 — 10 —   I usually
behave this way.

Evidence:

4. I am a flexible thinker. I seek new and different perspectives and can change my mind.

Not yet, but
I'm learning.   — 1 — 2 — 3 — 4 — 5 — 6 — 7 — 8 — 9 — 10 —   I usually
behave this way.

Evidence:

5. I am aware of how I am thinking (metacognition) when I am trying to solve a problem.

Not yet, but
I'm learning.   — 1 — 2 — 3 — 4 — 5 — 6 — 7 — 8 — 9 — 10 —   I usually
behave this way.

Evidence:

6. I check my work for quality and try to be accurate and precise in everything I do.

Not yet, but
I'm learning. $- 1 - 2 - 3 - 4 - 5 - 6 - 7 - 8 - 9 - 10 -$ I usually
behave this way.

Evidence:

7. I ask questions, search for data to support conclusions, and inquire into intriguing ideas.

Not yet, but
I'm learning. $- 1 - 2 - 3 - 4 - 5 - 6 - 7 - 8 - 9 - 10 -$ I usually
behave this way.

Evidence:

8. I draw on what I have learned and apply it to new situations to solve problems.

Not yet, but
I'm learning. $- 1 - 2 - 3 - 4 - 5 - 6 - 7 - 8 - 9 - 10 -$ I usually
behave this way.

Evidence:

9. I am constantly adding new words to my vocabulary. I think about my words and choose them to communicate my ideas precisely.

Not yet, but
I'm learning. $- 1 - 2 - 3 - 4 - 5 - 6 - 7 - 8 - 9 - 10 -$ I usually
behave this way.

Evidence:

10. I use all my senses (sight, hearing, touching, smelling, tasting) to learn.

Not yet, but $-1-2-3-4-5-6-7-8-9-10-$ I usually
I'm learning.   behave this way.

Evidence:

11. I am a creative person and know how to generate ideas and processes.

Not yet, but $-1-2-3-4-5-6-7-8-9-10-$ I usually
I'm learning.   behave this way.

Evidence:

12. I am intrigued and have a sense of wonderment about the world. I enjoy finding problems to solve.

Not yet, but $-1-2-3-4-5-6-7-8-9-10-$ I usually
I'm learning.   behave this way.

Evidence:

13. I am willing to take calculated and responsible risks to venture into the unknown and to try new ideas and strategies.

Not yet, but $-1-2-3-4-5-6-7-8-9-10-$ I usually
I'm learning.   behave this way.

Evidence:

14. I can laugh at myself and find humor in many situations. I refrain from belittling or making fun of others.

Not yet, but $-1-2-3-4-5-6-7-8-9-10-$ I usually
I'm learning.   behave this way.

Evidence:

15. I collaborate with others, contributing to and learning from cooperative work

Not yet, but $-1-2-3-4-5-6-7-8-9-10-$ I usually
I'm learning   behave this way.

Evidence:

16. I am a continual learner. I reflect on and learn from my experiences and easily admit what I don't know.

Not yet, but $-1-2-3-4-5-6-7-8-9-10-$ I usually
I'm learning.   behave this way

Evidence:

Teaching the Habits of Mind

Use the following key to complete the table:

1 = Not yet   2 = Sometimes   3 = Usually   4 = Consistently

You may wish to focus only on those Habits of Mind that you have identified as priorities for your students.

Habits of Mind	In my classroom ...				
	This habit is an *explicitly* valued behavior for my students.	I plan lessons to give students opportunities to engage in this habit.	This habit is evaluated and reflected upon as a valued learning outcome.	I plan for the development and improvement of this habit in students.	A strategy or an idea I might use to improve my teaching of this habit could be ...
Persisting					
Managing impulsivity					
Listening with understanding and empathy					
Thinking flexibly					
Thinking about thinking (metacognition)					
Striving for accuracy					
Questioning and posing problems					
Applying past knowledge to new situations					
Thinking and communicating with clarity and precision					
Gathering data through all senses					
Creating, imagining, innovating					
Responding with wonderment and awe					
Taking responsible risks					
Finding humor					
Thinking interdependently					
Remaining open to continuous learning					

How Am I Doing?

Observable Indicators	Often	Sometimes	Not Yet
I teach toward the Habits of Mind.			
I consciously develop lessons intended to engage students' thinking processes and Habits of Mind.			
I hear myself employing Habits of Mind terminology in my discussions with students.			
I communicate with parents about their child's growth in thinking and Habits of Mind.			
I recognize and reinforce students when they display the use of effective thinking and Habits of Mind.			
If you were to come into my classroom, you would see indicators of my students learning the Habits of Mind.			
If you were to come into my classroom, you would see indicators of my teaching the Habits of Mind.			
I am aware of and assess students' increasing use of the Habits of Mind.			
I value and teach students how to assess their own performance of Habits of Mind.			

Appendix E:
Resources Related to
Habits of Mind

Australia
- www.habitsofmind.org
- Blog: www.mindfulbydesign.org

New Zealand
- www.spectrumeducation.com
- www.learningnetwork.ac.nz

Singapore
- www.artcostacentre.com

United Kingdom
- www.habitsofmind.co.uk

North America
- www.habits-of-mind.net
- www.instituteforhabitsofmind.net

Books and Kindles
- www.ascd.org

Discussion Site
- www.hom@ansn.edu.au register at www.habitsofmind.org

Australian National Schools Network. (2008). *Habits of mind: A resource kit for schools* (2nd ed.). Sydney: Author.

Boyes, K., & Watts, G. (2008). *Learning and living with habits of mind: The habits of mind learning tool.* Alexandria, VA: ASCD.

Carter, C., Bishop, J., & Kravits, S. (2008). *Keys to effective learning: Developing powerful habits of mind.* Upper Saddle River, NJ: Pearson.

Costa, A. (Ed.). (2000). *Developing minds: A resource book for teaching thinking.* Alexandria, VA: ASCD.

Costa, A. (2008). *The school as a home for the mind.* Thousand Oaks, CA: Corwin.

Costa, A., & Kallick, B. (2000). *Habits of mind: A developmental series. Book 1: Discovering and exploring habits of mind.* Book 2: *Activating and engaging habits of mind.* Book 3: *Assessing and reporting on habits of mind.* Book 4: *Integrating and sustaining habits of mind.* Alexandria, VA: ASCD.

Costa, A., & Kallick, B. (2004). *Assessment strategies for self-directed learning.* Thousand Oaks, CA: Corwin.

Jenson, G. (2008). *The habits of mind classroom series: An introduction to intelligent behaviours.* Melbourne, Australia: Hawker-Brownlow.

Marzano, R. J. (1992). *A different kind of classroom: Teaching with Dimensions of Learning.* Alexandria, VA: ASCD.

Renee, A. (2008). *The habits of mind classroom series: Practical ideas.* Melbourne, Australia: Hawker-Brownlow.

Renee, A. (2008). *The habits of mind classroom series: Thinking challenges.* Melbourne, Australia: Hawker-Brownlow.

Swartz, R., Costa, A., Beyer, B., Kallick, B., & Reagan, R. (2007). *Thinking-based learning.* Norwood, MA: Christopher Gordon.

Toi, H. (2006). *The habits of S.U.C.C.E.S.S.: Nurturing intelligent people @school @home @work.* Singapore: Art Costa Centre for Thinking.

Toi, H. (2008). *Sixteen habits of highly intelligent students.* Singapore: Art Costa Centre for Thinking.

Wiggins, G., & McTighe, J. (2007). *Schooling by design: Mission, action, and achievement.* Alexandria, VA: ASCD.

Index

The letter *f* following a page number denotes a figure.

ability, effort, and achievement, 7–8
acceptance without judgment, 106–115
accuracy, striving for
  achievement, indicators of, 182
  in communication, 300–302
  leadership and, 388
  meaning of, 25–26
  Thinking Maps and, 168
  word splash for, 121
achievement
  ability, effort, and, 7–8
  celebrating, 267–268
  coaching and, 279–280
  at Friendship Valley Elementary
    School, 339–340
  indicators of, defining, 177–178,
    189, 199*f*
adventure and risk, 34
agreement questions, 137
alertness, increasing, 61–62, 65–66*f*,
  196–197, 197*f*, 383–384
Alinsky, Saul, 39
allocentrism, 22
American Association for Gifted
  Children, 322
analytical intelligence, 10
assessment. *See also specific dimensions
  of growth*; student self-assessment
  dimensions of growth, 64–68*f*,
    196–197, 197*f*
  indicators of achievement, defining,
    177–178, 189, 199*f*
  of internalization by students, 74–76,
    81–83, 90–92, 92–94

assessment *(continued)*
  of vs. *for* learning, 190
  nested objectives for, 363–367, 368*f*
  planning matrix for collecting
    evidence, 218–219*f*
  reporting on growth, 258–268
  summative vs. formative, 190–191
  Tahoma School District standards
    of, 371, 372*f*
assessment, strategies of
  anecdotal record keeping, 213–215,
    214*f*
  balancing, 217, 218–219*f*, 220
  checklists, 199–202, 199*f*, 201*f*,
    400–401
  goal setting, 197–198
  interviews, 215–216
  journals and logs, 216–217
  performances and presentations,
    210–213, 212*f*
  portfolios, 202, 206–210
  rubrics, 202, 203–206*f*
assessment conferences, collaborative
  an account of one discussion from,
    240–247
  benefits of, questioning the,
    236–238, 255–256
  contextual information, purpose of
    withholding in, 248–250
  fundamental beliefs underlying,
    248, 251
  goal of participation in, 254
  judgment, withholding in, 239,
    250–252

assessment conferences *(continued)*
  protocol structure, 239–240
  purpose of, 249, 251
  questions raised, 252–254
  reflections on, 255–256
  wonder and the, 236–238, 254
associationist theory, 7
attending, Thinking Maps and, 158*f*,
  166–168
Auburn School District, 274
awareness, inner. *See* thinking about
  thinking (metacognition)
awe, responding with. *See* wonderment
  and awe, responding with

Barrymore, Ethyl, 188
Bellingham Public Schools, 259
Bleyl Junior High School, 274
body language, 98
book study practice, 282, 335–336
brain, the human, 97–98, 107, 153,
  157, 164
brainstorming webs, 154–155
Bread Loaf School of English, 248–250
Bright IDEA (Interest Development
  Early Abilities)
  future of, 329–331
  projects findings, 328–329
  rationale for, 320–326
  in summary, 331–332
  transformation, 326–328

capability dimension, 17*f*
capacities, expanding, 61, 64–65*f*,
  196–197, 197*f*, 381–382
celebrations, 267–268, 274–275
Charlevoix-Emmet Intermediate School
  District, 263–264
checklists for assessment, 199–202,
  199*f*, 201*f*, 400–401
Chesterton, G. K., 38
clarifying, 111–112
classroom discussions, 103, 106–108,
  224
classroom environment. *See also*
  thought-full environments
  Bright IDEA project, 325

classroom environment *(continued)*
  indicators of HOM embeddedness,
    391
  paired classrooms, 356
  reflective, 222–223
  rich and responsive, requirement for,
    101–102
  standards in Tahoma School
    District, 371, 372*f*
  trustful/nonjudgmental, 98, 106–115
classroom management
  mindful language and, 127–128
  Tahoma School District standards
    of, 371, 372*f*
  wait time and, 106–108, 167
classroom observation, 277, 325, 336–337
classrooms, paired, 356
closed questions, 137
coaching, 190–191, 277–280, 336–337
cognitive dissonance, creating, 135
cognitive modifiability theory, 9
Coles, Robert, 11
collaboration. *See* assessment
  conferences, collaborative; teamwork
commitment, building, 62, 67–68*f*,
  196–197, 197*f*, 386
commitment dimension of HOM, 17*f*
communication. *See also* feedback;
  language; listening with
  understanding and empathy; thinking
  and communicating with clarity and
  precision
  clarifying in, 111–112
  in conflict management, 356–357
  dialogue to create group norms,
    277–278, 335–336
  email form of, 300
  families, time for talk in, 117
  leadership and, 277–278, 300–302
  nonverbal, 98
  paraphrasing in, 109–110
  the purposeful pause in, 106–108
  roundtable dialogues, Friendship
    Valley Elementary School,
    335–336
community, the, 265–266, 284–288,
  357, 393

Community Council, Waikiki School, 357
community in schools, creating through
    dialogue to create group norms,
        277–278, 335–336
    enthusiasm and commitment,
        338–339
    learning communities, 280–282,
        291–292
    shared vision and common
        purposes, 43–44, 273, 311
    signals, recognitions, celebrations,
        and rituals, 273–274
    staff meetings, 277–278
community of thinkers, creating, 355–356
compassion, developing, 185
conflict management, 21, 356–357
consciousness, self-reflective, 24–25, 39
cooperation, 37, 206f, 356. See also
    teamwork
craftsmanship, 25–26, 151
creative intelligence, 10
creativity, 31–33, 35, 104–105
creativity, imagination, innovation
    achievement, indicators of, 185
    categorical questions, examples of,
        147
    coaching and, 279
    leadership and, 388
    meaning of, 31–32
    questions that stimulate, 141–143
    Thinking Maps and, 168–169
    word splash for, 122
criticism, openness to, 31–32, 37
Croton Elementary School, 229–230
culture, defined, 42, 352
curiosity. See learning, remaining open
    to continuous; wonderment and awe,
    responding with
curriculum design. See also
    instructional design
    indicators of HOM embeddedness,
        391–392
    integrating the HOM, 44–46, 52–58,
        69–71
    outcomes, nested levels of, 47–52, 48f
    systems of learning in, 46–47
curriculum mapping, 46

data, 127, 140–141, 191. See also sensory
    pathways, gathering data through
data-gathering questions, 138–140
Davis, Lisa, 99–100, 285–287
decision making, data for, 127
defensive questions, 137
discipline, mindful language for, 126
discourse analysis in language, 131–132
Dweck, Carol, 12–13

Eagle Rock School, 346
Edgemont High School, 208
educational management, historical
    influences on, 6–7
efficacy, 32, 40
effort, ability, and achievement, 7–8
egocentrism, 22
Einstein, Albert, 312
E. L. Furr High School, 274–275,
    342–347
emotional intelligence, 11
empathy, 22, 110–111. See also
    listening with understanding and
    empathy
Encinal High School, 274
engagement, 135, 247–248, 338–339
experience, learning from. See new
    situations, applying past knowledge to
experiential intelligence, 10
external data, 191

failure, risking, 34
families, time for talk in, 117
feedback, 112–115, 188, 190–195,
    210–213, 212f. See also
    communication
feedback spirals, 194–196, 195f
Feuerstein, Reuven, 9
field trips, 102, 345–346
Fierce Conversations (Scott), 313
fight-or-flight response, 107
First Break All the Rules (Buckingham
    and Coffman), 311
flow maps, 150–151
focus for leadership, 310
Friendship Valley Elementary School,
    149–151, 333–340
Fuller Elementary School, 236–238

Gardner, Howard, 9–10
general intelligence theory, 6–7
generating and Thinking Maps, 158f,
    168–170
genetics of intelligence, 10–11
gifted programs, 319–332
Glacier Park Elementary School, 371,
    373
goals, clarifying, setting, and assessing,
    192, 194, 197–198
Goethe, 312
Goleman, Daniel, 11, 12
graphic organizers, task-specific,
    155–156
group cooperation rubric, 206f

Habits of Mind. See also specific
    dimensions of the; specific HOM
    attributes
    additional resources, 76, 402–403
    attributes of, xx–xxi, 15–17
    building an action research agenda,
        288–289, 393
    defined, 16
    dimensions of the, 17f
    effective use of, 39
    as learning outcomes, 16–17
    tree map of, 158f
    word splash for the phrase, 119
Habits of Mind, incorporating
    assessment of, 395–401
    E. L. Furr High School, 342–347
    Friendship Valley Elementary
        School, 334–338
    indicators of, 390–394
    results of, 42–43
    successful, elements of, 269
    Tahoma School District, 362–377
    Thomasville Primary School,
        319–332
    time required for, 101
    Waikiki School, 348–361
Harvard Project Zero, 237
Highet, Gilbert, 1
HOPE (humility, options, persistence,
    everyone), 314
humor, finding, 35–36, 123, 169–170,
    187, 389

imagination, stimulating, 141–143. See
    also creativity, imagination,
    innovation
impulsivity
    examples of, 295–296
    risk taking and, 33–34
impulsivity, managing
    achievement, indicators of, 179
    categorical questions, examples of,
        146
    in gang members, 345–346
    leadership and, 295–297, 312–314,
        387
    meaning of, 19–20
    rubric for, 204f
    a teacher's reflection on, 227
    Thinking Maps and, 167
    wait time for, 106–108, 167
    word splash for, 120
inclination dimension of HOM, 17f
information, providing, 112–115
innovation and coaching, 279. See also
    creativity, imagination, innovation
instruction
    increasing intelligence through,
        8–13, 100–101, 319–332
    the purposeful pause in, 106–108
    quality standards in Tahoma School
        District, 371, 372f
instructional design
    book study practice for, 282
    indicators of HOM embeddedness,
        391–392
    integrating the HOM, 44–46, 52–58,
        69–71
    lesson study practice for, 281
    outcomes, nested levels of, 47–52, 48f
    primary goal of, 92
    studying student work practice for,
        282
    systems of learning in, 46–47
    at Tahoma School District, 367,
        369f, 370–371, 372–373f
    for teaching for the HOM
        building intuitive awareness and,
            74–76
        cognitively demanding tasks and,
            71–74

instructional design (continued)
    for teaching of the HOM
        building depth, complexity, and
            elegance, 86–92
        exploring meanings for, 76–83
        strategic application for, 83–86
    for teaching with the HOM
        diagnosing and assessing
            students' level of mastery, 92
        modeling for, 93–94
instructional thought, 278–279
intellect, structure of the, 9, 138, 139f
intelligence, 5–13, 100–101, 319–332
internal data, 191
internalization, journey toward. See also
    specific dimensions of growth
    assessing in students, 74–76, 81–83,
        90–94
    indicators of HOM embeddedness,
        391–394
    introduction, 59–60
    language in, 118
    mastering, 62–63, 100–101
    reflection and, 103
interviews, 215–216, 224
intuition/intuitive awareness, 23
intuition/intuitive awareness, building,
    74–76
invitational questions, 143–144

Javits Program, U.S. Department of
    Education, 322
Jindal, Bobby, 34
John Lyman Elementary School, 259,
    260f, 261f, 264–265
Jordan, Michael, 192
journals and logs, 103, 216–217, 225, 228
judgment, 106–115, 239, 250–252

Kallick, Bena, 225–228
Kelvin, Lord, 6
King, Peter, 56–57
knowledge
    applying to new situations, 28, 121,
        147, 170–171, 183–184, 388
    memory and, 164
    social construction of, 187–188
    visual tools for constructing, 153–157

language, 29, 117–118, 129, 131–132.
    See also communication; mindful
    language; thinking and
    communicating with clarity and
    precision
language refinement, 29
laughter, 35. See also humor, finding
leaders, systems-savvy
    communicating with precision and
        accuracy, 300–302
    importance of, 305
    impulsivity, managing, 295–297
    introduction, 291–294
    listening with understanding and
        empathy, 298–300
    persisting in, 294–295
    thinking interdependently, 302–305
leadership. See also under specific
    HOM attributes
    attributes overview, 387–389
    in building an action research
        agenda, 288–289
    the call to, 291–292, 305, 307–309
    classroom interactions and, 277
    coaching and, 277–280
    communication and, 277–278,
        298–300, 387, 388
    continual learning and, 282–283,
        314, 389
    distributed, 311, 335
    focus and, 310
    impulsivity, managing and, 295–297,
        312–314, 387
    indicators of HOM embeddedness,
        393–394
    metacognition and, 388
    modeling, 283–284
    persisting and, 294–295, 308,
        309–310, 313–314, 387
    pollinating and sustaining practices
        in, 283
    roles and responsibilities, generally,
        270–271, 275–276, 292–293, 307
    Tahoma School District, 371,
        373–376
    thinking flexibly for, 387
    thinking interdependently for,
        280–282, 389

The Leadership Engine (Tichy), 307
learners, self-directed, 192
learning
    attention to readiness and sequence
        for, 102–103
    data to energize, 191
    feedback spirals and, 194–196, 195f
    keeping track of, 103
    reflection and, 221–222
    risk taking and, 189
    systems of, 46–47
learning, remaining open to continuous
    achievement, indicators of, 188–189
    book study practice, 282
    categorical questions, examples of,
        146
    coaching and, 279
    feedback and, 112–115, 194–196,
        195f
    leadership and, 282–283, 314, 309
    meaning of, 37–38
    a teacher's reflection on, 227–228
    Thinking Maps and, 170–173
    word splash for, 123
learning communities, creating,
    280–282, 291–292
learning organizations, schools as, 192
lesson study practice, 281, 325
listening with understanding and
    empathy
    achievement, indicators of, 180,
        199f, 201f
    categorical questions, examples of,
        146
    examples of, 110–111
    leadership and, 298–300, 387
    meaning of, 20–21
    paraphrasing in, 109–110
    student journal excerpt, 80
    a teacher's reflection on, 226–227
    Thinking Maps and, 165–166
    word splash for, 120
literature circles, xxviii–xxx
Lupton, Phyllis, 330

Machado, Luis Alberto, 11
macrocentrism, 22–23
Mamaroneck Public Schools, 207, 211

Mann, Horace, 16
mapping, 45–46, 154–157. *See also*
    Thinking Maps
Marcy Open School, 261–262, 262f
Martinez, Susan, 264–265
Maryland Center for Thinking Studies,
    337–338
Meadowview Elementary School,
    265–266
meanings, exploring, 60–61, 64f, 76–83,
    196–197, 197f, 380–381
mediators, mindful, 356–357
memory, 164, 171
metacognition. *See* thinking about
    thinking (metacognition)
microcentrism, 23
mindful language. *See also* language
    building, 124–132
    instructional design for using,
        74–76
    reasons for using, 132–133
    at Waikiki School, 353–355
    word splashes, 118–123
mindful school culture
    benefits of, 358–360
    building an action research agenda,
        288–289
    creating, elements of, 271–275
    examples of benefits in a, 348–349
    Friendship Valley Elementary
        School, 334–338
    indicators of HOM embeddedness,
        392
    leadership roles and responsibilities,
        275–284
    parents and community in, 284–288
    Waikiki School, 348–361
Mindmapping, 154–155
modeling
    accepting without judgment, 106
    community example of, 266, 285
    graphic organizers for, 156
    instructional design for, 93–94
    interviews for, 216
    leadership, 283–284
    reflection, 225–229
    thoughtfulness, 108
moral intelligence, 11

motivation, using praise and rewards,
104–105
Mt. Airy Elementary School, 157,
159–162

narratives on report cards, 264
neural intelligence, 10
new situations, applying past knowledge
to. *See* knowledge, applying to new
situations
Niles North High School, 168
North Carolina Department of Public
Instruction, 322

organizers, task-specific, 155–156

paraphrasing, 109–110
parents
Bright IDEA project involvement,
326–327
involving in student growth, 213,
214*f*
mindfulness culture, creating in,
284–288, 357, 393
reporting to, 259–265
at Tahoma School District involving,
363, 366*f*
passivity, managing, 296–297
Patti Welder Middle School, 274
performances and presentations,
210–213, 212*f*, 265–266
Perkins, David, 10–11
persisting
achievement, indicators of,
178–179
categorical questions, examples of,
146
leadership and, 294–295, 308,
309–310, 313–314, 387
meaning of, 18
rubric for, 203*f*
skills and strategies map, 85*f*
student journal excerpt, 80
Thinking Maps and, 167
word splash for, 119–120
perspective. *See* listening with
understanding and empathy; thinking
flexibly

Philosophy for Children program,
355–356
Piercy, Thomasina DePinto, 157, 159–162
Pittsburgh Public Schools, 237
A Place Called School (Goodlad),
373–376
policy dimension of HOM, 17*f*
pollinating and sustaining practices,
283, 393–394
portfolios, 202, 206–210, 229, 265–266
The Power of Their Ideas (Meier), 43
practical intelligence, 10
praise and rewards, 104–105
precision. *See* accuracy, striving for;
thinking and communicating with
clarity and precision
presuppositions, 129–131
problems, posing. *See* questioning and
posing problems
professional development
Bright IDEA, 323–326
E. L. Furr High School, 346
Friendship Valley Elementary
School, 337–338
study practices, xxvii–xxx, 282,
335–336
Tahoma School District, 371, 373*f*
Waikiki School, 354
projecting and Thinking Maps, 158*f*,
170–173
Pugwash Conference, 271

questioning and posing problems,
26–27, 106–110, 121, 145–147,
182–183, 388
questioning while reading, 147, 148
questions
categorical, to engage HOM,
145–147
in collaborative assessment
conferences, 251–254
complex thinking, stimulating with,
138–143
engaging students using, 135–136
origin of, 247–248
powerful, composing, 143–145, 145*f*
reflection, creating with, 224
that miscue or stifle thinking, 136–137

reading, questioning while, 147, 148
recognitions, celebrations, rituals, and signals, 104–105, 274–275, 357
reflection
    coaching for, 278–279
    developmental issues, 229–230
    dimensions of growth, 60, 62
    documenting, 234–235
    facilitating, 222–225
    internalizing the HOM and, 103
    learning and, 221–222
    modeling, 225–229
    purpose of, 232, 233
    students' stages of, 231f
    teaching, 230–233, 231f
    Thinking Maps and, 158f, 162–166
    valuing, 222
    voices of, internal and external, 233–234
reflective intelligence, 10–11
Reilly, Kathleen, 208–209
relationship identification in language, 131–132
relationships, nurturing, 98
report cards, 259, 260f, 262f, 264
reporting systems, 258–268, 260f, 261f, 262f
Resnick, Lauren, 13
rewards and praise in the classroom, 104–105
rhetorical questions, 137
risk taking
    creativity and, 31–32
    learning and, 189
    responsible, 33–35, 123, 186–187, 313, 389
    Thinking Maps and, 171–172
rituals, signals, recognitions, and celebrations, 274–275, 357
Roach, Judi, 77–78
Roosevelt, Eleanor, 313
rubrics, 212f
    for cooperation, 206f
    for group cooperation, 206f
    for managing impulsivity, 204f
    for persisting, 203f
    for school report card, 260f, 261f

rubrics (continued)
    for thinking about thinking (metacognition), 203f
    for thinking flexibly, 205f
    using, 202

Sacred Hearts Academy, 267
scaffolding, 221
The School as a Home for the Mind (Costa), 333, 334
school board, reporting to, 265–266
school culture. See also mindful school culture
    defined, 352–353
    feedback and assessment systems in, 192–196, 195f
    integrating HOM into the, 271–275, 342–347
school districts integrating HOM, 362–377
schools as learning organizations, 192–196, 195f
Schools That Learn (Senge), 303
self-discipline. See impulsivity, managing
self-knowledge, 233
sensitivity, dimension of, 17f
sensory pathways, gathering data through
    achievement, indicators of, 185
    leadership and, 388
    meaning of, 30–31
    Thinking Maps and, 162–164
    visual imaging in the brain, 153
    word splash for, 122
signals, recognitions, celebrations, and rituals, 274–275, 357
Sir Francis Drake High School Communications Academy, 228–229
Skokie Intermediate School, 198
SMART (specific, measurable, attainable, realistic, timely) goals, 198
social intelligence, 12
Southampton Public Schools, 207
Spearman, Charles, 6
special needs students, 357–358
staff development, 337–338
Sternberg, Robert, 10

stress and the brain, 97–98
striving for accuracy. *See* accuracy, striving for
students
    assessing their internalization journey, 74–76, 81–83, 92–94
    celebrating success, 267–268
    community of thinkers, creating, 355–356
    engaging, 135, 338–339
    gifted programs for disadvantaged, 319–332
    reporting, involving in, 263–267
    special needs, 357–358
    21st century, preparing for the, xxiii
student self-assessment. *See also* assessment
    building depth, complexity, and elegance, 86–92
    checklists for, 199–202, 201*f*
    classroom discussion for, 103
    goals, setting and meeting in, 192, 197–198
    inventories and checklists, 395–399
    journals and logs for, 103, 216–217
    portfolios in, 206–210
    processes of, 192–193
    promoting, 266–267
    record-keeping in, 211
    reporting, involving for, 263–267
    rubrics for, 202
student work, studying, 282. *See also* assessment conferences, collaborative
Sunrise Valley Elementary School, 199–200, 199*f*

Tahoma School District, 214, 263, 362–377
Tamalpais Elementary School, 202
teacher-leaders, effective, 291–292, 307–308
teachers
    classroom observation of, 277
    coaching, 278–279
    learning communities, creating among, 281–282, 291–292
    nonjudgmental, response behaviors of, 106–115

teachers *(continued)*
    praise, effect on, 105
    professional development for, 282, 323–326
    self-assessment for the HOM, 400–401
teamwork. *See also* thinking interdependently
    coaching and, 279
    leadership and, 311, 314
    rubric for, 206*f*
    shared vision and common purposes, 273, 311
    think-pair-share strategy, 108, 172
    Waikiki School, 354
technology, in thought-full environments, 102
thinkers, incremental, 7–8
thinking
    complex, stimulating, 138–143
    creative and imaginative, 141–143
    inside and/or outside the box, 154–157
    language and, 29, 117–118
    skillful, cognitive tasks demanding, 50–51
    stress and, 98
    visualizing, 165–166
thinking about thinking (metacognition)
    achievement, indicators of, 181–182
    categorical questions, examples of, 146–147
    defined, 153
    expanding capacities, 61
    leadership and, 388
    meaning of, 23–25
    mindful language and, 128–129
    rubric for, 203*f*
    student journal excerpt, 80
    Thinking Maps and, 164–166
    visual tools of, 153–157
    word splash for, 120–121
thinking and communicating with clarity and precision. *See also* communication; language
    achievement, indicators of, 184
    categorical questions, examples of, 146–147

thinking and communicating with
    clarity and precision (continued)
        clarifying in, 111–112
        leadership and, 300–302, 388
        meaning of, 29
        Thinking Maps and, 167
        word splash for, 122
thinking flexibly
    achievement, indicators of, 180–181
    categorical questions, examples of,
        146
    leadership and, 387
    meaning of, 21–23
    rubric for, 205f
    a teacher's reflection on, 227
    Thinking Maps and, 168–169
    word splash for, 120
thinking interdependently
    achievement, indicators of, 187–188
    classroom example of, 349
    dialogue to create group norms,
        277–278, 335–336
    leadership and, 280–282, 302–305,
        314, 389
    meaning of, 36–37
    study practices, 281, 282
    Thinking Maps and, 172–173
    vision, creating a shared, 43–44, 273,
        274, 311, 313, 333–340, 346
    word splash for, 123
Thinking Maps. See also mapping
    attending and, 158f, 166–168
    cognitive processes of, 152f
    at Friendship Valley Elementary
        School, 338
    generating and, 158f, 168–170
    HOM and, framework for relating,
        157, 158f
    introduction, 149–152
    leadership seminar on, 173–174
    at Mt. Airy Elementary School, 157,
        159–162
    projecting and, 158f, 170–173
    reflecting and, 158f, 162–166
Thinking Maps language, 165
thinking-process maps, 156–157
thinking skills, 48–50
thinking words, 124–125

think-pair-share strategy, 108, 172
Thomasville Primary School, 319–332
Thorndike, Edward L., 6–7
thought-full environments
    accepting without judgment in,
        106–115
    attention to readiness and sequence
        in, 102–103
    beliefs underlying, 100–101
    classroom discussions, 103
    defined, 115
    introduction, 98–100
    learning in, 103
    modeling, 115
    praise and rewards in, 104–105
    requirements for, 101–102
    time's importance in, 101
thoughtfulness, modeling, 108
thoughts, monitoring while listening, 21
three-story intellect model, 138, 139f
trust, 98, 106–115
Turning Point Learning Center, 288
Tzur, Ron, 329–330

understanding, listening with. See
    listening with understanding and
    empathy
Understanding by Design (Wiggins &
    McTighe), 44
University Heights School, 229

value dimension of HOM, 17f
values, extending, 62, 66–67f, 196–197,
    197f, 384–385
venture and risk, 34
verification questions, 137
vision, creating a shared, 43–44, 273,
    274, 311, 313, 333–340, 346
visual tools. See also specific types of
    for constructing knowledge,
        153–157
    Friendship Valley Elementary
        School's use of, 338
    types of, 154f
voices of reflection, 233–234

Waikiki School, 274–275, 284, 348–361
wait time, 106–108, 167

Watson, Mary, 330
webbing, 154–155
West Orchard School, 285
Whimbey, Arthur, 8–9
wonder, 236–238, 254–255
wonderment and awe, responding with
    achievement, indicators of, 186
    categorical questions, examples of,
        146
    leadership and, 389
    meaning of, 32–33

wonderment and awe, responding with
    (continued)
    Thinking Maps and, 169–170
    word splash for, 122
    word splashes, 118–123
World War I, 6
writing, teaching. See assessment
    conferences, collaborative

Zelda's Tip Top Café, 266, 285
Zewail, Ahmed H., 32

About the Editors
and Other Contributors

Arthur L. Costa is an emeritus professor of education at California State University, Sacramento, and cofounder of the Institute for Intelligent Behavior in El Dorado Hills, California. He has served as a classroom teacher, a curriculum consultant, an assistant superintendent for instruction, and director of educational programs for the National Aeronautics and Space Administration. Costa has made presentations and conducted workshops in all 50 states as well as Mexico, Central and South America, Canada, Australia, New Zealand, Africa, Europe, the Middle East, Asia, and the Islands of the South Pacific.

Costa has devoted his career to improving education through more "thought-full" instruction and assessment. Author of numerous journal articles, he also edited *Developing Minds: A Resource Book for Teaching Thinking* and is the author of *The Enabling Behaviors* and *The School as a Home for the Mind.* He is coauthor (with Larry Lowery) of *Techniques for Teaching Thinking* and *Cognitive Coaching: A Foundation for Renaissance Schools* (with Bob Garmston); and coeditor of *Assessment in the Learning Organization, Assessment Strategies for Self-Directed Learning,* the Habits of Mind series (with Bena Kallick); the trilogy Process as Content (with Rosemarie Liebmann); and *Thinking-Based Learning* (with Robert Swartz, Bena Kallick, Barry Beyer, and Rebecca Reagan). His works have been translated into Dutch, Chinese, Spanish, Italian, Hebrew, and Arabic.

Active in many professional organizations, Costa served as president of the California Association for Supervision and Curriculum Development and was the national president of ASCD from 1988 to 1989. Costa and Kallick have started the Institute for Habits of Mind, providing products and services to schools throughout the world. Costa can be reached at 916-791-7304; e-mail: artcosta@aol.com.

 **Bena Kallick** is a private consultant providing services to school districts, state departments of education, professional organizations, and public agencies throughout the United States and abroad. Kallick received her doctorate in educational evaluation at Union Graduate School. Her areas of focus include group dynamics, creative and critical thinking, and alternative assessment strategies for the classroom. Her written work includes *Literature to Think About* (a whole language curriculum published with Weston Woods Studios); *Changing Schools into Communities for Thinking* (published by Technology Pathways); coeditor of *Assessment in the Learning Organization*, the Habits of Mind series, *Strategies for Self-Directed Learning* (co-authored with Arthur Costa), *Information Technology for Schools* (co-authored with James Wilson), *Thinking Based Learning* (with Robert Swartz, Arthur Costa, Barry Beyer, and Rebecca Reagan) and *Using Curriculum Mapping and Assessment to Improve Student Learning* (co-authored with Jeff Colosimo). Her works have been translated into Dutch, Chinese, Spanish, Italian, Hebrew, and Arabic.

Formerly a Teachers' Center director, Kallick also created a children's museum based on problem solving and invention. She was the coordinator of a high school alternative designed for at-risk students. She is cofounder of Performance Pathways, a company dedicated to providing easy to use software for curriculum mapping and assessment tracking and reporting, in an integrated suite. Kallick's teaching appointments have included Yale University School of Organization and Management, University of Massachusetts Center for Creative and Critical Thinking, and Union Graduate School. She was formerly on the board of the Apple

Foundation, the board of Jobs for the Future, and is presently on the board for Learning Effects and Weston Woods Institute. Kallick and Costa have founded the Institute for Habits of Mind, providing products and services to schools internationally. Kallick can be reached at 12 Crooked Mile Road, Westport, CT 06880 USA; phone/fax: 203-227-7261; e-mail: bkallick@aol.com.

Other Contributors

Jennifer Abrams is a national and international speaker and consultant who trains and coaches educators and other professionals in successful teaching practices, new teacher and employee support, generational savvy, supervision and evaluation, and collaboration skills. She has been a classroom teacher, a coach of new teachers, and a professional developer, and she has served as a consultant to design programs across the United States, Europe, and Asia. Her book, *Having Hard Conversations*, was scheduled for publication by Corwin Press in 2008. Abrams considers herself a "voice coach," helping professionals tap the power and effectiveness of their own voices—within groups, in front of classrooms, and in coaching or supervisory roles. She holds degrees from Tufts University and Stanford University and can be reached at jennifer@jenniferabrams.com.

James Anderson was a middle school teacher and curriculum coordinator at the Grange P–12 College in Hoppers Crossing, Victoria, Australia, where he was responsible for introducing and implementing a program for teaching thinking and Habits of Mind. Anderson is the founding director and principal consultant of MindfulbyDesign. He developed, launched, and led the first collaborative, generative network of educators dedicated to exploring the Habits of Mind. Since 2005, Anderson has led the growth of this network throughout Australia by supporting hundreds of schools both across Australia and abroad, and has helped to extend our understanding of the Habits of Mind through major events like the International Habits of Mind Expo in 2007 (the first of its kind anywhere in the world). Anderson is a highly experienced and engaging presenter with experience at all levels of schooling from early learning through to tertiary level. He has presented to business audiences and consulted extensively to schools. Anderson is Australia's leading authority on Habits of Mind and the regional director of Costa and Kallick's Institute for Habits of Mind and is endorsed to train and support schools and others in Habits of Mind. He offers consultancy and training services through his company Mindful by Design: www.mindfulbydesign.com.

Sandra Brace has been teaching since 1986. A graduate of UCLA with a degree in performing arts, she has taught at every level of education from kindergarten to college. During her professional teaching career, she has been resident "artist in the schools" for more than a dozen schools in California and Hawaii. She founded and administered a 501(c)3 non-profit dance collective on the Big Island of Hawaii and taught music in the public elementary schools there. She has served on the faculty at the University of the Pacific Stockton, directed the dance program at the award-winning Hamilton Performing Arts Magnet School in Stockton, and now teaches full-time at the Waikiki School in special education. A writer, composer, and choreographer as well, Brace has had dances, plays, and operas produced in California and Hawaii.

Kristin Edlund is a curriculum specialist in the Tahoma School District in Washington State and author of the middle school Habits of Mind curriculum. She has written social studies units that integrate the Habits of Mind and thinking skills, and she supports teachers in implementing this curriculum in the classroom. Edlund teaches classes in integrated curriculum, thinking skills, and Habits of Mind throughout western Washington and has presented at numerous state and national conferences. She worked as a teacher-librarian for 12 years before entering administration. She can be reached at the Tahoma School District office at kedlund@tahomasd.us.

Margaret Evans Gayle is executive director of the American Association for Gifted Children at Duke University and a noted futurist and author. She is project manager for Bright IDEA 2, a Jacob Javits Research grant awarded to the North Carolina Department of Public Instruction (NCDPI) by the U.S. Department of Education. She was the associate director of programs in early childhood and languages and chief consultant for media and technology at NCDPI. She is coauthor of *Schools of the Future*

(McGraw-Hill, 1985) and *Educational Renaissance* (St. Martins' Press, 1991) and is a curriculum developer for schools of the future. She was the project designer and director in NCDPI for the Lincoln School of Technology and the DownEast Instructional Telecommunications Network from 1985 to 1989. Gayle holds a BA in English (magna cum laude) and an MA in education from Western Carolina University. She has been a teacher, a media specialist, and a principal. She has presented more than 2,000 keynote addresses and seminars to business and education leaders about curriculum and education for the future.

Emilie Hard is the principal of Glacier Park Elementary School (GPES), which serves more than 900 students in the Tahoma School District in Maple Valley, Washington. She became principal at GPES in 2000 and is one of the main authors of the elementary curriculum units. She coauthored an integrated curriculum for the district with thinking skills and thinking habits at its core. She supports this curriculum by providing demonstration lessons, teacher inservice training, and instructional coaching through her role as principal. Hard has more than 20 years of elementary teaching experience in Oregon, Washington, and Alaska. She has also served on the Washington State Math Advisory Committee and was a member of the state's Classroom-Based Assessment Committee. She can be reached at the Tahoma School District Office, 23700 SE 280th St., Maple Valley, WA 98038; phone: 425-432-7294; fax: 425-432-6795; e-mail: ehard@tahomasd.us.

Mary "Valorie" P. Hargett was the state consultant for academically or intellectually gifted programs in the North Carolina Department of Public Instruction and a former systemwide staff developer, literacy specialist, talent development program specialist, curriculum writer, and education consultant specializing in the most up-to-date theories and practices. As the state consultant for gifted programs she is responsible for (1) program designs, implementation, and reviews; (2) facilitation of rigorous and challenging K–12 curricula; (3) advocacy for underserved populations in K–12 for honors and gifted classes; (4) professional development expertise in best instructional practices that promote student achievement and growth; and (5) licensure policies and development in gifted education. She was the designer for Project Bright IDEA 1 and serves as the co-investigator for Project Bright IDEA 2, a Jacob Javits Gifted Education grant funded by the U.S. Department of Education. The grant is a five-year study on changing the dispositions of teachers and increasing the cognitive and metacognitive thinking of students. She is a former teacher in the areas of gifted education, middle school, kindergarten, and English at the high school level. She holds a BS in education (summa cum laude) from Wingate College and an MEd from the University of North Carolina. Hargett may be reached by phone: 704-253-5513; or e-mail: vhargett@carolina.rr.com.

David Hyerle is an author, a consultant, and a researcher whose work focuses on integrating content learning, instruction in thinking processes, and assessment. In his doctoral work at the University of California–Berkeley and the Harvard Graduate School of Education, Hyerle refined a practical language of visual tools he created called Thinking Maps®. He has written and produced professional development resource guides, videos, and software packages based on Thinking Maps as tools for student-centered learning and whole-school change. He has also published articles and the ASCD books *Visual Tools for Constructing Knowledge* (1996) and *A Field Guide to Using Visual Tools* (2000). Hyerle can be reached at Designs for Thinking, 144 Goose Pond Rd., Lyme, NH 03768; phone/fax: 603-795-2757; e-mail: designs.thinking@valley.net.

Arnold Latti did his undergraduate studies at the University of Hawaii at Manoa in elementary education. After receiving his bachelor's degree, Latti received a professional diploma for elementary education in 1986. Inspired by the Habits of Mind, he received an MEd in educational foundations at the University of Hawaii at Manoa in 2001. He has taught elementary students for more than 20 years and has been on the faculty at Waikiki School since 1992.

Matt Lawrence has been at Waikiki School since 2000 and was introduced to the concept of the mindful school while there as a student teacher. He received a bachelor's degree in education from Illinois State University and a master's degree in educational psychology from the

University of Hawaii. He is currently teaching 6th grade, where integrating Habits of Mind into project-based units of instruction is his primary focus.

David Perkins, codirector of Harvard Project Zero, is a senior research associate at the Harvard Graduate School of Education. He is the author of several books, including *Smart Schools: From Training Memories to Educating Minds* and *Outsmarting IQ: The Emerging Science of Learnable Intelligence*; and many articles. He has helped to develop instructional programs and approaches for teaching understanding and thinking, including initiatives in South Africa, Israel, and Latin America. He is a former Guggenheim Fellow. Perkins can be reached at Project Zero, Harvard Graduate School of Education, 323 Longfellow Hall, 13 Appian Way, Cambridge, MA 02138; phone: 617-495-4342; fax: 617-496-4288; e-mail: David_Perkins@pz.harvard.edu.

Thommie DePinto Piercy was a public school teacher in grades K–5 for 18 years. She is the former vice principal of Friendship Valley Elementary School in Carroll County, Maryland, and currently teaches graduate courses in reading and writing. She has published articles about integrating reading comprehension with two of the Habits of Mind: (1) questioning and posing problems and (2) thinking about thinking (metacognition). She based her research on this topic at the University of Maryland and was honored with the International Reading Association's (IRA) Research Award. In 1999 she chaired and presented at the IRA Convention in San Diego with Regie Routman. DePinto Piercy has received the Bailor Award in recognition of her distinguished educational career. In her current role as principal of Mt. Airy Elementary School in Carroll County, Maryland, she has promoted a Habits of Mind culture as reflected in her new school's vision: "Success with a joy for learning and pride in a caring community." As author of a recent ALA publication, *Compelling Conversations: Connecting Leadership to Achievement*, and the Prekindergarten–Grade 12 Supervisor of Reading, she continues to strive to establish communities of learners who embrace common beliefs and practices aligned with the Habits of Mind. She can be reached at P.O. Box 1228, Harpers Ferry, WV 25425; phone: 304-725-3128; e-mail: tpiercy@ccpl.carr.org.

Curtis Schnorr is director of elementary schools in Carroll County, Westminster, Maryland. Previously, he was a school principal for 22 years. He spent seven years as principal at Friendship Valley Elementary School helping to create a "home for the mind." He has been a presenter at state and national conferences on incorporating the Habits of Mind into a school culture. Originally selected as principal for Friendship Valley, Schnorr has since had the opportunity to incorporate the Habits of Mind in his role as director of elementary schools. Schnorr can be reached at 517 Washington Rd., Westminster, MD 21157; phone: 410-876-1807; e-mail: ctschno@k12.carr.org.

Steve Seidel is the Bauman and Bryant Lecturer in Arts in Education and directs the Arts in Education Program and Project Zero at the Harvard Graduate School of Education. At Project Zero, Seidel has been principal investigator for projects that have studied learning in the arts, the close examination of student work, reflective practices in schools, and children as individual and group learners. Before becoming a researcher, Seidel taught high school theater and language arts for 17 years. He has also worked as a professional actor and stage director. He may be reached at steve_seidel@pz.harvard.edu.

Bertie Simmons is the principal of E.L. Furr High School, an inner-city school in Houston, Texas. She has had a long career in public education as an elementary and secondary teacher, as well as an elementary and high school principal. She has held numerous positions in central administration, including the role of teaching strategist, which required that she work with inner-city schools in the Houston Independent School District to facilitate desegregation. She served as superintendent of the east region of the district, assistant superintendent of the south region, and superintendent of District VIII. She retired in 1995 as the assistant superintendent of campus management, a position that provided her with an opportunity to work with all schools in the district. After five years of working as an educational consultant, Simmons was called upon to assume the role of principal at Furr, a troubled school with serious gang activity and little focus on academics. She has worked to create a student-centered environment where teachers and students strive for excellence and where the school's mission can be realized. That mission is "Furr High School: where high expectations are met and hopes and dreams come true."

Nancy Skerritt is the assistant superintendent for teaching and learning in the Tahoma School District in Maple Valley, Washington. She has worked in the district since 1990 and has designed and published a training model for writing integrated curriculum with thinking skills and Habits of Mind as the core. Skerritt has conducted workshops in curriculum integration and thinking skills instruction. She is a member of the Washington State Assessment Advisory Committee, which is implementing a statewide performance-based assessment system. Before her work in curriculum development, Skerritt was a secondary language arts teacher and a counselor. Skerritt can be reached at the Tahoma School District office, 25720 Maple Valley/Black Diamond Rd. SE, Maple Valley, WA 98038; phone: 425-432-4481; fax: 425-432-5792; e-mail: nskerritt@tahoma.wednet.edu

William A. Sommers lives in Austin, Texas, and is the director of Leadership and Organizational Development for Manor ISD. He has been a principal, university professor, and independent consultant for more than 30 years. Sommers is a senior fellow for the Urban Leadership Academy at the University of Minnesota. He served on the board of trustees for five years and is a past president for the National Staff Development Council.

Sommers is the former executive director for Secondary Curriculum and Professional Learning for Minneapolis Public Schools. Since 1990, he has been an associate trainer for the Center for Cognitive Coaching based in Denver, Colorado. Sommers has been a program director for an adolescent chemical dependency treatment center and on the board of a halfway house for 20 years.

He has co-authored six books, *Living on a Tightrope: A Survival Handbook for Principals*; *Being a Successful Principal: Riding the Wave of Change Without Drowning*; *Reflective Practice to Improve Schools: An Action Guide for Educators*; *A Trainer's Companion: Stories to Stimulate Reflection, Conversation, Action*; *Energizing Staff Development Using Film Clips: Memorable Movie Moments That Promote Reflection, Conversation, and Action*; and *Leading Professional Learning Communities: Voice from Research and Practice*.

In addition to writing many articles regarding coaching, assessment, and reflective thinking he also does training in poverty, leadership, organizational development, conflict management, brain research, and classroom management. Since 1970, Sommers has been in K–12 education as a teacher and principal in urban, suburban, and rural schools. He has served as an adjunct faculty member at Hamline University, the University of St. Thomas, St. Mary's University, the Union Institute, and Capella University.

Bonnie Tabor has been involved with Waikiki School since 1987, initially as a counselor and presently as the principal. She received her bachelor's degree from Case Western Reserve University, her master's degree in counseling from the University of Hawaii, and her master's in special education from the University of California. Throughout her professional career, she has found the Habits of Mind to be inspirational and fundamental to her vision of the purpose of education. As principal of Waikiki School, recently recognized as a State Blue Ribbon winner, she believes the Habits of Mind provide the vision, the direction, and the unity of purpose that have resulted in the school's status as a school of excellence.

Diane P. Zimmerman is superintendent of the Old Adobe Schools in Petaluma, California. She has worked as a teacher and an administrator in special education, as an elementary principal, and as assistant superintendent for human resources. Her work with job-embedded staff development has been featured in the joint ASCD-NSDC publication *A New Vision for Staff Development*. She has collaborated for more than 25 years with members of the cognitive coaching community and was identified as an early practitioner; she is featured in the ASCD video series *Another Set of Eyes: Conferencing Skills*. Zimmerman completed her PhD in organizational systems at the Fielding Institute in Santa Barbara, California. In her spare time, she continues to collaborate with colleagues and to write both articles and coauthored books.

Related ASCD Resources: Habits of Mind

At the time of publication, the following ASCD resources were available (ASCD stock numbers appear in parentheses). For up-to-date information about ASCD resources, go to www.ascd.org.

DVDs
How to Spiral Questions to Provoke Student Thinking (#605122 DVD)
Learning to Thinking . . . Thinking to Learn: The Pathway to Achievement (DVD and user guide #607087)

Networks
Visit the ASCD Web site (www.ascd.org) and click on About ASCD. Under the header of Your Partnership with ASCD, click on Networks for information about professional educators who have formed groups around topics, including "Character Education," "Overseas and International Schools," "Brain-Based Compatible Learning," and "Global Education." Look in the "Network Directory" for current facilitators' addresses and phone numbers.

Online Courses
Improving Student Achievement with Dimensions of Learning (#PD05OC50)

Print Products
Building Background Knowledge for Academic Achievement: Research on What Works in Schools Robert J. Marzano (#104017)
Developing Minds: A Resource Book for Teaching Thinking Arthur L. Costa (#101063)
Educating the Whole Child (action tool) John Brown (#709036)
Getting to "Got It!" Helping Struggling Students Learn How to Learn Betty K. Garner (#107024)
Habits of Mind Across the Curriculum: Practical and Creative Strategies for Teachers Arthur L. Costa and Bena Kallick (#108014)
A Teacher's Guide to Multisensory Learning: Improving Literacy By Engaging the Senses Lawrence Baines (#108009)
Teaching for Meaning (theme issue) *Educational Leadership* (#105028)
Teaching Students to Think (theme issue) *Educational Leadership* (#108024)

For more information: send e-mail to member@ascd.org; call 1-800-933-2723 or 703-578-9600, press 2; send a fax to 703-575-5400; or write to Information Services, ASCD, 1703 N. Beauregard St., Alexandria, VA 22311-1714 USA.